The Guardian
book of football

Manchester Guardian front, 1958

Guardian Sport front, 2008

Foreword by Sir Bobby Robson

The Guardian book of football

Edited by Mike Herd

First published in 2008 by
Guardian Books, 119 Farringdon Road, London EC1R 3ER
guardianbooks.co.uk

Guardian Books is an imprint of Guardian News and Media Ltd.

10 9 8 7 6 5 4 3 2 1

A CIP record for this book is available from the British Library.

ISBN: 978-0-85265-096-7

Design: Barry Ainslie

Printed and bound in China by C&C Offset Printing Co. Ltd

Contents

Foreword

As an England player and manager, Sir Bobby Robson has been steeped in football throughout this book's 50 years

Was it really half a century ago that I heard the abrupt, dreadful newsflash on the radio? *"United plane crash. Players feared dead"*. Some of the Busby Babes were my friends and work colleagues and they had been decimated in the blinking of an eye. I tried hard to fight the truth, even as I turned on the television set at my home in West Bromwich and saw the Aston Villa manager, Eric Houghton, reading his own solemn tribute.

Those gifted, talented, courageous Manchester United players were people I knew, not just famous names I'd read about. Just nine weeks previously I had made my England debut alongside Tommy Taylor, Duncan Edwards and Roger Byrne. We had beaten France 4-0 at Wembley; I'd scored the second and fourth goals, Tommy the first and third. As the shocking news sunk in, painfully, distressingly, I realised my first England match would be their last, even though Duncan fought valiantly for his life until the end.

It was only three months later that I found myself on a plane sitting next to one of the survivors, Bobby Charlton. He hadn't flown since Munich but we were England team-mates going to the World Cup in Sweden and I willingly took on the role of elder brother. Poor Bobby was sweating and looking a bit anxious as we hit some turbulence while making our final descent into Stockholm Airport.

"You all right, Bob?" I asked gently.

"I'll be OK, just let's get this bloody thing down safely," he replied. I didn't want to imagine what memories might have been going through his mind.

Because of people like Bobby Charlton, Manchester United and English football have not only survived the Munich disaster, they have in many ways flourished. I know the football industry has changed beyond all recognition and not all of it for the better, but the game itself has spent 50 years improving and is more exciting and entertaining now than it's ever been. The pitches, the ball, the stadiums, the training facilities, the medical equipment — all of them better. As a result, players are fitter, stronger and, yes, more skilful.

Of course Tom Finney and Johnny Haynes could have played

Sir Bobby maintains that, had Bryan Robson been fit, he could have trumped Sir Alf Ramsey and won two World Cups ...

in today's game. But Cristiano Ronaldo and Steven Gerrard would have been fine ambassadors for the game in any era as well.

Remember that, in 1958, players had to cope with a heavy leather ball on mud pitches. Floodlit stadiums were a rarity, too — I remember playing for England at two o'clock on a weekday afternoon so we would finish before it got dark. Players were on a maximum wage of £20 a week; when Johnny Haynes became the first £100-a-week player and employed an agent, Bagenal Harvey, to get him a contract advertising Brylcreem, it seemed as if it was the most exotic thing on earth.

I loved the game then but I love it just as much now. I defy anyone not to feel a surge of excitement when Ronaldo lines up a free-kick or when Adebayor goes up for a goalscoring header. And I've been so lucky to have enjoyed a career in the spotlight. As the England manager going into two World Cups, I knew I held a massive responsibility. It would have been daunting had it not been so exciting.

How did I know about that responsibility? Because I used to

Bobby Robson, right, challenges Duncan Edwards during training for the only England match they played together, against France in 1957

read the newspapers every day and they made it pretty clear. Don't believe people in football when they say they don't read the papers. They did then and they do now. I looked at them all, including *The Guardian*, whose chief football correspondent David Lacey was a must-read, particularly with his Monday round-up. Frank Keating was another favourite.

I am delighted that some of my finest moments are included in this book. How can I forget winning the Uefa Cup with Ipswich in 1981? The irony of our victory against Alkmaar was that two of our best players were Dutch: Arnold Muhren and Frans Thijssen. Signing Arnold was an example of a manager thinking on his feet. His wife didn't want to leave Holland and I was so frightened of missing out on the signing that I hired a small plane to fly Arnie and his wife over Suffolk, to show them what a lovely part of the world it was. In fact, I didn't give permission to land until she'd agreed to live there!

The big World Cup games featured in this book against Argentina in 1986 and West Germany in 1990 are bittersweet, of course. To go so close to winning the biggest prize in football made me immensely proud, but losing those games was terribly painful. I still maintain that, if we'd had Bryan Robson fit for 1986 and 1990, I could have trumped Sir Alf Ramsey and won two World Cups! Bryan was our best player, no doubt about it; someone who could stop goals, create goals and score goals. There is no way Diego Maradona would have scored that wonderful solo goal if Bryan had been on the pitch. Not sure about the Hand of God, though …

It was a shame we didn't win in 1990 because I remember how excited the country was when Alf won the World Cup in 1966 — and boys like Lineker, Beardsley, Shilton, Gascoigne and Butcher deserved to become icons just like Bobby Moore and the other boys of '66.

If Bryan was the best British player I managed, Brazil's Ronaldo was the best I ever managed, full stop. I tried to sign Alan Shearer for Barcelona in 1996 but, when he chose Newcastle, I persuaded the Barcelona president to gamble on this untried Brazilian youngster from PSV. He was simply sensational. It is a very rare player who can score a match-winning goal on his own; George Best could and so could Ronaldo.

I was privileged to play with greats like Duncan Edwards, Bobby Charlton and Johnny Haynes and to manage the likes of Gary Lineker, Paul Gascoigne, Romario, Ronaldo, Ruud van Nistelrooy and Alan Shearer. Pitting my wits against Shankly, Paisley, Revie, Clough, Beckenbauer and Sir Alex Ferguson was also an incredible challenge.

Cloughie was a one-off, of course. I went to see him in his office after we'd drawn an FA Cup tie against Nottingham Forest and he was sitting there in pitch darkness. At first I thought I'd wandered into the broom cupboard by mistake. Then I asked him if he'd consider putting the replay back 24 hours because we both had a couple of players carrying knocks.

"Get out, I'd play you tomorrow on f***ing Felixstowe Beach if I could!" he thundered. I beat a hasty retreat — but I had the last laugh. We won the replay 1-0, Arnie Muhren scoring the winner if I remember.

The game has given me so much. It's why I've always tried to act with dignity, whatever the pressures from the newspapers. The game is bigger than the prize because, for every winner, there has to be a loser. It's why I clenched my teeth and faced the TV cameras seconds after being knocked out of the World Cup semi-final on penalties. It wasn't easy but I had a responsibility.

I remember, too, being knocked out of the FA Cup semi-final by West Ham in 1975, after a dubious refereeing decision. The papers might have wanted me to lash out, I don't know, but all I could say was: "Out of adversity some good may come." Thankfully I went to Wembley three years later and my Ipswich side beat Arsenal to win the FA Cup.

One headline that made me laugh as well as cry came after my England team was held to a draw by Saudi Arabia. "*In the name of Allah, Go!*" it screamed. It wasn't in *The Guardian*.

If I had more space, I could write down a million more memories. Thankfully you don't have to rely on me. *Guardian* journalists have been publishing their own accounts of memorable matches and personalities, and here is a selection of the best from the last 50 years. Enjoy the read and remember, for true football fans, the game is always greater than any prize.

Sir Bobby Robson
February 2008

Chapter one
United, from tragedy to triumph

Eight Manchester United players were among the 23 people killed when a BEA Elizabethan crashed on take-off in snow at Munich

07|02|1958
Airliner hits house

Victor Zorza, Munich

Twenty-one of the 44 passengers and crew of the British European Airways airliner which crashed yesterday near Munich carrying the Manchester United football team are feared dead. About eight others are in hospital, seriously injured. A report from Associated Press said the aircraft crashed on to a hut full of oil and petrol. It was the fire from this which did the greatest damage. The plane itself did not explode.

Bobby Charlton, one of the members of the Manchester United team who is in hospital in Munich, described how the crash took place. He said the aircraft tried to take off and had even got as far as the end of the runway but there appeared to be something wrong and it came back.

All the passengers got out and went into the waiting-rooms, where they waited for some 10 minutes. They were then told that whatever had been wrong had been put right and they got back into the aircraft, which taxied to the runway and made another attempt to get off the ground. But just as it approached the airport boundary something went wrong again and it caught the edge of the house with its wing just outside the airport.

The driver of a German car saw the aircraft hit the house, then go up and down in the air, coming to rest between two houses. Almost immediately one of the houses, on which part of the tail had come to rest, was on fire. Another German eye-witness, a lorry driver who happened to be standing at the back of his house when he heard the crash, ran towards the aircraft straight away: when he got there, there was already a car standing there and a child who had been thrown out of the aircraft, apparently only slightly injured, was being carried to the car to be taken away.

An injured member of the crew had also got out and was trying to pull one of the passengers out. The aircraft had broken into two parts. The right wing and the right part of the cockpit were relatively undamaged but the left wing was broken off at the point where the engine had been. People who had been thrown clear, and some who had by now been pulled out, were lying about on the snow. It had been snowing at the time of the crash and it was still snowing in the evening after the rescue operations had been completed.

Mr Peter Howard, a *Daily Mail* photographer who was stated to be the only journalist aboard the aircraft in a condition to describe what happened, telephoned this description of the crash to Manchester last night, after going back into the wreckage to do what he could in the rescue attempt. As he talked, ambulance men were waiting to take him to hospital to be treated for shock.

"It was snowing when we landed at Munich. We went off for refreshments and then back to the aircraft to continue the flight. I was sitting in the front row of seats on the starboard side. When the pilot tried to take off there seemed to be some kind of slight fault with the engines. He stopped. Then he tried a second take-off. That did not seem satisfactory, so he taxied back to the apron to get things checked up. It was on the third take-off that we crashed. I think we were at the end of the runway only a bit above the ground.

"The plane suddenly appeared to be breaking up. It was a rolling sensation and all sorts of stuff started coming down on top of us. There wasn't time to think. No one cried out. No one spoke – just a deadly silence for what could only have been seconds. I can't remember whether there was a bang or not. Everything stopped all at once. I was so dazed I just scrambled about. Then I found a hole in the wreckage and crawled out on hands and knees.

"I turned and saw Harry Gregg, the goalkeeper, and he and myself went back into the wreckage. It looked as though those who had been sitting in the forward part of the plane were the lucky ones who got out. The luckiest of all were those in backward facing seats. Part of the engines of the airliner had gone forward for 450 yards and hit a small house, which burst into flames but the fuselage did not catch fire."

14|02|1958
Duncan Edwards conscious

Duncan Edwards, one of the three most seriously injured survivors of the Munich air crash, showed a "dramatic improvement" yesterday. Dr Graham Taylor, the British European Airways doctor in Munich, said: "Edwards is conscious and talking. He asked for a drink and for an apple. He was given a glass of lemonade." He pointed out, however, that Edwards was still on the danger list.

The improvement began yesterday after Edwards had an artificial kidney linked to his blood stream in an attempt to take the strain off his injured kidneys.

The funerals took place yesterday of Alf Clarke, of the *Manchester Evening Chronicle*, and HD Davies, of the *Manchester Guardian*, at Manchester; Mr George Follows, of the *Daily Herald*, at Wolverhampton; Tommy Taylor at Barnsley; Geoffrey Bent at Pendlebury; and Mr Tom Curry, United's trainer, at Stretford.

22|02|1958
Edwards: body will be flown to England today

The body of Duncan Edwards, who died early yesterday in the Rechts der Isar Hospital in Munich, will be flown to England this afternoon. The funeral is expected to take place at Dudley, his home, on Wednesday. His parents and fiancée, Miss Molly Leach, flew from Munich to London yesterday and went on to Dudley in a car provided by British European Airways.

Mr Walter Winterbottom, the England team manager, said of Edwards yesterday: "He was a great footballer and he had the promise of becoming the greatest of his day. He played with tremendous joy and his spirit stimulated the whole England team. It was in his character and spirit that I saw the true revival of British football."

30|01|1998
Dance before death
The prelude to Munich

Paul Hayward

There were 63,000 people at Highbury and children were passed along a floor of flat caps to sit on the cinder track: a set of babes on either side of the touchline, one on a path to doom. Forty years ago on Sunday potentially the greatest of all Manchester United sides left the pitch after an epic 5-4 victory over Arsenal. It was the last time many of them were to perform in England.

The 40th anniversary of the Munich air disaster falls a week from today and Highbury will be filled with its own contingent of ghosts this weekend when Arsenal meet Southampton. Next Friday a memorial service will be held in Manchester Cathedral to remember the 23 dead. Eight were members of the original Busby Babes, the guiding spirit behind United's present youth policy; eight were journalists who had filed their last full stop. Copy ends.

"United plane crash ... many dead" ran the stop press in the morning papers of February 7, 1958. The raw chill, the collapsing stomach that comes with shock, must have been felt by many of the 63,000 crushed into Highbury, a ground packed to the lightbulbs these days with only 38,500. One spectator who was at Highbury aged nine says: "When I heard the news I remember thinking, no, that can't be right. I only saw them a week ago. It was impossible for a child's mind to comprehend." The headline above the match report in this newspaper was "Arsenal Go Down Bravely". The report itself was a paean to the team that was about to fly to Belgrade to draw 3-3 with Red Star in the European Cup and thus advance confidently to the semi-finals. They were the English champions, youthful and masterly in all they did.

The decimation of Matt Busby's first masterwork was not about a football team being destroyed. It was about 23 men losing their lives and their families waking to desolation. In one sense it is obscene to elevate the death of a footballer above the death of a pilot or travel agent. But the loss of something so fresh and creative was a different kind of calamity. It allowed those not connected with the club or its victims to experience death as more than an abstract tragedy, another grim news item.

It can still be felt now, even by those of us who were not born when the BEA Elizabethan failed to take off after a refuelling stop in Munich and overshot the runway that wintry afternoon.

Before United play Bolton next Saturday, some of the survivors of Munich will gather at Old Trafford to pay tribute to the dead. Last year they travelled to Munich for the European Cup final, which United narrowly failed to make, and visited the Rechts der Isar Hospital, where the dead and wounded were treated 39 years before. A 40th anniversary does not normally carry quite the resonance of a 50th but this time, in the side Alex Ferguson has assembled, there is an unmistakable echo of Busby's own achievement in scouring the country for the best of British youth. The average age of the players who died at Munich was 24.

Sir Bobby Charlton was quoted 12 months ago in Munich as saying: "There isn't a day that goes by I don't remember what happened and the people who are gone. The fact that the players are not here and are never going to be judged is sad. They'll never grow old."

Forty years ago at Highbury, when the maximum wage was £17 a week, Charlton attracted professorial praise in these pages. "In less than a year," wrote our correspondent, "R Charlton has grown from a limited, left-sided player of little pace into a brilliant inside forward." In that 5-4 win "R Charlton drove lustily into goal" as United surged into a 3-0 lead by half-time. Arsenal recovered to 3-3 before United snatched the game back again.

The *Manchester Guardian* report is enough to confirm the legend of that team's destructive powers. United kept "one or both wing-halves always poised on the frontal limit of defence, ready to move forward and make a sixth or seventh forward". This left large gaps in defence but "always Manchester's forwards promised to score more goals than their defence yielded".

From *The Team That Wouldn't Die*, John Roberts's definitive account of the crash, come impossibly poignant reminders of how much was lost amid the wreckage. Eddie Colman's cousin, Albert Valentine, remembers hearing confirmation of Colman's death: "I told the family and then left the house. I just had to go out. I don't remember anything until I suddenly realised I was standing in Piccadilly, Manchester, after three in the morning, soaked to the skin without a coat and still wearing my slippers. After that I didn't eat for two weeks and I just could not settle to anything for two years. I couldn't sleep at night. I was shattered." Thirteen days later United played Sheffield Wednesday in the FA Cup fifth round at Old Trafford. When the team sheets came through, United's was empty. Almost until the kick-off the club was unsure who would be able or willing to play.

At Bolton next Saturday, as Sir Bobby Charlton and the others gather at Old Trafford, the match programme will be awash with colour and the names of those now carrying youth's flame into Europe. The long goodbye continues at Highbury tomorrow.

20|02|1958
The dream comes true
United win Cup tie

Our own reporter

....

There has never been a more unlikely result in football or one more fervently hoped for. Manchester United, in their first game since the Munich air disaster, beat Sheffield Wednesday by three goals to nil under floodlights at Old Trafford last night in the fifth-round Cup tie put back from Saturday. It was a dream come true.

Supporters thronged to the ground to watch the young, makeshift team tackle what seemed an insuperable task. Only two of the great combination that had taken the club to the football heights were playing last night: Harry Gregg and Billy Foulkes, both survivors of the disaster. The only other well-known names were Stan Crowther, signed for United from Aston Villa only an hour or two before the match, Ernie Taylor, the former Blackpool player, and Webster, who had made many appearances in the United first team. But how would inexperienced players like Greaves, Goodwin, Cope, Dawson, Pearson and Brennan fare? The answer was: magnificently.

Apart from the 60,000 who got in there were up to five thousand people without tickets who waited outside the ground throughout the game so as to hear at least the sounds of this historic encounter. After their long period of mourning for the players lost in the crash it was – among many other things – a chance for them to pick up the threads of normal football life again.

The shout of welcome when the players came out, led by the new captain, Foulkes, mingled with a great sigh of relief that United were playing again. However the team shaped, it was a start at least. With the floodlights slanting on the Old Trafford turf and the densely packed crowd surging restlessly as the ball swung from end to end of the field, the scene was well set to suit the occasion.

Outside the ground the thousands without tickets continued to try to beg them until well after half-time. There were a few black-market ticket salesmen and they found it easy to get 10 times the face value of the ticket. Many in the crowd, like the players, were wearing black armbands. Before the kick-off the crowd stood for a minute's silence to commemorate the late United players. At the end mourning was forgotten. The "team of the century" was gone but its successor had taken its place in a way not even the most fervent supporter – and they were all over the world last night – could have dared imagine.

It was not only the victory which was so unexpected; the manner in which United won was perhaps even more heartening and significant. From start to finish the untried team played with far more confidence and skill than Sheffield Wednesday. There will be good news to add to the bad when the decision is finally taken to tell Matt Busby the full details of the disaster.

Bill Foulkes, right, and Sheffield Wednesday's Albert Quixall shake hands before the first match after the crash. United won 3-0

Again it was Connelly who bemused Cavern with his swift change of direction and from his pass in the closing minutes of the first half Pereira leapt to his left to palm away one of the shots for which Charlton is known the world over. But as this match pulsed with excitement into the second half there was a resurgence of spirit from Benfica.

This was all too short, though, and too often Benfica were left with only a hopeful long shot that was stopped by a wall of United defenders. But there was disappointment for United in the 52nd minute as Brennan, attempting to keep the ball from Eusebio, hooked it to the right of Gregg and it rolled into his own net.

There was almost another on the hour when a back pass from Brennan fell short of Gregg and the goalkeeper only just won a race for the ball with Torres. But gradually United regained control and Charlton, Best, Connelly and Herd worked together finely. Herd, rather too carefree, however, sent the ball wide.

Then it was Law's turn. He sent Pereira flying to tip away a fierce shot. Again Best was the provider in one of the moves that made the match one to savour. And there were still United's two final goals to come – the fourth 10 minutes from time when Crerand pounced on to a perfectly timed pass from Law which opened up Benfica's defence, and seconds from time when Charlton went through the defence and delayed his shot with almost a touch of insolence.

11|04|1966
Bill Foulkes – and a dental parallel

Eric Todd

....

Only when the news was announced that Manchester United had rested Bill Foulkes on Saturday did I realise fully how much I missed the front tooth from which a dentist separated me a few days earlier. The replacements for both, however adequate, could not possibly be quite the same as the originals. That incisor had been as valuable to me in its own way as Foulkes to United these many years. It had been filled several times of necessity, as Foulkes's place has been. It looked less important than its gold-crowned companions but it could cope with anything, however tough – as Foulkes can among shining colleagues. That tooth finally broke under the strain of extraction; and, if Foulkes' physical endurance did so under the strain of hard labour in the field, his spirit did not. I dare say I shall be able to get another tooth of sorts to fill the gap. United will be hard pressed to get another Foulkes.

14|10|1967
Growing up with United

Playwright Keith Dewhurst tells how the last crowds of Cottonopolis taught him the joy of emotional expression

....

Twenty-one years ago this autumn, when I was 14, I saw Manchester United for the first time. They beat Middlesbrough 1-0 at Maine Road before a huge, grey, rain-sodden crowd of 65,000. I sat with my boarding school friend Peter, and his brother David, in what were then the 4s 6d seats at the front of the stand and I was amazed that the players were men and not schoolboys. Their speed and violence made me gasp and the violence of the crowd (their emotions as much as their pushing and stamping) frightened and thrilled me. I was shocked when a man stood up and shouted: "Look at them silly buggers on the stand" – the roof at the Platt Lane end gleamed with rain and two or three men were slithering down it.

The girders and massed people below were dark and the pitch had a different, more leaden gleam, over which Charlie Mitten's feet flickered like cat's paws. Wilf Mannion jumped to avoid a slashing tackle. His golden hair burns in my memory. Jack Rowley wheels to score the only goal, Jack Warner comes off with a gashed head (in that light the blood was black) and goes back on with a sticking plaster, and my own heart aches. I yearn in my memory to be free.

Supporter

We left early and at the brink of the steps I turned to look back at the match. Shouting men towered round me. On the field Charlie Mitten had his head up, looking where to put the ball. The crowd bayed at a finer point that escaped me and it was in that instant that I determined to make myself a connoisseur and realised that at the football match people expressed what they felt directly, without check or distortion.

I had found for the first time outside books values different from those of home and a rugby-playing boarding school. I was clever, poor at games and by temperament, being an only child, conceited and rebellious. I was pimply and afraid of the dark masses of whom I knew nothing and had never really seen. In 1945 I saw Labour landslide election results chalked on a board in Kendal Milne's department store and ladies in expensive coats groaned as they must have done in 1917 in St Petersburg. So it is not surprising the crowd at United frightened me, although I should say with hindsight that the people in the 4s 6d seats were not so much the unwashed masses as small-time Jewish businessmen, the storm petrels of free enterprise. They shouted and screamed nonetheless. What sad lives we have led, to demand this release at the football; and what dreams we have dreamed, to see their noble shadows in an athlete.

Thus for five years of my pathetic life my most serious definition of myself would have been " Manchester United supporter". At school we ordered the Manchester football papers and collected them on Sunday to read in a milk bar where, to the hiss of the urn, we educated boys laughed at the journalese: "Frank Swift jumped literally from nowhere ..." Peter had a cuttings book which he gave me and I still read.

When we were at home and could go to the match we arrived two hours before the kick-off, to ensure good positions at a crush barrier or over one of the popular side-entrance tunnels. From there we saw the classic 5-0 defeat of Burnley on New Year's Day, 1948, and the rout of Chelsea the week before United won the Cup. This Cup campaign, and the delightful attacking skill of United's play generally, seemed to justify all our bragging and moral assertions. United really were the best team.

At the same time we learned a larger poetry. From the cheap seats at the top of the Maine Road stand I saw Tom Finney's snow dance when he destroyed Manchester City on his own. I saw Bobby Langton score in seven seconds while Swift was still adjusting his laces; and, agonising because it was against United,

Fans with rattles enjoy a match in 1948: 'frightening and thrilling'. Old Trafford crowds now are charged with being too quiet

I saw Peter Doherty with his arm in plaster lead a great Huddersfield rally and equalise in the dying minutes; and I saw Dennis Viollet's first game for United, when the crowd jeered at him and Dennis was only a boy, but already his face had that drawn and cynical smile. Once when United lost I sat near Matt Busby, and I could not understand why his face expressed nothing, why I was desperate with rage and he puffed easily at his pipe.

When I went to Cambridge my interest faded but it returned later because I could not find a way in life and the football helped me. This time I wrote about it for newspapers and I needed it psychologically, I suppose, as the drama which showed that provincial life lay nearer to the truth than any other – the black roofs of the stand, the rain drifting, the red shirts valiant. We were the producers of the industrial revolution and other people the consumers.

Reporter

What a volume of avenged disappointment there was in the roar that sustained United against Bilbao: for the great, ruthlessly drilled side that won the League in 1956 and 1957 and made those forays into Europe had support as mystically local as Liverpool's is now. Those crowds were the last expression of Cottonopolis, the last assertion after slumps and dismal wars that Manchester was one of the great cities of history.

Even that vanity was pulled down at Munich. Alf Clarke, whose reports I had read in the milk bar, was killed in the airplane and I took his job. I dictated the fractured English running reports and rode in the team bus. It was a schoolboy dream come crudely and freakishly true.

Now, after another 10 years, I am in a different profession and, when I see United today, it is from the terraces again. If I stand there with anything, it is with a pang of exile because now my identity is my own. I see on the field what I see when my wife is acting or when a friend like John Hopkins has written the script: I see the hearts of Matt Busby and my hero Jimmy Murphy and I know what it has cost them.

They will never again have a team like the one before Munich. They have lost the pride, the ambition and the willingness to risk their emotions on years of boring, repetitive coaching. They are too sorrowful to tempt the gods twice. Their emphasis today is upon individual talent and it is a great mistake to call this second best. Individual talent has always been the essence of their vision, and in my opinion the part of it that twines down to the very source of football's fascination. Murphy says that a player is great when he plays the game in his own time. Moments which prove this, like Wilf Mannion's little jump to avoid the tackle, are the ones that remain. Is not this conquest of time, this flutter of immortality, the aesthetic heart of any sport? If Busby and Murphy were poets we would say that United's style expresses a profound acceptance of the sadness of life, and the reiteration against it of human values, especially beauty. But since it is football we say that no one in Europe has ball players to touch them.

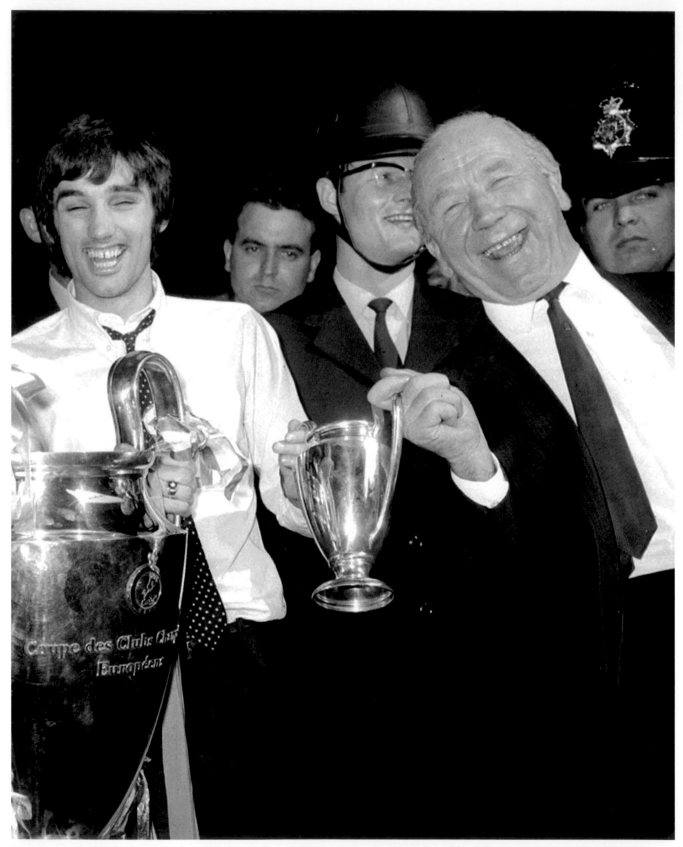

Matt Busby, sharing the European Cup with George Best, fulfils the dream that Munich could not shatter. He was shortly knighted

30|05|1968

Busby dream comes true at long last

European Cup final
Manchester United 4 Benfica 1
(aet; 1-1 at 90min)
Eric Todd, Wembley

....

The football might of Benfica, indeed of Portugal itself, was brought low by Manchester United at Wembley last night. In the presence of 100,000 frenzied spectators who had paid heaven knows what prices for admission, United won 4-1 after extra time and, for the first time in the 13 years of the competition, the European Champions' Cup has come to England. Better still to Lancashire. And, perhaps best of all, to Manchester United.

As a corollary rather than as a relevant postscript, Manchester City at present are spreading the gospel in the Americas as recently crowned champions of the Football League. If only West Bromwich had been situated in Lancashire instead of in Staffordshire, the County Palatine would have had a memorable hat-trick.

It was written that more things are wrought by prayer than this world dreams of, and Manchester United and their countless admirers will testify to the efficacy of that belief. Ever since United removed Real Madrid from the semi-finals, football enthusiasts in this country and in remote lands beyond the seas have entreated the gods to look favourably on Old Trafford, with particular reference to the team and to Matt Busby, its manager.

No matter that those gods chose to ignore similar sup-plications on behalf of Tottenham Hotspur, Wolverhampton Wanderers, Ipswich Town, Burnley, Liverpool and Everton in seasons past. Nor, for that matter, those on behalf of United, who had fought losing battles in three previous semi-finals — on the road to one of which, in 1966, they thrashed Benfica on aggregate 8-3.

This time surely they would not be denied, in spite of the menace of the incomparable Eusebio, of whom nearly as much has been written these past few days as has been allocated to the other 21 players put together. Which is saying a lot. Nor the fact that Benfica's forward line was that which played for Portugal in the World Cup two years ago. Speculation was rife as the crowds closed in from every side.

If the scenes after the match defied adequate description, those before challenged it seriously. With several hours to go, United's followers captured the heights around the stadium and slept a perspiring sleep through the hot afternoon.

Touts, who would flog tickets for the next world given the opportunity, reaped another rich harvest, as did purveyors of unofficial programmes, all unmindful of the terrible warnings of retribution and eternal damnation carried on sandwich boards. The Stretfordenders of Old Trafford, present in their legions, were concerned only with the damnation of Benfica. And so it proved, although their heroes made rather harder work of it than they need have done.

Best flattened

United had most of the play in the first half but many of their attacks ended abruptly with the flattening of Best, three times by Cruz — who once trod on Best's face for an encore — and three times by Humberto, who finally had his name taken. Sadler went very close to scoring on two occasions, although he blundered in the 28th minute when, after receiving a perfect pass from Kidd, he shot wide from 10 yards.

Benfica, when they were not attending to Best, attacked fitfully, without causing Stepney any anxiety until he made a smart save after the deflection by one of six United players when Eusebio took a free-kick. In taking another free-kick, Eusebio failed narrowly to be the first man so far as I know who has dis-patched the ball over the stands. All eyes, of course, were on Eusebio, who produced the best shot of the first half. Stepney was given no time to move. He could only stand and hope as the ball rattled against his crossbar.

Early in the second half Aston, playing the game of his young life, tested Henrique with two fine shots. Then, in the 53rd minute, it happened — Dunne to Sadler, Sadler a lob of geometri-

25

cal precision into the Benfica goalmouth, where Charlton, leaping up, flicked the ball into the net with his balding head.

"We shall not be moved," roared the United followers, and it certainly seemed that Benfica – Eusebio excepted – would not move anyone. If United had taken all their chances, Benfica would have been beyond redemption by half-time.

Ten minutes from the end, however, United faltered and Stiles thumped the ground in anguish after Augusto and Torres had paved the way for a goal by Graca. It was unbelievable after United's domination. Almost as unbelievable were two saves in the last five minutes by Stepney from tremendous shots by Eusebio, who was gracious enough to congratulate United's goalkeeper.

In seven minutes of the first period of extra-time, however, United destroyed Benfica with further goals from Best, Kidd (19 yesterday) and Charlton. Apart from a few thunderbolts hurled by Eusebio and treated almost with contempt by Stepney, Benfica were out of the hunt.

Inevitably it was a night for tears, rejoicing, memories and maybe pathos as well. Yet I suspect that the emotion transcending all others was that of unqualified universal pleasure for one man – Matt Busby, manager of Manchester United. Busby, who once might have joined them as a player for a transfer fee of £150 and who, in 1945, visited the then chairman of the club and inquired almost nonchalantly: "I believe you are seeking a team manager? Well, I am interested."

There is no need here to recount his exploits as a player and as a manager. They are known by heart anyway. Now the European Cup has been added to Old Trafford's bulging cupboards. What next? The world club championship? An eventual seat on the board for Matt Busby? Sufficient unto the day are the honours thereof.

Wonderful support

And when we are "old and grey and full of sleep and nodding by the fire", what, I wonder, will be the most clearly defined memory of Wembley, May 29 1968? That of the bemused spectator who, seeing United in all-blue strip, demanded to know: "How's Chelsea got into this act?" Of the wonderful vocal encouragement of the oft-maligned supporters of United? United's missed chances? Eusebio's lethal shooting? Foulkes, th'owd chain horse, playing Torres out of the game? Or of Matt Busby marching on to the pitch at the final whistle and shaking hands with the Benfica players and officials before turning to his own men?

Or will it be the memory of Matt Busby, the man who "learned to labour and to wait", embracing his magnificent backroom boys and then watching his men do a lap of honour? And did he look up briefly at the heavens as if seeking – and getting, no doubt – the approval of the spirits of Munich? And did he look, too, with pride on his bright young men, his hopes for years to come, and maybe more so on Charlton and Foulkes, who have been with him almost since they learned to kick a football?

Home are the hunters, home from the hill. At last.

29|10|1971
George is the best in the world

Football diary
Albert Barham

George Best had police protection again on Saturday, not from the adoring worshippers of this modern man cult but far more sinister, a threat on his life. Best these days is enjoying, and Manchester United are benefiting from, the refereeing decisions which prevent the hatchet men crippling him from behind.

Whatever one thinks of his image, or the flaws in his soccer character of sudden bubbling retaliation, childish taunts and provocation, plus the mischievous confrontation with authority, there is the opinion, which I offer, that he is the greatest player in the world.

Yet asked, as once he was, whether this was so, he said no, he was not but he could be if he became obsessed with the game as some of the other players were. "I like to enjoy myself – to get pleasure out of the money I've made," he has said often enough. When he feels right and at his sharpest, he says he can do anything with the ball no matter what the opposition.

One can quote other masters – Matthews, Finney, Di Stefano, who is Best's top man, Garrincha of the corkscrew legs, Pele, now just going past his best, or Mueller. But they cannot be compared for they are not all of the same era nor have they played in the same competitive spirit, for the tragedy of Best is that he comes from Northern Ireland, who are so badly placed that they can scarcely ever qualify for a major international competition.

Best is at his best anywhere along the line of forward positions. He is a finisher and creator. He has quick appreciation of a situation. Armchair television critics, who may disagree, seldom see the telling pass stabbed often at long distance and to pinpoint accuracy. Few of his colleagues can complain that they get a pass from Best when in a bad position – he keeps the ball and responsibility. He is deft, unpredictable, in that his range of variable moves is unmatched, and has a disregard for personal safety.

When Best first came to Old Trafford the edict went out from Sir Matt that the boy's style was not to be changed: he was to be allowed to develop and the rest would come in time. That time has come. Sir Matt summed him up best. "He is the greatest player on the ball I have ever seen," he said. "You can recall Matthews, Finney, Mannion and all the great players of the past but I cannot think of one who takes the ball so close to an opponent and beats him with it as does Best." As a rival manager once said of Best: "All the rest are just footballers."

26|11|2005

Yesterday in Belfast, the most poignant sadness

Michael Walker

Back where it all began the snow crunched underfoot around Belfast's Cregagh estate yesterday morning. Lowry-like figures hugged themselves against the worst as they made their way to and from the shops on Greenway, where Mawhinney's the butcher proclaims "Meat to please you" and where the flags and murals shout of Ulster loyalism. Down on Burren Way, where the Cregagh's most famous resident used to practise with a tennis ball against his parents' doorknob, the waiting went on. Then at lunchtime, the end: George Best was dead.

There was no ceremony. Best had not lived in this sprawling 1940s housing estate for nearly half a century. Yet to those of us who grew up in this corner of Belfast it always felt as if George,

A well-wisher pays last respects to George, 'always just George', during the cortege in Belfast, when tens of thousands turned out

always just George, maintained a presence. We wallowed in the warmth of his golden shadow. Yesterday was cold, tearful, distressing, but when Belfast regains composure it will be to say that he was one of us, always will be. It will be to say they can take his body away but that George Best will never die.

You cannot bury a legend and, since the day in December 1972 when Best played his last match for Manchester United, that is what he has been, a beautiful, living football memory. There were moments after that when he rekindled the flame – notably for Northern Ireland against Johan Cruyff's Holland in 1976 – but Best the meaningful footballer finished in 1972. From there his career, his life, was drowned in drink and we cannot forget the pain he inflicted verbally and physically when in thrall to alcohol, not least on his family.

Belfast is not a city noted for forgiveness but where George Best was concerned, among the public, it was a bottomless well. To local politicians it was different, though of course now there is a notion that the proposed new national stadium should be named after him.

It is too late. It should have been done years ago. Unofficially Best must have known what he meant to Belfast but it would have been good for him to see it in bronze. Recognition was a problem for him: he had too much of it from those who could offer him little, not enough of it from those who could shape him. He said the captaincy of United might have changed his life. Instead he began a pattern of departure. As the poet said: "We live our lives forever taking leave."

Best had first slipped away from the Cregagh in the summer of 1961. He was 15 years old when he got on the Liverpool ferry to go on trial at United. He had never before worn long trousers. Famously he came back days later citing homesickness and was met by his bemused father Dickie, on July-fortnight holiday from Harland and Wolff shipyard. "That's all right, son," Dickie said, "grown men get homesick."

George soon left again for Old Trafford and after that returned to Burren Way infrequently. Now he will make one last journey from there. Looking up from the house where Dickie has lived for

56 years you can see the Castlereagh Hills. They were wreathed in snow yesterday and it is believed that this is where Best will go, to lie in the Roselawn cemetery beside his mother Ann. It will be a day of unspeakable pain for Dickie and family. While George's memory will shine on, to many it will also feel like the interment of part of their own lives. That is how Best affected people.

For Dickie it will be tragic. He will bury his son alongside his wife in the knowledge that both died of alcohol abuse. Almost a decade ago I met Dickie in Burren Way and, as we talked on his doorstep on the way out, he sighed and said of the alcoholism that has surrounded him: "I've become an expert in something I never wanted to know anything about."

Dickie Best said then that it was George's daily regret that he had not done more to help his mother. The father had been a useful amateur footballer but George always said it was from his mother that he got his athleticism. From her son, Anne Best got the downside of fame as much as the flickering pleasure. Later she acquired a fondness for alcohol – she did not drink before she was 40, it is said – and in October 1978 she died in the house on Burren Way. The previous day George, now 32 and in a contractual dispute with Los Angeles Aztecs, was banned by Fifa. His career looked to have reached a full stop.

Best left California for the Cregagh. Ann Best's funeral, if memory serves, was large. It must have been on a Saturday because along with the other 12-year-olds of Rosetta Boys we had gathered as we always did outside the shops on Greenway. We stood there with our boots in hand preparing to go and play and saw for the first time in the flesh the man who lit up our lives.

If it is possible to love a stranger then we loved George Best. Those of us who went to school at Lisnasharragh would always ask others who their most famous ex-pupil was – so that they would ask back – and we revelled in the tales. There was the "genius" telegram sent by the scout Bob Bishop to Matt Busby, then there was the scout from Leeds United who turned up late for a trial match, but from Dickie came the best, how he listened to the famous "fifth Beatle" Benfica game on the radio in the shipyard: "I was on the night shift at the time. I turned on the radio and there was this voice saying: 'And George Best has two goals'. There was only about seven minutes gone. That was one of the most important nights for George. Afterwards the press and the locals went daft for him."

In Dickie's hand that day was a letter with a German stamp and postmark. It was addressed to "George Best. Footballer. Belfast". It was 23 years after George's last United game. "I get them all the time," Dickie said.

Then one day a lad we had not seen before joined the team. He had the flaxen mane of Rod Stewart and suddenly we were handed a new kit. Then a photographer from *Shoot* magazine appeared. Rod Stewart, it turned out, was Ian Best, youngest of George's five siblings. Ian's middle name is Busby.

But there could be only one George in the Best family. There could be only one George Best.

Chapter two
England, 1966 and all that

24|02|1966

England outlook is dim with such a ragged army

England 1 West Germany 0

Eric Todd, Wembley

England's collection of strikers, sweepers-up and linkmen beat West Germany 1-0 last night at Wembley. It was more a triumph of disorganisation than of improvisation or tactical supremacy, and imagination itself is fearful of what will happen to England if they produce this apology for football in the World Cup.

A critic, admittedly one of the "old guard " who in recent weeks had waxed fat on such entertainment and skill as were provided by Chelsea and Leeds United, Rotherham United and Manchester United, and Carlisle United and Shrewsbury Town, for example, demanded of nobody in particular: "What has happened to our lovely game of football?" So far as I know there was no effective answer. This, of course, is one of the penalties of being old-fashioned and orthodox.

Most of us have resigned ourselves to the fact that the game these days is essentially a tactical exercise in which numbers on jerseys and their wearers are used principally as decoys. It is a good idea to deceive any enemy in every way possible; when that deception spreads among the originators to such an extent that none of the players knows his own functions, let alone that of his colleagues, then it becomes a different matter. England's display last night was a travesty of football and a slight on the great players who wore the white jersey in days gone by.

It is all very well protesting that this plan or that plan should be given a chance. No plan, however good in theory, is of the least practical use unless there are players capable of carrying it out. But last night England covered vast areas without getting anywhere. Ball and Cohen alone looked as if they meant business.

R Charlton as usual was wasted and looked thoroughly unhappy while his brother was beaten nine times by Held in the first half-hour. After that I gave up counting. Goodness only knows how J Charlton would have fared if Seeler had been fit to play. But the Leeds centre-half could console himself with the knowledge that he was by no means the most ineffective of the England players. There was plenty of competition for that unenviable distinction.

Too harsh? Too unsympathetic? Better be both, surely, than create even the slightest impression that any encouragement could be derived from this performance. West Germany, weakened as they were by the absence of four of their best players, were much the more methodical side and Netzer did more work in an orthodox part than did the whole of the England forward line, Ball always excepted. They moved the ball intelligently and repeatedly found gaps in the England rearguard, whose members repeatedly deliberated which of them were supposed to be defenders and which attackers.

If the Germans' finishing had been as good as their approach work, England would almost certainly have been beaten, and deservedly so. Even when Heiss, who came on as substitute for Hornig, drove the ball magnificently past Banks in the second half the goal was disallowed. The referee consulted a linesman after supplications by English players and ruled that Netzer, the provider of the centre, had first taken the ball out of play. As consolation the Germans were nevertheless awarded a corner.

The only other items worthy of record are that Newton had a sorry baptism in international football — he was removed on a stretcher with a badly bruised leg in the first half and will have it x-rayed today — and that Stiles scored the goal in the 40th minute after Tilkowski had fumbled a header by Hunt. Manchester United v Burnley on Saturday will, with luck, start to erase memories of one of the most painful nights spent watching England.

> R Charlton as usual was wasted and looked thoroughly unhappy

02|07|1966
Bitter lemons or Eros?

Leading article

This month Britain will be inundated with visitors coming to see the World Cup. The foreign football fans will descend on us as tourists, wallets bulging with foreign currencies. But does anyone entertain the naive belief that all those hot Latins will be here merely to watch the football? Of course not. The message of *Time* about swinging London has by now percolated in garbled fashion all over the globe.

The objective of many of our visitors will be, as one report stated bluntly, "looking for a good time in the West End" between matches. Or, to put it another way, they will watch the football if they can bear to tear themselves away from delights elsewhere. This is the moment Scotland Yard has decided that swinging London is to be "cleaned up". The vice squads are moving in. The clip joints are being raided. And all over England, if local police forces follow Scotland Yard's example, strippers and others will meet with chilly disapproval. No longer will it be possible to buy a glass of lemonade for £5 in those clubs staffed with provoking but unrewarding hostesses. For the duration of the World Cup matches, the girls will be expected to play fair and not cheat their guests. But once the football is over, presumably, they will go back to their former ways.

To extend such courtesy to our foreign visitors is commendable and not unknown in the rites of primitive tribes. But we seem to have to go to strange lengths to match the obligations of hospitality with our reputation for being " with it". The price of swinging is eternal vigilance.

14|07|1966
Swede under pressure

A complaint about cramped conditions for journalists covering World Cup matches at Goodison Park, Liverpool, is published in today's *Dagens Nyheter*, Scandinavia's most widely circulated newspaper.

"This is the first report ever written by a journalist in a mousehole," writes the paper's correspondent, Torsten Ehrenmark. "I am wedged firmly between two planks and two cigar-smoking Brazilians in yellow sombreros, and my typewriter is resting on the head of a Bulgarian journalist who winces every time I touch the keyboard. They have tried to find places in a box that was designed for the local press for 800 journalists from all over the world . It means that if I turn my head I swallow a burning cigar."

Mr Ehrenmark balances this with a tribute to the people of Liverpool. "This is the football city of England – not stiff and serious London, where you can hardly tell there is a World Cup competition going on.

"The people here are really the supporters and friends of football ... I don't think I have ever heard a football crowd enjoy themselves as much as they did in last night's game between Brazil and Bulgaria."

20|07|1966
North Koreans profit by Italy's misfortune

North Korea 1 Italy 0

David Lacey, Ayresome Park

The North Koreans have done it. Incredibly the little men from North of the 38th parallel, whose only previous success in the World Cup was two victories over Australia, beat Italy, one of the world's most expensive and complex sides, 1-0 in Group 4 at Ayresome Park last night. It is the biggest shock in the World Cup since that day 16 years ago when the United States beat England by the same score at Belo Horizonte, Brazil.

Let it be said at once that the Italians would probably have won had it not been for the loss of Bulgarelli, who was carried off in the 35th minute with torn knee ligaments after colliding with Pak Seung Zin in midfield. Bulgarelli is the strongest link in this Italian side, and without him they fell apart.

But all credit to North Korea for seizing their chance. Seven minutes after Bulgarelli had gone off Pak Doo Ik put them ahead and from then on they never looked back. It is almost unbelievable: Rivera, Mazzola, Facchetti, out of the World Cup while Doo Ik, Im Seung Hwi, Han Bong Zin and company are still in and will play in the quarter-finals on Saturday if Russia do not lose to Chile at Roker Park this evening.

The North Koreans had already impressed as a fast and fit side but last night they rose to their greatest height, the culmination of three years of intensive preparation. In the second half Shin Yung Kyoo, Ha Yung Won and Oh Yoon Kyung were the equals of Mazzola, Perani and Barison. The Italians had had their chances in the first half-hour when they could have won the match with ease. Once behind their sole hopes rested with the individual brilliance of Rivera, and once he faded they looked well beaten.

Geoff Hurst, dubbed 'England's World Cup hat-trick hero' from 1966, was dubbed again as a knight 32 years later

Wilson, I hear you're trying to get in touch with me." Wilson was possibly the first modern full-back. Before the 60s full-backs were big bruisers pitted against speedy, nimble wingers. It made no sense. So full-backs became fast and nimble, like Wilson, and could overlap and attack in their own right.

Wilson meets me at Huddersfield train station. Big woolly hat, sweater, boots, grey beard, bald head and stony, blue eyes. He drives me to his house, a cottage alone in a field. Wilson is tough, funny, warm and surprisingly vulnerable. He grew up in east Derbyshire and is the only one from 66 to tell me he had an unhappy childhood. His mother and father split up when he was seven. "Very few people split up in those days. My mother had a fair character and saw things she didn't like, so they split. Then she went to work away as a chef," he says. "I was shipped about, staying with aunties and uncles who didn't particularly want me, which I can understand; they had children of their own."

"I didn't like school. I played hooky for about six weeks and, when they caught me and took me back into school, nobody had missed me. Hehehe!" It's a painful laugh. "Almost suicidal, isn't it? I was about 13." Eventually his mother returned home with a new man and young Ray settled down with them. "He was a smashing bloke, a hairdresser, and I lived with them and my life was better for that."

At 15 Wilson went to work on the railways, repairing wagons in Shirebrook. At 17 a schoolteacher recommended him to Huddersfield Town FC. His experience had toughened him, maybe too much. When he got called for national service in Egypt, he came across young men – boys, really – who couldn't cope. "Some of the sergeant majors were cruel bastards. In the barracks at night you could hear at least a dozen of the kids crying themselves to sleep. And I used to say, 'For fuck's sake, shut up.'" He wouldn't be like that any more, he says. "Thank God."

His strength as a player, Wilson reckons, was being a decent reader of the game. "I had the equipment to be a full-back. I never used to dive in, I was booked only once in my career and I was gifted by being quick. George [Cohen] was remarkably quick for a big lad. To be honest, I think the only thing I had over George was that I was a better player." It sounds as if he's joking, but he's not – his ability on the ball counted for little in the grand scheme of things.

By 1966 Wilson was England's most experienced player. The morning of the World Cup final he and Bobby Charlton decided to go for a walk. "We woke up pretty early. We strolled in from the Hendon Hall Hotel and walked up to London and back again. Nobody recognised me but obviously one or two recognised Bobby. I used to dread going anywhere with Bobby. Everybody would be [he whispers] 'Bobby Charlton'. Because you could forget Bobby Moore and all that; you were looking along the same line as bloody Garrincha and Pele. When we went to Chile in 62, we stayed in this little mining village where I don't think they'd ever seen a football match and as soon as we arrived it was 'Bobby Charlton, Bobby Charlton'. It didn't matter where you went." Did

he like it? "I don't think he did, no. I don't think anybody with any sense would enjoy that."

Wilson thinks the 1966 final is, with hindsight, overrated. "I don't think it was that much of a game, to be honest. People just get overwhelmed by the finish, the extra-time, was it a goal, wasn't it a goal?"

How hard was it for Jimmy Greaves not being picked? "Oh, he's done bloody well to cope with it. If he said, 'I've got over it, it doesn't bother me,' I'd find it difficult to believe him."

In the end, though, its impact on Hunt might have been equally devastating. He played for Liverpool and at the time, Wilson says there was a huge north-south divide among fans. "Roger got some awful stick. All these people with no memory who think Roger took Jimmy's place – they forget it was Geoff, because he scored the hat-trick and he's a Londoner. It was embarrassing. They used to sometimes boo Roger. He stopped playing for England, told Alf he'd had enough."

Wilson was rarely recognised as England hero Ray Wilson. That's the way things were in those days – few footballers were celebrities and no full-backs were. In the close season he began working with his father-in-law, a joiner-cum-undertaker, and eventually ended up running the business. He's retired now. The thing about the funeral business, he says, is that it takes only one tiny thing to go wrong to spoil the occasion. "I tell you what, son, playing football is a lot easier than directing a funeral." He thinks. "Mind you, I suppose I was more gifted at the football."

A player gives me Gordon Banks' number. "Good luck," he says. Banksy is still widely regarded as the world's greatest goalkeeper. Not long after the 1970 World Cup he lost an eye in a car crash. These days he does some after-dinner talking and is on the Pools Panel with Roger Hunt.

"Hi, is that Gordon?"

"Yes."

"My name is Simon Hattenstone . I'm doing this piece on the boys from 66. I've already met Geoff and Martin and George and ..."

"Is there a fee involved?" he asks.

"No, I'm sorry, we don't pay money but ..."

"I'm not interested then."

The phone goes dead. I try my number for Hunt. He is away. I try again and again, until I feel like a stalker. Weeks later I get through. He doesn't say much but he's friendly. By now I've no pride left and beg him. "The trouble is, I think everything there is to be said has been said. I'll think about it and ring you back ..." Hunt finished his career at Liverpool and went to work in his father's road haulage firm. He sounds lovely. I wonder why he is so resistant. Is it because of his final unhappy chapter with the England fans? I never get to find out. He doesn't call back.

But Jack Charlton does. "I'll meet you at the station, son." Even at 70, he looks like a stopper. He's 6ft 2in, red-faced and all jutting bones. He lights a Lambert & Butler and starts the car. He lives half an hour outside Newcastle and, as he drives,

It was everything you wanted to do in your life. When I stopped playing, people said, 'D'you miss playing?' What? Miss playing? It was the most ..." And he stops. He can't find a superlative quite superlative enough. "I had the most incredible years, just training, laughing, playing football in the morning, then getting paid at the end of the week, and paid more if you won — come on! I knew how lucky I was. My father made sure I did." He lived up to his name in the final — a ball of flaming energy, chasing, harrying, tackling and running to the end. What is his memory? "The final whistle. We'd done it. All I kept thinking about was me, after being rejected not 3½ years before, proving myself right to my dad."

After Ball finished playing he had mixed success as a manager. He always seemed to be in charge of clubs on the precipice — sometimes he hauled them back, sometimes he chased them straight over. By the time he was managing, he says, attitudes of players had changed. How? "Money. Getting vast amounts takes away the hunger, that little edge. Players of today say, 'I go out and play with the same desire ...' Nah. It cannot possibly be that way when the comfort zone comes so quickly and so easily. As an older player I don't have one ounce of regret because I've had the best."

It is two years since Ball's wife, Lesley, died. They had been together since before 66 and he always talked about them as a team. How have the past few years changed him? "It's changed me in that you know you have to come to terms with this life. It is a beautiful life, and an incredible world, but you've also got to be aware of what's round the corner and in the big scheme of things football isn't that important." Before I leave, Ball takes me into his office, "the treasure trove". The only trophy on display is for golf but there are wonderful historic football pictures on the wall — mates like Mick Channon and Charlie George, heroes like Nat Lofthouse and Denis Law and, of course, Hursty and Mooro and all the 66 boys.

What made them so strong as characters and as a team? "I tell you what made us what we were — we had this wonderful feeling that we were still part of the people. Every street in England had a footballer living in it. Not any more. They're behind big barbed wire fences, they've got security, they've got blacked-out windows, they hire clubs to go and have a night out. We were ordinary, approachable people. You were welcome to walk the streets, you were patted on the back, you were touchable, reachable."

Chapter three
Local heroes, Scottish legends

26|05|1967

Relentless attack captures European Cup

European Cup final
Celtic 2 Inter Milan 1
Albert Barham, Lisbon

Celtic flags flew triumphantly in the evening shadows here yesterday. At last, like the World Cup, the European Cup comes home to Britain. Celtic are the new champions and worthy ones at that, having beaten Inter Milan 2-1 in the final by sheer determination when all seemed stacked against them, when frustration and defeat stared them in the eye.

There is no individual hero. Every man gave his all. No other British club has ever reached the final, let alone won Europe's most coveted prize. It was a remarkable finish as, five minutes away from extra-time, Celtic scored the winning goal. After that it seemed the final minutes would never pass for their 7,000 supporters. It was like Wembley all over again after the Scottish victory against England. Jubilation was everywhere as the supporters cavorted around their heroes.

But hope had been slim for so long. Not for an hour could the despairing Scots break the defensive wall Inter built round their goal. Inter have done it so often, so successfully, it seemed Celtic, for all Johnstone's cunning and Murdoch's support of the forwards, had not the key to prise apart the tall Facchetti from his cohorts, Burgnich, Guarneri and Bedin. But the assistance from the backs and particularly the shooting of Gemmell from outside the wall, was rewarded in the end.

Jubilation was everywhere. There was no individual hero. Every man gave his all

For all the expectation of high tension no one could have expected it to erupt so sharply or suddenly. Within six minutes Celtic were a goal down to a penalty. It came after Craig fouled Cappellini and was scored by Mazzola for whom this must have been an emotional experience for his father played his last match here before dying in the air crash afterwards. Inter, for all their leisurely approach, snapped into action near goal with surprising speed and seconds before the goal Cappellini had sprinted down the wing and Mazzola's low header glanced off Simpson's knees.

From that disastrous goal Celtic gained in strength, forcing Inter back into a familiar pattern of massed defence behind which stalked Sarti, plucking high balls out of the air. There was seemingly no way through for Celtic and no way over the wall either. It was a case of getting round the sides or finding a chink. Incident piled upon incident, thrill upon thrill as Auld hit the crossbar and a low left-foot shot from Johnstone was smothered by Sarti, who in the next minute tipped a header from Johnstone over the crossbar.

Nine men were pulled back to stem the tide as Inter were well content and determined to hold what they had. It demanded defence of the highest order against an attack as consistent and resolute as Celtic's. Sarti just managed to smother one free-kick, which Gemmell deflected off this wall of defence. Later, lobbing speculatively, Gemmell hit the bar as the evening sun glinted in Sarti's eyes. And all the while Inter had not threatened again. And when they needed to come from their defensive box they could not.

Gemmell claimed the goal which brought Celtic level after an hour and a beautifully taken goal it was, coming from the clever understanding of Murdoch and Craig. This time the groping fingers of Sarti could not touch Gemmell's fierce, first-time shot. With the goal came renewed hope for, in spite of Inter's stubborn defence, Celtic were back with a real chance. It did not come until five minutes from time, whereupon Chalmers was submerged by his jubilant colleagues. He had scored the most crucial goal of his career. And so on to the rejoicing.

Jimmy Johnstone turns in elation as Steve Chalmers, out of shot, ensures immortality for the treble-winning Lisbon Lions

07|05|1974

No end in sight to Celtic's run

Vincent Parker

Celtic's acquisition of yet another Scottish FA Cup and Scottish Championship – their fifth double in eight years – has been received by the footballing public of Scotland with about as much excitement as one could expect to find in the Isle of Skye on any wet Sabbath. Every additional honour seems to multiply the indifference.

The club's official magazine *Celtic View* caught the mood with a remarkable photograph taken seconds after the tame draw 1-1 at Falkirk, which had extended their supremacy for yet another year. As the players left the pitch there was not a smile to be seen on the faces of this permanently triumphant team. The side, it would appear, takes glory as a matter of course.

The statisticians rolled out another fact, which helped to remind Scotland of the achievement of its champions. Nine successive national titles equal the European record held jointly

Kenny Dalglish flies for Celtic as he helps them to their fifth double in eight years with cup victory over Dundee United

by MTK Budapest and CSKA Sofia and few bookmakers would be prepared to wager against Celtic holding the record on their own in 12 months' time. They are, by the length of Sauciehall Street, the most successful club in Scottish, even British, football history.

It is only the poverty of the challenge presented to them by their rivals which takes some of the gloss away from their latest championship . Celtic quietly covet praise from English sources and frequently believe their talents go unnoticed South of the Border but until their domestic challengers improve outsiders will always be ready to devalue their performances.

"This was one of the more difficult ones – although it does not look that way on paper," their manager, Jock Stein, was quick to say after the Falkirk match. Celtic's ninth title was gained in spite of many setbacks, which Rangers, Hibernian and Aberdeen were unable to exploit as they missed the chance of knocking down the champions during one of their more hesitant periods.

During the course of the league programme one international, Davie Hay, asked to leave the club and was actually involved in transfer negotiations with Tottenham Hotspur. Another, George Connelly, walked out of the club for a period and he too wished a transfer. Serious injuries to the young McLoughlin, as well as to other international players, Lennox and McGrain, also tested the Celtic resources. Their goalkeeper, Alistair Hunter had a sudden and strange lapse of form while Jimmy Johnstone, still the joker in the pack, started to reveal his talents only in the last handful of matches after being out of the team for three months.

Such misfortune would have crippled any other club. Celtic had much in hand. Stein's paternalistic management remained sharp and alert . He alone of Scottish managers has built up a pool of such strength that replacements can always be found. He has, unsung, built up a youth policy far more comprehensive than any in the country and, with success breeding success, today's youngsters of all denominations want to play for the only champions they can remember.

While Celtic floundered in the League Cup final and failed to overcome Atlético Madrid's highly dubious tactics in the European Cup, their league success was never in doubt. Dixie Deans ended the season as leading goalscorer, in front of the superb Dalglish. Steve Murray, signed from Aberdeen a year ago, added drive from midfield. In a team which cost less than £200,000, the captain Billy McNeill, at 31, looked as good as ever. But he was rarely pressed.

Celtic are unlikely to surrender their position at the top of Scottish football in the foreseeable future. Stein has already defied the football truism, that teams cannot be broken up and remodelled while they are still at the top. This is his third different side since he began at Parkhead more than 10 years ago while the fourth and fifth are already on the drawing board.

Thus Celtic can look forward confidently – they are likely

to supply at least four members of Scotland's World Cup party – but the rest of Scottish football seems incapable of living with them. Rangers are a shadow of the side that won so many titles before the Stein era and the low points of this season came with defeats at Ibrox by East Fife and Arbroath. While Celtic show a slight drop in attendances (familiarity breeding contempt) the position of Rangers is alarming, with no more than 10,000 people turning out for recent home matches.

Hibernian, under the care of Eddie Turnbull, lack reserve resources and like other Scottish teams are prone to inconsistency. But they, together with Aberdeen, remain the only other genuine challengers. The rest act as nurseries to the English game, always ready to sell their brightest young players once the money is right.

Suggestions that the Scottish championship be run on a handicap system with Celtic as the back markers were made at last winter's seminars on league reorganisation. Instead next season will see Division One run along traditional lines for the last time before the introduction of the Premier League for 1975-76. If Celtic, under Jock Stein, make it 10 in succession, they will have set a record which can surely never be beaten.

08|05|1997

Rangers make it nine in a row

Dundee United 0 Rangers 1

Glenn Gibbons, Tannadice

....

Rangers last night secured the result which gave them their ninth successive championship to equal Celtic's record from 1966-1974, releasing their supporters from the shackles of doubt that had immobilised them since Monday's defeat by Motherwell.

Brian Laudrup scored the early goal, which eased the pressure, but Paul Gascoigne, who surprisingly started and almost finished the match, deserved his ovation on a night when he paraded the full range of his talents.

As well as being the most potent force in Scottish football Rangers have been the season's great kidologists. They were at it again recently, faltering like jaded steeplechasers and sometimes giving the impression that the obstacles between them and another triumph would not be negotiated.

But Rangers went to Tannadice last night and easily dealt

with a side who had beaten them in their previous two meetings. Those defeats had stoked the possibility of Rangers being usurped after a lengthy term in government but there was never the slightest danger of United repeating the dose.

Laudrup scored after 11 minutes but Gascoigne turned out to be the main man. The England midfielder had been a surprise starter, as Walter Smith had insisted on Tuesday that a thigh strain was so inhibiting that Gascoigne could not last 90 minutes. In fact he lasted a little longer, being replaced by Derek McInnes in stoppage time. It was a gesture by Smith that not only allowed his substitute to participate in the celebrations at the finish but ensured that Gascoigne received the crowd's warm applause.

It was a pity that one moment of virtuosity in the second half did not bring the goal it merited. Gordon Durie's cross from the right had been handled by the United defender Steven Pressley, but the referee allowed the advantage as the ball ran to Gascoigne. A little burst with that famous tiptoeing gait took him to the edge of the area and his low right-foot shot snaked past the goalkeeper Sieb Dykstra, thudded against a post and bounced away to safety.

A goal then would have been meaningless in terms of the result or the championship but it would have been an apposite return for Gascoigne's contribution. Laudrup, the most significant influence over the course of the season – Gascoigne having missed 14 weeks from the end of January because of injury – was, however, an appropriate scorer. His bulleted header to the right of Dykstra after receiving an impeccable cross from the midfielder Charlie Miller on the left put an end to any idea that Rangers' retention of the title would not be determined until Saturday, the last day of the season.

Rangers' captain, Richard Gough, was in civvies when he accepted the trophy at the end, having missed the match because of injury. He will now leave the club after 10 years and finish his career with Kansas City Wizards in America's Major League Soccer.

Smith found time to sympathise with Tommy Burns, sacked as manager of Celtic last Friday as the Parkhead club conceded that Rangers would win the 100th Scottish League championship this week. "Maybe there was a bit too much pressure. Celtic had a lot to do and it has cost the fellow his job," he said.

Gascoigne deserved his ovation. He paraded the full range of his talents

Archie Gemmill celebrates his goal that unlocked in turn the Dutch defence and the delirium of Scotland's followers

12|06|1978

Gemmill's magic too late

World Cup
Scotland 3 Holland 2
David Lacey, Mendoza

At least it was a marvellous funeral. Scotland, forgetting all the troubles which have beset them since their arrival in Argentina, made a brave if belated attempt to stay in the World Cup yesterday and finished by beating Holland, the runners-up last time, 3-2 in Mendoza yesterday, the game they had been least expected to win.

For eight minutes in the second half the Scots, who needed to beat the Dutch by three goals to qualify for the next stage, were in sight of their apparently hopeless target. A marvellous goal by Archie Gemmill, one of the best seen in the tournament so far, gave them a 3-1 lead and the delirious band of Scottish supporters, not to mention their manager, Ally MacLeod, began to believe that the miracle which had been freely spoken about but hardly expected was going to happen. Then Rep scored for Holland with a superb shot, the Dutch held on and for Scotland that was that.

Much to the frustration of their supporters, Scotland showed yesterday that they did after all possess the means to make progress in this tournament. At the last MacLeod decided to play Souness in midfield and the Liverpool player's timing of his passes, along with his sense of openings, complemented the bustle of Gemmill and Hartford.

The Dutch had sacrificed one of their midfield, Haan, so as to bring in an extra forward, Rep, but their side badly lost its balance in the 10th minute when Neeskens hurt himself trying to tackle Rioch and was taken off on a stretcher for attention. Eventually he was replaced by Boskamp but Holland, so

badly in need of Cruyff's inspiration, never really got their game together. Instead it was Scotland who were playing with greater purpose, showing the more positive attitude.

At the outset it seemed that Scotland's only serious hope of getting the goals they needed was to score early and the chances of this happening looked surprisingly good. In the fifth minute the Dutch defence went with Jordan as Souness centred from the right and Rioch headed against the bar.

Three minutes after Neeskens had gone off, with the Dutch reduced to 10 men for a time, Krol misheaded a through-ball backwards and Dalglish swooped on to it to beat Jongbloed but the Austrian referee decided he had used his elbows and what could have been a crucial goal was disallowed.

Certainly Scotland, showing such enthusiasm that Johnston's drug test and all those stories of ill-discipline at Alta Garcia might never have happened, did not deserve to fall behind 10 minutes before half-time. A through-ball from Willy van de Kerkhof caught the Scottish defence square but Rough and Kennedy went to stop Rep and whether or not the goalkeeper just beat the full-back to bring him down was immaterial. Rensenbrink scored from the penalty.

The game seemed to be taking the familiar fateful course for the Scots but two minutes before half-time Jordan headed down a neat chip from Souness and Dalglish sent the Scots into the interval full of hope while Dutch doubts were renewed.

Two minutes into the second half Souness, going for a high ball in the Dutch penalty area, was bundled over and Gemmill scored the second penalty of the game. Now the Dutch were looking in need of assistance. Four minutes past the hour, following a free-kick for Scotland on the right, Gemmill collected the ball just outside the Dutch penalty area and proceeded to bob and weave his way through the defence on the right before scoring a goal that will be remembered for a long time.

Now the Scottish supporters, so disgusted with their team after the defeat by Peru and the draw with Iran, were singing: "We'll support you ever more". Support, however, was just not enough and 18 minutes from the end Rep sent in a marvellous swerving shot from 25 yards that Rough got his hands to but could not stop. Symbolically one of the last Scottish attempts ended when the referee spotted Jordan reaching up for a centre with the hand that had finished Wales. It was a last ironical twist to a story that had a bitter climax but a gallant epilogue.

❝

Ally MacLeod, their manager, began to believe the miracle was going to happen

❞

11|09|1985

Jock Stein, Scotland's guiding hand, is dead

Obituary

Jock Stein, the 62-year-old Scotland manager, collapsed with a heart attack as he watched his team virtually ensure a place in next summer's World Cup finals by drawing 1-1 with Wales, and died a few minutes after the game had ended.

In spite of immediate attention from the Scottish team doctor, Stuart Hillis, who is a leading cardiologist, and his Welsh counterpart, Graham Jones, Stein died in the treatment room at Ninian Park. Some 15,000 celebrating Scottish fans left the ground singing their delight at the result, unaware of the death of one of the greatest figures in British football.

Willie Miller, the Scotland captain, said: "It's unbelievable. What more can I say?" Another Scottish player, Chelsea's David Speedie, said: "It's a great result for Scotland but the evening has been ruined by the news of Jock's death."

The secretary of the Welsh FA, Alun Evans, said: "The game has lost a true man of football who will be missed not only in Scotland but throughout world football. When you consider what he has done for British football then everything this evening pales into total insignificance."

Denis Law, who was commenting on the game for BBC radio, said: "The first thing you'd think of are Jock's wife and family. He had a boy and a girl, both married, and I know the family well."

The Labour party leader, Neil Kinnock, who was at the match, said he was "deeply shocked and saddened" by Stein's death. "I and countless others knew Jock Stein to be such a good and kindly man and his death will grieve thousands of people inside and outside football," he said.

Stein, sitting on the Scottish bench, became agitated in the closing minutes of the game as, with the score 1-1, photographers began to crowd in for their reaction shots. According to Mike England, the Welsh manager, who was sitting close by, "I saw Jock collapse. The whistle went for a free-kick and I thought it was full-time. I saw photographers bothering him and he put out a hand to try and move one of them away. As

Jock Stein in Celtic's counting house: the European Cup and 10 league titles, nine in succession, were won in his reign

soon as Jock turned round I knew something was wrong – he clutched at his chest and I thought he had had a heart attack."

Jock Stein CBE achieved his greatest success with Celtic, whom he led to victory in the European Cup final of 1967 – the first British club to win the trophy. But if the Big Man's achievements were unrivalled in the Scottish game, his origins were humble.

His father was a coal miner who was a miner's son, and the young Stein went down the pit at the age of 16. Meanwhile his playing career was blossoming with Blantyre Victoria, a junior club in the family's home village in the Lanarkshire coalfield.

He progressed to playing semi-pro with Albion Rovers, before turning his back on mining and accepting an offer of £12 to play for the Welsh club Llanelli. He spent 18 months there before a £1,200 fee took him in 1951 to the club with whom he was to become synonymous, Celtic.

Bought originally as cover for the regular centre-half, Stein soon became captain and led the club to league and cup honours. When injury ended his career, he was put in charge of the reserves, the prelude to four years as manager of Dunfermline. He took the Fife club to Scottish Cup success for the first time in their history and had a brief spell with Hibernian before being asked to return to Celtic.

Stein became only their fourth manager. He was a Protestant, and the Celtic chairman, the late Sir Robert Kelly, was fond of joking that. although his club had Catholic origins, a quarter of the men at the helm had been Protestant. No matter, Stein's Celtic blended players of both persuasions and they became one of the most formidable sides in British soccer history.

At home the team of Murdoch and McNeill, Johnstone and Auld, Simpson and Gemmell swept all before them. Under Stein Celtic won 10 Scottish championships, nine of them in succession. But it was the European Cup triumph, a 2-1 victory in Lisbon over the arch-disciples of defensive football, Inter Milan, which confirmed Stein's and Celtic's greatness.

Bill Shankly, who shared a mining background with Stein, is said to have forced his way through the euphoric dressing-room to shake his hand. "John," said Shankly, "you're immortal."

With players like McGrain and Dalglish coming through, Celtic's success was sustained until the mid-Seventies. But after a car crash, in which he almost died, in 1975 Stein discovered that even those who rise above mere mortality are dispensable. Celtic asked him to become promotions manager to make way for Billy McNeill. The sense of rejection drove him south of the border for the first time at the age of 55 to try his luck with Leeds. Recommended for the job by his friend Don Revie, Stein's attempt to clear up the mess left by Revie's departure lasted 44 days. A call to succeed Ally MacLeod as manager of Scotland — a post he had held briefly in 1966 — proved irresistible.

He steered the national side to the World Cup finals in 1982 and, although unable to duplicate the success he enjoyed at club level, was on the verge of leading Scotland to the Mexico finals. Alex Ferguson, Aberdeen's manager, was appointed Stein's assistant last year, and is likely to take over now.

> ❝
> Stein's death will grieve thousands inside and outside football. He was such a kindly man
> ❞

14|03|2006

Jinky the green man gave the go-ahead to legends

Kevin McCarra

Jimmy Johnstone died yesterday of motor neurone disease. Of late supporters have taken to calling him the greatest player in Celtic's history. I am not sure I agree with that but he is the most loved player the club has known. The winger's final game for them took place 31 years ago but the memories seem to have been getting fresher. Johnstone implanted himself in the consciousness of Glasgow and the west of Scotland.

There children of a certain background are taught about the green man symbol by being told that they must not cross at the traffic lights until they see Jinky. Johnstone himself, however, had to commit himself to risk-taking. Few reflect on just how dirty a sport football was in the 60s, when full-backs were usually permitted to sink the boot into wingers they were not good enough to tackle properly. The better the footballer, the greater the danger. Johnstone was, therefore, in a whole lot of trouble. During the infamous 1974 European Cup semi-final with Atletico Madrid, three of the visiting team were sent off in Glasgow and I recall Johnstone taking a kick to the testicles.

He had worked to turn himself into an unbreakable athlete. As a 16-year-old in 1961 he was 5ft 2in and weighed little more than six stone. His height could increase only slightly but Johnstone built muscle by donning his father's heavy pit boots and running every day in the fields behind his house.

Such dedication was not commonly associated with him in adulthood, where a boisterous private life provoked Celtic to part with him when he was 30, but fellow players were in awe of his courage even more than they were of his talent. They watched him getting hacked down, calling for the ball from the free-kick and taking on the man who had just hurt him. Johnstone was a superb dribbler whose turns and jinks, those sudden changes of direction, made the greatest defender queasy.

The anecdote is being dusted down once more of the occasion in 1974 when, not far from breakfast time, the Scotland squad emerged from a pub in Largs and he was pushed out in a rowing boat that happened not to possess any oars. There was a cascade of bad coverage. It is less commonly recalled that Johnstone played beautifully in a 2-0 victory over England a mere four days later. As he left the pitch, the winger made a gesture to the Hampden press box that, just conceivably, was indicating the number of goals. He got himself into further trouble and was not picked for any of Scotland's games at that summer's World Cup finals. Considering that a little unorthodoxy could have tipped a goalless draw with Brazil into a win, his country may have been punished by the decision more than he was.

The honours had mounted up for Johnstone in any case but it is the sheer pleasure he gave that counted most. He was not the kind who, in retirement, turns into the curator of his career. I remember asking him about the 1967 Scottish Cup final with Aberdeen. "We lost that one, didn't we?" he ventured. Every Celtic supporter has it tattooed on his or her brain that the club completed a clean sweep of five tournaments that season, from the Glasgow Cup to the European Cup. Every supporter except Jimmy. I wound up standing on his fireside rug trying to recreate his contribution to a goal against Aberdeen that day.

There was never any need for him to highlight his achievements. The legend and the anecdotes were handed down. Generations to come will continue to hear how Johnstone, who was frightened of flying, struck a deal with the manager Jock Stein that he would be excused the second leg of a European Cup tie with Red Star Belgrade in 1968 so long as Celtic won the first by a four-goal margin. The winger, having scored twice and made two others, ran down the field shouting "I'm no' going" when the score reached 5-1. It was moving then to hear he had conquered the phobia and boarded a flight so he could get treatment for his motor neurone disease in the United States.

People were drawn to this unique, ordinary character. The 2004 documentary Lord of the Wing captures it well, showing Johnstone walking towards the main entrance at Celtic Park one match day while fans flock to him from all over the car park. Kids so young as to have heard more about him from their grandfathers than their dads lead the charge. They just wanted to be close to him. Individuals rallied round purposefully as well. On that same DVD Johnstone talked about the drink problems he had been through and, in addition to the help of his family, he was aided considerably by the businessman and Celtic shareholder Willie Haughey.

The bonds with him were not to be broken. The crowd will feel closer than ever to Johnstone at Celtic's CIS Cup final with Dunfermline on Sunday and it would be in keeping with the sheer fun he inspired if it was a happy commemoration. He epitomised an innocent virtuosity and an image springs to mind of the amusing, inflatable Johnstone dolls that were waggled from the terracings around 1970. If any Glaswegian entrepreneur can get some manufactured this week he'll make a tidy sum.

21|06|2007
Scotland's future is bright with past master Smith in place

Nicky Campbell

Stephen Hawking argues that time travel cannot be possible. If it were, or should I say if it ever will be or ever was, where are all the time travellers? Where are the hordes of future folk nipping back to now and then for a glimpse of our collective lunacy?

Fast forward to this time next week. It is the first official day for the new chief executive of the Scottish Football Association – a remarkable case of poacher turned gamekeeper. Gordon Smith, the former striker, coach, assistant manager, TV pundit and, latterly, football agent (cue Victorian melodrama music), will be donning the ceremonial blue blazer worn previously by some of the most spectacularly mediocre figures in Scottish football's long and colourful history. "Ladies and gentlemen, if you care to look out of your windows you will see that we have arrived in the 21st century."

I rang Gordon to congratulate him and, given that he has a fuller plate than a Floridian at a buffet, I wanted to get a sense of how he was going to tackle the big issues facing the game. The national team? Grass-roots participation? And, yes, sectarianism? But he was the one who brought up metaphysics. "If they ever invent a time machine, count me in," he chuckled.

Back to May 1983, then. "And Smith must score," declaimed the commentary. I asked Gordon about his notorious last-minute miss for Brighton in the FA Cup final against Manchester United because I've always wondered if Chris Waddle, Stuart Pearce and others, despite the inner steel that got them to the top in the first place, ever stop hurting deep inside.

I've spoken to Waddle about his penalty miss against West Germany in 1990 and he is a fantastically phlegmatic character who went on to have an outstanding season with Marseille in 1991. He once said: "There were two ways to react: basically you can do a Lord Lucan and disappear or stick your chest out and prove to everybody you're a good footballer. That's the one I opted for. I certainly don't dwell on the memory." There is a hint, though, in the last bit. I wonder if, in the darkest night, the memory still comes knocking.

Smith is candid. "There were difficult times in the early days when it had a real effect on me." Not long after the Cup final he found himself in a woebegone reserve match and some nonentity started taunting him. Smith calmly looked in the guy's eyes and said: "What does the Cup final look like on TV because it's great to play in." After he retired he got a job in financial services in London and recalls the boss's phone calls. "We've got an ex-footballer, Gordon Smith, working for us now." And then the sotto voce "Yes, that's the one."

Smith's memory of the final is priceless, by turns the stuff of boyhood dreams and adult nightmares. He had put Brighton 1-0 up, remember. Imagine coming off at half-time and seeing your name on the scoreboard. "I thought, 'I'll be remembered for this game.'" How right he was. So what happened?

"It had got to extra-time and we were in the last minute. I thought low and hard would take him by surprise but he blocked it and smothered the rebound. What would I do differently? Definitely wait and see if he committed himself." "He", of course, is Gary Bailey, a man still miffed that the commentator did not say: "What a save by Bailey!"

"I turned away and thought, shit, I could have scored there," remembers Smith. "It would have been the winning goal in the Cup final. It would have won the Cup for Brighton. I should have done better." Brighton lost the replay 4-0 but the next season Smith was Manchester City's top scorer in their promotion drive. As Waddle said, it's all down to how you respond. Smith pointed something else out as I listened earnestly. "The next season I signed a record-breaking 10-grand deal with Adidas." "Did you?" "Yeah. To wear Nike."

Now he is running the SFA and it is great news for the Scottish game. He is an impressive man and I'd hazard that's in no small part thanks to a blond-haired South African goalkeeper. Gordon, give that Tardis a wide berth.

Gordon Smith did not score to win the FA Cup for Brighton in 1983 but he did with the Scottish Football Association

Braveheart campaign ends in failure ... just don't call it glorious

Euro 2008 qualifiers
Scotland 1 Italy 2
Andy Hunter, Hampden Park

A campaign that had given so much had breathed its last but Scotland would not let go. For 30 minutes after hope had expired the Tartan Army stood firm, singing through its anger, despair and tears for an encore which eventually arrived when James McFadden led the team on not so much a lap of honour as a funeral march. In the bowels of the stadium the talk was defiant, of new beginnings rather than another agonising ending, but the words came from the players, the officials and supporters involved in the revival. They were not so convincing from the manager.

Alex McLeish will witness tangible evidence of his successful international reign when he travels to South Africa for a World Cup qualifying draw on Sunday with Scotland among its second seeds. It may feel an empty consolation, now that his nation's more prized reward has gone, and the manager may be tempted to go with it.

A place in next summer's European Championship would have completed the transformation of a country which was convinced of miracles until Christian Panucci's stoppage-time header looped over Craig Gordon and brought Scotland back to grim reality. In a group containing the proven pedigree of Italy and France there could be no outside help towards qualification.

An appointment in Austria and Switzerland would also have dispelled the uncertainty surrounding McLeish's future. Without it, and without a competitive fixture until next autumn, Scotland are prey to a Premier League club who attempt to capitalise on his desire to work in England's upper tier. Such offers were conspicuous by their absence in the nine months he was out of work after his departure from Rangers, where seven trophies went unacknowledged after his final fraught season. The challenge facing the Scottish Football Association will be as immense as the one its team faced against the world champions.

"You can understand the boss being in demand and I'm sure there will be big Premiership teams looking at what he has done with us and they will be after him," said Darren Fletcher. "We can only hope he stays because it is a young team and we are ready for another couple of campaigns. There are positives to be taken from this campaign but, once again, we were just that one step short of qualifying."

McLeish echoed the sentiment that this Scotland squad could make the final leap but was noncommittal on his part in the process. "I am happy in the job just now. I really enjoy it, I enjoy working with the players and the backroom staff," he began. "But you know how football is. It's the type of business where you can never say it is going to be a definite. At the moment I am very much committed to Scotland but I don't think this is the day to talk about my future. I'm gutted for my players and for my staff and for Scotland."

A drunk who stood in George Square at midnight arguing that Scotland would still qualify if France lose to Ukraine on Wednesday was symptomatic of the underdog refusing to accept the truth but Scotland came close to the incredible at Hampden. In the 20 or so minutes between Barry Ferguson's poached equaliser and the erroneous decision of the Spanish assistant referee, Juan Carlos Yuste Jimenez, to penalise Alan Hutton for taking an elbow from Giorgio Chiellini, a free-kick award which produced Panucci's winner, they played with a purpose, some style and a belief in the victory they needed to advance. The sight of the world champions desperately clearing their lines in the closing stages, of Hutton rampaging down the right and the Scotland midfield belatedly gaining the upper hand provided further evidence of their quality.

Yet it was not enough to deny an impressive Italy, an international team who again drew strength from turmoil, and for all the injustices raged at Jimenez — "If it was a player making a terrible decision in a game or a big mistake, he probably would not be playing the next game," McLeish said. "The guy, for me, doesn't deserve to be officiating at a high level" — Scotland's frustration stemmed from their own failings, too. Four players were oblivious to danger from a throw-in after only 70 seconds, allowing Antonio di Natale to cross for Luca Toni to flick into the top corner and to send the raindrops on the Hampden net exploding into the evening sky.

Thereafter the Scots toiled to find space behind the Milan midfield and were indebted to the Spanish officials for having a fighting chance when they disallowed a fair goal from Di Natale for offside and allowed Ferguson to level from a suspect position. A handball appeal against Gianluca Zambrotta and a glaring miss from McFadden with the scores level increased despair. Panucci then inflicted the agony.

A glorious failure? As the kids who traipsed from Hampden with tears rolling down their painted faces testified, there was nothing glorious about it.

Chapter four
Liverpool's bootroom revolution

06|12|1999

Way back when ... the Reds were struggling

Liverpool were a Second Division club in a vulnerable industrial city – then along came Bill Shankly. By Frank Keating

Forty years ago today Bill Shankly and his wife Nessie were househunting in Formby. It was the start of something new and English club football was never to be the same.

The week before, on Tuesday December 1 1959, the local *Echo* had announced that Shankly was to be the manager of Liverpool FC, then in the Second Division, and that he would begin duty on New Year's Day, his present club Huddersfield Town having demanded he work out a month's notice.

The paper said the 46-year-old former Scottish international had beaten the other shortlisted candidates Harry Catterick, Jimmy Murphy, Peter Doherty and Jimmy Hagan for the job and that his annual salary of £2,500 was £500 more than he was getting at Huddersfield.

The sports editor, Leslie Edwards, wrote prophetically: "Liverpool are getting the man they want. He is a 100% club man, an expert and enthusiast rolled into one, in fact a one-man combination that will not rest till Liverpool are in the First Division."

In fact, within days of his resignation Huddersfield, desperately sorry to lose him, relented on the month's notice. Early on the morning of Monday December 14 Shankly parked his Austin A40 in the tiny car park behind Anfield's gabled main stand. He had bought a new suit. He announced himself at the front office – "I am your new manager, lassie" – and was told to go upstairs where the imposing chairman, Tom Williams, and club secretary, Jimmy McInnes, awaited him, as well as a photographer from the *Echo* who at once posed the trio shaking hands and "sharing a joke", although Shankly was not smiling.

"Now we'll show you around," said Williams. "No need," said Shankly, "I saw all I needed on Saturday after I watched the reserves play." The two Liverpool men were taken aback.

On Saturday they had been with the first team at Bristol Rovers, and it was news to them when Shankly announced that the reserves had beaten Manchester City's "stiffs" by 5-0. "Did you know you've some useful players in the reserves?" he told them. They were already thinking they had made the right choice.

Anfield was as run down as the club, which had been consigned to the Second Division since 1954 and earlier in 1959 had been a national laughing stock when beaten in the third round of the FA Cup by non-League Worcester City. But Shankly's reasons for leaving Huddersfield – after a 10-year apprenticeship as manager at Carlisle, Workington and Grimsby – had been the obvious potential of a big city club.

He wanted to stir a giant, however slothful, and felt he was ready to do so. Mind you, in 1959 the city of Liverpool itself

A bronze of Bill Shankly, who laid the bootroom foundations for Liverpool's greatness, is unveiled at Anfield in 1997

had yet to stir from the postwar industrial depression, even though Harold Macmillan had that year won a general election for the Tory party on the slogan "You've never had it so good".

Socialist Shankly knew better than that. The once great port of his new city was economically dispirited and on that very day the *Echo* printed the photograph of his arrival at Anfield the paper led on the forecast that the city's 800 male juveniles on the dole would rise in number tenfold within three years.

Nor had Liverpool remotely realised its cultural potential for the new decade. That first week in December, Cliff Richard and the Shadows were playing at the local Empire and only their best friends knew that a group of lads had formed their first pop group, about to rename themselves the Silver Beetles.

Williams and McInnes took Shankly down to meet Anfield's small staff once they had all reported for work that morning. Although their new manager had not yet mentioned it, they presumed, as was the custom, that he would be bringing in his own lieutenants and that Liverpool's lot (recruited under the previous manager Phil Taylor, who had retired through ill-health) would be leaving.

Again, Williams and McInnes were mightily surprised that Shankly treated the group of men sweating on their jobs almost as blood brothers. He had played with and against trainer Bob Paisley, a fellow devotee of American boxing, and he embraced him. He knew Reuben Bennett through his own brother Bob when they played together at Dundee. He had tried to sign Joe Fagan years ago for Grimsby when Fagan was playing for Manchester City, and he warmly told old Albert Shelley, who had cleaned the dressing rooms for years, that he was a legend in the game.

In Stephen F Kelly's biography *Shankly*, the author writes: "On that first morning Shankly was to make the wisest decision he was ever to make in his entire Anfield career. He guaranteed every man their jobs ... at a stroke he had Paisley's supporting role and tactical knowledge, Fagan's psychology, Bennett's Scottishness, Shelley's loyalty. All of them, including Shankly, had been forged in the same hard-knocks school of life ... and they had all learned the lessons of common decency, honesty and pride."

Shankly sat them down that morning. "Fellows, your jobs are safe. Some managers bring their own people with them. Not me. I have my own system and it will work in co-operation with you. I will lay down the plans and gradually we will all be on the same wavelength. I demand only one thing: loyalty. Nobody must carry stories about anybody else. If anyone tells me a story about anybody else, that man with the story will get the sack, and I don't care if he has been here 50 years. Every one of us must be loyal to each other — and every single thing we do must be for Liverpool football club." The legendary ethos of Anfield's bootroom was born. And so was the most successful football club England has ever had.

17|12|1968

The fighting philosophy of Shankly

Eric Todd talks to the Liverpool manager — a players' man who has always been 'daft about fitba'

Like the state of holy matrimony, an interview with Bill Shankly, manager of Liverpool, is not to be entered lightly. There is an element of chance about them both; in neither is the course of events predictable. Shankly has to be heard to be appreciated. Like Jim Sims, that much-loved slow bowler for Middlesex in years gone by, he expresses himself through the corner of his mouth. There the comparison ends. Sims favoured the confidential drawl, Shankly fires his words as if with a Gatling gun. And he does not often miss.

Thirty years have passed since my first sight of Shankly playing at Deepdale in the company of the Beatties (not related), the O'Donnells (brothers), Jimmy Milne, Jimmy Dougal and Harry Holdcroft, that most handsome of goalkeepers. Even in those days Shankly was a busy, fussy character who always played with his palms turned outwards, creating the remote illusion of a sailing ship striving for that little extra help from the wind.

"Naw, naw," protested Shankly, when I suggested that analogy. "It gave me strength. Did ye notice too that ah played on ma toes all the time? Like a ballet dancer? That gave me strength in ma calves, and ah've still got it. Preston was only a sma' place — Jim Taylor, the North End chairman, called us a village team — but it was a fine club who believed in modern methods. Ah lairned a great deal wi' Preston and ah've always tried tae pass on some o' those lessons.

"Ah was always daft about fitba'. Ah went tae Carlisle whan ah was 17 an' a half, moved tae Preston in 1933, an' finished pleyin' in 1949 when ah went tae Carlisle as their manager. They were a useful side but they hadnae a great deal o' ambition. But ah had. So when ah had the offer tae take over at Grimsby because they ware strugglin', ah went an' took less wages. Frae Grimsby ah went tae Workington, who were facin' extermination. They offered me a bonus if ah could save them. Ah got ma bonus. Then ah went as assistant tae Andy Beattie at Huddersfield an', when he left, ah took his place. Ah was made manager o' Liverpool in 1959 an' the rest you know. An' by the by, ah was never sacked in the whole o' ma life.

Shankly sipped his tea, long since cold, before he set off on a new theme. "People often ask me if ah ever made a mistake. Well, tae my mind 'mistake' is a misused word, especially in fitba'. For example, ye might say it was a mistake for a club tae buy such an' such a player but that is nae necessarily true. The player might not be able tae settle down or to fit in. He might no' suit his environment. Just bad luck. A fitballer's no' like a hat or a coat that you can leave at a shop if it doesna' fit or suit ye."

"Mind you, there are some managers ah've known who have gone about things the wrong way. The manager above all things should be solely responsible for the playing and training staffs and all tactics. He must be able tae coach and tae explain such basic things as how tae kick a ball and how tae pass it an' control it. In other words, he must know what he's talking about. What good is it tae go tae a golf professional for lessons if he disna' know the game? The same wi' a fitba' manager."

"Mind you, ah wouldna' say the best players make the best managers, although ah think that's been more the case in recent years – but a manager makes things so much harder for himself if he can't explain the game to his players. An' even that's only half the battle. Tae get the best out of his men, the manager has tae work tae a tactical plan they understand which need not necessarily be the one he'd like himself. For instance, at Liverpool we have Ian Callaghan and Peter Thompson, two of the best wingers in the game. They are as near tae the old orthodox wingers as there are, so why should they be used in any other way? It wouldn'a be fair for one thing. Natural ability is far too precious tae be messed about wi'."

Law had everything

"Before ah forget ah must just tell ye about Denis Law. When ah went tae Huddersfield, ah had charge o' the resairves, an' this wee boy o' 15 was one of them. Ye wouldna' hae thought so tae look at him but he had everything. He was fiery an' he was talented an' he was earmarked tae be a star. He was tae become one o' the greatest players ah ever set eyes on. Aye, he was that."

After this diversion Shankly picked up his management thread as if he had never left it. "As for me, if they're no' satisfied wi' me, they'll get rid o' me. We have a responsibility tae the people o' Liverpool. There was a great potential at Anfield when ah went there and ah like tae think ah have helped tae realise that potential. We have got tae try and maintain the high standard we have set, keepin' in line wi' other teams wi' ambition, an' mebbe winnin' the League Championship again. That would gi' us a record haul of eight league titles, one more than Manchester United and Arsenal."

Shankly is young enough to have expectations of seeing that day, successful enough to withstand those tribulations to which so many of his kind have succumbed, patient enough to go on making a living until he can retire and take Nessie, his long-suffering wife, on their first real holiday in 25 years. When they went to a football match during their honeymoon, Nessie had a hint of what was in store in the years ahead. "A wonderful, understanding woman," said Shankly, whose present idea of a holiday is to stay in bed until mid-morning.

Sense of humour

He neither smokes nor drinks but sees no reason why others should not do so – in moderation – and he has a lively sense of humour, although he is not conscious of it. If he were asked to think of something funny, he would be a slow starter. He is, however, master of the "off the cuff" type of humour and frequently reduces his players and press conference to hysterics with asides he had meant to be taken seriously. The sayings of Shankly are as forthright and weighty as the sayings of Mao. In the streets around Anfield they are also much more respected.

Shankly is not impressed easily nor is he a willing subject for embarrassment. When he put through his own goal in Tom Finney's testimonial, he was no more remorseful than a lad caught pinching jam from the larder. Only once, perhaps, did he go close to blushing. He played in a game alongside Frank Soo of Stoke City and afterwards a Scottish selector among the crowd went up and put his arm round Shankly's shoulder. "Well done, Soo," he said. "You played a blinder." "He thought ah was the Chinese because of the way ma hair was cut," explains Shankly, and his chuckle is that of a corncrake in search of a mate.

I think it would be an exaggeration to say that Shankly is regarded generally as a "popular" manager – except at Anfield, where the Kop acknowledges him to be omnipotent. He is not as aloof as he used to be but he is not easy to know, not easy to draw out. His conversation, like the man himself, is fitful. He speaks in Morse, as it were. But for all that he is, and always has been, among the genuinely dedicated managers and his success as a player and as a manager has been achieved the hard way. He has in his time made mistakes over transfers – that is my view, not his – but he covered them up effectively. Above all, Shankly is a players' man who knows that if he fights for them, they will fight for him. It seems a sound philosophy.

The Duke of Wellington is reported to have made sure personally that his troops – who did most of the work – had comfortable billets. Shankly subscribes to the same principles and now squeezes the duties of accommodation inspector into his already congested schedule.

Before I left him, Shankly summoned the manager of a hotel and gave him his instructions. "There'll be, eh, 17, in the party," he said. "So, eh, that'll be 17 fillet steaks – ah'll let ye know how we want them done when we arrive – wi' chips. For afterwards, eh, there'll be 17 fresh fruit salads an' fresh cream. Right? Then for breakfast, eh ..." A players' man indeed.

27|05|1977

Glory, glory Liverpool

European Cup final
Liverpool 3 Borussia Mönchengladbach 1
David Lacey, Rome

Liverpool gained their ultimate reward for 13 years of dogged perseverance in Continental competitions when they became the second English and third British club to win the European Cup last night.

After taking the lead and dominating the first half they conceded a goal early in the second and for a time were in danger of being overwhelmed by the West German champions' formidable attacking skill. But Tommy Smith put them back in front with his first goal of the season, probably the last and certainly most important of his long career at Anfield, and Neal completed a famous British victory with a penalty.

As the game finished, the 20,000 Liverpool supporters who had regaled the Olympic stadium throughout with songs from home, reacted not with relief but with the jubilation of those who had known all along that the result would be right.

In some ways the match followed the course that many had predicted for last Saturday's FA Cup final. At times Gladbach produced some breathtaking moments in attack and after they had drawn level, Bonhof, the outstanding individual on the night, looked as if he might haul the Germans to victory.

But their defence made error after error, each one more elementary than the last. Gladbach were always in danger of being severely punished for Wittkamp's weakness in the air, Klinkhammers's carelessness and the fact that on a warm heavy evening Vogts was worn down by Keegan's speed and quick changes of direction.

In the end Vogts gave away a weary penalty by bringing down Keegan to finish any hope that Gladbach might have had of achieving yet another remarkable West German escape.

The German team hit a post before Liverpool scored and might have had another two goals but for the quick reactions of Clemence. But no one could deny the English champions their full credit.

Liverpool have been criticised for playing predictable football which owes more to determination and organisation than to the sort of varied skill shown by the leading continental teams. But they have just won the League, were unlucky in losing the Cup to Manchester United and have now seen off a side regarded as being among the best in the world. No English club will ever come closer to the treble without actually winning it.

The pattern of play so closely resembled the Wembley match that Liverpool's performance could almost be summed up in the same words. Again Kennedy, McDermott and Case, wonderfully supported by Callaghan, held the midfield for long periods. The difference this time was that Liverpool found space in the penalty area easy to come by and that, when they made mistakes themselves, they survived, that is with one notable exception.

The Germans hardly achieved a serious attack for 20 minutes but, when they did, they nearly scored. Stielike and Heynckes worked the ball quickly up the left and found Bonhof running on the inside for a 20-yard shot that rebounded from the foot of the near post. In the 25th minute Kulik replaced Wimmer, who appeared to have strained a thigh muscle, and three minutes later Liverpool were ahead. Callaghan pushed the ball forward to Heighway near the right-hand corner of the penalty area. As this was happening McDermott ran into a huge gap Heighway found him with a cool pass and Kneib could do little to stop McDermott's shot low to his right.

The Kop spent half-time singing "Come On You Mighty Reds" but within six minutes of the second half the mighty had fallen, albeit temporarily. Case passed to Neal without looking and found to his horror that he had put Simonsen through. The little Dane held off Smith impudently before unleashing a marvellous shot high into the far corner.

For the Germans it was as if someone had flicked a master switch to animate their previously pedestrian movements. Just past the hour a superb movement, instigated by Bonhof, ended with Simonsen sending Heynckes clear but Clemence sprinted off his line to block the shot and two minutes later Liverpool were back in the lead. Klinkhammer needlessly conceded a corner on the left, Heighway sent the ball in towards the near post and Smith timed his arrival perfectly to head past Kneib.

After that Liverpool virtually regained their earlier command, although Clemence had to make another desperate save near the edge of his penalty area, pushing the ball away from Simonsen. Seven minutes from the end Keegan sprinted past Vogts on the inside, was brought down, and Neal scored with another of his calm penalties.

There was just time for Stielike to be cautioned for a foul on Keegan and it was all over. "Liverpool are the winners," announced a female voice — but the sea of red and white spreading halfway round the stadium told its own story.

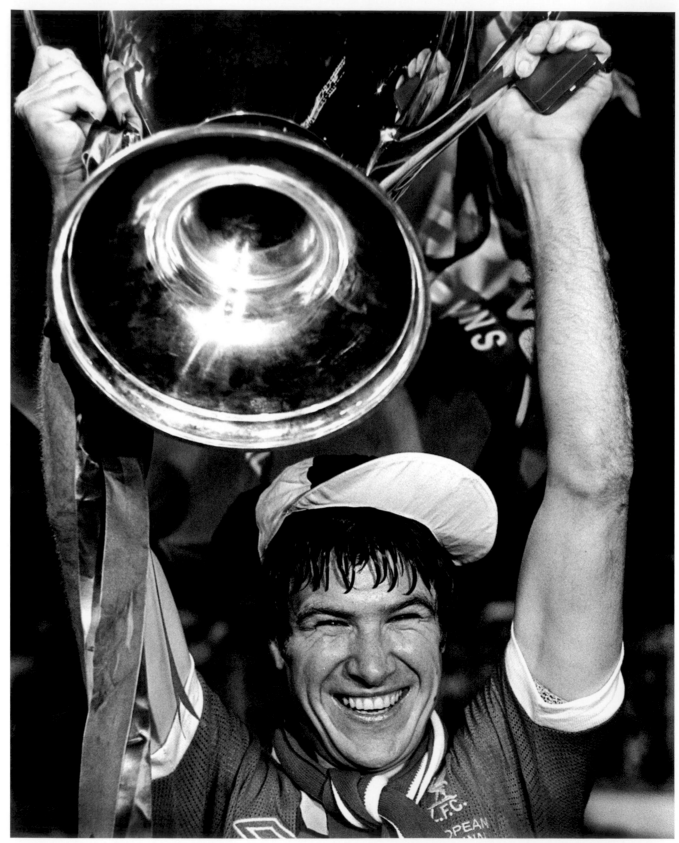

An ecstatic Emlyn Hughes, captain as Liverpool retained the European Cup in 1978, wears his heart on his head and neck

11|05|1978

King Kenny keeps crown

European Cup final
Liverpool 1 Bruges 0
David Lacey, Wembley

Liverpool, playing marvellously co-ordinated football at times, retained the European Cup when they defeated Bruges, the Belgian champions, 1-0 at Wembley last night to rapturous accompaniment from their supporters, whose songs of rejoicing rang loud and long into a warm, clear London night.

After struggling for a time to disentangle themselves from their opponents' tight marking and outwit their offside tactics, Liverpool's football found something, though by no means all, of the quality of Rome where they won the European Cup a year ago. Birger Jensen, Bruges' Danish goalkeeper, thwarted them for a time but 25 minutes from the end Kenny Dalglish won Liverpool the match with his 30th goal of the season and, apart from one precarious moment when the ball was cleared off the line, it was all over bar the singing.

If Liverpool did not achieve quite the simple, ritualistic victory that many had expected and while none of their players became the dominant figure that Kevin Keegan had been in Rome, they still produced an intelligent performance which in some ways was more creditable than their defeat of Borussia Mönchengladbach, who fell far below their potential.

Bruges were more awkward opponents. They were without Courant's skilful influence in midfield and the possibility of the injured Lambert making an appearance in attack could only have been a rumour put about to disconcert the enemy. Lacking two such important players, they decided to concentrate on stifling Liverpool's movements with dedicated man-to-man marking and an offside trap ever improving in efficiency.

The way Liverpool set about defeating these negative but for a time highly effective tactics was the most interesting aspect of their performance and demonstrated the change in the English champions' make-up that has been taking place during the season just ended. There was a time when a Liverpool side presented with such opposition would have become nervous and impatient, ballooning the ball upfield and becoming over-reliant on corners and free-kicks for scoring chances.

Last night they solved the problem amid the full flow of play. Souness, with his beautifully struck, finely weighted passes, began the process of dismantling the Bruges cover and McDermott, his positioning and perception on the ball again an integral part of Liverpool's success, completed it. Kennedy was not as strong an influence as he had been in earlier rounds but Fairclough's persistent harrying of the Belgian defence more than compensated for this.

The overall impression of Liverpool's performance last night was of an accomplished team, strong in tradition and experience, confident of victory and patient in its pursuit. Only twice did Bruges offer them a serious threat. Early in the second half an excellent crossfield ball from Vandereycken gave Sorensen the chance to slip past Hughes. The Dane was blocked before he could shoot, but the ball was not cleared and Clemence nearly lost a race for possession with Ku, a Hungarian brought in at the last moment by Ernst Happel, the Bruges coach.

Five minutes from the end Sorensen unnerved the Liverpool defence by running straight at them with the ball, again he was stopped but, with Clemence off his line and Simoen taking aim, the possibility of extra-time loomed briefly. Thompson, however, was behind the goalkeeper to block.

Liverpool suffered a multitude of near misses, most of them in the 30 minutes straddling half-time when their football reached its height. Kennedy volleyed the ball across the face of goal; Case's thunderous free-kick was punched away by Jensen, who in the closing minutes of the first half first blocked Fairclough as he ran through, then tipped over a Hansen header.

Early in the second half Jensen flung himself at the feet of McDermott who had started and seemed likely to finish an exquisite passing movement with Souness and Dalglish that had the Bruges cover looking statuesque, the offside trap gaping in astonishment.

Bruges made a couple of substitutions, Sanders replacing Ku and Volders coming on for Maes, but Bob Paisley's replacement of Case by Heighway, newly recovered from an injured rib, was more significant because Liverpool's attacks had much more width once the Irishman had been introduced.

Heighway had not been on the field a minute before Liverpool scored with a goal that summed up their thoughtful mood of the night. There seemed minimal danger to Bruges as Neal held the ball in a confined space near the right-hand corner flag. Then the full-back released it to McDermott and a marvellous little chip found its way along the byline for Dalglish to open up all manner of possibilities. The ball went back to Souness, who held it long enough for everyone to move onside, then squeezed his most telling pass of the game through to Dalglish, whose shot went wide of Jensen's despairing right hand.

Case and Vandereycken were cautioned during a brief spell of mutual frustration in the first half but generally it was a clean fought encounter, not the best European Cup final there has been but by no means the worst, and for Liverpool the ultimate confirmation of their present status as the most successful English club of all time.

Paisley blamed Bruges for the lack of excitement. He said: "It takes two teams to make a game into a spectacle and Bruges only seemed to be concerned with keeping the score down."

23|02|1991
The winner who was happiest when his boots did the talking

A shining light on the pitch, Kenny Dalglish was never at ease in the glare of management, writes Steve Bierley

A few weeks ago, in the middle of an after-match conference at Villa Park during which Kenny Dalglish was being typically oblique, an interloper suddenly sprang an irrelevant and impertinent question. "Kenny," he demanded, "in that European Cup final did you really mean to score against Bruges or were you trying to cross the ball?"

Not surprisingly the fan did not receive an answer and the bizarre little incident would have been relegated to the smallest scrapbook of football history until yesterday morning when Dalglish, still a few days short of his 40th birthday, announced that the pressure had all become too much.

It was then that the words of Bob Paisley came to mind, words that described the immediate aftermath of the single Dalglish goal that had won the 1978 European Cup final for Liverpool at Wembley. "He celebrated as if it was the first one he had ever scored. The arch-professional suddenly lost out to the football nut. The arms flew high and wide, the smile cracked the face in half, the eyes sparkled and he sprinted away faster than he had moved all night."

This was Dalglish the majestic, Dalglish the players' player, Dalglish the goalscorer par excellence. The hackneyed phrase "his record speaks for itself" might have been coined for him. He made 324 appearances for Celtic and scored 167 goals; played in 515 matches for Liverpool and scored 173 goals. "When Kenny shines," said Paisley, "the whole team is illuminated."

Dalglish, the scorer of breathtaking goals and purveyor of the most perfectly weighted passes, was a player that anyone, Liverpool supporter or not, could take to the heart, for his was a genius all too rare in the modern game.

Dalglish the manager, the moulder of men and teams, was an altogether different persona and one that few could fathom. The right-arm salute and the huge grin were there for all to see whenever he celebrated a Liverpool goal from the match-day dug-out. But when it came to the public relations side of management he reflected his early schooling at Celtic under the tutelage of Jock Stein: say little and trust nobody.

Such was the legend of Shankly and the phenomenal success of Paisley that Dalglish was on a hiding to nothing when he was appointed player-manager, succeeding Joe Fagan on May 31 1985, immediately after the Heysel tragedy. Yet within a year, with Paisley at his side, he had pulled off what no other Liverpool manager had achieved: the League and Cup double.

It was the stuff of fiction. And so it had been from the moment Dalglish exchanged his green and white hoops for a red shirt in August 1977 for a fee of £440,000. That sum was a British transfer record but the seemingly irreplaceable Kevin Keegan was still being mourned and there were those, particularly outside Scotland, who wondered whether "one-paced" Kenny would succeed in the land of the Anglos. The answer was swift: he scored on his League debut at Ayresome Park and three days later treated the Kop to his first home goal in the 2-0 defeat of Newcastle. The No7 shirt was his and Anfield was in seventh heaven. It was not long before his goals were being greeted with a wave of home-made banners on the Kop, their message adapting the old song with the words "Kenny's from heaven".

There was no domestic title in his first season but on that warm May evening of 1978, in an otherwise largely forgettable match, Dalglish stole up on the blind side of the Belgian defence, took a pass from Graeme Souness and delicately chipped the Bruges goalkeeper.

Thereafter medals chased medals. "He is level-headed in all things," said Paisley after Dalglish had been voted Footballer of the Year in 1979. He added, significantly in hindsight, that the Scot was "not interested in publicity or talking about himself. He concentrates on just two things: his football and his family."

To say that his resignation yesterday was a shock would be an understatement. The players, on arriving for training, sensed that something was in the air but assumed another Anfield cloak-and-dagger transfer was imminent. "Nobody remotely guessed the gaffer was going to call it a day," said Ronnie Whelan.

The talking point on Merseyside was still that marvellous FA Cup tie at Goodison on Wednesday and lips were being licked at the prospect of the next replay. Suddenly, startlingly, it was forgotten.

There were tears in the eyes of Dalglish as he departed and within minutes, predictably enough, the rumour machine had lurched into overdrive. The words he had so often uttered, whenever a cloud had temporarily passed over the Liverpool sun, echoed back: "This is a matter for Liverpool Football Club and will be dealt with internally."

No doubt it will be, but there must be a thousand would-be interlopers who would just love to catch Dalglish at his front door this morning and ask: "Kenny, why did you really leave?"

28|05|1981
Five in a row for English raiders

European Cup final
Liverpool 1 Real Madrid 0
David Lacey, Paris

....

Liverpool became the first British club to win the European Cup three times when they defeated Real Madrid 1-0 in Paris last night in a final which, while it seldom approached the high standards set in the competition's early years, produced an increasingly interesting contest of many contrasts.

A late goal by Alan Kennedy kept the trophy in England for a fifth year and the end came with the Kop reminding the Parc des Princes that neither they nor their team would ever walk alone. In truth Liverpool always seemed the more likely winners and victory came after they had walked through not so much a storm as a series of squally showers of the type that Parisians had been avoiding all day.

Yet, if ever one man could have denied Liverpool their triumph, he had to be Juanito. The little Spaniard, one of the architects of England's humiliation at Wembley in March, challenged Liverpool's authority in midfield in the first half and in the second started to run at their defence to such good effect that he seemed capable of defying the logic of the game's pattern, most of which suggested a British success.

Liverpool's victory owed everything to their long years of experience in Continental competition. Real, for all their fine traditions in the European Cup, looked comparatively raw and especially in defence. From the outset Liverpool whittled away at Madrid's man-to-man marking. Souness, once he had run off the effects of an early foul by Sabido, was as profound an influence as ever, Lee chased and harried on the right, the full-backs, Neal and Alan Kennedy, were ever ready to move forward and Hansen and Thompson stood firm during an awkward period in the second half when Real threatened to snatch a goal.

In the first half Dalglish, held back the first time he twisted away from Cortes but seldom held thereafter, was a constant danger in the Real penalty area and this advantage ought to have brought Liverpool an earlier goal. After half-time Dalglish played deeper, seeking to draw defenders so that maximum use could be made of McDermott's runs deep into the Real cover. As Liverpool had not scored when they were dominating, the game became more intriguingly balanced the longer it went on.

Liverpool might have gone ahead in the opening half-hour, when Agustin pushed wide a low, skidding shot from Alan Kennedy, McDermott lifted a chance over the bar and Dalglish produced another sharp turn to confound Cortes but could not finish with sufficient strength to worry the goalkeeper.

It took Real some time to achieve similar co-ordination. Nevertheless there was danger lurking for Liverpool once Juanito started to look for opportunities to send colleagues running on to passes lobbed through the Liverpool defence. One such ball found Camacho slipping inside Hansen to clip a shot wide with Clemence off his line and out of position.

Cunningham's role was often peripheral. Once or twice his skill and acceleration threatened to turn either of Liverpool's flanks but little came of even his most promising advances.

A few minutes before half-time Neal, attacking on the right, found Dalglish, who held the ball craftily before rolling it into the path of Souness, running late and unnoticed through the Real defence. Agustin could not hold the shot and the Scot just failed to reach the rebound.

Liverpool either seemed likely to win by methodical means or lose through a moment of carelessness and, when Juanito began to assert his skill on the game, these moments seemed more likely to occur. Early in the second half Liverpool stopped for an offside decision against Cunningham that was not given and allowed Camacho a free run at Clemence. The goalkeeper, racing off his line, was beaten by a prodigious lob and shared the general British relief at seeing the ball dip over the bar.

In the end the game was won for Liverpool by a combination of Kennedys. Ray took a throw on the left which Cortes was in a position to cover. However the ball reached Alan , whose surge up the touchline took Real by surprise. Cortes made an indifferent challenge and Alan Kennedy's momentum carried him on for a thunderous left-footed shot into the far corner. After that Liverpool might have gone further ahead as Real Madrid sacrificed almost everything in defence for the sake of a goal and Agustin had to make a number of brave saves in succession.

Francesco Graziani's penalty shaves the bar with 'wobbly kneed' Bruce Grobbelaar stranded, and a fourth European Cup is imminent

31/05/1984

Grobbelaar keeps the Romans out

European Cup final
Roma 1 Liverpool 1 (*aet; Liverpool win 4-2 on pens*)
David Lacey, Rome

The European Cup returned to Anfield last night by its most tortuous and nerve-racked route yet, Liverpool defeating Roma 4-2 on penalties after the teams had fought out a 1-1 draw over two exhausting hours in the Stadio Olimpico in the Italian capital.

Liverpool's fourth triumph in the competition — now only Real Madrid have won the European Cup more times — was thoroughly deserved despite the closeness of the finish. Indeed so superior was much of their teamwork and so obviously greater their resilience that when the game went into extra-time the likely identity of the winners did not take too much guessing.

However, the additional half-hour seemed to be an equal drain on Liverpool's stamina, the inexhaustible Souness apart. A spent Dalglish was soon replaced by Robinson but a decisive goal for either team appeared less imminent as the 1984 final completed its absorbing if seldom compelling course.

The onset of penalties did not fill Liverpool's supporters with fresh optimism, far from it. Liverpool's record from the spot is erratic and when Nicol, who had replaced Johnston 19 minutes from the end of normal time, put the opening kick wildly over the bar the Roman hordes shrieked with joy.

Di Bartolomei, the Roma captain, took the ball off Graziani, who was marching up to the penalty spot, and calmly beat Grobbelaar off two paces. Neal, the scorer of Liverpool's goal in the game proper, kept them in the tie-break with a modicum of hope, hope which soared when Conti sent the most casual of kicks over the top.

Souness gave Liverpool the lead, Righetti and Rush made it 3-2 and now, at last, came Graziani's turn. With Grobbelaar on his knees and starting to go the wrong way the unfortunate Graziani saw his shot graze the upper side of the bar on its way over. Alan Kennedy, whose goal against Real Madrid won the European Cup for Liverpool in 1981, sent Tancredi the wrong way. The Liverpool players went as barmy as their supporters and the rest of Rome went into mourning.

When everything had calmed down it seemed a wretched way to have decided a competition of this importance. However, unlike Tottenham's victory on penalties over Anderlecht in the Uefa Cup final — hard-won and dramatic though it was — Liverpool's success did not leave one with the feeling that the better side had lost.

To be fair, Roma displayed something of the excellent technique with which Italian football, not to mention Brazilian, is readily associated. But for large parts this quality was not matched by their organisation and on its own was not enough to enable them to challenge Liverpool's teamwork and experience to any lasting effect.

Once again Souness was the dominant figure. His authority had been the prime force behind the successes Liverpool had achieved in the earlier rounds against the hostile background of Bilbao, Lisbon and Bucharest. Last night he responded to the flags and fireworks, drums and klaxons of a fiercely partisan, but often sporting, Rome crowd with a deliciously phlegmatic performance.

While Liverpool were often able to control the pace and rhythm of the game, they were not allowed to assert themselves in all the usual positions. For example, Rush was well contained by Righetti for much of the evening and Dalglish was unable to find the spark and speed of reaction which earlier this season had still made him such a marvellous player to watch.

However, Lawrenson and Hansen were rarely disturbed in the middle of the defence and even less so after Pruzzo, having brought the scores level at the end of the first half, limped off around the hour to be replaced by the energetic but less accomplished Chierico.

From the start the game went according to the plan Liverpool had laid for it. They had to reduce the tempo to the sort of pace that would prey on the already taut nerves of the Roma players. Grobbelaar had to hold a couple of crosses from Graziani early on but this proved to be merely the prelude to Liverpool taking the lead on the quarter hour.

> Grobbelaar and the players went as barmy as their fans, Rome into mourning

Souness and Lee combined to send Johnston away on the right, his high centre found Tancredi strongly challenged by Whelan at the far post and the rest was a succession of Roman catastrophes. Tancredi dropped the ball, Bonetti tried in vain to head it behind and Nappi's attempt at a clearance bounced off the goalkeeper's back to Neal, the only survivor of Liverpool's 1977 team, and he scored simply.

At that moment the mind was full of 1977 and Liverpool's first European Cup triumph in which Neal had scored one of the goals from the penalty spot. Soon, however, it became obvious that the right back's lack of pace on the turn might prevent Liverpool's success being repeated in the same stadium. Conti switched wings to be able to use his speed to maximum advantage and he was often well supported by Nela's powerful runs from left-back.

Neal completed a momentous 15 minutes by being cautioned for bringing down Conti but Liverpool seemed to have survived the first bout of pressure by Roma. Two minutes before half-time however, the scores were level.

Almost inevitably the goal stemmed from a movement on the left. Nela gave Conti the chance to run at Neal once more but the right-back, with Lawrenson covering him, appeared to be about to avert the danger. Then Conti's first attempt at a centre came back to him off Lawrenson and Pruzzo met his cross with a glancing header which sailed out of Grobbelaar's reach and in under the bar.

The goal could hardly have come at a better time for Roma. They began the second half with the air of a team who had just discovered that Liverpool were mortal after all and it was during this period that the omnipotent presence of Lawrenson became crucial to the English champion's cause. His was the tackle that prevented Nela getting a clear run at goal.

For 10 minutes or so the night was heavy with the combined beat of Italian and Brazilian rhythms as Falcao, with one shot rammed into Grobbelaar's hands from 25 yards, and Cerezo began to look as though they might achieve some kind of parity with Souness and the Liverpool midfield.

However, Roma'a attacks quickly subsided and for the last 25 minutes of normal time Liverpool steadily reasserted their earlier grip on the game. The arrival of Nicol gave them a fresh pair of legs and four minutes from the end Dalglish appeared to have sent him in for the winning goal but Tancredi blocked the shot.

Ideally the final could have been settled in that moment. Until the penalty competition the rest tended to be a little weary and anti-climactic.

If any player could have won the game for Roma in extra-time it had to be Conti as he resumed the teasing of Neal which for some unaccountable reason Roma had abandoned in the second half. It was ironic that in the end two of their more effective players should have missed the penalties that cost Roma the final.

22/02/1996

Humble man who never walked alone

Frank Keating

Good Bob Paisley was laid to rest in his parish churchyard yesterday as Liverpool supporters respected his family's request for privacy, and there were fewer than 100 gathered outside when the simple coffin, adorned with red and white roses, was carried into St Peter's, Woolton. There will be a more acclaiming memorial service in the city in the spring.

His widow Jessie, their three children and seven grandchildren led the mourners, who included a number of players from Paisley's record-breaking teams as well as the four managers who succeeded him — Joe Fagan, Kenny Dalglish, Graeme Souness and Roy Evans.

Two of those, Fagan and Evans, would have been ruminating

Bob Paisley got used to celebrating — three European Cups, six League titles — and nowhere better than the bootroom

through moist eyes on the days when all the blazing red fires that were too hot for Europe were lit in the Anfield bootroom, which, legend has it, was instituted by the late Bill Shankly after he arrived to manage the dingy Second Division club at Christmas 1959 and kept on the two backroom boys from the previous regime, Fagan and Paisley.

By touching fluke this very day is published a biography, *Shankly* by Stephen F Kelly, which celebrates the founder of the feast. Kelly writes: "If there was any magic, it came from that small group who gathered within its four walls … and all that came out of that bootroom was plain common sense."

And you can just picture it: a pot of tea on the hob, Shankly in his woolly cardie, Paisley in his slippers, Fagan and Ronnie Moran still in their tracksuits. "Young so-and-so didn't look too bright this morning," Paisley would mutter in his north-east vernacular. "Probably out too late last night," someone else would suggest. "Better have a word," Shankly would add. "Or give him a run in the reserves …"

Cosy little natters at elevens which, in their way, girdled the globe — as pictures of yesterday's funeral will have.

The Geordie adopted — and how! — by the Scousers knew he would be buried at St Peter's, which he and Jessie attended each Sunday for years. St Peter's! To the end he would tell of the finest night of his career, after Liverpool had won the first of their European Cups, soundly thrashing Borussia Mönchengladbach in Rome. The party afterwards was at the Holiday Inn, just down from St Peter's itself. It was the last of its type. It was still (just) the age of soccer's innocence then. The press were invited and the world and his wife were allowed to gatecrash so long as they were decked in red.

A number of the obits to Paisley mentioned that, however much the champagne bubbled, the beaming manager bursting out of his ill-fitting Burton's blue suit refused to take a drink, so he could "drink in the atmosphere and the achievement".

Well, true in fact but not in theory. Halfway through the do a big mitt gripped my arm fondly. "A Keating's a boy who should know," said Bob. "D'you think there's any chance of getting a bottle of Guinness round here?" I searched every nook. The St Peter's Holiday Inn did not stock Guinness. "Ah me," said Bob, "that means only me and the Pope up the road and Horace [Yates, the teetotal sports editor of the *Liverpool Daily Post*] over there are the only three sober men in Rome tonight."

By then the joint was dancing. Lo and behold, they struck up the Gay Gordons. Paisley joined in one set with us, grin on full beam, then went to bed, a happy man, the very happiest of men. Before he pattered off to the lift to get into those favourite slippers he had said something passingly matter-of-fact and prophetic. No football club in those days was sponsored but the spivs were talking such revolution. "Sponsors?" Bob winced as we walked to the lift. "Sign up with them and they'll be picking the team for you inside a fortnight." And so it has come to pass. RIP.

26/05/2005

Gerrard drives the Reds to a stunning comeback

European Cup final
Milan 3 Liverpool 3
(aet; Liverpool win 3-2 on pens)
Kevin McCarra, Istanbul

The glory of Liverpool is reborn. They are not merely champions of Europe once more but the indefatigable creators of a victory that will be talked about so long as football exists. Though the win came in a penalty shoot-out, the triumph took place long before, when Rafael Benítez's inspired side were rapidly overhauling a 3-0 half-time deficit.

Milan, for whom Paolo Maldini had scored at the very start of the night, were broken in spirit as extra-time came to a close. Serginho missed the first penalty and Andriy Shevchenko himself had their fourth saved, which meant that the substitute Vladimir Smicer, with his last touch of the ball before his expected departure from the club, gave Liverpool a European Cup to remember him by.

The whole team transcended itself. To start at the very beginning of the line-up, Jerzy Dudek not only reached Shevchenko's penalty but in the 117th minute of the game had made an uncanny double save from the Ukrainian's header and point-blank effort from the rebound.

The only man in the Ataturk Olympic Stadium composed enough to set down Liverpool's heroics methodically, though, would have been Benítez, who greeted this conclusion to his first season at Anfield with an air of mild contentment. Even he, though, must have gone through moments when he had to resist screaming his praise of, say, Steven Gerrard.

The captain was voted man of the match. It was his passion and belief that whipped Liverpool on after the interval and he himself headed home a John Arne Riise cross for the goal that saw a defence viewed as the world's best shredded in six historic minutes. So great was Gerrard's contribution that he suffered cramp and spent extra-time confined to a wing-back's role. He was not fit enough to take a penalty in the shoot-out but further cheered Liverpool supporters after the match by announcing that he would stay on at the club.

Liverpool were supposed to have been incapable of the kind of fire and verve he had kindled, especially with Benítez pledged to teaching the team restraint. For this match the Spaniard had shown a touch of adventure by picking Harry Kewell ahead of Dietmar Hamann but the Australian lasted 23 minutes before a groin strain claimed him and Smicer took over.

The first half had been full of woe that would have made a lesser club, back in the final after 20 years, feel that they did not belong here. Milan's immediate breakthrough disrupted a daunting acclimatisation process that had scarcely begun. The goal had something to do, as well, with stage fright in the English side that let their opponents strut the boards. The extraordinary comeback was beyond imagination then.

Steven Gerrard leads the celebrations in Istanbul as he did Liverpool's remarkable recovery from half-time oblivion

Djimi Traoré, who would boot a Shevchenko effort off the line in extra-time, fouled Kaka in the first minute. Andrea Pirlo pulled his free-kick slightly behind the main group of attackers and the 36-year-old Maldini hit it hard enough with his right foot from 12 yards to ensure that it flew past Dudek on the bounce.

Xabi Alonso and Gerrard, ultimately acclaimed with good reason, were left for a while on the sidelines of a midfield packed with marvellously articulated moves by Carlo Ancelotti's players. Minds left in a spin by Maldini's goal needed time before they could steady again.

In the 14th minute the Argentine striker Hernán Crespo, well before he scored his goals, met a Pirlo corner with a header that was blocked on the line by Luis García. Clarence Seedorf then found Kaka in the 39th minute, and his beautiful pass inside Traoré freed Shevchenko to set up Crespo to finish at the far post. A minute before half-time, Kaka again split the Liverpool defence with a raking ball and Crespo, the man loaned out by Chelsea, was on the loose to dink it stylishly over Dudek.

Facing humiliation

Hamann, brought on for the second half, excised any regret over his initial exclusion. A complacent Milan, for their part, were unprepared for a Liverpool urgency founded on desperation. Facing humiliation, they reacted with enough pride to give the club arguably the greatest achievement of its rich history.

Milan's marking was as lax at Gerrard's 54th-minute goal as Liverpool's had been at the outset and the consequences were just as extreme. It was Ancelotti's turn to gaze in disbelief. Milan had no chance to regain poise immediately.

All the conviction was Liverpool's as they passed the ball along the edge of the penalty area four minutes later until Hamann, who has come to the end of his Liverpool contract, put it into the path of Smicer. From 20 yards he angled a low finish across and beyond Dida.

A rout was turning into a near miracle. The play roared towards an equaliser. All the gaps were in the Milan side as Gerrard, with an hour gone, drove straight through the middle until Rino Gattuso brought him down for a penalty. Dida leapt to his right to save Xabi Alonso's kick but the Spaniard smashed in the rebound with his left foot.

The run of the ball was a piece of luck but fortune had bowed to the will of this Liverpool team. Even if Milan had the better of extra-time, Benítez's men had already endured so much that it was as if no more harm could befall them. The fight-back they had staged was not to be eclipsed.

There must be one more reward for Liverpool. Even if they finished outside the Premiership's top four, Uefa should allow the team that have given it the greatest European Cup final of modern times the opportunity to defend their title.

31|05|2007

Two to one Shankly would have loved the US dollars

Nicky Campbell

I know exactly how the Royal retinue must have felt when Kate Middleton's former air-hostess mother showed her lack of breeding and allegedly used the word "toilet". I feel veritably faint. As we sat broadcasting from a bar in Syntagma Square, Athens, last week we pressed our headphones to our ears amid the din and clatter of scouse patter to hear George Gillett and Tom Hicks talking to us live from a nearby hotel suite.

Thus it was, 13 hours before Liverpool's chances went down the U-bend, that the two Americans drawled their score prediction — "two to one". We winced and sniggered like those toothy mates William hangs with at Twickers. "At least it won't be going to overtime with field goals then," phnnnnr-arred a colleague, with a haughty snort.

Why did them good ol' boys think it was going to be (I can hardly bear to say it] "two to one?" Because, as George revealed, they had consulted a ouija board. This gem has been somewhat overlooked in the post-match brouhaha, but the incubi and succubae were bang on the satanic money and Gillett, to be fair, had injected a sage note of caution. "It did come up two to one and we certainly hope it to be in our favour."

George W's billionaire-buddy Hicks and Gillett were full of praise for Rafa which, given their occult dabblings, brings a whole new meaning to the phrase "a vote of confidence from the board". In their defence, or as they would say "dee-fence", the Americans seemed genuinely caught up in the rapture of the occasion and Gillett struggled to think of anything like it.

"I suppose the Stanley Cup play-off rounds in Montreal would come close — we have a tremendously passionate fan base there but I don't think we've seen numbers like this." Hicks inner-jected: "We know we are lucky to be here. We had a dinner with our families last night on the roof of the hotel and we could see the lighted Parthenon in the distance and we could hear our fans singing below us, and we said this is as good as it ever gets."

As the strains of Rodgers and Hammerstein's You'll Never Walk Alone filled the fetid morning air, I thought of another musical. Lerner and Loewe's Camelot. King Arthur stares from his castle at his contented subjects in the fields below and wonders — what do the simple folk do?

"I have been informed by those who know them well, they find relief in quite a clever way. When they're sorely pressed, they whistle for a spell and whistling seems to brighten up their day."

Sitting listening to this was another guest, a delightful woman called Karen Gill. She is an English teacher, lives in Athens and had a grandfather called Bill Shankly. As the two owners of the franchise spoke, I thought of the long road from Bill to Tom and George — a road to perdition, some say.

Shanks once said: "Now when I hear of the money that's bandied about, the thousands of pounds a week people hold out for, it makes my blood boil. There are men with tennis courts and swimming pools who haven't even got a championship medal ... not one." He saw the game, through his exclusively red-tinted eyes, as "a kind of socialism".

What would he have made of the Benítez spending plans or today's superstar wage packets? He would have gone with it because he wanted the best for the institution he loved and worked so hard to build. He would have no truck with real socialism, as espoused by the writer John Reid in *Reclaim the Game*.

"Players would receive wages tied to the average wage of a skilled worker, with differentials based on the level of league they play in ... Sky TV, and all cable, digital and commercial TV should be nationalised under democratic workers' control and management ... The greed-is-good league should be scrapped. Football revenue including the monies from TV should be shared out more evenly between all the teams in the four divisions."

Right now Shankly would be desperate to get his hands on as many of Tom's and George's greenbacks as possible. I bet you. Two to One? Never mind the Americanism, the spiritualism, the capitalism, the feudalism or the socialism, the only relevant-ism is Darwinism — adapting to survive. My colleague Jonathan Ledgard told me Hicks had the look in his eyes of someone who, when he wants something, gets it. Like Shanks? The great man will no doubt tell me if I am wrong. Now where did I put that ouija board?

Chapter five
The magic of Pele and Cruyff

Alfredo Di Stefano lashes in the second of his three goals, which on the historic night was second best to Ferenc Puskas's four

19|05|2007

'At the end we stayed to cheer for an hour'

On this day in 1960: the future Scotland manager Craig Brown saw Real Madrid beat Eintracht Frankfurt 7-3 in Glasgow

Looking back, it's probably the best match I've ever seen. You remember the brilliance of Di Stefano and Puskas, who scored all the goals. Real Madrid were just sensational. When you're fiercely patriotic and you're Scottish, maybe when Celtic beat Leeds in 1970 might come close, but nothing could beat this.

I was 20 then, which gives you an idea how old I am now, and I was on loan from Rangers to Dundee. It was a very good, hospitable, friendly club and they took most of their staff down to the game and got us tickets. I think we came down the night before and stayed in the Ivanhoe hotel, where we always went on trips to Glasgow. Our manager then was Bob Shankly, who took Dundee to the semi-finals of the European Cup three years later. People forget that before Bill Shankly had his great success at Liverpool his older brother had done so well in Europe.

The atmosphere was tremendous but it didn't look like a big match today. The big difference between crowds back then and now is that in those days, supporters didn't wear replica kit. Nowadays the crowd is very colourful but then they were quite dull. It was a sea of people, all in their jackets and with their bonnets on. You'd maybe have a scarf but no more than that.

I think there were about 130,000 people there, and quite a few thought Frankfurt were the favourites after they beat Rangers in the semis. They had that strength and discipline and maybe Real Madrid would have difficulty against the Teutonic efficiency. Not a bit of it. The quality and technical ability of these guys was incredible. Di Stefano scored one by himself, running 50 yards with the ball. Gento had superb pace and creativity. Puskas was one of the greatest players of all time.

At the end we stayed to cheer, for perhaps an hour. There was no point going because you couldn't get out of the car park. For us young guys it was awesome. Real's all-white outfit made them look huge and glamorous and us young guys were talking about it for days. In fact, we're still talking about it now.

07|10|1969

The courage of Pele

Football Diary

When one talks of Brazil, of artistry, of ingenuity, one thinks naturally of Edson Arantes do Nascimento — Pele to you and me. One of many internationals with the highest opinion of Pele is Billy Bremner, captain of Scotland and Leeds United.

In his new book Bremner describes how he tried to shadow Pele. "No matter how tightly I tried to mark him, he was still able to make space for himself virtually out of nothing."

Bremner does not think there is a professional in the world who could mark Pele so tightly as to eliminate him from the game. And, he says, Pele has not only ability but courage and determination. He did not draw back from the fiercest of challenges — from one of which Bremner emerged with a black eye.

But Bremner's opinion is vastly different of Gianni Rivera. He has skill too but Bremner was vastly surprised when Rivera, the so-called "golden boy" of Italian football, just accepted tight marking and hard tackling. Never once did he let Bremner know that he, too, could go in hard for the ball.

"It seemed," says Bremner, "that, if I were so intent on breathing down his neck, then that was how it had to be. He seemed quite content to be played out of the game." And that, to Bremner, was inexcusable.

Pele did not draw back from any challenges, one of which left Bremner with a black eye

22|06|1970

On top of the world

World Cup final
Brazil 4 Italy 1
Albert Barham, Mexico City

Brazil, masterly in their ability to fashion goals from a hint, a flick or mere intuition, triumphed here as perhaps the majority of the world hoped they would. This was the great confrontation between the finest attack in the world and Italy, masters of defence. That attack should succeed is all to the good.

Thus the Jules Rimet trophy goes home to stay in Rio de Janeiro and with it the best wishes of all football followers. Brazil have given to all the World Cup finals colour and flamboyance. They have lent the competition dignity and introduced a sparkle into football when its image was beginning to be tarnished throughout the globe.

Brazil have won the trophy three times — in 1938, 1962 and again now — and with no real change in their methods. They have had belief and confidence in their own style and all credit to them for persisting with it in the face of some hostile criticisms. Naturally they have placed a little more emphasis on a tighter defence but this is not their game. They can still cause the heart to stop with some of their odder quirks. They did so here, giving away a goal and bringing the Italians level. But just when this vast colourful stadium, solidly behind them in support, thought that perhaps Brazil were slowing down a little they suddenly burst into action. It seems to be another facet to Brazilian methods that they lull the opposition into a false sense of security, then strike suddenly and brilliantly.

Two goals came after such a spell as this. It was during these 10 minutes that the Jules Rimet Trophy was really won and lost. Every match has its turning point and this was the turning point of one of the finest finals I can recall. The rest was the endorsement of success, the icing on the cake, the demonstration of Brazilian superiority. Once Brazil get on top no country can stop them. They toyed with and destroyed Italy in the last 20 minutes.

Perhaps the great efforts the Italians made in extra-time in the semi-final to beat West Germany 4-3 had something to do with this defeat. But in essence they were just not quite good enough to succeed. And as some of the crowd carried off their heroes and the thunde rflashes rumbled the song of victory, one could feel just a little sorry for Pele. This must surely be his last World Cup appearance.

Apprehension enveloped the Italians like a shroud at the start of this match as the ingenuity of the Brazilians, with their pattern of attack varied so subtly, prised open this fine Italian defence. Yet the first shot in this fascinating battle came from Riva, which brought a thrilling save from Felix, arching his body like a bow to flip the ball over the crossbar.

With Rosato shadowing Tostao and Pele being closely watched the Italian defence needed no reminding where the great danger lay. But these were just the warning shots as, after 10 minutes, Carlos Alberto loped up the wing and Tostao slid forward and almost gave Brazil the lead.

Brazil's first goal eventually came from Pele himself, leaping like a salmon to reach a high pass by the far post after a move created by Tostao and Rivelino. It was a carbon copy of a move which brought the finest save I have ever seen when England played Brazil in the group matches. But Albertosi, good goalkeeper though he is, had not the reaction or the reflexes of Banks and he was left stranded.

The Italians came back strongly but found the defence a little less susceptible to Mazzola's probing, the speed of Boninsegna and the wiles of Riva than they may have expected. Almost always the Italians were crowded out by sheer manpower before they could strike.

Eight minutes before halftime Brazil, in one of their lazier moods, made an awful hash of what should have been a simple pass forward. Clodoaldo, deep in his own defence, casually backheeled the ball to no one in particular — though this nonchalant passing always had in the past and in the rest of this game found a Brazilian expecting it. Boninsegna pounced like a leopard, took the ball clear of Piazza, exchanged a pass with Riva and carefully placed the ball into the net, again demonstrating the vulnerability of the Brazilians' defence.

Then, after 65 minutes, Brazil regained the lead with a goal which deserved to win the trophy. Carlos Alberto began a bout of neat interpassing and the ball was played between Gerson to Everaldo, on to Jairzinho and back to Gerson who, turning on a sixpence, flashed a shot into the far corner of the net. Five minutes later the World Cup was won and lost. Once again it was Gerson, the great provider, who made the goal. Pele, running

Carlos Alberto leaps with joy at scoring Brazil's fourth goal. The world's finest attack had destroyed the masters of defence

backwards, headed across goal to Jairzinho who, almost missing his kick, managed to slice the ball into the net to complete the feat of scoring in every round.

The Italians were now being ripped apart. They were unfortunate too, for Bertini injured his groin and was replaced by Juliano and it was too late to make their customary tactical switch by replacing Mazzola with Rivera.

With four minutes to go Brazil underlined their overwhelming individual advantage. Clodoaldo, with a fine display of ball control, beat four Italians around the halfway line. He sent Rivelino racing down the left wing, Rivelino cut in towards the goal and touched on the ball to Jairzinho. With all the Italian defence drawn out of position, a gap yawned on the right and, via a precision pass from Pele, there was Carlos Alberto bursting forward and swerving in a fine shot for the last goal. The Italians, the European champions, were well beaten and knew it. Brazil were without question the great team of the tournament, as they have been before.

19|03|1971
International football to lose Pele

David Lacey

....

The decision of Pele to retire from international football after Brazil's friendly match against Austria on July 11 is, like the exit of Henry Cooper, no less sad for its inevitability. The World Cup, which at times has ill-used the singular talents of Edson Arantes do Nascimento, will be poorer without him.

Pele is to Brazilian football what Bradman was to Australian cricket. His scoring feats, more than a thousand goals, are unparalleled, his ability to win matches virtually single-handed unequalled. When a European club tried to sign him the Brazilian government, knowing that if Pele left the country they might as well follow, passed an Act of Parliament preventing it.

To most people, if only because of the distance involved, Pele represents a remote ideal, the ultimate co-ordination of mind and muscle, the perfect footballer or as near perfect as makes no difference. If this sounds sycophantic, then examine his record: more than 1,000 goals at an average of 77 a year with a top score of 125 in 1959. Even allowing that Pele plays in something like 100 matches a season, the figures are remarkable.

Now 30, Pele, the son of an unsuccessful footballer, joined Santos when he was 15 and was playing regularly for their first team a year later. At 17 Pele appeared in his first World Cup, the 1958 finals in Sweden, when he combined with Didi, Garrincha and the rest to take Brazil to the first of their three triumphs. He saw little of the 1962 finals in Chile, pulling a muscle early on, and in 1966 in England he was hacked into oblivion by the cynical Portuguese under the benign gaze of the English referee.

The doleful figure trudging off the field at Goodison, raincoat slung round his shoulders, eyes rolling back reproachfully at his assailants, made a sorry picture. Fortunately there was another reel to come. In Mexico Pele emerged as almost a father figure – Gerson being the grandfather – in midfield, leaving the pyrotechnics to Tostao and Jairzinho. But the old scoring power was still there. Against England his header led to that remarkable save by Banks; in the final a similar header proved too good for Albertosi of Italy and Brazil were on the way to winning the Jules Rimet Trophy for good.

Yet even then, perversely perhaps, one remembers Pele for a pass rather than a goal. The relaxed manner in which he turned and rolled the ball into the path of Carlos Alberto for Brazil's fourth goal of the 1970 final summed up, simply, absolute mastery of his sport. And those at Guadalajara recall with relish how, seeing the Romanian goalkeeper off his line, Pele sent a prodigious lob from the centre circle over the man's head. Unfortunately for World Cup history the ball went past a post.

"I play football because I love a ball," Pele said this week. "To enter the field wearing the Brazil team jersey in front of a full stadium is just as thrilling for a veteran as for a novice. I am going to leave all this with nostalgia but I must spend more time with my family while I am still young."

Pele has not infrequently fallen out with the various Brazilian managers' scheme of things and one has a sneaking sympathy for anyone who, in theory at least, is placed over him. It is always hard to plan for living legends. The stories about Pele are legion. Once, after scoring four goals in the first half, he was replaced after the interval only for the crowd to invade the pitch demanding his recall: the game could not continue until Pele, by that time soaking in the bath came back on to the field.

On another occasion Pele, after being fouled continuously in a league match lost his temper, retaliated and was sent off. He asked for a personal hearing and was cleared by the disciplinary committee. The referee was suspended for 30 days.

Pele has scored direct from a kick-off, beaten nine men and the goalkeeper, flicked the ball up on to his right instep and

A turn and rolled pass in the final summed up Pele's absolute mastery of his sport

hopped over the line on his left leg. Hillsborough will remember the penalty he took when Santos beat Sheffield Wednesday 4-2 in 1962, a hip-swinging double-shuffle affair which left poor Ron Springett feeling as though he was facing a creature from another planet. Sir Alf Ramsey will remember Pele's five-minute destruction of one of his early England teams in the "little World Cup" in Rio in 1964, when Brazil won 3-1.

Pele's 1,000th goal also came from a penalty, taken against Vasco da Gama in Rio. Wearing a jersey with the number 1,000 on its back, he was carried shoulder high on a lap of honour by players of both sides, and later he unveiled a commemorative plaque in the stadium which read: "1,000 by Pele - 19 November". He was given a football made of gold and the Brazilian Post Office struck a special stamp in his honour.

Pele says he intends playing three more years for Santos. It is good to know he is not completely lost to the game and that for a little while yet the transistor radios of Brazil will still scream forth the commentator's clarion call: "PELEEEEEEE!"

08|07|1974
Vogts snuffs Dutch fire

World Cup final
West Germany 2 Holland 1
David Lacey, Munich

West Germany found the answer to Johan Cruyff and won the 1974 World Cup amid much rejoicing, and some relief. After falling behind before they had touched the ball they defeated Holland with the sort of performance that had made them such overwhelming favourites before the marvellous all-round qualities of the Dutch side sowed seeds of doubt in German minds.

The game, which was extremely rough in parts with several cautions given by the English referee, Jack Taylor, seldom reached the heights of skill achieved by the Brazilians in the 1970 final nor did it equal the dramas of Wembley in 1966. But the willingness of both teams to throw men forward in attack ensured the football was rarely dull.

If one player was responsible for Germany's victory it was Berti Vogts, the stocky blond defender who was detailed to stop Cruyff and won one of the World Cup's most telling duels. Late in the game Cruyff moved into the middle of the Dutch attack only to encounter Beckenbauer at his most masterful.

With Cruyff halted, the Dutch football, while remaining skilful, seemed grey and unimaginative in comparison with what had gone before. It was as if somebody had ploughed over a tulip field. The other ingredients were there – Neeskens with his stamina and courage, Van Hanegem's wickedly swerving passes, the energy and quick eye of Jansen and the overlapping of Suurbier and Krol. But for long periods, even though Holland had possession, Rep, Rensenbrink and Van de Kerkhof, who replaced Rensenbrink for the second half, did not get their usual opportunities near goal. When they did, either the shots were inaccurate or Maier steadfastly blocked the way.

West Germany have tended throughout to get results when they most wanted them, often improving after unimpressive openings. So it was here. Many teams would have been unnerved to the point of defeat after Holland had taken the lead with a penalty after a minute's play, less because of the goal than the manner of its arrival. Having kicked off, the Dutch strung more than a dozen passes around the centre of the field at a walking pace, suggesting they were looking for mines rather than goals. But suddenly Cruyff broke into a sprint, tried to force his way between Hoeness and Bonhof and was brought down. Neeskens walloped the penalty past Maier and for the next 20 minutes the Germans played as if in a stupor of disbelief.

Misguidedly Holland continued to slow the rhythm of their game, content to stop Overath getting his passes through, block the wings and seal the middle. Perhaps they thought they could win the World Cup without allowing Germany to play in the final. If so, it was a rash assumption, for the Germans needed only a goal to recover their poise.

This is what happened. As the Germans began to run wider, making it less easy for the Dutch to maintain their casual cover, Holzenbein raced into the penalty area from the left and was brought down by Jansen, who had hared back 40 yards to make the tackle. Breitner scored with the penalty and from then the crowd in the Olympic Stadium began to recognise their team.

Once more the German system of double wings was an important factor. Hoeness covered huge areas as he worked in turn with Holzenbein and Grabowski to wear down the Dutch flanks. At last Suurbier and Krol, who have had such a splendid tournament as attacking backs, were outmanoeuvred by players of superior pace and wit. In the 36th minute Beckenbauer had Jongbloed stretching back desperately to push a delicate lob of a free-kick over the cross-bar. Seven minutes later Germany were ahead with the goal that was to win the World Cup.

A smart early ball by Grabowski and a shrewd run into space by Bonhof opened up the right wing and, though the low centre ran behind Müller in front of goal, the striker had time to check, retrieve and slip his shot past Jongbloed.

Only occasionally thereafter did Holland swing from penalty area to penalty area with the effortless running and passing which has made them such a pleasure to watch. And they found Beckenbauer at his most imperious. They did have chances, most notably Neeskens who saw his close-range volley marvellously saved by Maier, but almost before they knew it the German captain was holding the new Fifa Trophy aloft, leaving the Dutch with the consolation of knowing they had been beaten by the only team who truly had the talent to match their own.

27|01|2004

Reign in Spain

When Johan Cruyff moved to Barcelona the people thought he was an angel, writes Geoffrey Macnab

In early 1970s Catalonia the resentment against General Franco was profound and deep. The local people still felt as if they were under foreign occupation. One of the few public places where they could speak their own language was the Nou Camp, the Barcelona football stadium. That was why the arrival of the Dutch footballer Johan Cruyff to play for Barcelona in August 1973 was treated almost as if it was a second coming. He had been lured to Barcelona by his former coach at Ajax, Rinus Michels. The team was languishing and in desperate need of a saviour, which is precisely what Cruyff turned out to be. "This gaunt, gangly little fellow who smoked like a chimney gave us back our pride," says an elderly Catalan interviewed in Ramon Gieling's new documentary, Johan Cruyff: At a Given Moment.

A series of coincidences helped cement the Dutchman's relationship with the Catalan public. Cruyff's wife was heavily pregnant. The birth was induced a few days early, so he could play in the most important game of all, against Real Madrid at the Bernabéu. Largely thanks to Cruyff, Barcelona won 5-0 in a game that even now few Catalans can talk about without getting goosebumps. Then, simply because he and his wife liked the name, they decided to call their new son Jordi. This, it turned out, was the name of the patron saint of Catalonia and was forbidden under Franco's laws. When Cruyff tried to register the birth, the clerks told him he should call his son Jorge. He refused. As Jordi had been born in Holland, the authorities were powerless to stop Cruyff using the name. "But he was not aware of the immense political meaning of the name," Gieling says.

In those early months in Barcelona Cruyff played his greatest football, but only very slowly did he begin to appreciate the real nature of the Catalan people. "Being a Catalan is as exquisite as having an orgasm," one man suggests when asked to express

the essence of the Catalonian spirit and culture. "Bit by bit, you learn what makes them tick . . . Soccer here wasn't just a sport but a political affair, an escape valve," Cruyff says now as he looks back on his arrival in Spain on a sweltering August afternoon 31 years ago. When he first helped Barcelona win the league passers-by would stop him on the street. They would not congratulate him but would thank him instead, as if he was the hero who had delivered them from their oppressors. Not that they were always dismayed when Barcelona was defeated, just as long as they had a few sublime moments.

At a Given Moment is not a conventional sports documentary. Although the film ends with a long interview with the footballer, Gieling's real focus is on the Catalan people. Elderly waiters, the doctors who operated on the Dutchman following his heart bypass, taxi drivers, journalists, housewives, flamenco guitarists and one or two of his old opponents (including the former Real Madrid player Emilio Butragueno) are invited to share their favourite Cruyff moment.

We see fleeting images of Cruyff in action, scoring wildly improbable goals, ghosting past defenders. We meet the chef and waiters at his favourite Barcelona restaurant. We see the ad Cruyff shot for TV after his heart operation in which he says that he had two addictions: football and smoking. "One made my life, the other almost took it away." A musician talks about Cruyff and "*duende*", a term that roughly means an uncanny inspiration, charm or magnetism. Everyone has a favourite Cruyff moment. For Gieling it is from one of his games for Ajax: "When he takes the ball from behind with his heel. He is really like a kind of angel. He's not running, he is floating."

Johan Cruyff turns with his signature salute on scoring for Barcelona, where he was a law unto his magical self

The language the interviewees use to describe Cruyff is invariably lyrical and reverential. "A painting, a play, a poem can create an experience when suddenly you feel lifted up by a great feeling of joy," Butragueno tells Gieling, adding that his former opponent gave him a similar feeling, "a feeling that goes beyond admiration and that's comparable to an artistic experience". We see old men clumsily trying to imitate some of Cruyff's great tricks. We meet women who have never married because to do so would be to betray their idol.

What intrigued Gieling was the gulf between the mythical figure Cruyff became to the Catalan people and the deadpan, down-to-earth footballer he went to meet last year at his home in Spain. The film opens with Cruyff in shirt, trousers and loafers kicking around a ball on a patch of grass high in the mountains. He tells the kid in goal he is going to blast the ball, hits it and it spirals off into the sky. We then see it bouncing down the road all the way back to Barcelona. "I thought the ball should take us from character to character. God kicks the ball back into the city."

Even today, if Cruyff makes the most banal remark, it is treated by the Catalan people as if it is a Delphic utterance. Cruyff is not exactly a holy innocent but Gieling maintains that there is still a naïveté about him. He was born with a gift, he says, "but from the age of 18 he became suspicious because he knew that people saw something in him that maybe he had not been aware of. In a way he is still very innocent. When you sit in front of him, he'll tell you everything."

It seems there is little snobbery or arrogance about Cruyff. Gieling speculates that his humility is attributable to his background. He was 12 years old when his father died. His mother was forced to work, cleaning the locker rooms at Ajax. "That's why, to me, locker rooms are still a kind of holy place," he tells Gieling.

Not that the Dutchman was ever entirely unworldly. He loved money. In the mid-1990s the relationship with Barcelona soured. He was sacked as trainer. "They kicked me when I was down and tried to discredit me," he says of his traumatic break with the club whose fortunes he had revived.

The fact that Cruyff ended up being so badly treated by Barcelona only adds to the myth surrounding him. The defeats and setbacks lend pathos to his story. As he tells Gieling, the low point was losing the World Cup final with Holland in 1974. He now lives in the hills above Barcelona. He still does not speak a word of Catalan but that has not lessened the awe in which he is still held.

Cruyff's gift as a footballer, he tells Gieling, was that he mastered the art of being in the right place at the right time. "He was the philosopher of going your own way without any compromise," Gieling says. "Every Sunday he did what he thought he should do. He never listened to public opinion. If he lost, he lost on his own terms. You can never fail if you go your own way."

21|03|1997

Happy return for magical Magyar

Frank Keating meets Ferenc Puskas, who celebrated his 70th birthday at the scene of Hungary's historic win in 1953

Puskas came back to Wembley yesterday to celebrate his 70th birthday, all of 44 years after his Hungarian team's apocalyptic defeat of England in 1953. A sparkling springtime sunlight illuminated the old stadium as the tubby ancient doodled about with a football for the photographers – only his left foot of course – and he chewed the fat later with three of the five survivors of the England side which had been given such a lesson on that grey November afternoon long ago.

Puskas is one of that tiny band of immortals with no need of a forename the world over – Pele, Eusebio and Maradona, for instance. To welcome him back to north London's emerald field of dreams was another all-time legend of this amphitheatre as well as lore itself, and one who needs no surname for identification, England's nonpareil Sir Stanley. It was a privilege to eavesdrop.

In 1953 England had never been beaten by foreign opposition at Wembley. In less than an hour these glistening Hungarians were 6-2 up and cruising. They won 6-3. An aberration, said Fleet Street. Four months later England went to Budapest for revenge. They lost 7-1.

The two old men grinned with recognition across half the pitch, hurried towards each other and embraced for a long time. Puskas planted a succulent kiss on each of Sir Stanley's cheeks. It must be said that England's octogenarian knight looked fitter, certainly more dapper and trim than the rotund podge now living back in Budapest. But bright-eyed they both were.

Puskas laughed and called over his interpreter to translate: "I remember we stayed at Marble Arch and had to train at Queens Park Rangers; you would not let us practise once at Wembley. And your English footballs, they were heavy like blocks of wood."

Said Sir Stanley: "We never thought we could lose at Wembley. They were an eye-opener, all right, with their interchanging attack. My Blackpool captain Harry Johnston was centre-half. At half-time he came to me and said, 'Oh dear, Stan, what can I do, who do I mark?' Nobody told him, certainly I don't think Walter (Winterbottom, the manager) did. I can still see Puskas's third goal in my mind's eye. It was quite remarkable."

The Hungarian had bamboozled England's captain Billy Wright, dragging the ball back with the sole of his left foot and pirouetting to crack it into the roof of the net.

Wembley's directors yesterday threw a lunch and replayed that flickering sequence in fuzzy monochrome on a television. You still had to draw breath and "Wow!" when you saw it – and then, with coffee and cigars, a queue formed wanting the great man to sign his new and evocative autobiography. Top of the queue were Jackie Sewell and George Robb, both silvery-haired and full of the joys, two others who played that day.

Robb was the only English player who had seen the Hungarians play. As an amateur he had watched them win the Olympic title the year before. "Oh, how they sparkled, had all the suggestions of greatness. Mind you, we were confident of beating them. They looked the part before the kick-off, juggling the ball and playing little keepy-uppy, and then they just continued like that during the game.

"Four of their goals were whizz-bangs from outside the penalty area. Puskas's left foot must have been the greatest in all football."

Sewell still says that it was a privilege to have been on the same field. "It was, truly, even though in both matches I simply chased them about all over the place, trying to work out their mesmerising little passing triangles out of which they'd suddenly explode. Honestly, that match was the beginning of changes in the whole concept of soccer tactics all round the world."

The two other survivors, Sir Alf Ramsey and the goalkeeper Gil Merrick – "It would have been 12 but for Mr Merrick," said Puskas – were unable to attend the lunch. In a way it is a 5-5 draw – for as well, only five Hungarians of the team also survive. Puskas says he meets them often enough at home – sometimes even in the popular bar alongside one of Budapest's Grand Danube bridges.

The bar is called, simply, "6-3". Said Puskas, embracing Matthews and beaming, "We are all old men now but old men still madly in love with our football."

Chapter six
Brian Clough, the whole story

09|05|1972
Derby are champions

Michael Carey

Celebrations were held in Derby last night to mark Derby County's winning of the First Division championship. The results of the Leeds and Liverpool games were even announced at a church service where Father Trevor Huddleston was preaching, and there was a spontaneous outburst of applause.

County's manager, Brian Clough, on holiday in the Isles of Scilly, said: "It is incredible. I do not believe in miracles but one has occurred tonight. I believe they played four-and-a-half minutes of injury time at Molineux — it seemed like four-and-a-half years to me. There is nothing I can say to sum up my feelings adequately, although I suppose we could have won the Cup as well.

"For a team and town like Derby to win the title is a credit to all concerned. This has given me far more pleasure than I can adequately express. It makes you appreciate what a job you and your players have done. And my players have given blood this season. In fact no team has given more. Even so, although they are now on holiday in Majorca, I want them to remember that they are still Derby County players and to behave accordingly."

For Clough and his assistant manager, Peter Taylor, the men who have guided Derby County to the top, the First Division championship is not merely an accolade. Nor is it just the culmination of five years' work. It is solid proof that their methods, their principles, their attitudes, are the ones on which to build the foundations of a successful football club.

Clough's realistic and abrasive approach has not always endeared him to other people in a profession that has much of show business's "love thy neighbour" attitude. But it is this same honesty — with his players, with his directors, above all with himself — that has been a vital part of his remarkable climb to the pinnacle of football power.

From the poverty of Hartlepool to the First Division title and the European Cup competition in five years is an ascent that can rarely, if ever, have been equalled.

Soon after taking over at Derby, Clough went with his team on a pre-season tour of the Continent. After two matches he told his directors characteristically: "This lot will get us nowhere except the Third Division." He was so nearly right. In spite of wholesale comings and goings Derby had their only taste of mediocrity under Clough in that first season.

But he knew what was wanted. The signing of Dave Mackay was what he termed the missing piece of the jigsaw puzzle before Derby stylishly won promotion. Yet Clough was as quick to let Mackay move on at a time when, perhaps, other managers might have been blinded by sentiment.

He has been equally ruthless on other occasions. Players basking in the contentment of what they considered a good performance have been jolted by a well chosen, Anglo-Saxon-flavoured phrase pinpointing something which other managers might have overlooked in a moment of euphoria. Only this season one Derby player sat in the dressing-room just before a game, gloomy faced after being dropped. He was told by Clough: "Get a smile on your face or …. off out of here." He went.

Above all, though, Clough is a warm human being. Perhaps because his own career was cut off in its prime by injury, he feels for his players, protects them, laughs with them, groans for them. As one of them once memorably said: "Sometimes you think the man is an absolute bastard but you would give him your last half-crown."

13|04|1973
Clough harms image of English football

David Lacey

A rash remark by Brian Clough, which he must surely have regretted the moment he said it, has done no small harm to the image of English football in Italy and, more particularly, in Turin, where the England team will wind up a wearying summer tour with an international in the Stadio Communale on June 14.

After Derby County had lost disappointingly 3-1 to Juventus in the first leg of their European Cup semi-final on Wednesday,

Clough was immediately besieged by Italian journalists who wanted to know his views on the game and had the assistance of an Italian-speaking English sports writer acting as interpreter. "Tell them," snapped the Derby manager, "that I do not want to talk to any cheating bastards."

Clough, who in fact was more angry with the refereeing of the West German Gunther Schulemberg than with any of the Italian players, not to mention its journalists, later calmed down and re-emerged to give the Italian press a friendly interview – but by then, of course, the damage had been done.

And so, yesterday morning's *Gazzetta del Popolo*, the second biggest of Turin's daily papers, ran the headline "Clough: All Italians are Bastards and Cheats" over an article which referred to the "legend" of English fair play and described Clough as " volcanic", saying that he reacted "like a sulphur match".

The situation had already been made unnecessarily tense by an incident at half-time between Peter Taylor and Helmut Haller, the former West German international whose appearance as substitute after an hour's play was a strong factor in Derby's defeat. Taylor had heard that Haller went into Schulemberg's dressing-room before the match and, when he saw the player embrace the referee at the end of the first-half, he followed him off the pitch and there was a clash between the pair in which the police were involved.

Both Clough's outburst and the earlier incident did nothing for the reputation of English teams, which was rather hard on the Derby players whose behaviour, if not perfect, had been a good deal more mature than that of some of their predecessors in Europe. It was also a pity that this had to happen in Turin, where the affinity with the English game is particularly strong.

John Charles, after his distinguished career with Juventus, is an excellent ambassador for any Football League team visiting the city and after the Manchester United air crash in Munich in 1958 the people of Turin felt that a bond had been formed with England, the talented Torino side having been wiped out in the Superga air crash of 1949. An apology would help to clear up what is essentially a series of misunderstandings; neither Clough nor Taylor is the kind of person to bear malice.

 'I do not believe in miracles but one has occurred tonight,' said Derby's manager

25|09|2007

A few Chelsea fans with a banner – call that a protest?

John Sadler

Pardon me for asking but where were the protests that followed the departure of Jose Mourinho from Chelsea – a sacking if ever I saw one? A relative handful of supporters, chanting behind a blue-and-white banner outside Stamford Bridge and a few tears shed by Didier Drogba. Despite the expected outcry in the media and a murmur or two at Old Trafford on Sunday, this was about the sum of the anger, outrage and resentment expressed immediately after the parting of Chelsea and the finest manager they ever employed – the manager who guided them to back-to-back league titles and had masterminded the winning of six trophies, mostly endearing himself to the public despite an inclination to attract deserved criticism through a series of unpleasant incidents. A few chants and a trickle of tears? Call that a protest?

I'll give you a protest and it is offered with no apology for once more mentioning the name of my dear friend Brian Clough who, you will remember, with his assistant, Peter Taylor, steered unfashionable Derby County to the championship in 1972 only to resign in high dudgeon 18 months later. By comparison the Chelsea protests look no more intimidating than grandma's final wave through the window as the 5.30 express pulls out of St Pancras.

Allow me to take you back to those unforgettable days in the autumn of 1973 when, for days on end, the street outside Derby's ramshackle Baseball Ground was jammed with media and fans. The place was under siege while, inside, the players were seriously planning a sit-down strike – a blank refusal to take part in a home match against Leicester scheduled for the Saturday. I was among a handful of newspapermen privileged to report the revolution from inside the premises where the players stormed through the place yelling their dissatisfaction and demands that Clough be reinstated.

The former England winger Alan Hinton appeared from the kitchen, holding aloft a tea urn and predicting: "This, gentlemen, is the only bloody silverware we'll ever get our hands on from now on." Clough, who was behind much of the protest without exactly orchestrating it, eventually persuaded the players against the strike which, by now, had made the front pages. He, too, turned up on the Saturday but only to wave to the masses with their scores of banners pleading for "Clough in, Longson out" – a reference to the belligerent old chairman, Sam Longson, with whom Clough later offered to bury the hatchet, "right in the back of Sam Longson's head". The inevitable victory did not quell the mood of fans or players - or the town itself, through which thousands marched for the official protest movement which held countless meetings and recruited the enthusiastic support of the Labour MP Phillip Whitehead. Now that's what you call a protest.

Even when Longson and friends let it be known that Dave Mackay was to be installed as Clough's successor the anarchy raged on. The lights, cameras, microphones, notebooks and fans converged on the ground and jammed the street again, tipped off that the players were against Mackay's appointment despite him being a former team-mate of several. They threatened a sit-in and their mood was such that the club secretary and a director locked themselves in the boardroom where, too afraid to sneak to the toilet, they peed into an ice-bucket, probably the one in which they had chilled the title-winning champagne the previous year.

I read at the weekend that Mourinho had reportedly mentioned the attitude of the captain, John Terry, as a contributory factor in his departure. Hardly a parallel with the furore at Derby where Roy McFarland – like Terry, the club skipper and England's centre-half – telephoned Mackay and warned him not to take the job, saying: "There's a lot of turmoil and we think we can get Cloughie and Taylor back. We don't want you here." Being Dave Mackay, of course, he took no notice. He stuck out that barrel chest, threatened to play the reserves instead and went on to shape Derby's next league title triumph two seasons later.

All this, remember, was about a manager who had not been fired or ejected with that curious excuse of "mutual agreement" but who had voluntarily walked out on a newly signed four-year contract. As Clough later observed: "Things blow over – even turmoil on such an unprecedented scale. Eventually players realise they have enough on their plate keeping fit, getting in the side and staying there and looking after the money they make from doing it." Times do change, though, and perhaps there is a reason why the Chelsea protests were so low-key. Perhaps the fans are fearful of driving away the billionaire who made all things possible. And perhaps there is less opportunity for complaint when players receive in excess of £100,000 a week and live in a mansions with Ferraris at the bottom of the garden.

Francis lifts Forest to the summit

European Cup final
Nottingham Forest 1 Malmö 0
David Lacey, Munich

Nottingham Forest kept the European Cup in England last night when they defeated Malmö 1-0 on a warm Munich evening in a final notable for much Swedish obduracy and a performance of all-round competence from the winners stimulated by the occasional touch of class.

Fittingly Trevor Francis, easily the outstanding player of an often disappointing game, scored the decisive goal when he headed past Moller at the end of the first half. If the match is remembered for anything it could well be the fact that Britain's first £1m player was introduced to Europe's first £1m final and produced a performance worthy of the setting.

Otherwise, looking round the Olympic stadium at the end, as 25,000 Nottingham supporters greeted their team with all the familiar footballing anthems, one was left to admire the achievement rather than dwell on a rather anticlimactic denouement. Brian Clough and Peter Taylor, grey-sweatered and anonymous amid all the colour and celebration, stood for a moment on a bench calmly observing the mafficking. Theirs has been an outstanding achievement that it is hard to see being repeated – from Second Division to the summit of European football in three seasons. Moreover, English football now holds the unique distinction of providing three different winners of the Champions' Cup.

Last night's game was nearer in mood and pattern to Liverpool's patient, unspectacular victory over Bruges at Wembley last season than either their inspired conquest of Borussia Mönchengladbach in Rome the year before or Manchester United's highly emotional success against Benfica in 1968. Malmö, like Bruges, set out to disrupt the English team's rhythm and

Garry Birtles, £2,000 from Long Eaton United, is on the ball 2½ years later, winning the European Cup against Malmö

stop them moving forward. Unlike Bruges they could offer mitigating circumstance for tactics which were dour in the extreme. With their limited resources and in spite of their English coach, Bob Houghton, their only hope lay in exasperating Forest into making errors and then catching them on the break.

In the end all that really worked for the Swedes was their offside trap. Forest were caught 15 times and it was credit to their discipline and patience that they did not allow their concentration to be disturbed by this. Without intending any disrespect to Malmö or Meadow Lane, it must have been rather like coming across Notts County looking for a replay in a third-round Cup tie.

Many of Forest's familiar virtues were there. McGovern and Bowyer, strategist and handyman, calmly overcame the lack of Gemmill and O'Neill in midfield. Burns, apart from a dangerous back header to Shilton early in the game, was almost flawless in the centre of defence. And in attack, Woodcock and Robertson persevered in tight spaces full of lunging Malmö legs.

However, the only times that the match began to live up to its calling and approach the traditions of excellence set by those early free-scoring European Cup finals were when Francis moved easily and elegantly past the left of the Malmö defence. After a couple of tentative runs he announced his presence midway through the first half with a marvellous piece of play which saw him swerve past Erlandsson and Jonsson before laying in a ball that Malmö were happy to hoof away from the goalmouth for a corner.

With the midfield crowded and the jaws of the offside trap well lubricated, quality of this sort was seldom sustained and, as McGovern, Bowyer and Woodcock all came close towards half-time but without achieving the luck or the final touch needed to score, it seemed that Malmö would go in with the important psychological advantage of having kept Forest out for 45 minutes.

In the 45th minute, however, Bowyer found Robertson in space on the left and Francis, who had followed the movement from the start, arrived at the far post at precisely the right moment to head in from Robertson's hanging centre. Since Malmö had not looked remotely like scoring, apart from a low ball from Roland Andersson that evaded Shilton and shot across an empty goalmouth, it was hard to see how they were going to draw level and Nottingham's relaxed grip on the play suggested that similar thoughts were going through their minds.

So the second half was often a drowsy, predictable affair still punctuated by the continuing excellence of Francis who just past the hour moved to the byline once more before giving Robertson the chance of a shot which he sent low against the near post. Several times after that there were suggestions of further Forest goals but the outcome was a foregone conclusion long before the end. Indeed it had been that after the semi-finals, once Forest knew that their opponents would be the part-time Swedes and not FK Austria.

29|05|1980

Shilton is supreme

European Cup final
Nottingham Forest 1 Hamburg 0
David Lacey, Madrid

Nottingham Forest retained the European Cup to keep the trophy in England for a fourth successive year when they defeated Hamburg in Madrid last night.

The winning goal was a typical piece of audacity by John Robertson midway through the first half, but Forest's latest success will be better remembered for the organisation and composure of their defence and, above all for Shilton's goalkeeping which together enabled them to withstand wave upon wave of attacks by Hamburg.

The West German side drove forward for almost the entire match and several times appeared to be on the point of saving the game. However, for all Keegan's industry and the variety of skills around him, Hamburg simply could not outwit a Forest team now well accustomed to preserving a narrow lead against accomplished opposition. Burns, Lloyd and McGovern, solidly supported by all around them, frustrated Hamburg time and again and the only real piece of fortune that the holders enjoyed came in the second half when Kaltz hit a post.

The pattern of the final was much as one had expected. Without Francis, Nottingham Forest were more or less forced into a game of containment and counter-attack and, while they might well have adopted similar tactics even if he had been fit, the lack of choice in the matter meant that their plan was operating on an extremely fine margin of error.

In fact they won because they seldom made mistakes where it mattered. Their worst period came at the start of the match, when, with Hamburg flooding forward as Keegan had promised, Shilton was exposed once or twice by some uncertainty in front of him. He made a number of outstanding saves during the evening but none so important as when he tipped wide a shot from Magath in the ninth minute after Lloyd's clumsy foul on Keegan had given Hamburg a free-kick near the penalty area.

Hrubesch, the power at the centre of the Hamburg attack, came on only for the second half and even then he was obviously feeling the effects of his recent ankle injury. This meant that for half the game Keegan found himself having to operate in a more advanced position than usual and that helped Forest, who did not so much mark the little man – although Burns was cautioned for fouling him – as blockade him: that is to say they concentrated on isolating Keegan from his colleagues.

By the time Hrubesch had replaced Hieronymus, enabling Keegan to steam wider and deeper, Forest had settled into their trenches for a long war. Their goal arrived after 20 minutes and was simplicity itself, showing as it did the weakness of man-to-man marking in that when one marker is beaten there is sometimes no one ready to take over the responsibility for meeting the danger.

Robertson casually exchanged passes with Birtles on the left, drifted inside Kaltz and, with no one else near enough to make a tackle, advanced to the penalty area before beating Kargus with a shot which went in off the right-hand post.

Within a minute Shilton was beaten by Reiman after blocking a shot from Magath but a linesman's flag went up for offside first, and for Hamburg the rest of the game was all frustration. Ten minutes before half-time Keegan made his most significant contribution to the evening when he chested a ball from Kaltz down to Milewski, whose shot produced another marvellous save from Shilton, again turning the ball wide.

Hamburg, for all their efforts in the second half, were seldom so incisive again. Almost every corner and centre seemed to home in on to the head of Burns; Lloyd blocked a likely header from Magath in the goalmouth; there was another agile save from Shilton, pushing high and wide a long shot from Nogly, and he was even covering the drive from Kaltz that cannoned against the right-hand post around the hour.

Hamburg's last realistic chance came and went 10 minutes from the end when O'Neill's clearance was intercepted by Buljan, whose immediate shot went wide from barely five yards' range.

To the last Keegan ran and ran, goaded and coaxed, but it was all to no avail for Hamburg. Forest, with the experienced O'Hare on for Mills and Gunn replacing a limping Gray, held out although a number of the team were obviously tiring rapidly. They might even have scored a further goal when O'Neill, almost on his knees after an evening of concentrated effort, sent Birtles clear but the centre-forward, who had suffered a number of heavy tackles in his lone battle against the Hamburg defence, simply did not have the energy to shoot before Kaltz made his tackle.

Brian Clough admitted afterwards that Hamburg might have had the edge on Forest in technique but added: "We beat them for application, determination and pride – all the things that portray our football."

Clough went on to say that he did not consider that Forest had been lucky. "If you have to defend you have to do it well," he said. "It's as important as attacking. At half-time I wondered how we could last. Mills was one of only three players we could have taken off. In fact Birtles did not have enough strength to remove his shin pads when he came off at the end."

Peter Shilton, unbeaten for the second European Cup final running, enjoys his moment with the trophy

31/08/1984
Clough scores off the Post
Guardian Diary

Alan Rusbridger

This should be a rather good test of Mr Robert Maxwell's sympathies with the trade union movement. What will he do about Mr Brian Clough's new column in the *Daily Mirror* now that Mr Clough has decided to go down the Dimbleby road by striking up links with the blacked *Nottingham Evening Post*?

The National Union of journalists views as a heinous offence any contact with the *NEP*, which sacked all its striking NUJ employees in the provincial journalists' strike some six years ago and which has caused nothing but trouble for David

Dimbleby since he started printing his papers on the company's presses. At first Brian Clough nobly refused to have anything to do with the *NEP* but on Wednesday he started writing a new sports column for the paper. The *NEP* is trying to play down the significance of this move but no sooner did the NUJ headquarters learn of the venture than they were on to the *Mirror* NUJ officials, who will doubtless be asked to black Mr Clough's weekly column for the *Mirror*.

04|09|1984
On the ball

Guardian Diary

If Brian Clough appears to be adopting a low profile in the weeks to come it is because he has decided not to speak to journalists any more – not ones that belong to the NUJ anyway.

Mr Clough was sick as a parrot at last week's Diary item calling attention to his new column in the NUJ-blacked *Nottingham Evening Post* and suggesting that the union would take a dim view of his decision to associate himself with the paper. I will tell you how sick he was. He telephoned on Friday, swore like, well, a parrot for some 15 minutes and announced he had cancelled his order for *The Guardian*. Write this down, he said. We wrote it down. 'I'm going to stop talking to any of your ----ing members. You can all ---- off. I'm a ----ing football manager. I haven't got time for all this ----ing union bull----.' Mr Clough added that he was henceforth going to discontinue both his columns for the *Nottingham Evening Post* and the *Daily Mirror*.

He then tracked down the general secretary of the NUJ, Ken Ashton, who was at an executive meeting , to explain personally that he was never going to speak to an NUJ member again.

All this is most puzzling. When the NUJ's dispute with the *NEP* started - six years and a third of a million pounds ago - Mr Clough made it a point of honour to deal only with the NUJ members who had been dismissed by the *NEP* and who set up their own rival paper.

I'm not talking to you. I'm a football manager. I haven't got time for this union bull ...

06|09|1984
Subscription cancelled

Guardian Diary

I may not quite have done justice to the extent of Mr Brian Clough's psittacine sickness, for he now writes to confirm officially his drastic clampdown on contacts with journalists who are members of the NUJ as well as his shock decision to quit writing columns for both the *Nottingham Evening Post* and the Mirror Group and, finally, the cancellation of his *Guardian* subscription. The world will be a duller place but we must all struggle on as best we can.

14|01|2006
Brian Clough hits out
On this day ... in 1989

Forest fan Sean O'Hara

A few of us were at the Littlewoods Cup quarter-final between Nottingham Forest and QPR at the City Ground on the Wednesday night. It was in the days when every club took the competition seriously and we were a big team back then. Lee Chapman scored four as Forest won 5-2 and we all decided to make a quick exit five minutes before the end.

There were quite a few young lads like us – I was 20 at the time – hanging around at the bottom of the Main Stand. They were all ready to race on to the pitch at the final whistle. A couple of us jumped on Chapman but out of the corner of my eye I saw Steve Hodge and decided to make a run for him. Before I knew it I felt a big blow on the back of my head. It was a real solid punch. There had been a little bit of trouble between Forest and QPR supporters that night and I thought it was one of the away fans. But when I turned round, I knew exactly who it was. There was Brian Clough, screaming: "Get off the bloody pitch!" My head was still ringing when I met my mates outside.

I was living with my parents at the time and when I got home my dad was asking me where I'd been that night. I'd borrowed a tenner off him for two tickets but had told him it was to buy nappies for my son Shane and that I was going to spend the evening with him and my girlfriend Sandra. But he told me he'd seen me getting clobbered on the news. He recognised the green and red coat he'd given me for Christmas.

The next day a mate rang Central News and they came to do a piece with us. We also called the *Mirror*, who came to take some pictures. It was all a bit of a laugh and we just thought it'd make a small story but the News at Ten ran it as their lead. It was stupid – the next item was about George Bush being sworn in as US president. Then I was on the front page of the *Mirror*.

A few days afterwards I got a call from BBC East Midlands saying they wanted me to meet Cloughie. They collected me and the other guy who got hit and took us to the ground. We were having champagne when Cloughie walked in, apologised and said: "Give us a kiss!" He was an absolutely lovely bloke. I was heartbroken when he died. He was one of my true idols.
Then what happened: Clough was fined £5,000 for bringing the game into disrepute. "I just wanted to help the police to clear the pitch as quickly as possible," he said. Sean O'Hara went on to manage a charity shop in Nottingham.

30|09|1993

Downfall of a legend

John Mullin and Lawrence Donegan trace the decline of Brian Clough from a man revered to a life in turmoil

....

Chocolates and flowers for his players' wives. Fish and chips every day for striking miners. Exclusive stories for journalists setting up in opposition to the city's strike-bound evening newspaper. Brian Clough would take his players to Rampton high-security mental hospital. He took them to the Nottinghamshire coalfields, making them crawl 300 yards in the dust in tiny tunnels way beneath the surface. "He wanted us to remember how lucky we were when things weren't going well," said Ian Wallace, a centre-forward he signed for £1.2m in 1980.

He helped local charities. His former secretary, Carol Washington, can detail numerous acts of kindness. Above all, he was a winner.

How they hero-worshipped him. Had he accepted moves to nominate him as a Labour parliamentary candidate, he would have walked home. After all he had brought the European Cup to Nottingham (twice), as well as the Football League title (immediately after promotion) and the League Cup four times. Then there was the Anglo-Scottish Cup in 1976-77, a trophy which must have made small fry like Nottingham Forest think they were in seventh heaven.

He won a lot of them with Peter Taylor, the Middlesbrough reserve team goalkeeper who had singled out the 20-year-old fifth-string centre-forward as something special. He could hit a ball cleanly any way it came to him and blast it with the merest backswing.

The pair went on to work at Hartlepool, then Derby County. They took that unfashionable club to one Football League championship and were kept out of the 1973 European Cup final only by a bent referee. They walked into the City Ground in 1975 when Nottingham Forest languished in Division Two. How they loved Brian Clough in Nottingham. They made him the city's 30th Freeman five months ago. He was still seen as a good man. But even his fans admitted he had "gone" as a manager.

Yet the calls to BBC Radio Nottingham's afternoon phone-in on the day after this week's World In Action allegations that he profited from the sale of Cup Final tickets still split 10 to one in Clough's favour. Nick Brunger, station programme organiser, says: "There were people who remembered only his acts of kindness locally. One dissident said Nottingham had an over-sentimental view of the man. Another said he had always been a rogue."

Andy Lowe, editor of the Tricky Tree, one of three Forest fanzines, says: "Most of the calls in favour were little old ladies who remember him visiting him in hospital." Sheldon Miller, who heads the *Trent Times*, born in 1975, the year Clough came to the City ground, admits: "We thought he was an immortal, infallible character. I suppose we had a blind allegiance to him."

Rumours of heavy drinking had been circulating for several years. They were to be followed by more unsavoury tales. Among them that Forest was the side that would play anywhere for cash. Clough would joke that he could walk on the Trent. Now there are those who would be happy to see him fall in the drink. So when did it all go wrong for the most popular manager in English football?

Many who could suggest an answer are unwilling to be named. Some out of loyalty, some out of fear. One journalist, who has covered Midlands football for a dozen years, says: "I still live near Nottingham and there are a lot of people who still like him – I do – and I don't want them knocking on my door and saying 'What's all this shit you're talking about Cloughie?'"

A former player, a key member of Clough's European triumphs, says: "It's not on to put the boot in. Anyway, you don't know what your gaffer gets up to, do you? It was the same for us back then." Another former protégé believes Clough was unable to keep up with the modern game. His famous passing game was becoming an anachronism in the hurly-burly of the fitness fanaticism afflicting English football.

Clough was always prone to arrogance. Born in Middlesbrough in 1934, he was the only one in a family of nine to fail the 11-plus, Tony Francis recalls in his excellent biography. But Tony Rowell, a teacher at Marton Grove, says: "In 40 years I must have taught thousands of boys but Brian Clough sticks out in my memory for several reasons. He was bright and alert and seemed to have an opinion on everything. He would argue with the teachers, which was rare in a 13-year-old."

According to those who know him well, there were three crucial points in Clough's life: the premature end of his playing career; his falling out with Taylor, who died three years ago without any reconciliation; and his inability to find anything to fill the void outside football. As Taylor had put it after Clough had been out of work for three months when his playing career ended: "If it had been any longer, he'd have gone to pot. He was a no-hoper: jobless, boozing heavily and on his way out."

Clough scored 251 goals in 271 games for Middlesbrough and Sunderland. It was a post-war record. But it ended on Boxing Day 1962, when his right knee collapsed with a sickening crunch when he was challenging for a 50-50 ball. He never achieved what he could have done: he returned almost two years later to score his solitary goal in the First Division. He had played only twice for England. His son Nigel, now at Liverpool, has many of the attributes his father lacked, particularly the ability to turn.

There was a vicious falling-out with Taylor in 1983. Taylor had resigned at Forest because the strain had been too much. Then he returned to the football limelight – back at near-neighbours Derby County. Clough felt cheated. Worse was to come. Taylor cheekily pinched John Robertson, Clough's Scottish left-winger, under freedom of contract when his old partner was trudging around the Pennines on a charity walk. One of the most telling phrases on the day he was made Freeman of Nottingham concerned Taylor: "I wish Peter were with me on this lovely day."

Clough was apparently drinking heavily then. He had always been keen on a tipple. He once tried to sack Stuart Webb, the Derby County secretary, because he refused to allow him the keys to the drinks cabinet. When he made a bold attempt to sign Bobby Moore and Trevor Brooking from West Ham in 1973, Ron Greenwood, then West Ham manager, remembers him disappearing for 20 minutes into the kitchen, after finding out drink was there, before the negotiations.

Journalists knew he drank but one remembers the first time seeing him affected in public. It was when he was receiving an honorary degree at Nottingham four years ago. "We were all in the big hall. Cloughie didn't know what he was walking into or what he was supposed to be doing. He came off the stage afterwards. He turned round and his suit was wet through. I looked at him and thought, 'By gum, lad, you look a bit rough today,

Brian Clough found various ways of helping players relax. This did the trick at training before a European Cup final

a bit red around the face.' Whether he had just had a couple to steady his nerves on the day I don't know."

The respect Clough won in the glory years helped maintain his public reputation when there were problems on the field. But the facade began to crumble publicly on April 25 1993, with the publication of two stories in Sunday newspapers. One alleged the Forest manager had been found asleep in a field near his home. "On the day in question I had a kip in a field because I was tired. I've walked the Pennine Way on numerous occasions and slept in fields 20 or 25 times and no one said owt about it," he later told the *Sun* journalist John Sadler, an old friend and confidant.

But a second story, based on allegations about heavy drinking made by the former Forest director Chris Wootton, signalled the end of Clough's 18-year reign at the City Ground. Despite his previously stated determination to see out the last 18 months of his contract, Clough announced his retirement the following day. He pronounced himself ready for the role of doting granddad. "I'm delighted to get out, to make the break. Nobody is going to be on the phone saying 'Get in here, we have a problem, Pearcey's injured'," he told Sadler.

Retirement brought an end to worries about groin strains. But if the ex-Forest manager thought he was rid of the beautiful game for ever he reckoned without the mud that was about to fly in the Terry Venables/Alan Sugar affair at Tottenham Hotspur. In an affidavit read in the High Court in June Sugar claimed there had been irregularities in the £2.1m transfer of Teddy Sheringham from Forest to Spurs. "I was told by Mr Venables that Mr Clough likes 'a bung'. I told him I thought this was outrageous and that I would not run my company like this. I was told the usual thing was to meet him in a motorway cafe and he would be handed a bag full of money," the Spurs chairman claimed. Both Clough and Venables immediately denied Sugar's allegations. Worse was to follow for both.

Venables stands accused of fraudulently obtaining part of the money he used to purchase his stake in Tottenham. Clough's tenure at Forest was called into question by Granada's World In Action. The programme claimed Clough's reign at Forest was riddled with irregular practices, including the mishandling of match demands and cash payments to the former manager for friendly matches.

Andrew Plumb, the club's former ticket office manager, alleged he gave Clough nearly 2,000 tickets for the 1992 Rumbelows Cup final, worth £20,000, which later appeared on the black market — and their sale, it is claimed, caused the skirmishes between the two opposing sets of supporters — Forest and Manchester United — who found themselves seated in the same section of the stadium. The programme further claimed that Clough received £1,500 in cash after a testimonial match against Scunthorpe and had demanded £1,000 cash for a friendly game against non-league King's Lynn.

Clough issued a typically short, but forceful, denial: "I have not had 2,000 tickets in 18 years at the club." His friends were in more expansive mood. "I don't believe a bloody word of it," one said. "Why would a man who has made a couple of million pounds out football want to get involved in selling 2,000 tickets through the touts, just to end up with a percentage?"

There was little sign yesterday of Clough at his mock Georgian mansion in Quarndon, four miles from Derby. According to yesterday's *Daily Express*, he was prone to sit around in his dressing gown all day, drinking heavily. Peter Batt, a reporter who has known him for a quarter of a century, publicly pleaded with the man he described as an active alcoholic to seek help. During a telephone conversation a few days ago Clough sang to Batt, a reformed alcoholic, down the phone. "I've got you under my skin," he crooned. Batt said: "Clough is in the throes of incurable illness. He is fast approaching the point of physical, mental and spiritual bankruptcy."

But not financial. The Elms, with six bedrooms, is set in six acres. His blue Mercedes stood by the garden. He told one reporter after the World In Action allegations: "Clear off my lawn, young man."

They are the trappings of a wealthy man. His fortune dates from his dismissal after 44 days at Leeds United in 1974. He got a £100,000 pay-off. There followed lucrative deals with the Sun, a paper out of kilter with the political views he professed. He advertised electricity and Shredded Wheat. He bought a newsagent's — source, it is suspected, for many of the chocolates handed out. As Taylor once said: "He will be the richest man in Derby cemetery when he goes."

The team that Brian built and the shadow he leaves

Bungs or no bungs, what Cloughie did for Forest was nothing short of a miracle. By Richard Williams

It would have been nicer, perhaps, if Brian Clough had died with Nottingham Forest's record of 42 consecutive league matches unbeaten still intact. But at least when Arsenal finally surpassed it just under four weeks ago the old magician's name returned to the sports pages for the right reasons.

Bungs or no bungs, what Cloughie did for Forest was nothing short of a miracle. He took an old and proud but stagnant club and, with the minimum of resources, lifted it to the pinnacle of European football for two years running. While a statue inside the City Ground and his name on a grandstand are the visible signs of his 18 years there, his enduring place in the hearts of supporters ensures that all his successors will be measured by his achievements.

Yet the news of Clough's appointment in 1975 was not met with unanimous delight. To many he was the loud-mouthed upstart who, while rescuing the hated rivals Derby County from near oblivion, had stolen the heart of Johnny Carey's fine Forest side of the late 60s. Terry Hennessey and Alan Hinton were among those who swapped the red shirts for the white as Clough drove Derby to promotion from the Second Division and then to the League Championship.

Worst of all, during the 1970-71 season Clough staged a raid aimed at enticing Ian Storey-Moore, Forest's dashing left-winger and leading goalscorer, to the Baseball Ground. He paraded Storey-Moore at half-time during one of Derby's home games. But the contracts had not been signed, and such was the uproar at the other end of the A52 that Forest's directors were forced to withdraw and sell the prized player to Manchester United instead.

It took several months and the arrival of Peter Taylor, his old Derby assistant, for Clough to win the wholehearted support of the City Ground. Now players began to flow the other way, although the early arrivals of John McGovern and John O'Hare from Derby via Leeds, followed by Archie Gemmill direct from the Baseball Ground, were greeted with initial suspicion.

It gradually became apparent that Clough was building a team of substance. Peter Shilton moved from Stoke to fill the goalmouth. At right-back the gangling Viv Anderson left the nearby Fairham Comprehensive to start a career that would make him England's first black player. Larry Lloyd, discarded by Liverpool then Coventry, formed a solid partnership in central defence with Kenny Burns, who was transformed from Birmingham's thuggish centre-forward into a sort of Franz Beckenbauer of the East Midlands. The veteran Frank Clark completed the rearguard, replacing the promising but ill-fated Colin Barrett, plucked respectively from Newcastle and Manchester City.

With McGovern as the water-carrier, the midfield creativity was supplied by the bustling Gemmill, the thoughtful Martin O'Neill and the Scottish left-winger John Robertson – who, along with Burns, was the finest example of Clough's ability to persuade a talent to express itself. The "little fat lad" who beat players through guile and wit would play a crucial role in both Forest's European Cup wins.

Up front were the sparkling Tony Woodcock and the powerful Peter Withe, the latter replaced by the unknown Garry Birtles one unforgettable European night against Liverpool. Later came Trevor Francis, whose fee fell a few coppers short of £1m because that was how Cloughie wanted it and who got on the end of Robertson's cross to win the first European final.

As Clough's eye for a deal began to take precedence over his eye for talent, the failures of Ian Wallace, Justin Fashanu, Peter Ward and others began to chip away at the facade. But the fans continued to enjoy teams packed with players as gifted as Des Walker, Johnny Metgod, Peter Davenport, Stuart Pearce, Franz Carr, Hans van Breukelen, Roy Keane, Chris Fairclough, Steve Hodge and Clough's son, Nigel.

Many of those will be queuing up today to express their gratitude for his influence. Perhaps they will be joined by the two young fans whose ears he boxed when they tried to invade the pitch during a League Cup match at the City Ground one night 15 years ago, earning himself a fine and touchline ban merely for treating them as if they were his own sons.

In the end he stayed too long and had to be eased out. But no manager has left a newly relegated club more wreathed in admiration and gratitude, and few will cast a longer shadow.

Frightening, eccentric — and kind

Forest's European Cup-winning striker Trevor Francis pays tribute to an outrageous genius, who has died at 69

When Brian Clough signed me from Birmingham City in early 1979 Nottingham Forest were the only team that could challenge Liverpool at the time and I joined them to progress my career. More importantly, they had a manager whom I regarded it a privilege and honour to play for.

He was recognised as one of the outstanding English managers and should have been in charge of the national team. But that was never going to happen. I had played at various levels for England and I came to realise that, although he was the best, the way he managed football clubs – from top to bottom – meant he could never have done that with the FA.

Though I was to go on and win 52 caps and Cloughie was always the popular choice for the England job, sadly he would never get the chance. The FA would never have put up with some of the things he did. There were times when his behaviour bordered on the eccentric but that was part of his genius.

He even seemed to jeopardise our date with destiny in May 1979, because one of our players tried to get on the team bus covered in stubble. We arrived late for the European Cup final in Munich as a result, because the boss insisted that Garry Birtles went back to his room and shaved.

"What's that on your chin?" Cloughie asked Garry as we got on the bus. "I want to look mean," he replied, but the boss was having none of it and told him: "You're not playing in my team until you get a shave."

In the end we got to the stadium about 45 minutes before kick-off but his treatment of Garry was typical of the standards he demanded. I think it was also his way of helping us relax

The proud father, nine months before his death in 2004, supports his son Nigel, manager of Burton Albion

before the game. It was as though he was saying this match is just like any other and that there is no hurry to get there.

Another game I remember well was my Forest debut at Ipswich earlier that year although, if it was forgettable in terms of the way I played, the Ipswich fans loved it. They didn't stop chanting "What a waste of money", but something did happen that I'll never forget.

I couldn't reach a cross with my head, so I punched the ball into the net, though I didn't get away with it during the game. And afterwards the boss gave me the biggest dressing down of my career. He told me in no uncertain terms that, if I was going to play for Forest, then I played the game in the right spirit and according to the laws.

But, while the boss insisted on high standards from the players, especially punctuality, appointments could be moveable feasts for him, not least when he signed me. He arrived late because he had been playing squash. I guess for him it was just another day at the office but it was the opportunity of a lifetime for me.

He made players want to play for him, though, and had an uncanny knack of bringing the best out of them. Although he frightened some, he could be kind-hearted and make them relax. I think that, plus the respect he commanded, was his secret.

It was still all too apparent when I last saw him. It was only in May, a dinner to celebrate the 25th anniversary of winning the European Cup. All my old team-mates were there and the boss was as well. He was in great form and made an off-the-cuff speech.

I never saw this day coming at all. I'm in shock.

Chapter seven
Before the Premiership: of cups and characters

Second Division Sunderland mob their goalscorer, Ian Porterfield. Mick Jones, a winner the previous year, is not amused

07|05|1973

Flag flies for Sunderland underdogs

FA Cup final
Sunderland 1 Leeds United 0
Albert Barham, Wembley

Between the ecstasy of Wembley on Saturday afternoon and the less watchful hours of dawn, a large red-and-white flag was planted on my lawn by neighbours who have strong and long connections with Sunderland. It is still flying, a pennant of penance, for it was the head, not the heart, which had led one to imply that Sunderland would not beat Leeds United. Now the world knows that they did, well and truly, in a magical final which did a power of good for English football.

Sunderland and Bob Stokoe, the Messiah of Wearside, deserve every adjectival twist and every peon of praise, not only for the manner in which they held off Leeds at the end to become the first Second Division club to win the FA Cup since West Bromwich Albion in 1931 but because they have breathed new life into a competition which has been dominated for so long by the familiar elite units of the First Division.

But spare a moment for Leeds, once more so near, once more beaten at the last. Does this signify that their professionalism has been taken beyond the point where self-expression, a flash of intuition or a moment of unorthodoxy can win? "Because we keep going down at the end and because we shall be back next season, that's why we are a great side" – those were brave words from the losing captain, Billy Bremner.

Sunderland won this remarkable final with a goal from Porterfield, sweat almost staining away the No10 on his back, who scored with his "wrong foot" after 31 minutes: a good example of making the most of an opportunity suddenly presented. It was superbly taken by a man foot-sure on a pitch made capricious and slippery after early torrential rain.

Yet this was not the turning point. That came on the hour.

First Watson, a fair candidate for man of the match, cut across Bremner, the Leeds captain fell flat on his face but it was no penalty. Then Jones, Giles and Reaney swept remorselessly forward again, weaving an intricate pattern that ended with Cherry diving to head the ball towards goal. Montgomery leapt sideways and beat away the ball. Lorimer lashed it back and the goalkeeper, looking hopelessly out of position, twisted his body and diverted the ball on to the underside of the bar. Leeds were astounded as were the crowd, whose collective gasp was followed by a triumphal roar for Montgomery. Sunderland had been saved by the bounce, which might as well have gone a yard inside the net as outside.

The Sunderland goal had come almost with the first dangerous move they made. A wicked, if speculative, lob by Kerr, the indefatigable captain, dropped just short of Harvey's crossbar and the keeper turned the ball carefully over. Hughes curled over the corner, Watson bustled forward, taking Leeds players with him, and Porterfield had time to bring down the ball from his knee and volley it in.

Leeds, the Cup holders, were seemingly at half-power in the first period, and one waited for an explosion which never came. The passing of Giles was erratic; Jones and Clarke were worn down by Watson and Pitt, while Gray was simply grey. That he was taken off 13 minutes from the end and replaced by Yorath was a tribute to Malone's work in covering him.

Sunderland chased and harried as expected but they were also too sharp in interception for Leeds. Seldom were the favourites allowed to play the game they wanted. Late in the match, when Sunderland were tiring and Leeds pounding away, Watson, Pitt, Malone and young Horswill prevented the breakthrough. There were many harrowing moments: shots ricocheted and whined away, an interception by Pitt made Clarke appear slow. Yet, when the pressure was eased, there was time for a little audacity from Sunderland, Hughes leading them in a series of back-heel flicks.

None worked harder to give Leeds their break than Madeley. Reaney, so hard to beat, and Cherry went marauding more and more often but the men who a few months ago were almost unknown outside their own province – Montgomery, Hughes, Horswill and the others – were a match for the best of Leeds.

When Stokoe left the comparative safety of Blackpool to go to Sunderland, he said simply: "I'm going home." At home he has helped recreate the fervour of Wearside. A collection of players have been given their self-respect, worked hard and gained their reward. Now they will compete in Europe, though the target must be to return to the First Division where a team and a club like this belong.

The strain will be tremendous, for only more success will be expected. Yesterday William Hill made them 4-1 favourites for the Second Division championship. Today Sunderland meet Cardiff City in a match which will settle relegation. Only then can they return for the civic junketings.

26|04|1974

The master adds to his glittering record

Leeds, the outstanding side of the past decade, regain the League thanks to Don Revie's fanatical belief. By Eric Todd

The surrender of three points by Liverpool in their last two home games finally extinguished their hopes of retaining the League Championship but it would be unfair to suggest that Leeds United captured it by default. Not everyone loves Leeds; in fact many people hate them as they used to hate Arsenal, Huddersfield Town, Manchester United and Tottenham Hotspur in their days of almost monotonous success. Not that Leeds will worry. They have been the outstanding team in most of the past 10 seasons since they left the Second Division.

The handbooks for 1965 make interesting reading and the photograph of the Leeds promotion side embraces four players still on active service at Elland Road. Giles looks the picture of innocence and Hunter one of grim determination. Reaney looks bashful and Bremner, clad all in seraphic white, appears ready to launch into "O for the wings of a dove". According to one handbook: "Leeds gave many indications of their strength and there is little doubt that a lot more will be heard of them in the years ahead." And it was not even written by a Leeds man.

Those of us who have followed Leeds in the flesh as well as in the spirit for 50 years marvel at their transformation. Nobody could have foreseen it, remembering only their dreadful Cup

66

Though different characters, Revie remains to Leeds what Bill Shankly is to Liverpool

99

record in the 50s and early 60s. In 10 seasons running they were knocked out in the third round, thrice in succession at home by Cardiff. After promotion in 1956 they descended in 1960. In their first season after getting back up in 1964 they were beaten by Liverpool at Wembley and finished runners-up to Manchester United, the champions, who had a better goal average.

Leeds nevertheless had given notice of their intentions and, although the bad luck which denied them the double in 1964-65 has been their regular companion ever since, they have an enviable record, even though their collective and individual play sometimes has been frowned upon in high places. They have, however, accepted and survived their punishment – sometimes excessively severe – and proved what may be achieved by dedication and determination.

This season their wonderful run of 29 games without defeat suggested as long ago as mid-February that the championship was a foregone conclusion. Leeds then were nine points ahead of Liverpool, who had played one game fewer. Then came Leeds' first defeat at Stoke – after being two goals in front – and from then until they won at Bramall Lane on April 16 Leeds collected only eight points from nine matches. And they were beaten at home by Bristol City in the Cup. The rot had set in.

Liverpool, meantime, had been working up a head of steam, gathering 19 points from 12 games until, with a game in hand, they were only three points behind in mid-April. Leeds won at Sheffield and then defeated Ipswich but Liverpool had games in hand and the top of the table looked like depending on arithmetic before Everton drew at Anfield and Arsenal inflicted on Liverpool their only home defeat of the season. It was all over.

It was a pity, albeit understandable, that Leeds could not sustain their free-flowing, uninhibited style indefinitely. Indeed, there were occasions on which they were thoroughly bad, lacking in fight and reverting to niggling tactics of which we thought they had long been purged. Several players lost form at the same time, one or two began to sulk and it appeared that Leeds, but for their work earlier in the season, would be out of the race. To be fair, they were blighted by injury to such players as Giles, Cooper, Eddie Gray, Jones and Bates, and for other reasons they were not always at recognisable strength. Then Hunter proved yet again what a superb competitor he is and Bremner demonstrated what captaincy is all about. McQueen grew in stature as Jack Charlton's successor, Reaney regained the form he showed before he broke a leg and Harvey, in goal, surpassed all expectations after Sprake's departure to Birmingham City.

And then there was, and still is, Don Revie, who some years ago asked me to "sound" Manchester City with a view to returning to them as manager. Thankfully for Leeds the negotiations were stillborn and Revie remains to Leeds what Bill Shankly is to Liverpool – two contrasting characters with the same fanatical belief in their players, a belief that is reciprocated with interest. No other explanation is necessary for why Leeds United and Liverpool were neck and neck almost to the finishing post.

12|05|1980

Brooking's sting is deadly when it matters most

David Lacey reflects on West Ham's stylish 1-0 victory over Arsenal in an FA Cup final of late controversy

West Ham United became the third Second Division club in eight seasons to win the FA Cup because they retained the ability to think on their feet. Arsenal relinquished their hold on the trophy because on a warm Wembley afternoon they were asked to come from behind once too often. Their mental and physical responses, so reliable during the long semi-final with Liverpool, were unable to meet the demands of the bigger occasion.

In some ways, therefore, it was a sad result. It was hard to imagine that Arsenal, having worn down the league champions over seven hours, might still end the season with no tangible reward. However, such sympathy should not suffuse the abundant praise due to West Ham: they have won the Cup by defeating a top-class team beaten only once in 27 matches. They did so not by sacrificing their beliefs in the way the game should be played but by learning to live with them in a modern context.

Each of West Ham's three FA Cup successes has marked an important stage in their development over two decades. When they overcame Preston in the 1964 final the victory epitomised the philosophy of Ron Greenwood, who believes football should be allowed to breathe through its natural skills, that the sport is more a matter of creating space and not giving the ball away than simply preventing opponents from playing.

In 1975, with Greenwood still manager but John Lyall in charge of the team, West Ham gained a less cultured victory over Fulham in a final that caught the side in transition. Greenwood was still two years from his renaissance with England and Lyall was only starting to instil his own brand of pragmatism. True, he led West Ham out five years ago but Saturday's must surely have been a more satisfying triumph. While it was achieved, primarily, through football of high quality, the performance was sustained also by the sort of concentrated effort for which West Ham teams of the past have not always been noted.

Lyall gave a clue to his thinking 11 days before the final when he said the sort of players he wanted were those who could both play and compete. He did not want ball-players who failed to run for others; nor did he want runners who kept losing the ball. "Above all the zest for the game has got to be there," he said.

The most remarkable feature of Saturday's match was not that a Second Division side defeated one from the First – after all, West Ham had knocked out West Bromwich Albion, Aston Villa and Everton in previous rounds and were relegated only two seasons ago – but that Arsenal were beaten at their own game and shown a more stylish version of it. At times they must have felt that they were gazing into a distorting mirror.

No single player really dominated the match but one man's performance stood out. On Saturday morning in a popular newspaper Brian Clough had declared that on no account would he have Trevor Brooking in his team. Brooking, he declared, floated like a butterfly and stung like one too and it was because of his lack of consistent effort, along with that of other West Ham players, that the side had failed in recent years.

While certain members of recent West Ham teams have not qualified for Stakhanovite medals, it is hard to see how anybody could number Brooking among them. Far from contributing to West Ham's relegation in 1978, he delayed the inevitable for a year almost single-handed, hauling them through an unbeaten run of seven matches at the end of the 1976-77 season. Then there were his outstanding performances during West Ham's run to the Cup-winners' Cup final in 1974-75. It is true that in his early days at the club Brooking was a tentative player but for a long time now his skill and perception in using the ball have been backed by his ability to win it near his own penalty area.

However, Brooking's career has not, so far as one can recall, been notable for prolific scoring feats with his head and it is odd the way that Wembley sometimes disturbs comfortable assumptions about players. Manchester United's opening goal against Benfica in the 1968 European Cup final went in off Bobby Charlton's glistening and largely unsullied pate and on Saturday, after 13 minutes, Jennings was so swiftly beaten by Brooking's dark brow that probably neither the goalkeeper nor the scorer knew immediately what had hit them.

Yet the build-up to the goal was utterly logical and it neatly summed up the pattern that the match was always to follow. O'Leary brought the ball over the halfway line and seemed about to exchange passes with Stapleton. Instead the return ball found Sunderland, who was smartly dispossessed by Bonds.

With Arsenal scuttling back to cover, West Ham's counterattack flowed evenly from Brooking to Pearson to Devonshire on the left. Rice and Talbot moved across to meet the threat but were exposed by Devonshire's sudden acceleration to the byline. Jennings deflected the centre away from goal but the damage to Arsenal's defence was irreparable. A shot from Cross rebounded to Pearson, whose volley was turned in by Brooking, almost on his knees near the six-yard line.

Heads you win, though Trevor Brooking normally used his only for thinking. In 1980 it gave West Ham the FA Cup

12|07|1978
Handsome hombres heighten the senses

John Roberts

The rest of the spectacle was interesting rather than compelling. West Ham teams of the past might have lost concentration or left gaps in defence trying to embellish their victory. Lyall's did neither; they withdrew Pearson to midfield and spent much of the game tracking Arsenal down and wearing them out.

More and more it was like watching a tired heavyweight in the 15th round, who knows that he can still save the fight with one big punch but simply does not have the energy to land it. For all Brady's efforts and the willingness of Talbot and Price to go forward, Arsenal's attacks meant little with Stapleton balked and neither Rix nor Sunderland able to get in to the game.

All the while Brooking was pacing his game, knowing his ability to hold the ball would be of particular value in the closing stages. Three minutes from the end he sent Allen past Young and clear of a square defence and West Ham prepared to complete victory through the youngest player yet to appear in a final. Whether or not Allen would have scored is debatable – he still had Jennings to beat – but the question was never put as Young tripped him before the penalty area, acknowledging his caution with the professional's gesture of acceptance.

Some felt Young should have been sent off for ruining what might have been one of Wembley's long-remembered goals. That would have been a harsh end for a basically honest player but there have been similar incidents recently and the Football Association may consider it worthwhile informing referees of its full support should they decide, next season, to dismiss those who commit such cynical, squalid fouls, for which yellow cards and free-kicks are inadequate punishments.

The prospect of hastening towards a new soccer season does not seem so disenchanting now we can look forward to the arrival next weekend of those handsome hombres from Argentina, Osvaldo Ardiles and Ricardo Villa, welcomed, perhaps, by the evocative strains of Tim Rice and Andrew Lloyd Webber.

Tottenham Hotspur deserve full marks for enterprise in completing a deal which, at £750,000 for a pair of world-class players, would seem to be a steal and, when Keith Burkinshaw, the Tottenham manager, finalised the signings yesterday, it was confirmed by the Department of Employment, the Football Association and the Football League that no snags are likely to hinder the transfers.

Apart from a nervous twitch displayed by the Professional Footballers' Association, who expressed fears of a flood of importations from Latin America on hearing of the plan of Sheffield United to establish a transatlantic scouting link, utilising the contacts of their coach, Oscar Arce, the news was received with pleasure and excitement. Even the role of agent played by Antonio Rattin, the swarthy El Bandido of Wembley '66, was accepted with good humour.

Both players are 25 and play in midfield, though Ardiles, of Huracan, understandably cost a larger portion (£400,000) of the total fee than his friend Villa, of Racing Club of Buenos Aires.

Ardiles, diminutive and as sleek as a supporting player in one of those Astaire-Rogers Latin American romps, manipulated the strings behind Kempes and Luque as a major influence on Argentina's progress to World Cup triumph last month. He has been compared with Wilf Mannion and likened to an accelerated version of Paddy Crerand, though perhaps a more accurate description of Ardiles is that he is the type of player Danny Blanchflower aspired to be – which is the one that sprung readily from the lips of the former Tottenham captain yesterday.

Blanchflower, the intellectual of Tottenham's League and FA Cup double-winning team, who now has custody of the Northern Ireland national side, was eager to speak enthusiastically about his old club's pioneering. "This is a good move, a brave move and is to be applauded because the intention is good, whether it works or not," said this tireless campaigner for broader thinking by the soccer authorities of our cramped, insular island. "To do something is better than to do nothing. I would like to think that Spurs were a world club but I haven't been thinking that for two or three years. Now they are back on the ball."

There is, of course, an element of risk involved. As Blanchflower remarked: "It could be that the other lads at Tottenham find themselves playing a different game from Ardiles. If this happens, he'll have to go – on the basis that it's easier to find nine players than one. That's why Tottenham's move is such a brave one and why they deserve to be proved right.

"I don't believe we are near the Argentinians regarding skill. I played against Argentina in the late 1950s and I thought they had 30 fellows on the field. That was because they passed the ball better than we did. They have greater control of the ball and an awareness of where to send it for the best possible effect."

The optimistic side to this superiority is, Blanchflower believes, that some of the skill should, by virtue of association, rub off on the Tottenham players when they begin life afresh in the First Division, starting with the visit to Nottingham Forest, the League champions, on August 19.

"A player like Hoddle should benefit enormously from playing alongside Ardiles," Blanchflower said. "Hoddle has exceptional ability by our standards and the arrival of the Argentinians, especially Ardiles, should bring an extra edge of competitiveness within the team. Hoddle will be alongside the king, the master of moving forward and dictating the pattern and tempo, which is how I tried to play. Hoddle may, as a result, see the need to improve his game and learn the master's tricks, most particularly his positional sense. I don't think anyone else at Tottenham can teach Hoddle that.

"At the same time I still think Tottenham need to strengthen their defence. Two good midfield players may take a certain amount of pressure off a defence, but only for so long. If you pour a couple of cups of hot water into a bucket of cold water, they will raise the temperature all round for a while. But unless you keep adding hot water, it will all go cold again.

"By signing these players Tottenham have made a promise to their supporters and, if I were a supporter, I would be looking for a season ticket. The whole place has brightened up because Tottenham have gone out and had a good try and have come up with what appears to be a great bargain. If Ardiles had been transferred to a Spanish club for £1m, few eyebrows would have been raised."

Villa and Ardiles should be welcomed by the strains of Rice and Lloyd Webber

15|05|1981

Glorious Villa turns match of the century

FA Cup final replay
Manchester City 2 Tottenham Hotspur 3
David Lacey, Wembley

In the end the 100th FA Cup final produced the game of the century. After a match which enthralled Wembley, with the lead changing hands three times, Tottenham Hotspur defeated Manchester City 3-2 in last night's replay and the winning goal, scored by Ricky Villa, will always belong to football history.

Manchester City, who had drawn level within three minutes of Spurs taking an early lead, appeared to be on the threshold of victory for willpower and sheer perseverance when they led 2-1 after being awarded a penalty early in the second half. Then Crooks brought the scores level with 20 minutes to go and five minutes later Villa's second goal of the night provided the perfect climax to an unforgettable contest.

Before last night the 1948 final between Manchester United and Blackpool had been regarded as the outstanding example of attacking play to be seen at Wembley. Blackpool's 4-3 victory over Bolton in 1953, the Matthews final, has always been regarded as the best dramatised match. Last night's borrowed something from the yellowing scripts of both these and put them into a modern setting with Latin American accompaniment. Where Saturday's 1-1 draw had been a tensely fought affair, last night's match surpassed the wildest expectations.

Perhaps FA Cup final replays do not fit into the social calendar. Certainly the audience sounded and felt more like a footballing crowd and the players responded by playing open, positive and entertaining soccer, always prepared to get men forward, always looking for goals.

Spurs won the Cup for the sixth time because they improved their performance in those areas where on Saturday they had been lacking in aptitude and attitude. Hoddle was less inclined to drift out of the game between finely measured long passes and became increasingly committed as the game progressed.

Hughton, showing much more confidence last night, severely reduced the effectiveness of Hutchison on City's right and, while this was countered by Power's greater influence on the other flank, the Manchester team seldom managed to sustain an attack in the manner of the opposition.

The evening started and ended with Villa. On Saturday the big, bearded Argentinian plodded his crest-fallen path to the dressing room after being substituted with nearly half an hour of normal time remaining. Wisely Keith Burkinshaw, the Tottenham manager, thought this disappointment would galvanise Villa in the second game and so it proved.

He was always in space, always ready to support Crooks and Archibald, always willing to take men on with his swaying, shuffling runs. With Villa playing further forward and Ardiles, Galvin, Hoddle and Perryman giving Tottenham's movements speed, accuracy and width, City's chance of again stifling their attacks in midfield was usually slim.

Spurs took the lead in the seventh minute with a goal inspired and executed by their two Argentinians. Ardiles swerved in from the left, spotted a gap and his shot hit Archibald who was able to turn quickly on to the ball and produce another, this one blocked by Corrigan. With the nearest defender, Caton, powerless to do anything, Villa scored joyfully from the rebound.

Three minutes later, after a long kick from Ranson had been partly cleared, Hutchison headed square across the Tottenham penalty area and Mackenzie met the ball with a marvellous right-foot volley that rocketed past Aleksic from 20 yards. In spite of this Tottenham had distinctly the better of the rest of the first half and, but for the continuing excellence of Corrigan, would have been further ahead at the interval..

Four minutes into the second half, however, the whole complexion of the match changed as Manchester City took the lead with a penalty. Bennett's acceleration was on the point of taking him clear of a square Spurs defence when Miller closed in from behind and pushed the young City forward to the ground. Reeves scored calmly and firmly inside the right-hand post.

For a few moments the emotions of the evening boiled over. Then Tottenham drew level in the 70th minute with a goal typical of many they have scored this season. Hoddle prodded the ball forward to Archibald who appeared to have lost the chance when the ball rolled off the end of his foot. Crooks, however, was following up and just managed to push it past Corrigan.

Thus the scene was set for the perfect climax and it duly arrived five minutes later with a goal which in truth belonged not to Wembley but to the River Plate stadium in Buenos Aires. Villa gained possession and advanced into the penalty area to the left of goal. He swerved past Caton's lunge, cut in past a challenge from Ranson, swerved again to defeat Caton's covering tackle and in the same movement slipped the ball past Corrigan.

Tueart replaced MacDonald as City pushed forward to save the game, but this time the task was beyond them — and Tottenham's supporters roared their hallelujahs loud and long into the night air.

Robson's European dream comes true

Uefa Cup final
AZ'67 Alkmaar 4 Ipswich 2 (agg 4-5)
Robert Armstrong, Amsterdam

Bobby Robson realised the dream of a decade when Ipswich Town, a club he is considering leaving shortly, won their first European trophy last night.

For sheer skill, tension and courage the game at the Olympic stadium in Amsterdam will surely rank among the most memorable European finals. Although AZ Alkmaar ran out worthy 4-2 winners on the night, Ipswich emerged as proud possessors of the Uefa Cup with a 5-4 aggregate victory that owed everything to their early commitment to attack.

Apart from Robson's delight at adding a European trophy to the FA Cup Ipswich won three years ago, it was also a night of personal triumph for John Wark, whose first-half goal enabled the Scot to equal Jose Altafini's European scoring record of 14 goals, set for Milan back in 1963.

But even Wark's contribution, set amid a total of 37 goals this season, was overshadowed by the extraordinary display of Frans Thijssen, who wreaked havoc in the AZ defence when it mattered. He, like Robson, could leave Ipswich soon.

It takes two teams to bring unusual quality to a cup final and AZ played their part — despite trailing by an aggregate of four goals shortly after kick-off. When the Ipswich players paraded the trophy they had retrieved from the ruins of an elusive treble before those joyful hordes of blue and white, one had to feel a degree of sympathy for the dejected Dutchmen who performed so bravely without reward.

Bobby Robson nurses the Uefa Cup, won in Holland with Dutch influence. Fifteen months later he was manager of England

If it was never likely that Ipswich would sit back and attempt to defend their three-goal lead from the first leg, no one could have predicted that the Suffolk side would extend the aggregate score with a priceless away goal within three minutes of the start.

Ipswich's own Dutchmen, Muhren and Thijssen, clearly relished the opportunity to parade their cultured skills before their compatriots in the setting of their national stadium and it was the pair's close support of their forwards, ably abetted by Wark, that gave Ipswich their early lead. A clever inter-change on the right between Brazil and Thijssen culminated in a teasing cross from the Dutchman that Metgod hastily whipped away from Wark's feet, at the expense of a corner. When Gates took the flag kick from the left, the ball was only half-cleared to the edge of the penalty box and the industrious Thijssen was again on hand to send a superb volley past Treytel from 20 yards.

Now AZ had nothing to lose by committing everything to attack and English euphoria – colourfully expressed by thousands of their valuable supporters – was put in sober perspective when the Dutch quickly equalised. Their goal owed much to the composure of Metgod, who accepted a neat through-pass from Hovenkamp, dragged the ball away from the advancing Cooper and chipped a fine cross to the near post. Weizl, the Austrian winger who excelled as substitute in the first leg, scored with a firm downward header.

The battle for possession fluctuated wildly throughout the first half as both sides put the opposing goalkeepers under severe pressure with a series of high-quality attacks. No doubt Ipswich were less than satisfied with the marking and positional play of their centre-backs, Butcher and Osman, when the ubiquitous Metgod rose unhampered in the 25th minute to head home a right-wing cross by Peters. Before the half was out the visitors again lacked cover on their right as Metgod chipped a fine cross that Jonker flicked on for Tol to score off the inside of the left post.

But by then Ipswich had, on several occasions, almost casually split open the AZ rearguard and their second goal, in the 32nd minute, left the Dutch with a mountain to climb. In a game that often seemed under the creative control of Dutchmen at both ends, it was Thijssen who took a corner on the right that Mariner headed on for Wark to hook home at close range.

AZ fought desperately to save the final. After the interval they enjoyed territorial dominance – partly because of the striker Kist, who came on as substitute for Tol and immediately gave his side greater central penetration.

When Ipswich conceded a free-kick outside their penalty area the defensive wall had ample time to form up, yet Jonker bent his kick inside the left-hand post from 30 yards, scoring one of the finest goals seen in this season's competition. But even that was not enough.

27|05|1982

Glory night for Spink and Villa

European Cup final
Aston Villa 1 Bayern Munich 0
David Lacey, Rotterdam

Aston Villa kept the European Cup in England for the sixth consecutive year last night when they beat Bayern Munich 1-0 in Rotterdam in a final which, while the quality of football was at times less than distinguished, turned out to be one of the most eventful and exciting matches of its kind in recent seasons.

The goal that won the European Cup for Villa came in the 66th minute when Shaw and Morley gave Withe his only clear-cut chance of the night. But as in last Saturday's FA Cup final the real story concerned a young goalkeeper.

Nigel Spink, 23, who had made only one first-team appearance for Aston Villa and that 2½ seasons ago, replaced Rimmer in the 10th minute because Villa's regular goalkeeper was feeling the effects of a neck injury received in training on Tuesday and could not continue.

Far from being overawed by his sudden change of circumstances, brought from the hollow echoes of Central League football and thrust into a European Cup final to face some of the best strikers in West Germany's World Cup squad, Spink calmly took stock of the situation and then proceeded to thwart Bayern with a series of remarkable saves. When Hoeness at last managed to put the ball past him a couple of minutes from the end, it was only to find a linesman's flag raised for offside.

This final stroke of good fortune was the least Spink deserved because his resolution and agility had kept Aston Villa in the game when their football might have collapsed under the mounting pressure of Bayern's attacks.

Well might Bayern Munich, three times winners of the Champions Cup and unbeaten in their 12 previous European finals, sink to their knees and shake their heads in disbelief at the end of a match which – the longer it went on – seemed to be theirs for the taking.

Until Aston Villa scored – the excellence of Spink notwithstanding – it seemed increasingly likely that England's five-year hold on the trophy would be lost because Villa could not get sufficient accuracy into their football to wrest the game from the Germans.

Until that goal their challenges to the growing midfield mastery of Breitner were apt to be sporadic and the service to the front runners indifferent. In any case the control of Withe and Shaw was too loose to cause the Bayern defence serious concern and on the left wing Morley was a dormant threat.

Meanwhile Bayern fought out a private contest with Spink. On reflection Breitner and his colleagues must have regretted waiting 20 minutes before producing a shot to test Rimmer's understudy. By that time Spink had settled and he did his confidence a world of good with two saves in the space of less than 60 seconds.

First Durnberger cut in past Swain on the left and, although his low shot almost beat the goalkeeper, Spink was quick to reach back and grab the ball. In the next instant he blocked a shot by Rummenigge and Mathy's shot from the rebound cannoned back off Evans. A little later Rummenigge produced an acrobatic kick which beat Spink but went wide.

Towards half-time the influence of Breitner, and the ease with which he was getting past Mortimer, began to give Bayern a firm grip on the game and so it continued into the second half. Augenthaler beat Withe and Bremner as he ran two thirds of the length of the pitch, Evans slipped as he moved in to make a tackle but the German could only shoot wide of the far post. Durnberger was on target on the hour but Spink saved; Swain headed off the line from Augenthaler; Spink managed to grab the ball as Hoeness flicked out a foot at a low cross and, after Breitner had sent Horsman to the byline on the left, Hoeness arrived unmarked in the goalmouth, only to miss the ball completely.

Having survived all this without conceding a goal, Aston Villa had some reason for optimism. However, few could have expected them to score in quite the manner that they did. Shaw took advantage of a slip by Dremmler to find space on the left and sent the ball inside to Morley, who took on Augenthaler, swerving past the defender with a shrug of the shoulders and a sway of the hips. Finally he found Withe and the winning goal was scored via the near post.

Aston Villa's multitude of supporters then had to endure another 20 minutes of Bayern pressure, although in truth the Germans never produced the incisive play which earlier had looked like taking the European Cup back to Bavaria.

Peter Withe scored but the real story concerned Villa's young goalkeeper, Nigel Spink

07|05|1985
Singing the Blues
Everton Football Club are worthy champions

Leading article

Everton's accession to the Football League Championship yesterday marks more than glory for the "other" Liverpool team. On Merseyside that is important enough. For too long the Goodison loyalists and their Blues have played second fiddle to the Reds. Even now, before Everton kicked off yesterday, only their old rivals stood a chance of catching them. If Liverpool the club have had a relatively "poor" season, Liverpool the city is the undisputed centre of football achievement. It has two hugely successful sides, one on the threshold of triple greatness.

Economically, the city is still dominated by decline. Away from Goodison and Anfield it hits the headlines with factory closures, political revolt, riot, Heseltine, garden centres and, most recently, the Tate of the North. But the game goes on, ever more successfully, and where there were one and a half great teams, now there are two. Liverpool the city is down but never bowed. It lives on a spirit unequalled in the country. Would that prosperity could be created with such daunting efficiency.

Everton's achievement, after living so long in the shadow of their neighbours, has been built without flamboyance. In an age when footballers are mega-stars earning ridiculous wages, and seem irresistibly drawn to spending their riches in nightclubs and having public rows with their managers, Everton have, in the best way, avoided star quality. Their manager, Howard Kendall, is down-to-earth, spending more time preparing a good side than a good quote. Their players are not, by and large, household names. They too get on with their workrate and their victories. Neville Southall, the goalkeeper, is typical in that he washes his own jersey because he does not like the shiny ones the team provides, and rides a bicycle to the ground because he is scornful of flashy cars. No wonder he keeps a mean goal.

Further contradiction of the rule that success can only be bought lies in the boots of Andy Gray, who has contributed so much to Everton's championship. He was bought by Wolverhampton Wanderers (relegated on Saturday to the Third Division) for £1.2 million. Everton bought him last season for £250,000. Everton , whose fans do not riot, have restored sanity to our national game. We wish them well in their Cup-Winners' Cup final; and at Wembley for the FA Cup final. But we must be careful. There is a Manchester side there as well.

Scorer Andy Gray feels the weight off his arms in Rotterdam — but Manchester United would spoil Everton's treble at Wembley

16|05|1985

Patience and power drive Everton home

European Cup-Winners' Cup final
Everton 3 Rapid Vienna 1
David Lacey, Rotterdam

Everton brought the Cup-Winners' Cup to Merseyside for the first time last night and did so in the grandest of manners. They overwhelmed Rapid Vienna in Rotterdam and the only surprise feature of their 3-1 victory was that it took them so long to score.

Once they had gone ahead just before the hour any lingering doubts about Everton's ability to complete the middle part of the treble were dispelled. Their overjoyed supporters chanted "Celtic, Celtic" as Everton's all-round superiority, and especially the strength of their teamwork, demoralised and finally demolished the side who many felt should have gone out of the competition at Parkhead in the second round.

Faced with the powerful presence of the new English champions, Rapid Vienna became Vapid Vienna and this time there was no appeal. Indeed it seemed Everton might have had a harder preparation for Saturday's FA Cup final against Manchester United had they had to visit Watford this week instead. Then again Rapid, having talked their way past Celtic, had not reached the final by beating poor sides. The truth of last night was that Everton, as for most of the season, played with patience and intelligence and nicely controlled power.

Steven and the full-backs, Stevens and Van den Hauwe, were outstanding as Everton established a pattern of command at the outset that was never challenged for long. Rapid did not bring on Panenka, their main creative influence, until midway through the second half. The 37-year-old Czech had been carrying an injury and his passing and free-kicks were missed.

That Everton did not score before half-time was a major surprise, so utterly did they dominate the first 45 minutes. Perhaps one of the reasons was that they had so much space and time, especially on the wings. This might have accounted for the succession of predictable crosses that did not pose problems for the Rapid defence. Stevens' long, high, hanging throws from the right, which had brought about Bayern Munich's downfall in the semi-finals, were a greater danger during this period.

Konsel dealt well with an early Sheedy shot and for a long time that was the nearest Everton came to scoring. They thought they had done so seven minutes before half-time when Gray forced the ball past Konsel but Mountfield was offside.

Rapid began the second half showing more zest and confidence. But Everton maintained their attacking pattern and in the 49th minute Mountfield would surely have scored his 15th goal of the season had he been able to control Sheedy's free-kick first time after completing a late run through the defence to arrive unmarked barely three yards from the line.

When Everton did at last score after 57 minutes the goal owed a lot to Sharp's quick thinking. The Scot spotted a careless back-pass by Lainer and beat the goalkeeper to it. He dragged the ball clear of Konsel, stumbled but was still able to pull it back from the byline for Gray to score his 13th goal in 19 games.

Almost on cue, and perhaps not in the best possible taste in view of the Bradford tragedy, a green-and-white Viennese banner was set alight in the far corner of the ground. As Konsel tipped a rising shot from Steven over the bar after the best move of the night there seemed little hope for the Viennese and in the 72nd minute Sharp flicked on Sheedy's corner from the right, Mountfield dummied under the ball and it ran beyond the far post to Steven, who scored Everton's second.

Five minutes from the end Rapid at last produced a co-ordinated, penetrative attack. Kranjcar backheeled a through-ball from Gross for Krankl to round Southall and score only the second goal Everton had conceded in the competition. Yet immediately Gray and Sharp set up the chance for Sheedy to score Everton's third and complete another memorable night for Goodison Park.

"It was," said Howard Kendall, "a truly tremendous performance. In terms of possession football you will see nothing better. The treble is certainly on — our players have been rehearsing our record in the dressing room and we might even make the top 10."

18|12|1986
On pastures artificial: Luton Town appoints a club chaplain

Luton Town, beloved of the Prime Minister for being about the only team to act upon her entreaties to introduce membership cards and adopt a resolute approach to hooliganism, has gone a step further by taking on a club chaplain. Football has long been regarded as a religion to its more passionate supporters but this has seldom been taken to its literal conclusion. As far as they know at Luton, Hartlepool is the only other club to sign God but it might not be sensible to read that too pessimistically.

The Rev Mervyn Terrett, a Luton fan since he was eight, is about to take up his duties as pastor to the squad, offering counselling and encouragement whenever these may be sought. It will be a low-key presence – he will not be playing or, indeed, praying with the team – but will be "available" when required. There is no suggestion yet that the chaplain is insisting on the introduction of a "sin bin" (or repentance dug-out) for players committing fouls. But if the manager decides it would be more helpful for Mr Terrett to give the pre-match pep talk, the players may find themselves intoning this version of the Magnificat …

"My soul doth magnify the team: and my spirit hath rejoiced in John Moore, our manager.

For he hath regarded our current fifth place in Division One.

For behold, from the members-only family enclosure, all away fans shall be prohibited.

For the pitch, which is En-Tout-Cas, is artificial, and opponents cannot cope with it.

And the Prime Minister's mercy is upon her candidate for Welwyn Hatfield, our chairman.

He hath implemented our membership scheme and visiting supporters he hath sent empty away.

We have put down Everton and Liverpool from their seats: and have similarly beaten Nottingham Forest.

We have filled the Football League with confusion: and been expelled from the Littlewoods Cup.

But the FA in their mercy have allowed us to remain in their Cup: and television has come to the rescue of our home draw against Liverpool by deciding to screen the match live.

Glory be to the manager, and to the chairman and to Brian Stein, our leading scorer.

As it was before we were depleted, is now and ever shall be: heading for the Championship. Amen"

30|01|1988
Why uncle Roy is drawing a veil over the new Sproson

As Port Vale meet Spurs in the FA Cup, Frank Keating relates an extraordinary family tale of loyalty and resentment

Just like the old days it is a Cup tie Saturday in the Potteries. Us versus Them or, as we are allowed to say on these occasions, minnows and giants. Port Vale versus Tottenham Hotspur, the people against the gentry. Such matches were made for men called Sproson to get stuck in and do what a man had to do.

Phil Sproson, six foot bulwark of Port Vale's defence today against the strolling players of Spurs, is a one-club man, answering over 400 League and Cup calls to the colours. But that is not half the matches his Uncle Roy managed in a playing career that, almost unbelievably, spanned 1950 to 1971.

While the passionate "oohs" and "aahs" and cheers and sighs swirl all around nephew Phil in the muddy slop and slap and siege of the penalty area, some of them will be carried down on the chill winds from the bleak ridge of Burslem's Vale Park and be heard most certainly by Uncle Roy as he administers one of his three newsagent shops down the hill. Roy Sproson will pretend not to hear, intimate in his affable, bluff and comradely manner that he does not give a fig for football any more.

When Roy Sproson was sacked as Port Vale's manager after serving the club, man and boy, for 25 years he vowed never to set foot in the place again, never even to glance up at the tumbledown old arena as he passes it time and again each day. He has kept his resolution.

This afternoon it will be tested severely, I fancy. Roy is in his greying middle 50s, still a strapping man, as successful in business as he was down the years in his own half of a football field – more so, for when he drove away from Vale Park for the last time it was in a Cortina. Now he cruises about in a Mercedes.

"I never even looked back in the driving mirror. I'd worked

there a quarter of a century. I've never set foot in the place from that day to this and never will. I just can't, don't know why really. Other than Phil I couldn't even tell you this Saturday's team.

"A manager can smell the end of his time, you know. The whole club reeks with an imminent sacking. Not that they actually say, 'You're bloody fired.' It's all innuendo and muttering, you know, 'Things not going too well, are they?' But you know they're after your blood – and if truth was told you already had your bags packed for weeks."

C'mon, surely when you get up at five o'clock for the papers this Saturday morning, you'll make your cup of tea, look at the weather and think, "A good day for the Cup, eh?" and just get a bit misty-eyed and the old brain box will shuffle through a few of the memories? "No, I won't." Bet you will. "I won't, promise." I don't believe you, not even 1954 when Vale got to the semi-final? "No, all behind me now, that." Get away with you, fourth round of the Cup, 34 years ago to the very Saturday, Vale v Cup holders Blackpool, all the stars and Stan Matthews back at the Potteries?

The grin gets broader. "Oh yes, OK, if you force me, I can't forget that." The eyes glaze over. "I was marking Ernie Taylor. No disrespect but he was arrogant, jibing at me all through. When we looked like winning, I started getting back at him, 'Come and watch me in the next round, Mr Taylor,' I said. I was only a cocky kid then. At the end Taylor just walked off, wouldn't shake hands. Stanley took it very well, though, but I bet he was mad inside."

When he was a sprog at Oakhill School before the war Roy used to wait every day at the bus stop at Trent Vale for a sight of his hero going to Stoke for training. Once Matthews had got on the bus, the boy would hare to school. When he grew up he had to mark him in the Cup tie against Blackpool.

"Stan was even more of a genius close to. I fancied myself as a tackler. Suddenly he's coming at me down the touchline, jockeying, shimmying, his classic situation. Lo and behold he goes and shoves the ball too far in front of him: he's given it me. I smile to myself and think, 'Watch this, folks, I'm bloody taking the ball off Matthews.'

"Then bloody hell, unbelievable. Just as my toe was an eighth of an inch from the ball, he's found another gear, two ruddy gears, and his toe comes and sniffs it past me and he's skipping over my sliding leg and is away. I didn't just think I had him, I knew I had him – and now here I was flat on my backside realising genius is really genius, and the crowd all laughing."

We are in one of his shops at Cobridge. A few hundred yards away is Arnold Bennett's old house in Waterloo Road. A few doors along is a mosque. Up there Vale Park and its pylons look damply forlorn, plucking up courage for Saturday. Outside sit the sponsored cars emblazoned with the players' names. Phil is now the big man at the back. Twenty years ago or so he first went to watch his uncle play.

Roy Sproson, who marked Stanley Matthews in Port Vale's 1954 Cup defeat of Blackpool, stands tall with Jack Cunliffe

"It was against Brentford. I was so proud of him. Nobody believed he was my uncle till he came and tapped me on the head to prove it at the end. No, it's no matter he doesn't watch us now, he gives me advice whenever I've needed it."

The home dressing room is friendly, comfortable chairs and a carpet even. The visitors' room is like a barn. Cheerless, cold tiles, a slim bench round the walls and one large ancient bathtub. "This room's our secret weapon for Spurs," says Phil, "not forgetting their luke-warm pot of tea for half-time."

His uncle chortles when I pass on the tactic. "With any luck, Spurs might be in for a culture shock: out of their stockbroker houses and warm, snug luxury coach — straight into that cold room. There are omens too this week from that Blackpool match. It has rained all week and our rain can chill the marrow.

"It chilled Blackpool. We'd spent days drying out the pitch with coal sacks, wringing them with mangles, even shovelling water off, then forking and rolling so it looked quite reasonable till you trod on it and you'd sink in well over the tops of your boots. Might be like that this Saturday.

"Then we'd soaked the leather ball in water for 24 hours — filling one of those screw-lid buckets with warm water and screwing the ball down into it for a day. After lunch on Saturday out it comes, dry off the surface water and give it a coat of dubbin so it looked all right. But it weighed more than a cannonball. Then for the kick-in we gave Blackpool a few old balls, dry and light and pumped up like balloons. After that they could hardly kick the match ball off the deck."

So there you are, Roy — you see, it took me no time to get

you back in the mood for football? He grins some more and nods acknowledgement.

"Phil is a good stopper, more defensive than me perhaps, I started off as a wing-half, of course, a left-sider who could run all day. People complain about the players today, but they're all right, pretty good. But no, you still won't get me up there even to see that Waddle or Ardiles, can't really explain why, but I'll never go again.

"It was already a young man's game when I packed up at 41. But it had been a real good life. I came out of National Service and was suddenly earning £8 a week and £4 in the summers. That was more than my brother, Phil's dad, was getting as a skilled engineer."

He played 761 League games, only beaten narrowly by Trollope of Swindon (770) and Dickinson (764) of Portsmouth. "Might have beaten them: one season I was off injured for 21 games."

At 41 he tossed his muddy kit into the laundry skip and tried life in a collar and tie as the manager. "Any manager in football with a streak of reality or reason knows that sooner or later he's going to be crucified.

"I couldn't have been one of those blokes, good friends of mine too, you see at these annual get-togethers who just can't leave football alone. It's in their bloodstream like inky fingers are on newsagents' hands, and they scrimp and save for jobs scouting on wet Wednesdays on the Cheshire League and go round touching forelocks and cringing in front of directors. It's sad and pathetic, and there's an awful lot of them about, I'm afraid."

He will be up at five this morning and, OK, if you press him he might have a squint to see what the papers say about Port Vale's chances. By 9.30 he will be back home till the afternoon. Then, around four o'clock, he'll be driving back to organise the evening rush.

Won't he even glance up at the windswept paddock? "I doubt it." Not even switch on the radio for the half-time score? "Yes, I suppose I will, blast it" – and he laughs at himself for his cussedness. "Deep down, I really hope they do OK. I can't explain really why I couldn't bring myself to go but, like Arnold Bennett himself said somewhere, didn't he, 'Most things are to do with nothing but, in its way, football is to do with everything.'"

Stan was even more of a genius close to. I didn't just think I had him, I knew it ...

16|05|1988
Cup crazy in Wimbledon

Kathy Beach

There had been a couple of faintings, one policeman said, but otherwise it had been a great party.

Not even the burst of spring rain, breaking an otherwise glorious day, could dampen the spirits of the crowds toasting their local soccer team in a leafy London suburb better known for its tennis courts, its common and a furry Womble known as Uncle Bulgaria.

Wimbledon had brought the FA Cup home against all the odds and the 20,000 people who turned out to greet them yesterday would, as manager Bobby Gould ruefully admitted, have quadrupled the club's usual gate at its tiny Plough Lane ground.

Wimbledon's 1-0 victory over the League champions Liverpool at Wembley on Saturday was hardly to have been expected. But their supporters rose to the occasion, discovering shorts and T-shirts in the team's blue and yellow colours at the back of their wardrobes. The usually tranquil streets, filled with chanting fans holding beer cans high, resounded to a deafening chorus of car horns. No one could escape the festivities, from a babe in arms wearing only a Wimbledon scarf and a nappy to a bemused old man watching from a roadside bench.

'This'll teach the tennis toffs,' said one local with obvious satisfaction.

In the jam-packed pubs talk turned from the ins and outs of the match to the antics of jubilant fans who on Saturday night stopped the traffic by dropping their trousers. Police arrested 42 people that night, mainly for drink-related offences, but yesterday good cheer and tolerance reigned.

On the pavement outside the Alexandra pub the landlord roasted a whole pig on a spit, providing tough competition for the hot-dog stalls dotted around the streets.

The victory at Wembley capped an almost fairy-tale rise to the top for a team which started playing league soccer only 11 years ago and has climbed steadily up since then, entering the First Division in 1986. To reach the FA Cup final was in itself an achievement but to beat Liverpool, international kings of soccer, saving a penalty in the process, was beyond anyone's wildest dreams.

Earlier in the day the giantkillers paraded their trophy through Wimbledon in an open-top bus and were given a civic reception at the town hall — to the consternation only of the Wimbledon Choral Society, whose members had been hoping to squeeze in a last rehearsal for Bach's Mass in B Minor before the public performance tonight. In the jubilation of the moment, the choristers were summarily evicted to the cramped hall of the community centre around the corner.

On Wimbledon Common exhausted revellers sprawled out in the sunshine. Finding the going a bit tough was Rusty, an eight-year-old golden retriever who panted along the grass, his thick coat weighed down by the blue and yellow ribbons plaited through it.

21|10|1989

Second coming for the first Fashanu

Cynthia Bateman meets a man of style who has followed the way of God back from injury to action at Maine Road

Justin Fashanu is a Born Again Christian and this weekend a Born Again footballer. But if Christ has dictated the destiny and Fashanu's own grit been his salvation, Mel Machin, the Manchester City manager, must take credit for the resurrection.

On Tuesday Fashanu loped through the pink table-clothed pseud of Manchester's Ramada Renaissance hotel, wondering where his next five-star accommodation was coming from and seemingly as far away as ever from realising his ambition "to start a First Division game".

On Thursday, five years after Russell Osman's boot stud embedded itself in his knee, causing an infection that eventually forced him out of the game, Fashanu was offered a contract with City and named in the first-team squad for the game against Aston Villa at Maine Road tomorrow.

It is, at last, the pat on the head instead of the kick in the teeth from fate or God or whatever you believe in, which for Fashanu these past few years has had to be himself and the philosophy that, "if you really want something, you can get it. Your body will follow your mind."

But if Fashanu, the Dr Barnardo's foster boy, wears sackcloth and ashes in his head, the outward visible sign is of a high roller. "God has always allowed me to live in style and with

panache," he said. Giving up top-class soccer was bad enough and, if he was to have any chance of getting back, he had to hang on to the coat-tails, to feel he was still part of it. His younger brother John's success at Millwall and Wimbledon has helped. But image was all-important too – not to impress others but to impress himself, to keep in touch, to feed the dream while the hand of God moved in mysterious ways.

The lanky, soft-spoken striker uses his faith like a road map. It led after his injury to an invitation three years ago to spend a holiday with an American family in Los Angeles. Four weeks became two years.

In the early days there Fashanu was invited to watch the LA Lasers playing indoor soccer and, having been told by English doctors that he was lucky to be able to walk and would certainly not be able to play again, was invited to meet the Lasers' club doctor, who ran a clinic treating world-class stars.

'The doctor said, "Justin, you can play again but it will take a lot of rehabilitation" – not to mention a lot of money.

"I was relieved to find somebody as optimistic as I wanted to be," said Fashanu. "But the operation was 10,000 dollars and I wouldn't even be staying in overnight." God stepped in, the doctor waived his fee, the hospital reduced its rates and Fash the Dash was back on his feet.

The up and running took a good bit longer but, just as the living started to get easy in LA, with Fashanu getting paid to play and coach the LA Heat, God invoked the aid of the tabloid press. "LA was becoming a really fun place," Fashanu said. "I was driving a five-litre Mustang Convertible with car phone, meeting all the right people and going to all the right places, when the News of the World came out to do a piece on me."

Machin, who had Fashanu in his charge as a 19-year-old at Norwich and who last season was looking for strikers to get a tight-fisted City out of the Second Division, saw the story and gave him a call. Fashanu's heralded comeback was short-lived. "I came back too soon. I knew almost straight away the knee wasn't ready."

He returned to the States to "spend two months training in the sun" before the start of the Canadian season. He finished as the Edmonton Brickmen's 19-goal top scorer and Canada's "Most Valuable Player of the Year". He rang Machin to see if he could come back.

City granted training facilities and encouragement but no more. Machin admits: "I really only agreed to let him come back again out of sympathy. I didn't really believe that it could work for him. But he deserves it. He has worked hard and he's shown the guts and determination in trying to get back that he shows on the field. He is hungry and that is what I want."

Fashanu says he has "crept back into the country this time without all the ra-ra. I'm fitter and stronger now than I've ever been. I'm not the typical 28-year-old soccer player who is coming to the end of his playing life. My body has had five years to recuperate.

"But the biggest thing to combat is not my fitness but my lack of confidence. I still have fears. I still have doubts. The first few days of practice I felt like a new boy going out as I did 12 years ago. Now it is a lot better. I feel relaxed and comfortable."

A hat-trick in his first reserve team game was a good omen. But if Fashanu was in better shape, so were City. They had won promotion, had paid out £1m for Clive Allen and had a bunch of young forwards wanting to prove their worth. Getting in was going to be tougher.

But Machin said yesterday he believed Fashanu is a better player now than when he was a household name at Carrow Road. He made his League debut there at 17 and four years later went to Forest, where he believes Brian Clough's approach was quite wrong for him.

"I didn't have to train enough. He had older players, who perhaps didn't need to do too much, but it wasn't good for me. It was a silly move." He was billed as Fash the Flop, then missed out on a move to Manchester City under John Bond, before being "railroaded" into going to Notts County, where the injury interrupted his career. He played half a season for Brighton, who finally made him a free agent, and he has cost Machin nothing except a few hot showers and a phone call to the States.

But Fashanu's next concern is whether the reality will live up to the dream. "When I get back into the First Division, I don't know what my reactions will be. I don't know whether it's the fact that I'm playing or the road getting there that is important. I might probably retire next day."

Justin Fashanu began at Norwich in style but injury hit his career. In 1990 he came out as gay. In 1998 he took his life

05|05|1990

Goodbye to the great leveller

David Foot laments the end of an era as developers prepare to flatten Yeovil's pitch of historic upsets

So it's farewell to the climbing boots, the pitons and the skis, which mythmakers would have us believe are stored with the corner flags. Tears will cascade down Somerset's beloved mountainside. After today's match against Telford at Huish the slope is being dug up.

Alec Stock and many of his legendary side that beat Sunderland in 1949 will be there to see the last kick and eavesdrop on the last engaging exaggeration, in West Country burr, about non-League soccer's most famous field, where the incline, wing to wing, is said to be anything from three to 15 feet. Six is a fair compromise.

Here Yeovil and Petters played, and then Yeovil Town. Here glamorous footballers such as Len Shackleton stumbled and familiar cigarette-card faces turned ashen white as they stepped out of the team's coach for their first sight. Mostly they imagined it was all worse than it was, though a succession of outside-lefts from Louis Page through to Johnny Hartburn at times needed to be Olympian sprinters to keep the ball in play.

Stock magnified the menace of the slope to grateful reporters, as Bury and then Sunderland came and went in that romantic post-war winter. In retrospect he acknowledges the valid advantages of the slope: "We used to keep thumping the ball up to the winger on the top side and he would just blow his centres over."

A few of his successors in charge were rather embarrassed about all the talk of the pitch's eccentricities. Perhaps they were just jealous of Stocky, an unemployed miner's son from Somerset. His heart belonged to Huish like no other manager.

Now the ground is being sold. Yeovil are moving out to a £3.2million site where once the troops were stationed at Houndstowne camp. It is six times as large, complete with executive boxes, a gymnasium, administration block and sports shop. There will be seating for half the 9,000 capacity.

It is all commendably forward-thinking on the part of the village-boy chairman, Gerry Lock, from T S Eliot's East Coker, but, according to reactionaries, it is also a bit grand for the GM Vauxhall Conference.

Forty-one years ago I stood, a junior reporter, with Stock in his pokey office, where he paid the players, helped the bald trainer Stan Abbott make the tea in a large brown enamel pot and wondered whether he would ever have enough time left over to play on the Saturday. Now we were looking at the ground again, up the hill, swapping small-town gossip.

"Nick Collins, who kept the pub down the road, was the best we had. He's sadly very ill now. I visit him when I can ... Arthur Hickman, our big full-back ... ah, yes, his wife was Huish's most vociferous fan. After one game she told me she'd had a wonderful time. Someone in front of her had been shouting at Her Arthur and so she had her own back, burning holes in his overcoat with her cigarette end."

Stock is as companionable as ever. He has a story for every club he managed, every player he signed. "I liked Roma, you know, because they had the same colours as my home village, Peasedown ... Rodney Marsh? No real trouble you simply had to get inside his skin ... Stan Bowles? The only problem was his gambling, for heaven's sake." And then inevitably back to intimate Yeovil, where Alec and his teacher wife grew begonias and Dicky Dyke, the boy from the Bible class, took it so matter of fact when asked to play in the next round against Manchester United.

I walked from top to bottom of Huish the other day, stopping to pick the dandelions and blow the seeds away just as I had in the Thirties. Some of the advertisements were also the same as when I stood to watch Dave Halliday and Tommy Lynch.

My daughter has bought me a chunk of Huish turf for a birthday present. Alec approves especially if, in my own back garden, I get the angle right.

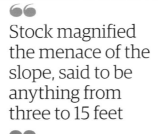

Stock magnified the menace of the slope, said to be anything from three to 15 feet

28|09|1991
Bidding sad farewell to all our Saturdays

David Lacey

Today's League programme should be cherished, for there will not be many more Saturday afternoons like it. Next weekend The Big Match returns in its Sunday slot and next season a Sunday television package of Premier League games has to be a possibility. 'The' Football League will become merely 'a' football league. Saturdays like this will just be another part of all our yesterdays.

So make the most of today, when all the First Division games will kick off at three o'clock as if TV and Elton Welsby had never been invented. White Hart Lane will be agog to see if Tottenham's latest attacking combination of Gary Lineker and Gordon Durie, which has so far produced 14 goals, can spoil the record of a Manchester United defence which in the First Division has conceded only two.

Entertaining matches are in prospect at Liverpool, Norwich, Nottingham Forest and Southampton, the Second Division has a gem of its own in the meeting of Middlesbrough and Sunderland, the Third is already warming to the prospect of West Brom and Birmingham City slugging it out at the top and the sight of Barnet in hot pursuit of Blackpool for promotion from the Fourth is intriguing if a trifle bizarre.

This does not look like a League which has remained in neutral for a hundred years – David Dein's words after Monday's extraordinary general meeting of clubs had voted to remove the last obstacle to the setting-up of a Premier League next season. The Arsenal vice-chairman also declared it "a historic day for football". But the sinking of the Titanic was a historic day for shipping.

Throw this afternoon's programme forward 12 months and you can see some of the problems that the rejected rump of the League will have in selling itself nationally. Once the League had lost its last battle Trevor Phillips, the marketing director, talked bravely about "repackaging the product and finding a different market in which to sell it".

This was how cinemas became bingo halls but there are only so many ways a football match can be sold and no one has managed to come up with a better sales pitch than a winning team. In losing the argument and having to acknowledge the imminence of the Premier League, the Football League has surely lost its biggest selling point, which was its own uniqueness.

Phillips is confident that the League's traditions and community links can form a solid commercial basis once the First Division has broken away. Today's confrontation at Ayresome Park is the sort of fixture the League will hope to sell to local sponsors and regional TV.

Nevertheless it still looks as if the Football League is going to be the small-beer league. No doubt a few prospective Premier Leaguers, freed from the shackles of the management committee, can already taste the champagne of big deals to come but the likelihood of the football improving in proportion to any increase in income must be open to doubt.

There has to be a danger that the Premier League, as well as making the richest clubs even richer, will create a bigger underclass than ever in the top division and that this will be reflected in the standard of the football. Goals are always welcome but there was a depressing predictability about the five Luton let in at Old Trafford.

Clubs such as Luton, faced with the huge costs of implementing the Taylor Report on all-seat stadiums, will find it difficult to keep up appearances in the Premier League, where transfer fees and players' salaries will soar anew. At least what is left of the old Football League will be able to cut its cloth with a clear conscience.

The greater the rewards for membership of the Premier League the higher will be the price of relegation from it. Fear of failure will become paranoic and the spectacle must suffer. Not that the television audience, engrossed in the doings of an assortment of Mighty Reds, will notice.

So it is hard to look forward to a devil-take-the-hindmost Premier League with unbridled optimism. Look what they've done to our game, Ma, look what they've done to our game.

Chapter eight
Death on the terraces

19|05|1967
Once upon a time ...

... a small boy said to his father: "I would like to go and watch a football match this afternoon." His father replied: "There is a First Division match at the Park. We will go together."

They joined the crowd and went through the turnstiles, where they were greeted courteously by the man who took their money. They stood on the terraces behind one of the goals and the little boy was amused by the comments of the spectators and impressed with their behaviour.

When the teams came on to the field they were applauded generously and impartially and, whenever one of the visiting players brought off a smart tackle or put in a good shot, the home supporters cheered him as if he had been one of their own.

There were no fouls, no obscene language and, when the game was over, the little boy said to his father: "I enjoyed every minute of it. Both sides played well and I thought that the referee was very fair, didn't you?"

"Yes, indeed," replied his father. "It was a grand afternoon's entertainment. A real football match, wasn't it?"

Once upon a time ...

04|01|1971
Tragedy at Ibrox Park

Leading article

The 66 people who died on the stairs at Ibrox Park were the victims of the environment in which they were and of the excitements of the match. They did not die because of hooliganism or as accidental victims of the grim, historic feud between Rangers and Celtic. They died because some of them were going home while others were coming back in the hope of seeing a winning goal. And stairway 13 could not digest them all. For Glasgow it has been a compounded tragedy. Celtic and Rangers had done their utmost to keep their supporters calm and they were successful. But, for all that, the crowd killed part of itself – blindly and unintentionally.

One reason, of course, was that it was a very large crowd indeed. Rangers have restricted admissions to Ibrox Park from 120,000 to 80,000 in the interests of safety. But even 80,000 people means a crowd nearly half as big as the British army. The problem is to prevent a very large number of excited people in a combined space from hurting themselves. It is an old problem, tragically and suddenly revived but familiar. In 1946 at Bolton some thousands who had not been able to get into the Wanderers' ground broke down a fence. The newcomers caused people on the terraces to lose their footing and 33 were suffocated or crushed to death against crush-barriers.

The inquiry into that disaster recommended the statutory licensing of football grounds. Clubs were to be made to satisfy local authorities that a crowd would not be able to do itself an injury. In fact the Government and clubs agreed in 1948 to make crowd safety a voluntary matter. The inquiry recommended various safety measures with which the clubs have since complied. It would be wrong to suggest that Rangers—or any other club—has not done what the report of the Bolton inquiry suggested. In the words of the more recent Lang Report "... these arrangements have generally been found to work satisfactorily."

Until Saturday, that is. The Ibrox tragedy proves that existing regulations and procedures are not safe enough. There have been two previous fatal accidents at matches on stairway 13 at Ibrox. Though they were far smaller than Saturday's disaster, and though Rangers can claim to have met all the existing requirements, the suspicion remains that watching football is still hazardous, and not just because of hooligans or passions.

The fact is that the law does not tell football clubs to do much to protect their paying guests. If theatres and cinemas invite the public to be entertained, they must first comply with an arduous set of rules and regulations which protect the audience against possible harm. But the audiences at cinemas and theatres are minute compared with those at big football matches. No cinema could accommodate half the Army. Nor is there much incentive to football fans to stay in their places. In Britain, which pioneered football, most spectators stand. Unless the press of people in the place where they begin is heavy, they can move around the stadium, coming and going as they please. This is what they were doing at Ibrox Park on Saturday.

In countries newer to football and with newer football grounds more spectators can sit. This is comfortable, though more expensive; but it also discourages movement until the match is over, and slows it down then. A crowd's movement is more easily controlled if the stadium authorities know when the surge is coming, as the Ibrox authorities did not on Saturday. British football clubs will not welcome suggestions that they should spend more on their grounds—as they would have to if they installed more seats—but the name of their game will suffer if it is seen to be unsafe to watch. One way or another, money will have to be found to protect the customers of football. The football pools do not at present contribute to football itself in the same way that bookmakers contribute to racing. But if money is needed, perhaps the pools should. A mass audience at a football match deserves as much and as rigorous protection as a small one in a theatre.

11|05|2005
Out of the inferno

Martin Fletcher went to watch Bradford City 20 years ago and was lucky to return alive. Four years later he was at Hillsborough. On the anniversary of the Valley Parade fire, he recalls the horror of that day and the lessons that were ignored

On my 20th annual pilgrimage to Bradford today it is impossible to recall the excitement with which I woke as a 12-year-old in 1985 to head north from Nottingham with my father, John, 34, and brother Andrew, 11, to watch Bradford City's unlikely coronation as Third Division champions, after 48 years in the Football League's lower reaches. We went with my uncle, Peter, 32, and grandfather, Eddie, 63. I would be the only one to return home.

As the crowd gathered at Valley Parade that May 11, cloud could not dampen a sunny atmosphere. The players received their trophy before the match and we cheered them on a lap of honour. They returned the favour at kick-off, each player holding up a board with the message "THANK YOU FANS". On this

The fire erupts in a wall of black smoke. Within a minute the entire stand was ablaze. Fifty-six people died

day of great expectation supporters spoke of the challenges promotion would bring. It would be a future 56 would not see.

It was 40 minutes into the game that smoke first rose from one end of the all-wooden main stand where my family and I were sitting. Uncertain if it was a fire but convinced the fire brigade would control it if it were, junior police officers ordered the section cleared into the stand's rear corridor, its only empty area . The 80 spectators in our section began to empty back as quickly as a stairwell one man wide would allow.

Just as we were about to move I looked down and saw large tips of flame dance beneath a crack in the stand. As a child might, I swore and Dad clipped my ear. I felt indignant and, when my uncle suggested the kids went ahead together, I agreed immediately it was a good idea.

I expected to return to my seat a few minutes later. Nobody anticipated having to escape a fire that was still to emerge from beneath the stand. Fans, expecting to be told to come back, massed in the area nearest their seats. When I arrived in the corridor to find a wall of people I was not concerned. I assumed it would clear. Only it did not.

At this point the teams were still playing and only the attentions of a linesman brought the game to a halt. By now flames had cut off the stairwell I had walked up, making it impassable. The nearest accessible stairwells, 9 and 13 metres away, were full of people. More spectators entered the corridor trying to make their way out and we became trapped at the end nearer the fire. Any attempts to have cleared the gridlock would have resulted in a deadly stampede.

Unable to move and unaware of what was happening, I eventually cried for dad. The corridor was so calm he not only heard me but I could turn to speak with him and he calmed my fears. Embarrassed by my behaviour, I apologised to the man beside me. He smiled back, pensively. At ease, I stood, having turned my back on my family, with no idea I had seen them alive for the last time.

Suddenly the gridlock cleared. But at the same time both

stairwells became cut off by fire and we headed towards the exit. Brisk walking turned to running as people tried to reach the nearest exit still some 25 metres away. I was at the front of the group heading for the turnstiles. Now, 75 seconds after the evacuation began, the fire erupted. In an instant clear air was replaced by an impenetrable wall of black smoke, laced with carbon monoxide. It brought with it instant death, killing 19 by the turnstiles before they reached an exit, 18 by the nearest exit and six more beyond it.

An eerie silence accompanied the blinding smoke, I could only sniff at my surroundings. My consciousness was painlessly crushed and I accepted death. It is almost impossible to explain what happened next but there was a flash of light, a sudden illuminated outline of an individual appeared before me. Just as quickly, it disappeared, but I chose to carry on, feeling my way along the wall of the block. I made my way alone and, with the exception of a brief solitary cry, the silence was unbroken. There were no flames in the corridor but when I reached the stairwell I was met by an advancing wall of fire that had enveloped the seating. I ran straight through the burning stand and reached the perimeter wall. I was dragged over it by fellow fans. Sprawled on the pitch, I got up and dashed for the safety of the terrace opposite. Within a minute the entire stand was ablaze.

In escaping one hell I entered another. Initially I was told that everyone had escaped the fire. Not until my family were identified two days later did anyone dare correct this impression. They had all perished in the corridor.

Later, at Warwick University, I developed skills that led me to study the legislation, transcripts and statements at the heart of the Bradford fire. It was the deaths of 66 supporters at Ibrox in 1971 that led to the first piece of legislation that offered protection to sports fans, the 1975 Safety of Sports Grounds Act. Government staggered the legislation's introduction: international and First Division grounds were designated first, with lower division grounds to follow later. Only they did not. After lobbying, the Thatcher government indefinitely postponed further designation because lower division grounds were not attended in sufficient numbers, even though any proposal that public safety legislation be abandoned at other public buildings that held thousands less would have brought uproar.

The unimplemented regulations anticipated stand fires. They stated that wooden stands should be capable of evacuation in 2½ minutes, no combustible material be left beneath them, any voids that caused such an accumulation be sealed and no one should be more than 30 metres from the nearest manned exit. None of these conditions was met at Bradford.

On June 5 1985, three days after we held a memorial service service for Dad and Andrew, the public inquiry opened into the disaster. It was so soon after the tragedy that most of the victims' relatives felt unable to attend. The inquiry's conclusions, based on five days' hearings, provided the superficial flawed answers that all craved. West Yorkshire's chief fire officer, Graham Karran, said it was "inexplicable" that his fire prevention team had never inspected the stand. Only they had inspected the clubhouse beside the stand in licensing it, while the brigade regularly visited the ground to water the pitch, undertake exercises and were even due to play a club's former XI there.

The fire authority knew of the stand's dangers. It held meetings about the ground with the Health and Safety Executive, which twice rated "fire" as a "substantial" risk . Fire prevention officer, Neville Byrom, received a detailed letter from a council engineer that warned, "The timber construction is a fire hazard". Yet the fire authority did nothing.

As it wrote to the club, the Executive had "emergency powers in relation to any sports ground", under the Safety at Sports Grounds and Fire Precautions Act. Claims that conditions were not serious enough to warrant their exercise were rejected at civil trial. Had the fire authority discharged its statutory duty the disaster would never have happened. Instead, in a gross dereliction of duty, it turned a blind eye to its now realised potential as a death trap.

What Bradford did prove was that the pitch provided the only emergency escape route. Had the 2,000 terrace spaces that flanked the stand's 2,000 seats been fenced, a death toll of 9/11 proportion would have resulted. As it was, only a gap in the Kop terrace fence adjacent to the stand allowed hundreds to escape. Both the FA chairman and Football League secretary immediately suggested a review of fencing policy. The Home Secretary, Leon Britton, promised parliament: "There is no question of simply putting up a fence which would create a trap".

Only on April 15 1989 as a Nottingham Forest fan I was at Hillsborough. From the Kop terrace, opposite the Leppings Lane end, I watched 96 die within such a trap, because the local authority had not held inspections, allowing unauthorised crush barrier modifications to go overlooked. I heard the sirens again and I clutched the fence beside me as fans tended and carried the dead. On returning home I became so distraught that nothing had clearly been learned that I hyper-ventilated. That weekend, the press began to doorstep my house again.

Unlike in Belgium, where the government fell after the Heysel stadium disaster, there would be no ministerial fall-out after England's twin disasters. Although both had clear grounds for gross negligence the authorities never considered manslaughter charges. If such failures carry no penalties, how can we expect their lessons to be learned?

I fear complacency has returned. This year I visited London Wasps rugby club where a locked gate meant my nearest available exit was a congested 50 metres away. I worry how effective current evacuation policies are in an age of global terrorism, how limited access points around new stadiums would cope if the unforeseeable happened and how clubs will get by when today's stadiums eventually crumble. Would our public authorities again gamble on forcing yet more innocents on the pilgrimage I make today?

19|03|2005

The Heysel tragedy
Photograph by Eamonn McCabe

I have photographed many similar skirmishes at big European finals, but this time would be very different. I know many will say, "Why didn't you stop shooting pictures and help?" – but I took two frames and got out of the way of the stewards and medical people. In truth, I was on some sort of autopilot.

My only explanation is that this picture, although conveying the horror on the faces of the Juventus fans, also holds out the hope that most people managed to get over the wall on to the pitch. I would like to think so. At the time I took the picture no one had died. By the end of the night 38 people had, and another later. I went that night as a sports photographer and ended up a news photographer.

This article and photograph appeared in a special Guardian Sport supplement to mark Liverpool's Champions League tie with Juventus, 20 years on from the European Cup final in Brussels

30|05|1985
Liverpool fade into the background

European Cup final
Liverpool 0 Juventus 1
David Lacey, Brussels

Liverpool lost the European Cup to Juventus last night but football has lost far, far more. In short, it died along with the 47 people trampled to death when a group of mainly Italian supporters stampeded to get away from rioting Liverpool fans and were crushed when first barriers, and then a wall, collapsed.

After the scenes of death, injury and destruction in the Heysel Stadium in Brussels, the result seems irrelevant, the details meaningless. How can a match be anything else when even as the players are winning their tackles, making their passes and producing their shots, the death toll continues to mount?

After the wretched affair had ended with the Juventus team doing a hurried half-lap of honour with the trophy, news came through that all 11 members of the Anderlecht youth team who had taken part in the warm-up game had perished.

Last night the horrors of crowd violence which have spread their tentacles from Britain to Europe for more than a decade overtook football on one of its most important occasions and the consequences for the game in general and English soccer in particular can only be severe.

Already we have had a season in which the Football Association has ordered an FA Cup tie to be played behind closed doors, and there has been violence at Chelsea in a Milk Cup semi-final and at Luton in an FA Cup quarter-final. The Bradford fire, in which 53 died, was in a category apart, but still added to the trail of mounting misery. We have seen football hooliganism in China of all places and this week 10 people died in Mexico City as a crowd tried to force its way into the national Cup Final.

It has all ended in a cry of anguish in Brussels. Liverpool, with one of the proudest records in Continental competition, now bear the scar of the worst rioting and the most tragic consequences ever seen in a European tournament. There is bound to be talk of banning all English clubs from European competitions until our game puts itself in order.

Yet only 24 hours earlier members of the Football Association voted out a proposal to harden up the rules on club responsibility which would have fallen into line with Government thinking. After the Bradford fire the cry went up: "Who pays?" In Brussels last night there was only one answer and they were lined up in a makeshift mortuary outside the Heysel Stadium.

The facts of the match can only sound hollow but have to be told. After Liverpool had dominated the opening half-hour and forced several urgent saves from Tacconi, they lost the game to a Michel Platini penalty 10 minutes into the second half, awarded after Boniek had been brought down by Gillespie (one of the Liverpool substitutes) nearly a yard outside the area. In the normal course of events this would have been the main talking point. As it was, one was glad something had happened to ensure the game did not last any longer than was necessary.

Inevitably the question of whether the match should have gone ahead remained the most urgent point of issue. In an ideal world it would have been cancelled immediately after the deaths on the terraces occurred. However, the decision to continue was probably the right one, even if it was made for the wrong reasons: the game had to be played to avoid the risk of further rioting, and in order to disperse the crowd of more than 50,000 as peacefully as possible.

What a way for Joe Fagan to end his short time as Liverpool manager. Poor Fagan – in all his years at Anfield he could hardly have envisaged beginning a European Cup final by walking out on to the arena wearing a No.13 Liverpool shirt to calm the fans. Both teams, to their credit, did their best to restore what dignity they could. In any other context one could have described it as one of the better European finals of recent years.

Lawrenson lasted only two minutes before aggravating the shoulder injury which had always threatened to put him out of the match, and Gillespie rejoined Hansen at centre-back. For a time this did not concern Liverpool overmuch as they moved forward in their patient, positive way, and prevented Platini running the match between the two penalty areas. Towards half-time, however, Briaschi switched from the right wing to the left in an effort to expose Neal and started to become a threat; and gradually Platini's influence grew.

Wark was cautioned for fouling Boniek when the Pole attempted to burst through the middle and in the 55th minute, when Platini at last managed to set Boniek at Liverpool's square defence, the moment proved decisive. Gillespie reached Boniek as he approached the penalty area and brought him down well outside it. But the Swiss referee, Andre Daina, was always going to give the penalty, and Platini sent the Juventus reporters into unrealistic ecstasies when he beat Grobbelaar.

> 66
> ### Joe Fagan had to walk out before the start wearing a Liverpool No13 shirt to calm fans
> 99

17|04|1989

Hillsborough: how could this happen again?

After football's past traumas, the worst tragedy in a British stadium begs one simple, awful question. By David Lacey

First the pain, then the anger, then the questions and as English football again counts its dead, this time after the worst tragedy in a British stadium, the biggest question of all is stark in its simplicity.

How was it possible, after all the previous disasters, inquiries, working parties, reports, recommendations and Acts of Parliament, for almost a hundred people to be crushed to death in a football ground which had a good safety record and was not full to capacity, while only a few yards away other spectators were moving around with room to spare?

Hillsborough was no Heysel because there was no riot, it was not a Bradford because there was no fire, it was not an Ibrox because there was no crush of fans going in opposite directions, and it was not a Bolton because the ground as a whole was not overwhelmed by weight of numbers.

Yet certain aspects of each tragedy are highly relevant to what happened at the start of Saturday's doomed FA Cup semi-final.

In Brussels four years ago an already terrible situation was exacerbated by the lack of liaison between groups of police inside and outside the stadium. For a few tragic minutes there appears to have been a similar breakdown of communications at Hillsborough.

Much is being made of the decision, taken by a police officer shortly before Saturday's kick-off, to open a gate at the Leppings Lane end of the ground in order to ease the crush of Liverpool fans, some with tickets, some without, trying to get in. Had he known of the crush already built up in the passageway leading from turnstile B to the small rectangle of terracing immediately behind the Liverpool goal the gates would surely have remained shut.

Yet high above the Leppings Lane end a closed-circuit television camera must have given the police control room inside the ground a full picture of crowd movements on the forecourt, and the naked eye could see what was developing on the terraces. Why did the police fail to act on the evidence of their eyes and at least get the kick-off delayed?

Any policeman with regular experience of controlling football crowds will tell you that, when a big match is played and people are coming through the turnstiles at the last minute, the most critical point occurs as the game kicks off and those outside, hearing the roar inside, will redouble their efforts to gain entrance. It was this that produced the fatal surge at Hillsborough. If the game had been put back half an hour nobody need have died.

One of the lessons of Bradford was that in times of emergency the pitch represents the spectators' best means of escape. At Hillsborough people were fenced in on three sides with only tiny gates giving them access to the pitch. It had always been feared that pens designed to segregate fans and prevent pitch invasions might one day become death traps. On Saturday anti-hooliganism measures cost lives.

The Ibrox disaster of 1971 led directly to the 1975 Safety of Sports Grounds Act which laid particular emphasis on spectators having safe access to and egress from stadiums as well as giving strict guidelines on how many people could safely be accommodated in a given area.

Hillsborough's flow of admissions is controlled by computers which told Mr Graham Mackrell, the Sheffield Wednesday secretary, that even as the disaster happened the crowd occupying the terraces at the Leppings Gate was still below capacity. So why were so many people crammed into one small space when there was room elsewhere?

Afterwards an inspection of that end of the ground in the company of Mr Richard Faulkner, deputy chairman of the Football Trust, suggested that, had the police been able to avoid the crush outside the perimeter gate, the late arrivals could easily have been accommodated on the terracing on either side of the disaster area.

Mr John Williams, a Football Trust research lecturer at the Leicester University Department of Sociology who has co-authored several books on the behaviour of soccer fans, could not understand why there had been so few police controlling the inflow at the Liverpool end. "Why weren't barriers set up at the end of the street so that the police could make a check on who had tickets?" Mr Williams asked. "There was a crush at the turnstiles at 2.30 and I could see ticketless fans sitting on the walls looking for a way in. It was already becoming a problem then."

Mr Williams had a stand seat which gave him a full view of the disaster. "We could see people being crushed against the barriers at the front of the terracing but others were still pressing in at the back. Then both police and spectators started to rip out the fencing in order to get supporters out of that section."

Logic suggests that Liverpool should not have been allocated that end of Hillsborough at all but should have been allowed to fill the huge expanse of terracing at the Penistone Road end. Yet for the second year running Nottingham Forest, with an average home attendance of just over 21,000, were allocated 28,000 tickets and spread themselves across the Spion Kop while Liverpool, whose average gate is nearer 40,000, were given 24,000 and a comparatively cramped enclosure.

Officially the Football Association decides the ticket allocation for semi-finals but it takes advice from the home club, Sheffield Wednesday in this case, who in turn act on the requirements of the police. At Hillsborough the prime concern of South Yorkshire Police appears to have been traffic flows. When it came to controlling a flow of people they were found wanting.

Nottingham Forest were allotted the Penistone Road end and Liverpool the Leppings Lane end on geographical grounds. The fact that this meant Anfield receiving 4,000 fewer tickets was merely incidental. Yet Mr Rogan Taylor, Liverpudlian head of the Football Supporters' Association, argued that the organisers should have taken differing strengths of support into account.

"Anyone who knows Liverpool fans should have realised that in this situation thousands would turn up without tickets. If you don't take support into account you are lighting the blue touch paper."

Apart from the odd idiot, usually young and at least alive, the abiding memory of Saturday's experience will be the immense dignity with which all involved conducted themselves. Not least were the Liverpool fans who used advertising boards as makeshift stretchers and ferried the injured and the dying to the ambulances with the speed and efficiency of highly trained paramedics.

Amid the chaos there were bound to be absurdities, asking spectators to clear the pitch, for example, when it was obvious that there was nowhere for them to go. The lack of information over the public-address system was deplorable. It was 50 minutes before Kenny Dalglish's voice was heard: "Obviously everyone knows that there have been one or two problems. Please co-operate ..."

It took a long time for the extent of the tragedy to reach the rest of the crowd. There was a roar of anger when a Liverpool supporter was spotted apparently demolishing the goal at the Leppings Lane end. In fact he had been hoisted on a policeman's shoulders to remove the net which was impeding the rescue operation.

Just after five o'clock, when in normal circumstances the winners would have been celebrating their success in reaching Wembley or the game would have been well into extra-time, a young couple wandered dazed across the deserted pitch – the woman in tears, the man comforting her in a numbed sort of way. The poignancy of that moment only hardened the opinion that the worst tragedy in British sport had also been the most avoidable.

There is the vaguest recollection of the front page of the old *Sunday Dispatch* on March 10 1946, covered with pictures of spectators crushed at Bolton after fans had broken through closed gates to see an FA Cup quarter-final against Stoke. Forty-three years ago the idea of 33 people being killed just because they went to a game of football left a hollow feeling inside and on Saturday, driving home, the feeling was there again.

Nobody should have to die in order to see Peter Beardsley hit the bar. English football grounds are many times safer than they were in the rickety days immediately after the Second World War, but the capacity for human error and faulty judgments in a crisis is undiminished. Hillsborough has proved that.

17|04|1989
Football's Kennedy clan learns how to walk on with hope in its heart

Matthew Engel

Anfield Road is much less grand than you might think, hardly more than a side street edged by Victorian villas. But opposite are the Bill Shankly Memorial Gates, above them the words 'You'll Never Walk Alone,' and next are the walls topped with the spikes, razor wire and broken glass that signify a modern football ground.

People began arriving there yesterday soon after dawn and by mid-morning there was an almost constant stream of mourners. They queued at the florist's stall outside the cemetery on the other side of Stanley Park, then cut through to place their flowers by the gates, and sometimes their scarves and bobble hats too.

At lunchtime the Liverpool directors decided to let the public inside the ground. The flowers were placed in the goal net at the Kop end, on the barriers behind and, as more people arrived with their tributes, along the Kop itself. Perhaps 1,000 people stood by the goal close by the 'Do not go on the pitch' sign. There was no sound except muffled sobbing.

Some moved on quickly, others stayed, staring numbly. A tough-looking man in a leather jacket stood crying, probably for the first time in years. An old man in a shabby coat waited close by, for at least two hours, moving only to help a couple of young lads tie their hats to the railings and then to take a long drink of whisky.

Four little girls in Sunday dresses came along with single tulips. But the more elaborate bunches had messages: "Everton FC Supporters. Our condolences. We pray for the lads who loved Liverpool FC"; "Look after them, Shanks, from all the lads at Kirkby"; and again and again and again: "You'll never walk alone."

No other football club has such a beautiful phrase so closely associated with it. And at no other club would the aftermath of a chance disaster to spectators focus so strongly on the club and not the dead and bereaved themselves. Liverpool have become the Kennedy family of sport, for whom great triumphs and great emotion have been sundered by great tragedies. But in Anfield, the district rather than the football ground, life was going on. Along with the mourners in Anfield Road there were men walking dogs and children on bicycles, as on any sunny Sunday.

Soon it was possible to hear the whistling and shouting of football matches coming from Stanley Park, 300 yards away, from where it is possible to see both the Liverpool and Everton grounds. The committee of the Anfield Junior Soccer League had decided there should be a minute's silence before the games but otherwise the semi-finals of the under 11s cup should go ahead.

"My lad was at Hillsborough," Ronnie Fawcett, one of the team managers, said. "It was three hours before I found out he's only hurt his leg. Someone was screaming at him for help but he was just carried forward on the surge and couldn't do anything. We both feel drained. But you've got to go on, otherwise when do you start? We shall all feel the same next Sunday."

So far as anyone knew, none of the under-11s due to play had been to Sheffield and not come back. But no one was certain. The city was subsisting on rumour and everyone knew someone who knew someone of whom they had heard nothing.

Just down the road at St Columba's, the local Roman Catholic church, a young preacher told his congregation that the suffering would not last for ever. "Because Jesus rose from the dead, we know death is not the end."

Only two months ago the Anglican Bishop of Liverpool evoked that image on another football matter: the identity-card debate in the House of Lords. "Many people have little sense of belonging or counting or identity," he said. "I don't want to exaggerate but following a football team gives you many of these experiences, something to be proud of, success that is yours to share in. Indeed, sometimes laps of honour, bringing the Cup home, have the feel of the liturgy of the Resurrection."

But the liturgy of football is usually altogether different. On the bridges along the M62 there are slogans placed by Liverpool's supporters to taunt Manchester United's fans: "Munich '58." Football slogans and songs have become the basest currency but perhaps Liverpool's now has it right: "Walk on, walk on, with hope in your heart." When the grieving ends, that is all anyone can do.

Fights, flares and little forgiveness

Dominic Fifield, Turin

A banner was unfurled on the curva sud an hour before kick-off here reminding, poignantly: "Easy to speak ... difficult to pardon." Painful memories of the Heysel Stadium disaster hung heavy in this arena last night, with the local mood summed up neatly in those simple white letters on a red background. For many in Turin it has not been possible to forget.

This was the first competitive meeting between these sides in this city since 39 Juventus supporters lost their lives when a wall collapsed after a charge by Liverpool fans before the 1985 European Cup final. Attempts to cultivate "*amicizia*" (friendship) in the first leg at Anfield last week had been greeted with derision by some Juve fans, their ultras turning their backs on the ceremony aimed at reconciliation. For a while here last night 20 years of simmering enmity threatened to boil over into violence.

There were ugly scenes both inside and outside the ground, with flares fired into the celebrating visiting supporters at the end as the reality of Liverpool's unlikely progress sank in. That maintained the snarling mood of the night and visiting fans were kept in the ground long after the final whistle.

Before kick-off a group of about 50 Juventus fans wielding batons clashed with riot police outside the stadium. The carabinieri, pelted with bottles and flares, took over 30 minutes to disperse the troublemakers – part of a larger group of about 150 locals – using tear gas. Two vehicles were left in flames. The offenders, wearing scarves over their faces to avoid identification, broke up into smaller groups as two police helicopters surveyed the scene.

Yet, though disturbances had been grimly anticipated outside the ground, events inside were shameful. A pitiful number of police and stewards had been stationed in the curva nord and they were utterly incapable of preventing the torrent of missiles flung initially from home fans over no-man's land into the lower section of the Liverpool support. The visitors responded, bottles arrowing back over the divide into the taunting Italians, with an extra line of riot police appearing only once kick-off approached. More stewards were belatedly deployed once the game was under way. Liverpool fans' mood was not improved by a banner referring to the Hillsborough disaster: "15.4.89. Sheffield. God Exists."

By then a message had twice been issued over the public address system, in Italian and English, warning that anyone caught throwing objects faced between six months and three years in prison. By the time that message was reissued at half-time the barrage had resumed, with a flare spouting fumes from the open terracing in front of the Juve fans.

Perhaps the scenes were to be expected. This tie was a nightmarish exercise in logistics for the authorities. Police had tightened security and drafted in undercover agents to help keep the peace, with the majority of English fans bussed to the stadium last night from accommodation well outside Turin.

Many were taken straight from the airport to restaurants and bars in neighbouring towns in order to separate the two sets of fans. The 72-hour alcohol ban apparently imposed in Turin centre — it applied only to bars and not hotels or supermarkets — dissuaded others from venturing into areas which might otherwise have proved perilous.

Even so, one fan had been attacked in a city pub by five Juventus supporters wielding bottles and baseball bats. "There was an argument and a Liverpool fan was hit on the head with a bat by one of the Juve fans," confirmed Cecilia Tartoni, a spokeswoman for Turin police. "The Liverpool fan received medical attention in the pub." He was later deemed fit enough to attend the game.

"Some 20 Juventus fans were stopped by the police," added Tartoni. "We searched vehicles and their homes and found baseball bats and other weapons. Eight have been detained for possession of arms."

That set a worrying tone which lingered into the match, for all that the majority of fans treated the memories of Heysel with much more dignity. Banners at the opposite end, where hoardings bearing the date 1985 are permanent, read: "The 39 angels look down with pride on us tonight" and "What is deep in the heart never dies".

Italian football could have done without last night's darker incidents. After Tuesday's disgraceful scenes in Milan, when Internazionale fans pelted the Milan goalkeeper Dida with flares, prompting the abandonment of their Champions League quarter-final, the prime minister Silvio Berlusconi had called for "drastic measures" to combat the upsurge of violence.

Berlusconi met the interior minister Giuseppe Pisanu to discuss the problem and later warned: "There is a clear risk of even more serious incidents in future, a risk which must be avoided by all possible means." Here last night, with emotions running high, risk became reality yet again.

Chapter nine
Maradona and the modern magicians

23|06|1986

The Hand of God strikes

World Cup quarter-final
Argentina 2 England 1
David Lacey, Mexico City

....

The sorcery, not to mention the sauce, of Diego Maradona ended England's World Cup hopes in the Azteca Stadium yesterday. Two goals from the magician early in the second half broke the resistance of Bobby Robson's defenders, and set Argentina on course for their second semi-final in three tournaments.

But Maradona could hardly claim he had nothing up his sleeve. Television evidence clearly shows that Argentina's first goal went in off Maradona's wrist after he had gone up for a high ball with Shilton. At the outset we all knew that each side possessed a world-class player, only one of whom could use his hands. In this context the name of Maradona did not spring immediately to mind.

Yet the England manager had no doubt what happened. "I saw the ball in the air and Maradona going for it," said Robson. "Shilton went for it too but Maradona handled the ball into the net. You don't expect decisions like that at World Cup level."

Since this was the consensus of Argentinian opinion after the West German referee, Rudolf Kreitlein, had sent off Antonio Rattin when they lost to England in the 1966 finals, some will argue that justice of a kind was done 20 years later. How extraordinary it is that England and Argentina cannot meet in a World Cup without some controversy ensuing.

A few minutes later Maradona scored one of the great World Cup goals when he left three defenders lying on the ground like broken dolls before slipping the ball past Shilton. "A brilliant goal," said Robson. "I didn't like it but I had to admire it."

A late header from Lineker, his sixth in this World Cup, briefly revived English hopes and he was only inches away from bringing the scores level. But in the end few could dispute that the winners had given a professional performance and on balance deserved their place in the last four.

After the early traumas of Monterrey England will not be too unhappy about going out of the tournament in this fashion — beaten controversially after defending solidly and attacking boldly whenever they could. They ended the match by reverting to Robson's original concept of two wingers after Waddle and Barnes had replaced Reid and Steven. For a moment or two

one felt that one of the remarkable recoveries was imminent. However, the Argentinians defended competently if not always with composure and nearly scored a third goal when a quick exchange of passes ended with Tapia hitting a post.

The renewal of the Falklands conflict on the terraces projected by some of the more fanciful headlines never materialised. There was a brief outbreak of fisticuffs at the start of the second half but generally English and Argentinian fans maintained a more or less peaceful coexistence.

Before the kick-off each England player received a pennant from a member of the Argentinian team. Unless they bore the words Malvinas Argentina it was a nice gesture.

Fenwick's first tackle on Maradona after 10 minutes was less diplomatic and after the Argentinian captain had gone flying the England defender was cautioned for the third time in the tournament. The booking seemed harsh at the time but was balanced when the Tunisian referee allowed Fenwick to stay on the field after later catching Maradona in the face with an elbow.

It was a long time before either attack achieved anything of similar impact. With the midfield crowded as the teams set out to close each other down the game was not unlike your average First Division fixture. In spite of Fenwick's early tackle England did not set out to mark Maradona individually. Instead they concentrated on interrupting his lines of communication with other Argentinians and in this they were successful until half-time, although there were signs in the last 10 minutes of Maradona taking control of the play between the penalty areas. Up to that point he had threatened England only with free-kicks near goal and nothing had caused Shilton serious problems.

However, all this had changed before the match was an hour old. In the 50th minute Maradona ploughed into the heart of the England defence before laying the ball out to his right. Valdano was unable to control properly, which gave Hodge the opportunity to flick the ball back over his head and back towards Shilton. Maradona immediately challenged the England goalkeeper and to the naked eye it seemed that he had achieved a legal touch in deflecting the ball into the net. Television, however, proved otherwise.

Bobby Robson had always said that Maradona was capable of winning a game on his own in five minutes. Maradona must have heard him for now he collected the ball on the right and

Diego Maradona's 'Hand of God' beats the honest arm of Peter Shilton to the ball and Argentina lead England 1-0

set off on a marvellous run. Stevens was beaten by a sway of the hips, Butcher with a shrug of the shoulders and Fenwick with contemptuous ease. Shilton was given no chance.

All that was left for England to do was to go on to the attack and this they did boldly and bravely. Pumpido had to move quickly to push a free-kick from Hoddle round a post and then Barnes, playing in the World Cup finals for the first time, worked his way to the left-hand byline before producing the centre from which Lineker headed in at the far post.

Six minutes later Lineker flung himself at a similar ball from Barnes but just failed to make contact. In that instant one could not help feeling that England were fated not to make further progress. Yesterday's match represented the watershed of their World Cup ambitions. Although they won the World Cup in 1966 they have yet to get past the quarter-finals in any of the other tournaments. Had Ali Ben Nasser been in the right place at the right time when the first goal went in yesterday, they might have reached the semi-finals – but on balance, probably not.

20|04|2004

Remember only the beauty

After years of drug abuse, the tortured genius Diego Maradona is in hospital fighting for his life. By Richard Williams

It is a crisp autumn evening in Buenos Aires but heavy sweat runs down the face of the corpulent middle-aged man in sunglasses and a black T-shirt who is struggling through a clamour of well-wishers and autograph hunters on his way into the football stadium. Behind the shades, beneath his unruly black curls, a pale, fleshy face is contorted into the familiar rictus of time-expired celebrity, that meaningless smile from which a form of existential panic has driven the last vestige of genuine pleasure.

For more than 10 years football fans have stared in horror at that face and then turned away in sadness as the apparently inexorable decline of the man sometimes called the greatest footballer of all time played itself out in the world's media, one hideous chapter after another. By comparison with Diego Armando Maradona, the descent of a George Best or a Paul Gascoigne seems almost decorous, just as his history of dalliances makes David Beckham's alleged extracurricular activities look like the adventures of a Boy Scout. You would need to turn to the darker side of show business – to the gruesome extended farewell of a Judy Garland, perhaps – to find a personal calamity made into such a public spectacle.

This time the pictures – taken on Sunday outside the Bombonera, or "chocolate box", the home of Boca Juniors, the club with which he made his name more than 20 years earlier – showed an almost unrecognisable figure. From the bloating of his face, the thickness of his neck and the extent of the multiple bellies wobbling beneath the black shirt, he looked to be carrying close to 20st on his 5ft 7in frame. And this was once the 10-year-old boy who entertained crowds with his joyful ball-juggling tricks at half-time during first division matches. Within a couple of hours the 43-year-old Maradona would be attached to a hospital's life-support system, his condition critical and his breathing sustained artificially as the news went around the world of the latest act in this long-running passion play.

Perhaps Maradona's condition really turned critical on the day in 1994 when he was thrown out of the World Cup after testing positive for various forms of ephedrine, a banned substance, in a random urine test following Argentina's 2-1 victory over Nigeria in Boston. He knew it, too. "They've killed me," he exclaimed, when told that he had been suspended from the remainder of the competition.

But "they" had not killed him, if by "they" he meant the officers of Fifa, football's international governing body. The long, slow process began the day such a phenomenal talent made its appearance in such a poverty-stricken environment, the day it became apparent that Maradona's genius was a goldmine to be worked and worked and worked again until it had given up its last glittering nugget. At the age of 10, for instance, he was being encouraged to use a false name to disguise his identity when he appeared in league matches between teams of a higher age group, for which he was not eligible under the rules of the Argentinian Football Association.

The last piece of significant exploitation took place in the months before the fateful 1994 urine test, when he was persuaded to return from Spain to prepare for his country's attempt to regain the trophy they had won, under his mesmerising leadership, eight years earlier. On arrival in Argentina he weighed a portly 92 kilograms. To play effectively he needed to be down to 77kg. By one means or another in a single month he shed almost a quarter of his body weight. Those who saw him at the time remarked that he looked like a jockey on a wasting regime.

Maradona, ruined by cocaine, went to Cuba for medical aid shortly before Fifa voted him the greatest player of all time

For a 33-year-old this was hardly the best preparation for a series of severe physical tests in the high temperatures of midsummer USA. The only man who knew how it had been achieved was Daniel Cerrini, a former champion bodybuilder and proprietor of a Buenos Aires gym. Cerrini took charge of the weight-loss regime, his methods including a crash diet, weight training and the extensive use of food supplements.

By the time the World Cup started Maradona was again surrounded by controversy. Newell's Old Boys, the Rosario club which had signed him on his return to Argentina, dismissed him after he had missed the team's training sessions once too often. Journalists attempting to doorstep his house were met with gunfire.

Nevertheless he reported fit for duty with Argentina. Masterminding their opening match, a 4-0 victory over Greece, he celebrated one of the goals by sprinting across to the nearest television camera and screaming into the lens. Broadcast around the world, his contorted features made him look like a lunatic, flying on a cocktail of adrenalin and every recreational drug known to man. Nevertheless the result of the match was enough to persuade the Argentinian people that a glorious finish to the story was not only possible but inevitable. Within a few days, however, he was weeping inconsolably after hearing the result of his test, and so were his fans.

His demoralised and leaderless team-mates crashed out of that World Cup but Maradona began a personal fall that nothing seemed capable of arresting. Banned for 15 months and fined £10,000, he returned to action as the manager of Deportivo

Mandiyu, a minor Argentinian club who were promptly relegated after a short reign during which Maradona called one referee a "thief and a liar". A similarly unsuccessful spell coaching Racing, one of Buenos Aires' great old clubs, was interrupted when he went missing on a drink and drugs binge. Having failed twice as a manager, he went back to the Bombonera, his spiritual home, and signed a new deal as a player with Boca Juniors, whom he had left 13 years earlier when he began his European adventure.

His return to Boca was going nowhere when he suddenly showed another side of his character. Out of the blue he summoned the world's media to a Paris hotel, where he announced his intention to form a trade union to represent the interests of leading footballers. Next to him on the podium were a group of stars including Eric Cantona, then in the middle of a nine-month ban for his attack on a Crystal Palace fan.

Although the idea of a couple of spoilt brats leading a labour movement might seem to verge on the surreal, and indeed bore no fruit beyond the immediate splurge of publicity, both men had already shown, in their different ways, a concern for wider issues. In Maradona's case he had twice urged football's governing body to reconsider the practice of kicking off World Cup matches in countries such as Mexico and Italy in the midday heat, sacrificing the players to the scheduling needs of television. His pleas for greater compassion to be extended to players found guilty of doping offences found a less sympathetic audience, although they came from the mouth of a player who had been built up on steroids in adolescence and pumped full of cortisone to keep him playing through injuries.

Drugs of a recreational kind had become a problem for Maradona when he moved from Barcelona to Naples in 1984, receiving a signing-on fee of $6m. This was the start of the most successful period of his career, in which he led Argentina to the 1986 World Cup (after beating England with those two notorious goals, one scored with the "hand of God") and then took his club to its first ever league championship in 1987, followed by the Uefa Cup victory in 1989 and a second league title in 1990. But Naples, lying under the heavy influence of the gangsters of the Camorra, was not a place that discouraged a thorough investigation of the pleasures of the flesh, and Maradona's nocturnal adventures inevitably drew him into a demi-monde of intrigue and clan warfare.

There was no shortage of kiss-and-tell episodes, both before and after his 1990 wedding in Buenos Aires to Claudia Villafane, in a ceremony whose ornate design would make an African emperor — or the scriptwriters of Footballers' Wives — blink in admiration. He was already at the centre of a police investigation into drugs and prostitution. And in the spring of 1991 a rare club dope test yielded traces of cocaine, leading to the imposition of a first 15-month suspension by the Italian authorities.

If that ban broke the back of his career, the second one, three years later, administered the coup de grâce. All attempts at a comeback were doomed to failure. His second spell with Boca Juniors brought little return for the club, interrupted first by treatment for addiction in a Swiss clinic in 1996 and then by another positive test for cocaine after Boca's opening match of the 1997 season. This time, 21 years after he had played his first professional match which was 10 days before his 16th birthday, his career as a footballer really was over.

In 2000 he was admitted to hospital in Uruguay, suffering from a severe heart condition that the doctors blamed on his heavy use of cocaine. Fidel Castro offered him the facilities of Cuba's excellent medical service and he landed in Havana for the first of several stays in an attempt to cure his addiction. His past, however, continued to dog him and two years ago he was ordered by a Naples court to cough up £18m in unpaid taxes and interest.

That same year Fifa, which had imposed the suspension that effectively terminated his career, voted him the greatest player in the game's history. Not everyone agreed, particularly those who took an Anglo-Saxon view of his respect for the laws of the game, but no one who saw him at anything close to his best would be inclined to put up too much resistance to the idea that he deserves to stand at least on the same level as Pele, Alfredo Di Stefano, Johan Cruyff, Michel Platini and Zinedine Zidane. Born into shanty-town poverty, a meal ticket for so many people who saw his genius only as a financial opportunity, Diego Maradona grew up in a world where rules were there to be bent. But the crowds outside the clinic in Buenos Aires yesterday, and many millions of football fans around the globe, remember only the beauty. That is our choice and his salvation.

That fateful left hand clasps the World Cup after Argentina's 3-2 victory over West Germany in 1986

25|06|1990
Eyewitness: Spell that *brrrrrrrrrought* the house down in football-crazed Nkondongo

Jocelyn Targett, Nkondongo

At the end of full-time, with the score in the most important football match ever jammed at 0-0, a middle-aged man in a safari suit whom I took to be quite mad, ran grinning and shouting into the bar where 30 or 40 of us were trying to watch Cameroon play Colombia.

He started jabbering nonsense at the top of his voice and the viewers joined in.

"*Brrrrrrrrr-Jah!*" he bellowed. "Oi!" the crowd replied. "*Brrrrrrrrr-Jah!*" he shouted, coiling up his body and springing out the sound. "Oi!" the crowd replied, punching the air.

On noticing me, the madman threw his face into a contortion of amazement. He embraced me, closed his eyes and squeezed me, all the time flicking out odes in Ewondo, one of the 24 indigenous languages Cameroonians can swear and be sworn at in. "You are a good omen," he said. "Wait here, I want to do something special with you."

He ran out into the rain, his flip-flops flicking the dissolving red earth road up the back of his trousers. "You have nothing to worry about," I was told once he had gone and play in Naples resumed. "He is only the witch-doctor."

I had watched most of the first half in another little bar but its down-valley transmitter packed up during the storm and we all had to run up the street to the nearest available television.

We didn't have to go far. In Cameroon there is on average only one television for every 500 people but in Nkondongo , a desperate slum of big-drinking football fanatics, every bar has to have one.

So far the game had passed with too little incident. We gasped at the Colombian near-misses, groaned at ours and snapped at the little boy sitting on a shelf holding the aerial whenever he moved too much.

Then, back came Appolinaire, the witch doctor, brandishing a candle. Everything was about to change. "To help break the deadlock," he said, "we need something out of the ordinary."

I was it.

As instructed, I lit the candle with someone else's half-smoked cigarette. Appolinaire murmured a spell, then began grinning again. A cheer went up. Then I had to follow him to the lorry park across the road and balance the candle on the rear axle of a defunct jalopy with go-faster rust down the side.

By the time we got back to the bar Roger Milla, the hero centre-forward, was just about to score a goal. When he did, we couldn't control our happiness. We jumped around all over the place, ran outside, inside, out and in again, yelled and hugged whoever came to hand. Even the aerial boy punched the air with his one redundant arm.

In my bar I was held solely responsible for the goal and was being mobbed as if I had scored it.

An eminent villa-dwelling lawyer had told me beforehand that I must watch the match with windows thrown open, so I could hear the roar of the city when Cameroon scored.

In Nkondongo the advice was useless. First, no one who lives there owns any windows; they have just got the indoors and the outdoors. Besides, Nkondongo was the roar and we could hear nothing for the deafening sound of our own song.

When Milla robbed the Colombians for a second goal minutes later, the witch-doctor came and grabbed my hand and took me back to where he was watching the match with at least 60 others in the motor mechanics' pit of the Mobil garage across the road, a huge television balanced on top of a row of oil drums.

Here fame of my magical properties preceded me. I was given a seat in pride of place and several women gathered around for a chance to kiss me.

No one spent any energy worrying when Colombia pulled a goal back a little later. In fact, it went virtually unnoticed. In the pit all manner of hollow metal objects were being bashed together. On the streets cars blazed by, madly toot-toot-tooting. "Brrrrrrrrr-Jah!" shouted Appolinaire. "Oi!" boomed the garage. No one even heard the final whistle. We just guessed, when the televison started showing adverts, that it must have sounded.

We ran a few hundred yards to Nkondongo's favourite night out, the Radio bar. The quick equatorial night started to fall and even before we could get the beers in it was disco-dark all over Yaounde.

At the Radio Cameroonian rhythms and trills were pumping out at hugest volume and families, lovers, friends, street sellers, policemen, taxi drivers and witch-doctors were jiving around getting very closely involved with each other.

A young woman I had never met before, her bottle of beer frothing on to me as she danced, gripped my left leg between hers and furiously jiggled her body up and down. I was beginning to feel quite flattered when she broke off and danced the same way with an old lady, a child, and three other men. Meanwhile I was getting shaken, rolled, pulsated, kneaded, beaten, primped and fricasseed by a never-ending supply of partners.

Appolinaire had been buying me pints of a mysterious

green liquid he tried to pass off as the local Export 33 beer and it wasn't long before I was Brrrrrrrrringing the house down with my ululations.

When Appolinaire, who turned out to be a prison officer, eventually insisted we go back to his place to "struggle", I slipped away into the city centre.

Here, as usual, an elderly woman was collecting discarded beer bottles in a bucket on her head so she could get the deposit back on them. She was doing good trade and, as she turned up the hill towards the distant beat of Nkondongo, she could expect to do even better.

20|06|1994

Houghton makes Italy feel the heat

World Cup, Group E
Republic of Ireland 1 Italy 0
Cynthia Bateman, New York

The temperature was 96F with 75 per cent humidity, yet suddenly the sweat trickling down the back was ice cold, the fervour and the pride and the unrealistic expectation had become an almost physical force.

The Irish had come in their thousands — 50,000 according to official reckoning — in their green shirts and painted faces and beating the bodhrain drums. But where were the Italians? There were supposed to be 20,000 of them among the 73,511 in the Giants Stadium.

Certainly one knew who they were by the end: they were the ones slipping away, some in tears, having confirmed their worst fears about a team and a manager in whom they have little confidence — in sporting terms a national disaster.

Those who thought that all the Republic had to offer were courage and lusty lungs, and they had plenty, knew nothing of Jack Charlton's tactical brain. Arrigo Sacchi had used 34 players in 23 matches leading up the finals and Charlton, who respects above all others the national side that eliminated Ireland from the 1990 World Cup quarter-finals, possibly had a better idea of the Italian manager's plans than he himself had.

Staunton gave notice of Irish intent after 11 seconds,

unmarked and with a clear view of goal. It was a wonderful but fleeting chance and he sliced his volley wide. A goal then would have been too much to hope for, a miracle rather than a blessing.

If Roberto Baggio, the 27-year-old wizard of Juventus and last year's Fifa Player of the Year, was in the mood, then the priority must be to cut off his supply lines. Baggio was most definitely in the mood. But so was Paul McGrath.

Playing just behind Signori, Baggio fed the Lazio striker with some superb passes that time and again in the opening minutes threatened the Irish goal. Each one, sometimes by only a centimetre, failed to pay off.

Yet by then McGrath, who was magnificent, had the measure of the pair of them. The Italians had warned they would attack down the centre and for a while McGrath coped with the threat single-handed, at one stage producing a miraculous block to deny Baggio a strike. As the match progressed, though, Phil Babb, winning only his sixth cap but encouraged by the success of his headers and challenges, came into his own.

Yet it was Irwin, clearing the lines with a long diagonal pass, who began the move that damaged the Italians most.

Coyne and Costacurta leapt for possession, the Italian nodding the ball to Baresi. The Milan defender, a veteran of 73 internationals, could only head lethargically away from goal. Houghton took the ball on his chest, carried it on two or three strides along the edge of the penalty box and turned to hit the sweetest of shots with his unfavoured left foot. Pagliuca, well off his line and knowing he was beaten, made only a token jump as the ball looped over him. From that moment, Sacchi said later, the Italians had lost the game.

"My wife and children were in the stadium and I looked for them but I couldn't see them," said Houghton. "I thought it was a dream."

Houghton had difficulty holding his club place at the end of last season and had almost been written out of Charlton's plans at the end of last year. It was his first international goal in five years.

The Irish had shown they were capable of penetrating Italy's defence, taken entirely from Milan. The question then was whether they could maintain their running and harrying in the heat.

The Italians continued to play slick, short passes to feet. Massaro, who many, including Sacchi afterwards, thought should have started in place of the midfielder Evani, came on up front, allowing Italy to dominate much of the rest of the match. But they became increasingly frustrated as they failed to find the equaliser, Bonner denying Signori with a superb save in the 67th minute, his only test in the match.

Houghton replied with a shot athletically saved at the foot of the post by Pagliuca, and seconds after McAteer, full of fresh running, had replaced him, the Republic produced a deft move which finished with Sheridan hitting the crossbar.

The closing moments, with a hard-to-credit four minutes of injury-time, were of almost unendurable length and tension, Baggio's final strike fatefully high.

Charlton lauded his players as "fantastic" before setting out to watch his next Group E opponents, Mexico, play Norway. It was, he said, a great beginning.

15|11|1995
Making a myth of the old sod

Vincent Hanna

Of course they know it's over. The Irish may dream but they rarely delude themselves. It is time for new ways and a new manager. But it's up to Big Jack to say when and how. He is owed that and more.

Did you hear the one about Jack's state funeral? John Bruton tells him they're building a mausoleum in Glasnevin cemetery and Charlton says: "Bugger off, what's the point? I'll only need it for three days." Whether or not he quits tonight, Jack Charlton's place in folklore is secure — up there with Collins and Pearse and Connolly and Arkle. The horse and himself are the exceptions to the rule that you're only a hero in Ireland in your lifetime when you're dead.

Charlton's place in the Celtic twilight is less about football than national self-respect but the record isn't bad: played 91, won 46, drew 30, lost 15. And two famous goals by Ray Houghton (in 1988 and 1994) that made it all worth while.

I was in Dublin in 1986 when they appointed him and a right pig's breakfast it was. The job was supposed to be Bob Paisley's but through a combination of ineptitude and back-stabbing Jack got the nod. So he sails into the Westbury Hotel, straightaway

Ray Houghton hit the sweetest of left-foot shots. 'I thought it was a dream,' he said

tells the hacks to mind their own business and invites Eamonn Dunphy outside to settle an argument. Which they never did.

At this point someone usually tells me how utterly charming Irish fans are, how much they love a drink and how did they ever warm to an Englishman. I mean, aren't they supposed to hate us for the Famine and couldn't you play for Charlton if you'd once owned an Irish setter?

Let us deconstruct a few myths. Jack is admired because he is English, not in spite of it. The Irish have a complicated relationship with their former colonisers, especially round Dublin where they get on better with them than with anyone else but would rather die than admit it. Sensitive to the least hint of a patronising remark, they have a compulsion to earn British respect.

In Dublin the working classes have two passions, Gaelic football and soccer. But not Irish soccer. In Dublin there are vast fan clubs for Manchester United, Liverpool and Arsenal. Jack unified them, made them feel important — almost as if Ireland could play in the Premier League, and him an English World Cup star too. And if Jack's soccer looks a bit like Gaelic football, so much the better, slap it into them, Jack.

On Sunday night members of the Ireland team and the All-Ireland champions Dublin had a night out together in the Baggot Inn in south Dublin. Different traditions, same fans, blended together by Jack. Oh yes, he owns a share in the pub, which is managed by his son John. He's a great man for the money, the sort they call a cute hoor in Dublin — but not to his face.

And what about all those players with so-called marginal Irish connections? For a century Ireland exported the best of her youth to Britain, the United States and Australia, creating an Irish diaspora 10 times the population of the island. Jack's team spun a thread between the two. When Charlie Haughey, ever a shrewd judge, called him an "honorary Irishman", he also carefully thanked him for "bringing Irishmen home".

There is the character too. Jack displays the truculence and independence that characterise many Irish heroes — Swift, Parnell, Behan, men who owed nobody and didn't give a damn. In 1943 Behan told a British officer in Regent Street: "Of course you'll beat Hitler. Didn't you nearly beat us?" That sort of thing.

Of course Ireland might win tonight. Or Northern Ireland might do him a favour. Or he might say, "Bugger off, I'm staying." No matter. *Slainte*, Jack.

Big Jack displays the truculence and independence that characterise many Irish heroes

05|12|1995

Every day's a Sunday when Weah's there

Richard Williams

Interesting chap, George Weah. Not long ago he was asked whether, as a practising Muslim, he prayed before a match — and if so, what he prayed for. "I ask God to make me victorious in the game and to make me score," he answered, "but only if those are the right things for me to be given. I always pray with that 'if'. You can't say to God, 'Give me money.' You can say, 'I'd like to have more money but only if it doesn't give me an unfair advantage.' He understands that."

Weah was on his knees in the centre circle as soon as the final whistle blew at Rome's Stadio Olimpico on Sunday afternoon, thanking his God — "a God of love and peace" — for what had happened four minutes earlier.

After a bright start Milan's game against Lazio was drifting to a goalless conclusion. Weah, who had blown the best of Milan's chances, was half-expecting to be pulled off.

But in the 87th minute Milan's goalkeeper Sebastiano Rossi bowled the ball to Stefano Eranio, a yard inside his own half on the right touchline. There was barely time to admire Rossi's distribution as Eranio pushed the ball to Weah, 15 yards ahead in the inside-right channel, faced by three defenders. And then came the explosion.

Weah brought it down with his right foot, nudged it on with his left knee as he hurdled Marcolin's wild lunge, pushed it across Nesta's attempted interception, touched it again as he sprinted past the bewildered Bergodi, then lengthened his stride and shot low from the 18-yard line past the left hand of Mancini, Lazio's keeper.

From Rossi to the back of the Lazio net the whole thing had taken 14 seconds. And what we saw from Weah was the player using his imagination to clarify rather than elaborate: a beautiful and instructive sight. Route One? More like the Via Veneto.

The 29-year-old Liberian has been doing this sort of thing on a regular basis all season since arriving from Paris St-Germain to succeed Marco van Basten in Milan's No9 shirt.

"Where will we find another such?" the Gazzetta dello Sport lamented on the day of the Dutchman's retirement. Three months later, after Weah had volleyed a wonder goal against Sparta Prague in the Uefa Cup, the Gazzetta's headline read: "Weah, you are Van Basten."

Last month Weah was presented with the African Player of the Year award for the third time. Before Christmas we will know whether he has also become the first African to win the award's European equivalent. If he wins it, he says, he will dedicate the victory to the peaceful outcome of next year's democratic elections in Liberia.

Weah left Monrovia in 1988, the year before the civil war broke out, to make his way to Italy via Yaounde, Monaco and Paris. Back home he lost friends, family and property in the conflict. But he helped half a dozen other Liberian footballers find clubs in France and with the proceeds of his own career he bought not just houses in New York and a restaurant in Brooklyn but also a football club, Junior Professional, in Monrovia.

"Football was what people had to make them forget the war," Weah said recently. "The day nobody plays football in Liberia will be the day there aren't any Liberians left." Now his image adorns a set of postage stamps and in January he will

> **The day nobody plays football in Liberia will be the day there are no Liberians left**

take leave of absence from Milan to represent his country in the African Cup.

So far Weah has scored five goals in Milan's progress to the top of Serie A but his unselfishness has won just as much praise. "As a player George has an extraordinary talent," Milan's coach, Fabio Capello, said on Sunday, "and he's also a great man — two qualities that don't generally go together."

A student of Martin Luther King and Malcolm X, Weah says that leaving Africa has made him think more about his own heritage. "At school we were given only European books to read. Now I'm rediscovering my culture. In Africa I became European. In Europe I've become African."

While he was in Paris he was asked why some matches seemed to motivate him more than others. "Football matches are like days of the week," he replied. "It can't be Sunday every day. There are also Mondays and Tuesdays" — a nice metaphor but flawed. Now, when Weah turns out for Milan, it seems to be nothing but one Sunday after another.

14|07|1998

Ronaldo: a 30-minute mystery

The striker, at first omitted but then restored to Brazil's World Cup final team, never looked fit, says Richard Williams

The million and a half French people thronging the Champs-Elysées on Sunday night were not to know it, and would not care if anyone had told them, but for Brazil a bitter post-mortem into their World Cup final defeat was only just beginning. Rumours emerged yesterday of pre-match rows inside their camp over the fitness of Ronaldo, their 21-year-old star, amid allegations of last-minute interference with the team selection.

Originally omitted from their line-up, as issued to the press an hour before kick-off, Ronaldo was reinstated in place of his apparent replacement Edmundo with barely half an hour to go. There had been stories of knee problems troubling the young forward and Ronaldo's eventual contribution to the match was marked by a complete absence of the speed and power that normally accompany his technical skills.

After the match the Brazil coach, Mario Zagallo, admitted that the other players had been "disturbed" when they learnt of Ronaldo's possible absence. But he refused to discuss Ronaldo's medical condition, angrily referring reporters to the squad's medical staff. "Ronaldo played because he played," he said. When questioned further he shouted, "I have my dignity," before storming out of the room.

But almost an hour after midnight, two hours after the end of the match, a statement was issued from the team's doctor, Lidio Toledo. "Regarding the health of Ronaldo," Toledo was quoted as saying, "he was not feeling well this afternoon, and now he's better. What happened to him? Quite simply he felt faint and after that, he went to rest. I stress that he is feeling better now."

Brazil's talisman Ronaldo is deep in thought before the World Cup final, for which he looked ill prepared. France won 3-0

Two pieces of paper were the only physical evidence of the cause of the catastrophe that had befallen Ronaldo and Brazil. They were two different versions of the official team sheets, containing the line-ups of Brazil and France as submitted to and ratified by the officials of Fifa.

On the first, printed at 19.48, 1hr 12 min ahead of the kick-off, the name of Ronaldo was to be found in the list of substitutes, replaced in the starting line-up by Edmundo. This list was the first to be issued to journalists, soon after 8pm, and was greeted with general astonishment. Unofficially journalists were told that Ronaldo was suffering from the effects of an ankle injury picked up in the semi-final against Holland five days earlier.

Soon, however, stories began circulating that Ronaldo would be included after all. And the second list, printed at 20.18, contained his name, with Edmundo back among the substitutes.

Meanwhile it was noticed that the team had not arrived on the pitch to go through their usual elaborate warm-up routine – a remarkable break with their standard practice. The France team completed their exercises and left the pitch. With five minutes to go both teams came out of the tunnel together and lined up for the national anthems, with Ronaldo in his usual place at the end of the Brazil line.

Ronaldo played the full 90 minutes without ever resembling the world's most feared striker. Uncharacteristically ponderous on the turn and slow to strike, he forced Fabien Barthez to make saves in the 21st and 55th minutes, and needed treatment after a heavy collision with France's goalkeeper after half an hour, but in general his efforts were smothered by the home defence with an ease which surprised onlookers. Around Ronaldo his team-mates appeared ill at ease and out of sorts with each other.

Before the match had long been over, stories were emerging from the Brazilian camp. Zagallo was said to have fretted long over Ronaldo's condition, eventually making up his mind to leave him out at around 5pm and informing Edmundo of his inclusion. At the team meeting he told the shocked players of his decision and reminded them of the example of the 1962 Brazil team, which lost Pele, their 21-year-old star, early in the tournament but went on to win the trophy. Zagallo had been a member of that team.

Selection countermanded

But then, according to a first report in the Rio daily newspaper *O Globo*, matters were taken out of Zagallo's hands. According to their report, the coach's selection was countermanded by Ricardo Teixeira, the controversial president of the CBF, the Brazilian football federation.

Teixeira, the son-in-law of Joao Havelange, the outgoing president of Fifa, is said to have reacted to the news of Ronaldo's omission by going to the dressing-room and calling an emergency meeting of the squad's management staff – his nephew, the CBF's general secretary Marco Antonio Teixeira, Zagallo, the coach Zico, the special coordinator Toledo, the

doctor and Americo Faria, the supervisor. All were told that Ronaldo had to play.

In the face of their objections the CBF president is said to have told them that he would take personal responsibility for Ronaldo's inclusion. And by this time, according to *O Globo*, Ronaldo had indicated that he wanted to play.

Another Brazilian daily, *O Folho*, quoted the Brazil full-back Roberto Carlos as saying that his room-mate, feeling unwell, had suddenly run out of the room at 20 past four in the afternoon to call a doctor.

"It was as if a malaise had come over him. Not even he knew what was wrong," Roberto Carlos said. "He had been in tears in the night, and in the afternoon he went yellower than our shirts."

Something had to give

Tellingly Roberto Carlos suggested a non-physical cause of the problem. "Here was a 21-year-old player, the best player in the world, surrounded by contracts and pressure," he said. "It was as if this was always going to happen to him. Something had to give. And when it did, it happened to be the day of the World Cup final."

Roberto Carlos's remarks may have been a reference to a reported £125million 10-year deal signed by the CBF president with Nike, widely criticised – not least by Dunga, the captain – for the control it gives the US sports-goods company over where and when the team play their friendly matches. As the team's most charismatic figure, Ronaldo is inevitably the focus of Nike's marketing campaigns.

Throughout the tournament questions had been asked about the state of Ronaldo's knees and about his weight, which was alleged to be higher than usual. His early performances were not of the standard expected and he was thought to be saving himself for the final stages.

But a pair of goals against Chile and two remarkable passes to create goals for Rivaldo and Bebeto in the match against Denmark, which Brazil won 3-2 after going behind, appeared to indicate that all would be well.

Ronaldo's absence from the squad's training sessions on Thursday and Friday was officially blamed on the ankle injury, although some suspected that this was a smoke-screen to disguise his continuing problems with tendinitis in both knees.

Edmundo, famous for his volatile temperament, is said to have reacted angrily to his last-minute displacement from the team. By the time he eventually appeared, sent on as a substitute for Cesar Sampaio with 15 minutes to go, the game was as good as lost.

More details of the events of Sunday are sure to emerge in an affair that will probably run all the way through to the next World Cup finals and seems likely to shake Brazilian football to its permanently unstable foundations.

06|07|1999
Pass Notes:
No 1433: Ronaldo (Jr)

Profession: Brazilian footballing sensation. Appearance: Tall, buck-toothed youngster

I know him. The bald one from the World Cup final. No. There are two Ronaldos in the Brazilian team. The one you are thinking about is 22 and, if not over the hill, at least nearing the crest. At 19 the new Ronaldo is the youngest player in the national squad and made his debut last week against Venezuela in the Copa America.

Is the new one any good? Two minutes after coming on he received a pass, flicked the ball over a defender and without letting it touch the ground, dribbled round another defender before scoring. It's already being compared with Pele's famous goal in the 1958 World Cup final.

But I thought the famous Ronaldo was the new Pele? He is, too. He equalled Pele's record of playing in the World Cup aged 17, and has already been voted world's best player two years running.

So there are a lot of Ronaldos in Brazil, then? Loads. Over the last few years, no fewer than four have worn the yellow national strip.

How do I know who's who? The first was a defender, who became known as Ronaldao, or Big Ronaldo. The second, also a defender, was plain Ronaldo. And the famous Inter Milan striker was nicknamed by the Brazilian press Ronaldinho, or Little Ronaldo, because he was younger.

What does that make the even littler Ronaldo? By rights he should be *Ronaldinhozinho*, or Little Little Ronaldo. But the original Ronaldinho is being promoted to Ronaldo, his younger teammate earning the name Ronaldinho Gaucho because he is from the state near the Argentinian border.

Why don't they use their surnames? That would be more confusing. The current squad has four Silvas and four Santoses. Nicknames are more fun anyway: the women's World Cup team features Marvellous and Ant. Dunga, who captained the 1994 World Cup-winning team, is named after the equivalent of Dopey in Snow White and the Seven Dwarfs.

Do say: "Hello, I'm from Nike, would you like 10 million dollars?"

Don't say: "Didn't your brother also play international football?"

01|07|2002
Free of demons and back in the land of the living

Ronaldo emerges from his France 98 nightmare as Brazil regain the World Cup, reports Richard Williams

When the final whistle blew Ronaldo was leaning on the canopy covering the substitutes' bench. He had been withdrawn from the action a couple of minutes earlier and was already weeping with exhaustion and relief. He knew that the shadows that had darkened his life for the past four years had finally been dispersed, and that life as he had known it before that dreadful evening in Paris could finally resume.

In the end it turned out to be one of the better finals, worthy of the occasion and the hype, but for almost the first 20 minutes yesterday every Brazilian outfield player appeared to have been struck by a recurrence of whatever nervous affliction turned Ronaldo into a zombie four years ago. A World Cup that began with an act of revolution when Senegal beat France was in danger of ending in the anticlimax of a victory for a workmanlike Germany.

In all areas of the pitch during that period Brazil were coming second to white-shirted men who sliced open the flanks at will and continually relaunched themselves by gobbling up the second ball. At this stage Brazil were being kept alive by their much maligned trio of central defenders.

But then, very slowly, the real Ronaldo began to appear before our eyes and the match started to assume its proper shape.

At the start he had been as tentative and imprecise as his team-mates. Three good chances went begging in the first half and for a while it seemed hideously possible that fate might be repeating itself. But when he finally scored, the way he did it — the intuitive dart to reach the rebound off Olivier Kahn's chest for 1-0 after 67 minutes, the calm touch to bring the ball under control before doubling the lead 12 minutes later — spoke of renewed self-belief.

With eight goals from this tournament Ronaldo has become the first man since Paolo Rossi in 1982 to win both the Golden Boot and a champion's medal at the tournament. He now has 12 World Cup goals in all, which puts him level with Pele and just behind Gerd Müller of Germany, the leader with 14, and Just Fontaine of France, whose 13 goals were amassed in one tournament. And at 25 Ronaldo has at least one more World Cup — perhaps two, with luck — left in him.

"I'm slowly realising just what happened. My happiness and my emotion are so great that it's difficult to understand," he said afterwards. "I've said before that my big victory was to play football again, to run again and to score goals again. This victory, for our fifth world title, has crowned my recovery and the work of the whole team. Above all it's a victory for the group. The whole team ran and battled and helped each other. No individual conquest can beat what the group achieved."

Gerard Saillant, the French surgeon who operated on his abused knee, was in the crowd as the guest of his patient. "This gives hope to everyone who is injured," Saillant said, "even those who aren't sportsmen, to see that by fighting you can make it. He's back to where he was. It's hugely satisfying and I am very moved."

In the view of Luiz Felipe Scolari, Brazil's coach, the final turned out to be a victory for individual players within a team game.

Ronaldo wraps himself in Brazil's flag of many colours after his two goals beat Germany in the 2002 World Cup final

"What made a big difference was the individual quality of each player," he said. "At certain times that was the factor that gave us superiority."

Not surprisingly Scolari praised the work of Lucio, Edmilson and Roque Junior in the centre of the defence. Edmilson, having been badly elbowed in the face early on by an unpunished Miroslav Klose, limped through the match after a collision in the 22nd minute. His mobility was impaired but he continued to exude tranquillity.

"The defence was so heavily criticised and it was really not that bad," Scolari said. "Maybe it is the best defence in the world."

The last laugh

A gift for ironic understatement was not among the coach's advertised qualities when he took the job two years ago with instructions to pull the disintegrating qualification campaign back together. Instead his militaristic tendencies were more widely noted. But, although Brazil used 77 players and four coaches to reach the finals, and suffered six defeats on the way, the signs of an improvement were present even before they arrived in the Far East.

Now Scolari has enjoyed the last laugh over those who campaigned for his removal. He has also earned the undying affection of the Brazilian people by producing an expressive squad who appear to conform in most respects to the ideals of the old days. It is a pity they were given no chance in Japan to test the belief that they may be a genuinely great side. For that they need great opposition, something that was not always easily visible in this tournament.

Germany were not that opposition, not by a long way. Their route to Yokohama was perhaps the easiest ever travelled by World Cup finalists. After the demolition of Saudi Arabia only the Republic of Ireland's last-gasp equaliser interrupted the string of parsimonious victories over Cameroon, Paraguay, the United States and South Korea. Nor in moral terms did they deserve victory yesterday, at least not since Michael Ballack publicly lamented his absence from the final through suspension by comparing his plight to that of Laurent Blanc four years ago.

Blanc, some will remember, lost his chance of a World Cup winner's medal after being sent off when Slaven Bilic of Croatia mimed a reaction to a non-existent infringement. His suspension was a terrible miscarriage of justice. Ballack's, however, was fully justified, since it came after he had intentionally fouled a South Korean opponent in order to preserve Germany's advantage.

Rudi Völler's defence of his player's decision to commit the foul merely added another bad smell to the tournament. Yesterday Ronaldo and the rest of Scolari's team — even Rivaldo, the artist with the morals of a pickpocket — blew the stench away.

01|07|2000

A leader among men

Zinedine Zidane is the quiet force who can silence Italy's followers in the final of Euro 2000, writes Richard Williams

In a team full of leaders Zinedine Zidane has become the patron. He may not wear the captain's armband and he seldom bothers to say much but he is the man to whom his team-mates turn for inspiration – and the man to whom the rest of Europe is looking to unlock the steel doors of the Italian defence in tomorrow night's Euro 2000 final, thus fulfilling the promise of a tournament which, until this week's semi-finals, appeared to have been dedicated to inaugurating an era of attacking football.

Those who know Zizou best say the introspection of old, the shyness of an immigrant's son from the housing projects who finds himself dining with presidents, has begun to fall away and that he is becoming more at ease with his celebrity. But he will always be a man whose eloquence is primarily in his feet.

Last week, in a rare flight of verbal fancy, he declared: "At 28 I'm at the pinnacle of my art." It sounded a bit pompous, a bit uncharacteristic, even a bit French, and two days later he had reconsidered the matter. "Maybe that was a little excessive," he said. "Let's just say I'm at the top of my form."

Yet his performances in the tournament suggest that Zidane is still finding new ways to express himself with a football. In the first half of the quarter-final against Spain he appeared to want to play the game only with the soles of his feet, stroking the ball with the blades of his boots simply because that gave him a more intimate contact with its surface – the difference between a punch and a caress. Against Portugal in the next round he showed another dimension, an ability to overcome double marking by setting off on long slaloms in which he seemed to be skimming across packed snow while his opponents were trying to run through sand dunes.

He is a big man, 6ft 1in and 12st 4lb, and his stooping gait can make him look ponderous, but his greatness lies in the delicacy of his touch and the subtlety of his mind. When he scored from a free-kick against Spain he seemed to be feeling the precise texture of the ball through his boot and stocking. When he took the "golden penalty" against Portugal he deployed the skills of a find-the-lady trickster, his eyes and his feet sending conflicting messages that hypnotised Vitor Baia into diving the wrong way. Earlier in the match he had set Bixente Lizarazu free on the left with a marvellously disguised six-foot backheel.

But his displays of unearthly skill are not Zidane's only contribution. During the squad's preparations for the tournament, while they were encamped at Bourg Saint-Maurice in the Savoy Alps, Roger Lemerre remarked: "When you see Zizou's appetite for work, his eagerness, his smile – well, that's reassuring." The coach was recognising that, unlike some superstars, Zidane is a vital ingredient in the social chemistry of a squad whose members relish their closeness so much that it seems as if as individuals they belong not to Juventus or Chelsea or Real Madrid or Arsenal but to a club called France. His special closeness is with Christophe Dugarry, a former Bordeaux team-mate with whom he shares ownership of a restaurant. To Dugarry's mother Zizou is "the sort of brother Christophe always wanted".

Born in La Castellane, a suburb of Marseille, the son of an Algerian father, he made his first division debut with Cannes at 17 before moving to Bordeaux in 1992. On his international debut in 1994 he scored both goals in a 2-2 draw with the Czech Republic. He joined Juventus after Euro 96 and won the Italian championship in his first season. The triumph at the Stade de France in 1998 brought him the title of the world footballer of the year to go with his Legion d'Honneur ribbon.

Naturally the two goals he scored with his head in the final against Brazil enhanced his already extraordinary status. When Zidane is not around, France are not the same side. Against Paraguay in the World Cup, while he was serving a suspension for trampling on a Saudi player, the team found themselves desperately lacking a creative force and were facing elimination until Laurent Blanc stepped forward to score a decisive goal in extra-time. England's fans will also remember the way Zidane presented the 18-year-old Nicolas Anelka with three goals (one of them unjustly disallowed) at Wembley two winters ago.

"This is certainly a better side than the France of 1998," he said after last week's quarter-final. "We've all got another two years of experience in the best leagues in Europe. And this time we've got five forwards, all with great qualities, which we didn't have during the World Cup. We've also shown that we're adaptable – there isn't one ideal system because each match offers different characteristics, which means that all the 22 players are involved. Against the Czech Republic, for example, Youri Djorkaeff came on and scored a vital goal after he'd been criticised for his performance against Denmark. And the spirit of Christophe Dugarry is an asset to us because he's happy to play in any position and to put himself at the service of the team."

143

In a tournament full of technical interest the main focus of tactical debate has been the general eclipse of the great playmaker, a majority of sides preferring to place their faith in collective movement. "I don't think the job of playmaker will disappear," Zidane offered, "because it's something that gives people a lot of pleasure. I know that many teams prefer to play without one but for me that diminishes the spectacle."

And whatever the importance of team play, the stroke of individual genius is still the most effective way of determining the course of a football match, with the No10 shirt carrying a special significance in that respect. When Liam Brady, invited last week to comment on Zidane's qualities as a playmaker, remarked admiringly that he saw the Frenchman as "a maker of goals rather than a maker of the game", he was perhaps ignoring the fact that goals make games. Zidane may not sit deep in the manner of a Gerson or a Brady, but his hands are just as firmly on the strings.

On Wednesday night in Brussels, in the five minutes of madness between the award of the decisive penalty and the taking of the kick, Zidane went off by himself to prepare for the task of finishing the match. Even after almost two hours of high-intensity action, his mind and his body were in perfect union.

Talking of his development as a player, he has credited Juventus's fitness team – currently embroiled in a controversy over their alleged use of bodybuilding substances – with increasing his explosive power by 30%. "But most of the improvement is psychological," he said. "Italian football is the best education in the world." And tomorrow night the pupil will attempt to teach his masters a lesson.

Zinedine Zidane made the case for the playmaker at Euro 2000, won by France. His fans think he is out of this world

11|07|2006
Zidane returns to adulation, intrigue and calls to tell all

Despite his World Cup final head-butt, 'Zizou' remains a hero at home. By Angelique Chrisafis and John Hooper

Under a haze of French flags and firecracker smoke the crowd of several thousand people filling Place de la Concorde yesterday afternoon chanted *"Zizou! Zizou!"* in a hero's welcome for Zinedine Zidane, the French football captain sent off for headbutting an Italian player as France lost the World Cup final.

At the same time Italian politicians, French anti-racism campaigners and a host of international lip-readers were trying to unravel the mystery of what Italy's Marco Materazzi might have said to provoke Zidane into violence, with some suggesting he might have called the son of Algerian immigrants "a dirty terrorist" and said his sister was a "whore".

Looking unmistakably sheepish, the man once nicknamed "Zidane President" waved down to the adoring Paris crowd who were keen to forgive their national hero for going out of his last ever match on a red card. Zidane, the immigrant warehouseman's son who practised his first shots against the grim concrete high rises of north Marseille, carried on his shoulders the weight of France's football success – not to mention championing racial integration, healing the country's bruised national image and boosting the economy by making people feel good – all the time advertising a host of national products.

President Jacques Chirac, in his own final hours at the helm and beset by problems, praised the captain unconditionally. "The match you played last night was full of talent and professionalism," he said. "I know you are sad and disappointed but what I want to tell you is that the whole country is extremely proud of you. You have honoured the country with your exceptional qualities and your fantastic fighting spirit, which was your strength in difficult times but also in winning times."

Post-mortem: Zidane shows frustration at having his header saved by Italy's Gianluigi Buffon. There was worse to come

A former Juventus player, Zidane would have understood any comment made in Italian. Speculation was rife on the streets of Paris yesterday that it was a racist or anti-Algerian comment, or a taunt at his mother, who is believed to be unwell, or his French-Spanish wife. One Italian lip-reader told the BBC that Materazzi said first: "I wish an ugly death to you and all your family," and then simply "go fuck yourself". Zidane is fiercely proud of his family and roots in the Algerian village of Taguemount in Kabylie and calls himself a non-practising Muslim.

In Italy a government MP said he was tabling a question in parliament after a report in *The Guardian* suggested that Materazzi had called Zidane a terrorist. Another said that, if the report was true, "it would represent a reprehensible episode".

The 32-year-old Italian defender Materazzi is viewed as the hardest of "hard men" in Serie A. In 2004 he was given one of the longest bans in Italian football for an unprovoked attack on a player in the tunnel. His victim, who was punched in the face, said Materazzi had taunted him throughout the game.

Materazzi said on his return to Italy: "It is absolutely not true that I called him a terrorist. I don't even know what it means. What happened was seen by everyone on live television."

A Brazilian television channel, Globo, quoted lip-readers as saying the Italian defender had twice called Zidane's sister a "whore" before launching an unspecified insult at the player.

Zidane's agent, Alain Migliaccio, said that the French captain had been "provoked" when Materazzi had said "something very grave". He told Radio Five Live: "He [Zidane] will not reveal what Materazzi said but he will in one or two days' time explain why he had such a reaction. When he is calmer he will speak. When I saw him at 2am he was very sad; he did not want to end his career like this."

Among the Algerian community on the streets near Paris's Gare du Nord yesterday the feeling was that Zidane was "unfairly abused". "Materazzi must have said something about his family," said 18-year-old Aziz, who started playing for the local football team aged 10 when Zidane led France to World Cup victory in 1998. "It's a shame that Zidane has sullied his career but he will always have a place in our hearts," he said. Some sections of the French press were less forgiving. The biggest selling sports daily, *L'Equipe*, asked in a front-page piece: "What should we tell our children, for whom you have become an example for ever? How could that happen to a man like you?"

Pascal Boniface, director of Paris's Institute for International and Strategic Relations and author of a recent book on football and globalisation, said Zidane's huge advertising contracts were probably safe. "Zidane must now come forward and explain. It won't kill off his contracts — it wasn't a line of coke. But it's good for us to see our national hero is fallible."

Despite France's joy that their team unexpectedly made the final, there was a grim sense that life was back to normal. The daily *Libération* mused: "For a month France was dreaming with Zidane. This morning, it wakes up to Chirac."

Chapter 10
Wenger and Mourinho: a foreign education

27|05|1989

Last-gasp Thomas ends the doubting

Liverpool 0 Arsenal 2

David Lacey, Anfield

Arsenal won the League Championship last night and denied Liverpool their second Double in four seasons because, when it mattered most, they marched towards the sound of the guns. The title has never been decided in more dramatic circumstances and amid such scenes of high excitement.

Needing to win by two goals to bring London its first title since 1971, George Graham's team made it in the second minute of injury-time when Michael Thomas, who had wasted a wonderful chance a little earlier, was given another and did not miss.

The teams finished level on points and goal difference but Arsenal scored eight more goals and that, in the end, was what mattered.

It was entirely fitting that Graham's team should triumph where they did, when they did and in the manner that they did. Arsenal's initial challenge had stemmed from their capacity to play positive, open football away from home, and this is what drove them on last night.

Just when it seemed that a series of poor results in home games, combined with Liverpool's unbeaten run of 24 matches, would again leave Arsenal in the role of also-rans, their team responded as a whole succession of Arsenal teams have done: with spirit, purpose and a refusal to accept that a cause is lost until the last of the final whistles.

The sudden twist of those closing seconds left Anfield and, yes, even the Kop dumbfounded. Seldom has such collective disbelief been written on 41,000-odd faces. The Arsenal fans must have pinched themselves for a moment or two.

Arsenal deserved their victory, no doubt about that, even if their first goal, scored by Smith early in the second half, was hotly contested by Liverpool. Yet there came a point when Liverpool's players, some of whom showed signs of weariness as they completed their eighth match in 23 days, looked as if they were being hauled towards the Double only by the strength

of will of their fans. The League Championship is an article of faith at Anfield and they were not going to let it go.

It was a marvellous night for English football. After the Hillsborough disaster and the subsequent crowd disorders, which had threatened to end the season with the game on its knees, the closest championship of all demanded a night to remember and that is what it was given.

From the outset last night Arsenal were determined never to let Liverpool settle into the rhythms which had swept all before them since New Year's Day. As early as the eighth minute Grobbelaar was unable to cut out Thomas's cross and Bould's far-post header was on target; Liverpool would have fallen behind then but for Nicol's interception.

After that Liverpool worked hard to raise their tempo but, with the Arsenal full-backs, Winterburn and Dixon, pressing up on the wings, it was difficult for Barnes and Nicol to assert their usual authority and stretch the opposition at the back.

Rush was forced off just after the half-hour with a groin strain and his replacement, Beardsley, looked jaded. McManaman never gave up trying to drive deep wedges into the Arsenal defence but their three centre-backs were solid throughout and, when Liverpool did outwit them late in the game, Houghton and Aldridge wasted simple scoring chances.

Smith's goal in the 53rd minute was followed by complaints and confusion. The Arsenal striker ducked into a gap to head Winterburn's indirect free-kick past Grobbelaar. Liverpool were convinced a linesman's flag had been raised, albeit briefly, possibly for a push by O'Leary.

Twenty minutes later Liverpool seemed to have survived

No comebacks: Michael Thomas ties up the Championship with the decisive goal in the second minute of injury-time

their worst moment when Winterburn, Smith and Merson worked the ball up to Richardson, whose final pass went through McMahon's legs and left Thomas with only the goalkeeper to beat. He froze on the chance and shot straight at Grobbelaar. In that moment the Double appeared won.

But in the 92nd minute Lukic threw the ball to Dixon to set in train a series of events during which time almost stood still. Dixon's pass found Smith, who deftly controlled the ball before slipping it through to Thomas haring past Ablett. Thomas showed admirable coolness in scoring one of the game's historic goals. The title had left Merseyside for the first time in eight seasons – and the Kop warmly applauded Liverpool's conquerors.

27|09|1996

Wenger learns the worst

Martin Thorpe samples Arsenal *à la Arsène* over four days of meets, greets and a defeat for the new manager

On Arsène Wenger's first visit to Arsenal's training ground last Monday the new manager was more than happy to be photographed with any of his adopted stars. Unfortunately there were few takers.

"No way," said Ian Wright out of Wenger's earshot. "I had my photograph taken with Bruce Rioch when he arrived and look what happened to him." What happened to him was that he made the mistake of falling out with Wright, the darling of Highbury. The photographic snub produced the clearest picture yet of the task Wenger faces in winning the players' trust.

Circumstances are loaded against Wenger in his task of winning over the Jack the Lad who is the English professional. He is foreign for a start. With his tall, lean frame and rimless spectacles he wears a scholarly look, spouts erudite sentences, has a degree in economics and fluency in five languages. There are not many of those in English dug-outs.

But Wenger is astute too, and this could be his passport to respect. He has already gone within the club for his No2, Pat Rice, who is steeped in the club's traditions, and he has shown a sensible flexibility on discipline by publicly praising Tony Adams's bravery in admitting his alcoholism.

What should mostly impress the squad are Wenger's dedication and knowledge. "Players judge a manager on whether he knows football," says the former Arsenal manager Don Howe. "The players will want to hear him talk about football and see if he knows about football. If he comes across as having good football intelligence, there will be no problem." In that case Wenger is home and dry. Football intelligence is his specialist subject. Trying to resuscitate Arsenal's European campaign at such short notice did prove too difficult – he watched them lose doughtily to Borussia Mönchengladbach on Wednesday evening – but, given time, the Wenger effect could be wholly different.

Glenn Hoddle decided to move into coaching after playing under Wenger at Monaco. "He is very impressive," says the England coach. "At Monaco he knew exactly what he wanted, what was the best thing for each individual to work at within the framework of the team and how to balance the team. He brought in five players and knew exactly what was needed. He got everything to gel. It was very refreshing and we won the title in my first season." Football is Wenger's life. The man's eagerness to fly halfway round the world and back to spend four days with his new team during a crucial European tie speaks volumes for his enthusiasm and loyalty to a club he hardly knows.

Born in Strasbourg 47 years ago, he is not the archetypal Frenchman. "He has an English mind but also a German mind, which is very disciplined," says Hoddle. He knows a lot about English football too, having studied it for years. Plus, perhaps crucially for future dressing-room confrontations, he understands English humour and employs it with native expertise.

Asked if he had sampled any of London's nightlife during his short visit, Wenger admitted, deadpan: "Yes. The other evening I watched the goal highlights on television." On Monday morning he introduced himself to the players with a five-minute speech, promising half-hour one-to-ones in a couple of weeks. What some of Arsenal's less cerebrally endowed players will find to talk about for half an hour is anyone's guess. But Hoddle says the players will discover Wenger to be honest, straightforward and approachable – but ruthless too, if required.

"He prepares a guideline on how the club should function on the playing side and how individuals should work," says

According to Hoddle, Wenger is honest and approachable – but ruthless, too

Hoddle, "and, if anyone steps out of line, he has a ruthless side to him. That's when the German side comes out."

The Arsenal board hopes that Wenger's record in seven years at Monaco — French champions, always in Europe — can be transplanted to Highbury. But to do that Wenger must succeed where the other foreign managers in English football — Ossie Ardiles and Jozef Venglos — failed.

"My challenge is to mix the English style to a more continental way," says Wenger. "Also I am conscious that I have to win over the supporters because they don't really know me and I am foreign. But if they reject me it will not be because I am foreign they will reject me if I don't do a good job." Don Howe agrees: "Sooner or later a continental manager is going to break through and get success in England and, if Wenger gets success, the Arsenal supporters will accept him like anyone else. Supporters are about seeing their team win."

Wenger's astuteness cautions him against seeking that success by immediately spending the £20 million he is reputed to have available for new signings. "First I want to give confidence to the players we have," he says, "to observe them a bit. If we are able to play well and the way I want, we will wait because there is quality in the team.

"Spending lots of money on players does not always mean you have a good team. Whatever happens, I want to keep what made Arsenal — the spirit, mental strength and character of the team. And for that I will need a majority of Englishmen." As for a tactical system, Tony Adams can keep raising his arm for a few seasons yet. "I play 4-4-2 if I can," says Wenger. "It is very adaptable because you can change easily to 4-3-3, 4-4-2 or 4-5-1. It is really strange because in all Europe people are going to the old English system of 4-4-2 and England is going the other way. But with three at the back you have to come a little deeper and I like offensive football and winning the ball early. It is much more difficult to pressurise up the field with three at the back." Then he gets technical: "Overall I like modern football, made of compact lines, of zones, of pressure and of quick, co-ordinated movements with a good technique." As for discipline off the pitch at what has become a scandal-strewn club, he says hopefully: "I believe the best discipline is always when a player understands it is in his best interests."

Criticism is something he does not reserve for others. "I am somebody who likes to meet challenges, has a passion for football, who likes to win and tries to improve himself," he says. "I am like every human — I have my weaknesses. But I would say to you I try every day to be better than the day before — that's a personal challenge. And if I have failings, I have one quality: I like to give." And as for Arsenal, Wenger is learning about them all the time. "Would you like some wine?" asked his chairman, Peter Hill-Wood, after Sunday's press conference. "Whatever you are having," said Wenger. "Oh, we only drink French here," came the reply. Vintage Arsenal.

11|05|2002

Wenger maps out life after the party

Jon Brodkin

....

While Arsenal's players were partying into the small hours of Thursday morning after their triumphant return from Old Trafford, Arsène Wenger was at home. Having shared a drink with his backroom staff, the manager sat down at 2am to watch a rerun of the win over Manchester United that had just clinched the Double. Let no one suggest the obsessive Frenchman does not know a good time.

Whether Wenger was scribbling notes is uncertain but, having retired to bed at 4am, he was up three hours later to leave for the office. "I had a lot of meetings," he explained yesterday. Before the present had been fully enjoyed it was time to plan for the future. There can be no let-up when dominating the Premiership and winning the Champions League is your ambition.

Wenger has privately identified the two players he wants to buy this summer and does not rule out a signing before the World Cup. A trip to Japan will constitute the 52-year-old's only holiday. He believes United "subconsciously" thought they had the title won at the start of the season and he is determined to avoid similar error.

"It is 3-2 to Manchester United [in championships] over the last five years and we want to equalise," he said. "When you have success you want to make sure you have that again. But the best way not to have success the season after is to enjoy it too much. You forget that people try to strengthen their team and then you lose. Today I am completely relaxed and enjoying it but already I want to know, can I deliver the Double again?"

Arsène Wenger watches intently in August 2002 knowing that, following Arsenal's 2002 Double, life will only get harder

Wenger is well aware that Sir Alex Ferguson, with whom he drank a glass of wine after Wednesday's game, will be highly motivated to redress the balance. He expects United to come back stronger. When Arsenal did the Double in 1998, Ferguson responded by winning the treble. Wenger, though, does not expect his players to become complacent.

"They are special human beings," he said. "They don't want to win one year and then say: 'We can relax now.' They want to win every year." Perhaps it was a reflection of Wenger's mentality that at 10am yesterday records of the 2002 triumphs were being engraved on the honours panel at the training ground.

There were traces of celebration there. Sylvain Wiltord turned 28 yesterday and his cake was a huge replica of the Premiership trophy. Wenger was in jovial, bullish mood. Yet he hardly needs reminding that the 1998 successes were followed by four fallow years.

"We won in '98 with eight players over 30," he noted. "Now we have a very young team. It's completely different and that's why I say we want to dominate. The biggest respect I have is for the team that wins the championship and I want as well to win the European Cup."

The success of Bayer Leverkusen, whom Arsenal drew with in Germany and then hammered 4-1, has strengthened Wenger's belief "that we can come back and win the European Cup next season". But the Champions League will not be his overriding focus. That, he feels, is where United went wrong.

"I can understand Manchester United [being obsessed with the Champions League] because they won the championship last year by 10 points," he said. "They bought Verón and Van Nistelrooy, so subconsciously it played on their mind: 'Anyway we will win the championship, let's concentrate on the European Cup.' And they were more convincing this year in the European Cup than the championship."

Wenger enjoys his verbal jousting with Ferguson, calling it "part of the game and part of what people expect". His feeling that this Double has eclipsed the previous one is plain. "We are unbeaten away, we have scored in every game and we have played exciting football," Wenger said. "We have won it in style and with an impressive record. I believe we will make 87 points and that's nearly 10 more than last time." Next season he wants much the same.

Unlike in 1998, we have a very young team now. That's why I say we want to dominate

16|07|2003
Agents rejoice as Abramovich turns on the money tap

Richard Williams

Just when it looked as though football was about to return to sharing the real world with the rest of us — when it seemed, for example, as though Steve McManaman might be able to endure the unspeakable pain of finishing his career on £20,000 a week rather than the £60,000 to which he had become accustomed — along comes Roman Abramovich with his oil tankers full of highly inflammable cash, ready to turn the dying embers of the transfer market back into a raging furnace.

No doubt many of Chelsea's fans are already intoxicated by the idea of Stamford Bridge becoming the Estadio Bernabéu of northern Europe, peopled exclusively by superstars. Christian Vieri, Patrick Vieira, Raul, Steven Gerrard, Edgar Davids, Alessandro Nesta and Andriy Shevchenko are just a few of the names "linked" with Chelsea in recent weeks, since Abramovich's ambitions became apparent. Who will end up wearing the blue strip at the beginning of the season is anybody's guess. But what Abramovich has certainly done is to breathe new hope into the almost lifeless bodies of the football agents, who were facing a summer in which David Beckham and Ronaldinho were providing virtually the only headline news in the transfer market.

Until Ken Bates and some of his fellow shareholders accepted Abramovich's offer, the Premiership clubs were virtually united in offering little comfort to an agent hoping to avail himself and his clients of the sort of largesse with which they had become familiar since television money took football to another economic level.

At certain clubs players were even accepting the need to take a reduction in their salaries, led by Vieri, Hernán Crespo and Alvaro Recoba, Internazionale's three star forwards.

A player such as the 34-year-old Dennis Bergkamp, his contract at an end, was forced to consider an offer of approximately 50% of his former wages for one more season with Arsenal. So far Bergkamp has chosen not to follow the example of the Inter trio. Others have seen things in a different, realistic light.

Abramovich, however, has turned the clock back all the way to the day before yesterday, when money gushed into football like oil from one of his wells and no one ever dreamed it could end. His desk must be piled high with faxes from agents alerting him to the qualities of players only too anxious to declare their allegiance to such a well-funded club.

So will he become the most influential figure in football since Rupert Murdoch, another foreign tycoon who transformed the economics of the game?

Or will his money merely enable a few lucky clubs to pay off creditors, put a smile back on their bankers' faces and look to the future with renewed confidence?

The only real victims of the recession of the last year are the players at the lower levels of the Nationwide League who have been released and find themselves floating in a market that no longer places a significant value on their services. Abramovich's money is unlikely to find its way down to their level, even in the merest trickle.

No doubt quite a significant proportion of it will be banked by the likes of Bernie Mandic, a previously unknown figure who allegedly has been or shortly will be in receipt of £2m for his part in Harry Kewell's move from Leeds to Liverpool. No doubt Mandic and his colleagues have families to feed. But the public cannot be blamed if they now view football agents with the sort of distrust and distaste normally reserved for lawyers and journalists.

As for Chelsea, it seems a pity that the policy pursued by Claudio Ranieri last season – best summarised as making the best use of the resources at hand, rather than throwing money at every problem – has been turned quite so spectacularly on its head.

Financial stringency was the mother of a more modest, inventive and consistent Chelsea last season, and it is easy to imagine another influx of would-be *galácticos* upsetting the balance.

The blossoming of Frank Lampard, quite against the expectations of some of us, is greatly to Ranieri's credit, as well as to England's benefit. The development of Carlton Cole and Mikael Forssell into an effective striking partnership would be another blow against profligacy and on behalf of common sense.

Let us hope that the quiet £6m capture of the highly promising Glen Johnson is a truer indication of the effect of the arrival of the petro-rouble as Chelsea's unit of currency than all the nonsense about Vieri, Vieira and the rest.

Abramovich has turned the clock back to when money gushed like oil from his wells

15|05|2004
Arsenal content if there are no twists to the plot

Today, the Gunners should become the first undefeated top-flight champions since Preston in 1889. By Kevin McCarra

Remember that drizzly afternoon when Thierry Henry used the dregs of his strength to get fractionally ahead of a defender and the full-time whistle, for the equaliser that saved Arsenal's unbeaten Premiership record? Nobody does. Nothing remotely like that has happened in a season when the club have turned the seemingly impossible into the virtually inevitable.

They have not needed much recourse to luck or histrionics and, presuming they deal with relegated Leicester City at Highbury this afternoon, Arsène Wenger's side will be the first champions to go through the top-flight programme undefeated since Preston North End in 1889.

Uncanny as the achievement is, the film rights would not fetch much at auction because there has been no suspense, no late twist to the plot. There was barely an outfield Arsenal player in shot for the sole cliffhanger, when Ruud van Nistelrooy hit the bar in stoppage-time with the penalty that would have given Manchester United victory in September.

Arsenal have never been behind in the last 20 minutes of any of their 37 matches. "More often it's been a case of clubs clawing us back rather than us catching up," said Wenger. The extraordinary feature of the team has been the consistency with which they demonstrate their superiority.

Even with a win today they will fall just short of the 91-point record that Manchester United set for the 20-club Premiership in 2000 but Sir Alex Ferguson's team lost three fixtures. Although the current Arsenal are more susceptible to draws, they rarely have a real off day.

This, as Wenger pointed out, is the second time in three seasons that Arsenal are unbeaten in away Premiership matches. The statistics smack of remorselessness but the team are celebrated because, with such players as Henry, Dennis Bergkamp and Robert Pires, they are a sheer pleasure to watch.

"Since I have been in football there has been a basic question to face," Wenger reflected. "Are you pretty or are you efficient? It's as if you have got to choose. What makes me very happy this season is that people have enjoyed watching us but we did win as well. That's good. What is dangerous for football is when people become convinced that you have to play a boring game to win."

There is no emergency plan at Highbury. Wenger wondered aloud yesterday if he might try his new signing Robin van Persie as a "target man" but the Dutchman is unlikely to score with a barging header from a hanging cross as the team resort to long-ball methods.

Wenger made his choice long ago and does not deviate from a fast-paced, highly technical approach. "It's more difficult for us in the winter when the pitch is not so good and it's windy," he conceded. "That can be a handicap. We play more of a summer game."

It was on a spring afternoon at Highbury five weeks ago that Arsenal looked as if they might not only be beaten by Liverpool but also blow the Premiership completely. In the previous few days they had been eliminated from the FA Cup and Champions League by, respectively, Manchester United and Chelsea.

"We were losing 2-1 to Liverpool at half-time and we could have taken a knockout blow there, after the right cross and left cross that had just hit us," Wenger recalled of the eventual 4-2 win. "When we got through that I felt we could go far."

Wenger, while a student, had completed a season undefeated with Mutzig in the French Third Division and, despite an utterly different degree of difficulty, he has always had in mind the possibility of Premiership invincibility.

He was even jeered for setting such a target last season but, a man of high ambition, sought his own equivalent to Milan's 1992 feat of going through the exacting Serie A fixture list with no defeats. Now he is set to savour fulfilment today.

"It would reflect how great the team has been this season and it would prepare us for next season, which we would start with the record still going," he said. "Recently we have been doing just enough not to lose but now we want to do enough to win. I would like the game to reflect the quality of the football that we have played over the season."

His thoughts cannot be reined in and he is already stepping into the next phase at Arsenal. He might be able to scrape together money for a right-back as cover for Lauren or a goalkeeper to understudy Jens Lehmann while Stuart Taylor is still trapped in a slow recovery from a shoulder injury.

There are also approaches from West Ham, West Bromwich, Bolton and Norwich to be considered now that the young midfielder David Bentley is to be sent out on loan for a year. Even the past cries out for Wenger's attention. He confirmed that the 37-year-old Martin Keown will leave to play at another club once an appearance today ensures one last League winner's medal.

Wenger marvelled at the sight of the veteran continuing to practise yesterday after training had officially ended. "He has that motivation," said the manager. "If you don't have that, you will never be a special player."

Judging by results, such commitment is rife at Highbury.

02|06|2004
Mourinho is bound by old ties to his backroom boys

Chelsea's new manager knows how to be successful and intends to repeat the process at the Bridge, writes Matt Scott

Jose Mourinho revealed earlier this season that the secret of Porto's success was "two years' hard work with the same players and the same coaching staff". He will crave such stability at Chelsea.

Mourinho will attempt to smooth the transition to London by surrounding himself with some of those who made his last season in Portugal so stunning. He has asked to bring with him three of his Porto coaching staff, men whose careers are closely tied to his own. The first, and most important, is his assistant Baltemar Brito.

The 53-year-old Brazilian has known Mourinho since the Portuguese was in his early teens. Having left his homeland to ply his footballing trade in Europe, Brito played towards the end of his career under Mourinho's father Felix at the small northern club Rio Ave.

A centre-half who acted as the on-pitch lieutenant of Mourinho Sr, he helped Rio Ave to the final of the 1984 Portuguese Cup and became a close family friend. But it is to Jose Mourinho's wife Tami that Brito owes the progression from friend to Champions League-winning coach. Brito is aware of his debt to Mrs Mourinho, referring to her as his "madrinha", or godmother, in recognition of her influence on his career.

Having been sacked by Benfica in October 2000, Mourinho headed for the more modest Uniao Leiria and was at a loss as to who should accompany him. When Tami reminded her husband of the commanding personality of Brito, he realised there was someone he could trust to act as his right-hand man.

That bond is something Mourinho always attempts to foster with his staff. Following Porto's Champions League semi-final win over Deportivo La Coruna, there appeared to be an emotion bordering on love in the eyes of Mourinho's devoted entourage as they stared fixedly at their mentor, a regard which is unusual in football.

Another to hold Mourinho in elevated esteem is Porto's 28-year-old fitness trainer Rui Faria, also wanted at Chelsea by Mourinho. Faria seems equally to have stumbled on his position at Porto. Born in the unexceptional central Portuguese town of Barcelos, he was, like Mourinho, a graduate in physical education who had never played football of any distinction. For Faria, as for Mourinho, that would not prevent him harbouring a burning ambition to work in the game.

It took him to a seminar day at Barcelona's Camp Nou, where his path was to cross Mourinho's, who was working at the time as Louis van Gaal's assistant manager.

The pair chatted and it became clear to Mourinho that his coaching philosophy matched that of the young PE graduate. Mourinho was impressed by the young man, stayed in touch and, when he took the job at Uniao Leiria in April 2001, appointed Faria fitness coach and video analyst.

Only a fortnight into his job, though, the then 25-year-old Faria thought he might be made redundant as abruptly as he had been hired. The Leiria chairman and his attendants came to the training ground to watch Mourinho's session one morning. There followed a stand-off between the coach and his superiors after Mourinho told the chairman to get out.

Though the chairman politely declined, Mourinho stood his ground and won the battle of wills. The callow Faria was convinced he would be sacked. "In all my life I had been employed only two weeks," he said.

If Mourinho adopts a similarly confrontational attitude with his new club's owner he will be in trouble. Roman Abramovich would not suffer such treatment and he is expected to be more interventionist than any of Mourinho's previous presidents. The Russian enjoys his European tours in search of new playing talent and it is not a role he is likely to relinquish.

Jose Mourinho makes an early statement of intent before winning the next two Premier League titles with Chelsea

27|11|2004

Defender cast in unwanted role of target man

Racist taunts may have got to Arsenal's left-back Ashley Cole but his spirit is undimmed, reports Michael Walker

How great it would have been to have sat down with Ashley Cole in interview room 15 at Arsenal's training ground and talked solely about football. How great it would be to write this piece without mentioning that Cole's mother, Sue, is white. How great it would be if Luis Aragones, the manager of Spain, was colour blind. Sadly Aragones's remark about Cole's Arsenal colleague Thierry Henry set in train events that culminated in the racist abuse heaped on England's black players in the Bernabéu Stadium 10 days ago, actions that continue to reverberate.

Consequently Cole's colour and culture became the subject of discussion. He responded politely and articulately, spoke forgivingly of racism he endured when young, of having Ledley King and Jlloyd Samuel as close friends then, of his love of Michael Jackson, Alexander O'Neal and his uncle's insistence on having Elvis Presley on in the car on the way to matches as a boy. None of which — certainly not Jackson and Presley — is black and white.

"At primary school you'd get kids who don't know what it means saying 'you black bastard', 'nigger'," Cole said. "You don't condone it but kids don't know what it means. My dad's from Barbados but I lived with my mum. She brought me up; my uncle took me to the football. I grew up in a white family, I'd say. It was Bow, east London, with Ledley, Jlloyd, just a lot of young people trying to get through life."

Cole is getting through. The title race rather than the human race would be his preferred topic — Arsenal's game tomorrow at Liverpool and Chelsea's Premiership challenge — but this day, blue was not the colour. Aragones had specified an Arsenal player's blackness. So uncomfortable questions are prompted.

Cole addressed it using a football cliché — with a twist. "At the end of the day," he said, "I'm human. I'm English — I was born here. Of course I'm a different colour from you but I'm still human. The main thing is, I'm human — like everyone else. Because I'm a different colour doesn't mean there is a difference."

It is a remarkable fact to have to assert in 2004 but the humanity of Cole and England's black players was questioned in the Bernabéu by people willing to paint them as members of the animal kingdom.

Spain shocked the 23-year-old and he was glad his mother had not travelled to the match. Back in England she turned off the television in disgust; back in England Cole felt as he should, at home. The abuse Dwight Yorke received at Ewood Park last Sunday is a reminder that there is long way to go in England too but Cole is positive about his country.

"I think England has become more tolerant," he said. "Walking down the street you don't hear things. In the Premiership I have not heard anything — Manchester, Liverpool, wherever you go, it's good. I think the foreigners can vouch for that and I think the T-shirts and campaigns have worked, definitely. But when you go away with your club team or your country it seems to be getting worse and worse. It's not changing. Thierry got most of it at PSV [two seasons ago]. I have had it for England in Slovakia, Macedonia, Albania, now Spain. It just seems to be everywhere apart from England."

As an example of England's tolerance, Cole said that his being the face of a new sportswear campaign was significant. He pointed out that two other players abused in Madrid, Rio Ferdinand and Jermaine Jenas, are fronting advertising for other brands. "It's good for me to be in the shop window — 20 years ago you maybe would not have seen a black person in the shop

Ashley Cole won two Premier League titles with Arsenal, before moving in acrimonious circumstances to Chelsea

window. As I said, I think times have changed and in England for the better. I'm happy with it. But there are white players doing things, too. It's equal in England."

In Spain, though, it is different. Cole's equanimity was shattered in Madrid and when a copy of last Friday's *El Mundo* was placed in front of him showing his 44th-minute face-to-face confrontation with Aragones, Cole's unease was plain. "Of course you don't want to hear racist chants but sometimes as a player you have to take it," he said. "But when you hear the manager saying things and not backing down then it does get to you a bit.

"When I went to get the ball there he pushed me. He pushed me first. As a coach you can't do that. I pushed him, which was stupid. I shouldn't have gone down to his level. But I was just shocked that he pushed me. I didn't understand why. I didn't do anything to him — I was just walking off to get the ball. I shouldn't have pushed him back but, with everything that was going on, I was a little bit mad and lost my head a bit."

Given what Cole had just endured, he had good reason to lose his cool. For him the pain of the whole Aragones affair was increased by the central presence in it of Jose Antonio Reyes, another valued and trusted Arsenal team-mate. Reyes was the player Aragones made the "black shit" remark to and Cole said Reyes left the Bernabéu wondering what the world would make of his country. "He was disappointed," Cole said. "It's his country. He was pretty down about it. He's not like that; he's so nice. We talked about it a bit but we couldn't laugh about it."

Laughter, one quickly discovers, is part of Cole's make-up and, as some of these questions provoked sighs, he was happy when they were finished.

Five years after his November debut for Arsenal, in a League Cup tie at Middlesbrough, Madrid capped an eventful month for Cole. Since late October's "Battle of Old Trafford", in which Cole was the victim of Ruud van Nistelrooy's violence and after which Cole was named as the pizza-thrower (strongly denied) in the tunnel, he has been in the eye of a tornado. It is probably just as well that, when Arsenal go back to Old Trafford next Wednesday in the League Cup, Arsène Wenger will be taking his young team.

"It's been an odd month," Cole said. "It always seems to be me. Of course I've done stupid things in my career and I do always seem to be in the paper but I hate seeing myself. Every time we play Man U something comes up.

"We lost the game and it is hard not to think about it because it's in every paper: who did this, who did that. And I was named — shock. It's just so annoying when you see your name in the paper for these things you didn't do. I didn't chuck anything. I weren't even there, nowhere near it. I was in the changing room. Soup! Crazy.

"Of course there were tackles, and there was the penalty, but passion runs high in these games and both teams are so eager to win. But I did think the media blew it out of proportion — a bit. Everyone saying we were chucking food or there was a big fight in the tunnel. It wasn't like that. Of course a few things happened that shouldn't have happened but tempers were running high. But I talk to Gary Neville and we laugh about it now. Yet it is still in the paper — "Pizza-throwing II" when we play them at Old Trafford."

After that come much bigger fixtures, at home to Rosenborg in the Champions League and then, a fortnight tomorrow, Chelsea. It reflects on Liverpool that the Chelsea fixture is already stalking the Arsenal horizon and Cole understands why: "Don't get me wrong, Liverpool is going to be a tough game. But I don't think it's got the spice it normally has. It's probably Arsenal and Chelsea who are the two now.

"Never count out Man U because they've got great players but it seems there's just something missing there, a little click. We've definitely got it and Chelsea definitely have it now. It seems like us and Chelsea. And regaining the title is definitely the main aim for us. Of course we want to do well in the Champions League but it's so hard to do well in both. Man U proved they can do it but they were quite lucky against Bayern Munich. If you asked the players here, they want to win the league. Just to prove that we are still around."

20|04|2005

Mourinho creates a title template which others are sure to copy

Kevin McCarra

....

Chelsea do not need to look at the league table to know that they will soon be champions. The first concession speeches are being made and they are grumpy rather than gracious. Arsenal's full-back Lauren goes to Stamford Bridge this evening with the aftertaste in his mouth of bitter words about the supposedly boring style with which Jose Mourinho's team have prevailed.

The champions elect can spare themselves the trouble of demanding apologies. If Chelsea only wait, they are bound to be flattered by imitation. Their forthcoming triumph will be the most influential in Premiership history and rivals will spend the summer analysing Mourinho's immediate mastery.

Where previous continental managers have floundered, he has triumphed by marrying traits from mainland Europe to the rumbustious habits of the Premiership. The foreign influence has revitalised the domestic scene before, particularly when Arsenal were in ravishingly "invincible" form, but rigour has not come easily to the Highbury club. They have conceded 33 goals in the Premiership this season.

Chelsea have been breached on only 12 occasions. Such a statistic encourages people such as Lauren to think that Arsenal can occupy the moral high ground even if they have been ejected from the top of the table. This misrepresents Mourinho, since his real purpose has been to attain a stability that the Premiership has never seen before.

His team are increasingly entertaining and only Arsenal, whose flair comes at the expense of durability, have scored more goals. It is Mourinho's aim to ensure that his side seldom have to attack out of desperation. With the defence so dependable, the players' patience is unruffled and nine of the 25 Premiership wins to date have come in games that were scoreless at the interval. If steady Chelsea gather 12 further points from the final six games, they will break the record of 92 set by Manchester United in 1994, when there were four matches more in the programme.

Rather than admit publicly that Mourinho has created a landscape in which rivals can no longer find their bearings, Arsène Wenger prefers the soothing thought that the Portuguese has merely extended Claudio Ranieri's work. "I don't see as big a difference as people make out," he said. "They have stabilised the defensive record. They have very influential players who are on the up, like Frank Lampard, John Terry and Eidur Gudjohnsen."

The Arsenal manager turns a blind eye to the manner in which conditions have been altered to make success possible at Chelsea, who were trophy-less under Ranieri. It was the defence which Mourinho reshaped most radically, even if Petr Cech had been signed before his appointment. A further £33m was spent in total to introduce Ricardo Carvalho and Paulo Ferreira to the back four.

The latter is so significant that the team have been noticeably more vulnerable since he cracked a metatarsal. Arsenal will thereby be heartened about their prospects tonight. It says everything about the nature of the new Chelsea that they coped more readily with the loss of the star attacker Arjen Robben. Though the personnel are interesting, the effectiveness arises from an un-English discipline. Mourinho's team is a series of many layers, with Claude Makelele ahead of the centre-backs, Lampard in front of him and Damien Duff a judicious distance adrift of Didier Drogba. The demarcations show the manager's preference for specialised roles.

It was already Makelele's instinct to cover the defence years before his arrival at Stamford Bridge but the focus on that task is tighter than ever under Mourinho's regime. There is little haste about Chelsea now. Unlike virtually any previous English club they are comfortable when holding the ball and waiting for a breakthrough.

Sir Alex Ferguson was struggling to engineer this method before the advent of Mourinho, but six goalless draws in the Premiership so far prove he has not yet discovered how to fend off torpor. United cannot quite notch necessary goals as Chelsea do. Those reluctant defenders Arsenal cannot quite keep clean sheets as Chelsea do.

Mourinho, realising there had to be some accommodation with the football society he had invaded, tailored his approach to the Premiership to a certain extent. The differences were always apparent to him and he was surprised, as Porto manager, when Spurs bought Helder Postiga from him for £6.25m. He could not picture the striker in the brawl of the English game.

Mourinho, at heavy expense, revealed his own concept of a centre-forward for the Premiership by signing Drogba for £24m. The Ivory Coast international, now fit and increasingly confident, should be important to Chelsea's prospects at the close of the Champions League, but his huskiness and disconcertingly deft moments have already delivered 16 goals in any case.

Wenger, pointing to half-ignored figures such as Scott Parker, Geremi, Alexey Smertin and Jiri Jarosik, highlighted the scale of the squad that Chelsea, unlike Arsenal, can afford. It is a fair observation, yet means present problems of their own and it is certainly no shortage of numbers or lack of investment in the transfer market that handicaps United.

Though his comments are occasionally excessive, Mourinho's labours are marked by a sense of proportion. Team selections, tactical switches and squad management are all steeped in common sense. The scale of operations is never impersonal either. With seven players who have appeared in 28 or more Premiership games so far, the bonds in the squad are strong at a club who used to be mocked.

A former gaggle of dilettantes have become role models as well as targets for all the teams left in their wake.

It was Makelele's instinct to cover the defence, but it is even more so under Mourinho

08|05|2006

A fond farewell to Highbury

Cheers, tears and a victory send-off: Sam Wollaston joins the crowd saying goodbye to Arsenal's spiritual home

To begin with it all goes according to the script. The sun is out, Highbury looks beautiful, Pires scores. This is the send-off Highbury is meant to have after 93 years as Arsenal's home. And it gets better, for Gooners anyway: news comes of a West Ham goal against Tottenham. Arsenal will claim that vital fourth place, there will be Champions League football next season in the new stadium, whatever happens next week in Paris.

"We're the North Bank, we're the North Bank, we're the North Bank Highbury," sings the North Bank, for the last time, giving Highbury the full, three-syllable treatment it requires to scan and deserves for its swan song.

"We're the Clock End, we're the Clock End, we're the Clock End, High-bur-ee," comes the echo, at volume 11 (there'll be no talk of the Highbury library today). It was never the greatest of football songs, either in tune or lyrics, but there is — was — something just right about it. Highbury is an old-style ground with open corners and four separate stands, each with its own character and distinct voice. Because of the tiny pitch the stands are not far from each other. Highbury can — could — sing in four parts.

Before the game, in the streets, there is a carnival atmosphere and also a sadness but it is seen to be a necessary sadness, like a favourite old tree having to be cut down. The three Sanger sisters, Frances, Marian and Betty, have been coming since the 70s — no before that, says Frances. "They used to open the gates 15 minutes before the end of the games and we used to sneak in," says Frances. And she remembers the Cassius Clay v Henry Cooper fight here in 1966, when she was 11. "The new stadium will be fantastic," she says, "but I'll miss this old place." They do not have tickets today. They have just come along to say goodbye.

Highbury may not match the scale of Old Trafford or the charged atmosphere of Anfield, but it is unique. The splendid art deco facade of the East Stand stays. The West Stand entrance is also reprieved but everything else goes. Where today 38,349

Thierry Henry scores the final goal at Highbury to sign off 93 years of history with a hat-trick in the 4-2 defeat of Wigan

tearful Gooners (and many more outside) are saying goodbye to the place that is their home from home, 711 new homes will soon go up, in seven-storey apartment blocks. There are a few still available, starting at £230,000.

And the pitch itself? When the award-winning groundsman Paul Burgess rumbles off with his fleet of mowers and rollers to his new Eden, 500 yards down the road, in will come the landscape architect Christopher Bradley-Hole, a gold medal winner at Chelsea – the flower show, not the football club. His garden will be calm and well-proportioned he says, and will combine the feeling of European spaces with English tradition (Arsène Wenger might approve). It is not known yet whether ball games will be allowed.

Back on the pitch someone forgot the script. Wigan equalise, then go one up. The news from Upton Park is not good either. Tottenham equalise, then Teddy Sheringham misses a penalty (when was Teddy ever going to score that one?). The sun goes in.

Highbury has seen a lot since Woolwich Arsenal first played Leicester Fosse here on September 6 1913 after moving from south of the river. March 9 1935, Arsenal v Sunderland, saw its biggest ever crowd – 73,295, mostly men in flat caps. In 1939 there was a murder on the pitch, albeit in a British film called The Arsenal Stadium Mystery. During the war it was used as an air-raid protection centre, but still took a heavy pounding, as did Henry Cooper in that fight. There have been cricket and baseball, possibly a dead horse (under the North Bank) and definitely a live squirrel.

There has been some football too: 13 League titles, three Doubles, a Fairs Cup. There is some football again on the pitch today. Someone – Thierry Henry, of course – remembers the script. He takes over, gets his hat trick and Arsenal win 4-2. The news at Upton Park is good. It is almost perfect except the sun does not come out again and Dennis Bergkamp's delicious flick goes just over.

After the final whistle a marching band returns to Highbury for the first time since ... well, no one remembers exactly when. Alex Morgan, the Police tenor from a long time ago, sings a song. And a procession of former players parades around the ground they used to play on: Steve Bould, Liam Brady, Cesar, Charlie George, Pat Jennings, Malcolm Macdonald, Graham Rix, Emmanuel Petit, it goes on and on, even Perry Groves turns up.

"Oh Rocky, Rocky. Rocky, Rocky, Rocky Rocastle," sings the crowd for one who cannot make it. I doubt if there is a dry eye in the house.

Roger Daltrey sings another song, a new one about Highbury, Henry gets his golden boot, fireworks are fired, red and white ticker tape streams down and then it is time to go. The carnival continues outside but suddenly Highbury is an empty place, echoing with memories and waiting for the diggers to come.

17|05|2007

Whatever happened to Jose Mourinho?

He introduced himself as 'a special one' and we agreed – but now we're not so sure. Barney Ronay asks why

....

Loathe him, hate him or just feel slightly irritated by him, for the past three years it has been almost impossible not to have an opinion of some sort about Jose Mourinho. In fact, that is not totally fair. Mourinho's period as manager of Chelsea has been measured out, not just in bold type headlines but in a public fascination that has taken in pretty much every emotional response it is possible to have to a haughty, infuriatingly handsome man in a well-cut dark suit. Most fanciable, richest, most widely imitated on prime-time comedy sketch shows: Jose has somehow managed to smuggle the grim business of football management into previously uncharted areas of the popular imagination.

In spite of which there is a growing sense that the tide of public affection may have begun to turn decisively against the world's most famous middle-aged Portuguese. The news this week that he had been arrested for arguing with policemen about his dog (he received a caution for obstructing the police in a row over his Yorkshire terrier's quarantine) had a weary inevitability about it, providing a kind of reductio ad absurdum of Mourinho's ludicrously feisty persona. Yeah, we thought to ourselves, that sounds about right.

The Yorkshire terrier affair followed closely the more serious business of losing the Premiership title his club had held for the past two years. The final whistle in the decisive draw at Arsenal saw Mourinho take to the pitch to make an unusual – and oddly unconvincing – "chin-up" gesture towards his players. At moments like these it is probably Chelsea's managerial tyro (still only 44) who really needs to keep his head. For the first time since he began his managerial career in earnest at Porto in 2002, Mourinho had not won a league championship. Success is key to his elaborately constructed persona. Without it Mourinho simply makes no sense. The unshakable conviction in his own superiority becomes not just boorish but ridiculous. Take away the trophies and he becomes a pantomime Brian Clough, a fading braggart, the boy who works down the chip shop and swears he is Elvis.

So where did the aura go? Partly it is physical. Looks have been a potent aspect of his appeal to a wider audience and Mourinho has undoubtedly begun to show the strain. When he arrived in Britain, he was the coming man: a spunky underdog with an excitingly modern take on the role of football manager. He looked like a vigorously youthful Hollywood gangster or like the cooler, sexier older brother of one of his players. This is no longer the case. Three years on, Mourinho looks exhausted, his eyes are deep set, his silky hair atrophied into a greying and often greasy bouffant. Suddenly he looks like a football manager and, as everybody knows, Jose was supposed to be so much more than that.

"Please don't call me arrogant but I'm European champion and I think I'm a special one," he declared at his first press conference after becoming Chelsea manager in June 2004. It was not exactly Oscar Wilde but in the neurotically guarded world of football management this was heady stuff. The Premiership swooned and over the next year the effect would seem to spread to pretty much everywhere else. Within weeks Mourinho had begun the impossible feat of transforming Roman Abramovich's monstrously constructed Chelsea footballing empire into something not just almost likable but weirdly cool.

The pattern of Mourinho's every public utterance finding its way on to both back and front pages of the papers was soon established. With Chelsea leading the table at the turn of the year he publicly mocked rumours the club were about to sign David Beckham, dismissing the England captain as "a Hollywood star". In January of his first season he produced his first devastating checkmate in English football's much trumpeted "mind games", through the simple device of shaking hands with each Manchester United player as they ran out on to the pitch for a Carling Cup quarter final – and Mourinho has a wonderful handshake, a pioneering mixture of neck-cuffs, cheek-pinches and high fives – as though conferring some lofty honour. To a man United looked utterly bemused. Chelsea won 2-1.

They went on to win the final, too, although not without Mourinho stealing the show by getting himself sent off for publicly "shushing" the Liverpool fans. But Mourinho's star was still very much on the rise. In April he was banned from the touchline and the dressing room for a Champions League tie against Bayern Munich but still managed to give his team talk through the extraordinary chutzpah, it later emerged, of having himself secreted inside a laundry basket to get into and out of the team's dressing room. In May his "lucky" overcoat fetched £22,000 at a charity auction in aid of the Indian ocean tsunami relief fund.

Ah yes, that coat. Mourinho's sense of style has received a hysterically favourable press during his spell in England. In truth, the overcoat, symbol of Mourinho the cosmopolitan, the urbane, the deep-thinking, is remarkable for only one thing: it is not a tracksuit. This seemed to be enough. In November he was voted best-dressed football manager of all time in a nationwide survey. That same December he was voted Britain's second best-dressed man by the style magazine *GQ*. He finished second again the following year, this time to Clive Owen, the editorial musing over how "he makes minimalism work in the everyday and by doing so makes it modern".

Mourinho was also installed as the *New Statesman*'s man of the year for 2005, rewarded by the political magazine for "his swagger, his sense of melodrama . . . his polyglot sophistication". These qualities were no doubt captured by the Mourinho waxwork unveiled at Madame Tussaud's two months later. Mourinho's comment that the statue was by far the better-looking of the two is perhaps not the best example of the wit which, in his early days at least, was often present as he transformed the dreaded football press conference into a form of light entertainment. In the flesh Mourinho has a rock star-ish magnetism, at least in the usually charisma-free world of the dug-out and the training ground. His voice is a playful drawl, alternating between thunderously outspoken and almost kittenishly mocking. He once claimed he was more worried about contracting avian flu than being caught in the Premiership by Manchester United. "For me pressure is bird flu. It's not fun and I'm more scared of it than football . . . I'll have to buy a mask."

Buoyant, made for TV and our first celebrity manager, he hurled his second Premiership winner's medal a year ago into the Stamford Bridge crowd, a gesture that seemed to combine arrogance, iconoclasm and reckless generosity. Even non-Chelsea fans, now, were smitten.

It was the following season that the tide finally began to turn and Mourinho got bogged down in spats, bust-ups, feuds and wars of words. In October 2006 he made his first real wrong move when he accused Berkshire emergency services of being too slow to arrive to treat one of his players, injured during a game against Reading, a remark that led to the Reading West MP, Martin Salter, accusing him of "taking a pop at hard-working NHS staff". October saw him sliding on the knees of his Hugo Boss suit past the Barcelona bench after a late equalising goal in the Camp Nou, an inflammatory and extraordinarily provocative celebration that managers just do not do. Since then the public set-tos have become wearyingly frequent: Arsène Wenger, Alex Ferguson and even the referee Mike Riley, whom Mourinho called a "filha de puta" ("son of whore") before extricating himself with trademark rakishness by claiming, dismissively, "I say this kind of word 10 times in every 15 words. I say it 50 times a game, 50 times in training".

And at times this season Mourinho has seemed to be repeating himself, banging on about the same things over and over. This has probably been the crux of his faltering appeal: the insistence on an anti-Chelsea conspiracy among referees, the

Gone is the back of an envelope. Jose Mourinho lays a personalised notebook on the wall of Chelsea's dug-out before the match

Premier League and the media; the post-match obsession with disputed penalty kicks; the accusation in October last year, subsequently retracted, that Everton's Andrew Johnson was a cheat; the frankly unpleasant remarks about the Manchester United winger Cristiano Ronaldo having "a tough childhood" and "no education". And the sense that the playfulness had begun to congeal into an unceasing tabloid polemic, that Mourinho was turning into just another football manager with a gripe – and we already have plenty of those. His attempts to wind up Liverpool players before Chelsea's losing Champions League semi-final led to the Reds' defender Jamie Carragher dismissing him (the impertinence!) as "the funniest thing to come out of London since Del Boy and Rodney". Rest assured nobody will be voting for Jose in any best-dressed or man of the year polls this year. The coat, the sneer, the offensive remarks: it all just seems a little bit tired.

But there may yet be another twist. Strangely, since the loss of the Premiership title earlier this month there is a sense that public opinion may have begun to shift again. Mourinho the loser: it is like a fascinating piece of rebranding for a high-end product that was looking past it. There have already been green shoots of a recovery. A section of Southampton fans were seen imitating the Mourinho "chin-up" gesture on Tuesday night during their team's defeat in the Championship play-offs. And Mourinho himself seems to have grasped the need for re-invention. "After all that has happened this season, and that is a lot, I've reached the conclusion that I am a good loser," he mused at the weekend. Yes, that sounds about right, too: Jose Mourinho, not just any old loser but the best-dressed, best-paid and best-looking loser in the world.

25/08/2007
Forget Vieira and Henry, meet the new superman

Four years after his arrival, talisman Cesc Fábregas tells Donald McRae why Thierry's loss may be the team's gain

"This is quite hard for me to believe," Cesc Fábregas says as he takes off his baseball cap and gently bends back its rim in a gesture of genuine surprise. "I came to London in September 2003 and so next week it will be four years since I left Barcelona for Arsenal. Everything has come so quickly that it's unbelievable. I was 16 then and now I am 20. A lot has changed."

The young Spanish midfielder, who symbolises the new heart of a football club caught in a state of unsettling flux, was once just another foreign apprentice trying to find his way in a strange country. But Fábregas has become the player they revere most at Arsenal, a figure second only to Arsène Wenger in terms of his symbolic significance to Arsenal's future. An unresolved battle over ownership of the club has been framed by the departure of David Dein, Wenger's great friend in the boardroom, and further losses on the field itself.

Thierry Henry's move to Barcelona at the start of the summer underlined Arsenal's dependence on Fábregas. If he had accepted a persistent offer from Real Madrid to line up against Henry in La Liga, Arsenal would have been in disarray. However, confirmed as their talisman, Fábregas believes the transfer of the French striker could usher in a defiantly positive transformation. He is intriguingly candid in admitting that Henry's mere presence often intimidated his team-mates.

"Thierry is the best I've ever played with. There's no doubt. But there was this other factor. He is Thierry Henry. When I came I felt I was low and he was high. It was a big difference and for a long time I was intimidated. When I had the ball I felt I had no choice but to look for him. I did this because, one, he is the best and, two, because I had the feeling I had to pass it to him. He has such a strong character that he almost made you feel this way. I needed him to say, 'Look, you don't always have to play the ball to me.' Once he said that, I was free and I gave him even more assists. Thierry is a very intelligent man and I wish him all the luck in the world at Barça."

Yet when Real pursued him, with the president Ramón Calderón calling Fábregas personally, was he not tempted to follow Henry back to Spain? "No. I always knew I would stay. Especially when Thierry went, I knew it would be a very important year for me at the club. It is a personal challenge but also a challenge for the team as well – to win something without Thierry. He was such a winner and of course we will miss that but we have other options now. And, if we can make it, then it will mean we are a great team. We are starting a new project without players like Thierry and Patrick [Vieira] but we are capable of something special."

Wenger's impact on his most glittering protégés – Vieira, Henry and Fábregas – is indisputable. It explains why Arsenal's entire future often seems to rest on their manager remaining at the club. "I believe Arsène will sign a new contract. Definitely. I think he will stay because he knows Arsenal will not be the same without him. This is perfect for me because I am learning from Arsène all the time. He speaks to me even more now. In the first years I was here he never put any pressure on me. But he has so much knowledge that all you have to do is listen."

Fábregas is understandably cautious when asked about Dein's acrimonious exit. "Well, that's when everybody started to think whether or not the boss would go or stay. I don't know whether that had anything to do with Thierry's decision but we must just think about football and winning matches and titles.

Who knows exactly what will happen in the future? But right now we are all together and we want to win. I definitely feel we can win something this season.

"I have been training with these guys a lot and this team has quality and desire. They get angry whenever we lose. We get upset with each other when we don't do things properly and you need this passion, this desire, to win things. This team has it. But it's no good me just saying it to you in the newspaper. We have to turn the words into reality."

And so, committed to both Wenger and the club, Fábregas plans to galvanise a youthful side renowned for producing sublime if often wasteful patterns of play into formidable challengers in both the Premier League and Europe. The last four years have instilled a toughness and an equilibrium which suggests he might prove equal to the task.

"I am proud of how I coped but I knew what I wanted even before I came here. I knew if I had to be alone for two years then I could do it - as long as it meant first-team football. If I could show everybody what I could do on the pitch then there would be no problem at all with the loneliness. But I want to think about Manchester City and Sparta Prague now."

Another big week looms for Fábregas and Arsenal. Following today's home game against City, the Premier League's unexpected leaders after three straight victories, the second leg of a Champions League qualifier against Sparta Prague awaits on Wednesday. In Prague, led by a combative Fábregas, Arsenal withstood an abrasive challenge to win 2-0. That should be a telling score, guaranteeing the Champions League millions which will go a little further in reducing the massive debt incurred by their new stadium. But defeat today would leave Arsenal eight points adrift of the league leaders with only one game in hand.

Fábregas reveals, with a wry laugh, how such urgency fuels an obsession with football that makes him sound positively Wenger-esque. "When I speak to my girlfriend [Carla] at home sometimes she shouts at me because, at the same time, I am watching a small game from Holland, between two ordinary Dutch teams. Or maybe I am watching a replay of a game I've already seen four times. She gets cross with me because it's football, football, football. But it has always been like this. Maybe when I am thinking about a game, or watching it again to see what I did wrong or right, then I take time to reflect."

It is a sign of Fábregas's intelligence that, despite his age, he is able to concede, "I am still a bit insecure about myself. Sometimes we finish the game and I feel I play bad, even if we win. Every training session I get angry because I think I didn't do well. But it is completely different when I have to show my character on the pitch. On the outside sometimes I feel worried and blah-blah but on the pitch I'm always confident."

And yet the insecurities still return occasionally, once the heat of a game has faded? "Definitely. I don't need to tell my family when I feel bad because they see straight away how I feel. They are my parents and so, because I'm still young, they are the first ones I turn to whether I'm happy or sad. My girlfriend knows that as well. As soon as they see my face they know how I am on the inside. I talk to them after four hours, when the bad feelings have gone and I am calmer."

His startling youth is confirmed by some of his more relaxed early memories at Arsenal. "When I scored my first goal, against Wolverhampton, I went home and celebrated by drinking a Coca-Cola and eating a Kinder Egg. Even now I go twice a month to visit my old Irish landlady. Noreen is a very nice lady who helped me and Philippe Senderos a lot when we lived with her and her sons. I spent 2½ years there and it was very special. The last 18 months I have been mostly living on my own. My girlfriend was studying in London last year and she was with me but now she has had to go back to Spain to finish her course."

Other familiar faces have also gone. "Apart from Gilberto, Kolo [Touré] and Jens [Lehmann] – only those three – the team has changed a lot since I came. But look at Barcelona. Three seasons ago they were a club undergoing lots of changes because they went six years without winning anything. They changed their team completely and started winning again. Sometimes you need change."

Part of that difference entails Arsenal's readiness to stand up to increasingly physical opposition. "It's true we didn't feel comfortable in the past going to places like Everton and Bolton. But you have to learn and it took two years for us to adapt to this way of thinking. Before, we would know Blackburn and Bolton and the others would play this way and we were not confident we could handle it. Now we are ready to fight. Our objective is to show everybody that it doesn't matter whether teams are physical against us, whether they play the long-ball or good football, we will not lose easily this season."

Even Arsenal's European opposition now attempt to bully them. Sparta's captain, Tomas Repka, a former West Ham hardman, had promised to leave Arsenal's footballers in a clattering heap. "We were having dinner in Prague," Fábregas remembers, "and Tomas Rosicky told us what Repka said. I don't like to hear these words from other teams."

Fábregas duly brought down Repka, forcing him to limp away from a spiky encounter. It looked as if he had taunted the defender when he lay on the ground. Did he relish the "Fábregas the Enforcer" headlines? "No!" he laughs with a bemused shake of his head. "I've been educated to play football, not to kick. Of course, sometimes you have to do it because you want to help your team but I can guarantee I will not change my game."

Yet Fábregas's desire to display the steel to match his visionary talent can only bolster Arsenal's previously fragile brilliance. Approaching the fourth anniversary of his arrival in London another stronger and tougher side to the boy-wonder is already evident, even when he smiles sweetly and protests that "I'm not hard against other people. I'm only hard on myself."

21|09|2007

For Abramovich, success on its own will never be enough

Richard Williams

Jose Mourinho was never the right man for Roman Abramovich, to whom the Premier League title turns out to be of little more value or relevance than the cup for the egg and spoon race at the local junior school's sports day. When it comes to football, Abramovich is not in it for the long, exacting grind that produces English champions. To him, that is merely a necessary launching pad for the far greater dream in which success would put all Europe at his feet.

Abramovich wants Chelsea to succeed on the biggest available stage and he wants that success now. Knowing little about the game, he thinks it can all be achieved more or less immediately through the correct application of money. He is right, in one sense, but he appears not to understand that spending vast sums on a football club guarantees only that you will achieve your ambition eventually, not according to the precise timetable of your choosing.

For the Russian billionaire England is merely a convenient and tax-friendly base of operations. For the Chelsea project to succeed in his terms, it must resonate as loudly in Paris, Rome, Madrid and Moscow as it does in London. And it must do so with a special cachet, among a particular class of people, creating the sort of glamorous ambience that made Vanessa Redgrave remark, about 15 years ago, that going to a big match at San Siro was like attending an opening night at La Scala.

To begin with, he must have thought Mourinho was the man of his dreams. Probably no other head coach in the world could have walked into Stamford Bridge in the summer of 2004 and, within 12 months, brought the club its first league title in half a century. It is true that the foundations had already been laid. Mourinho was bequeathed a useful squad by Claudio Ranieri and, for a while, enjoyed the freedom to spend Abramovich's fortune more or less as he wished. But the first thing Chelsea needed, if they were to start winning trophies, was the application of rigour that Mourinho was unusually well qualified to apply.

Those two league titles, and the various domestic cups picked up during the Mourinho era, represented a magnificent achievement that will always occupy a special place in the hearts of the club's long-term fans, who had waited so long for something that glittered attractively to reveal itself as real gold.

For a while Chelsea were Porto writ large. Their tactics represented a model of realistic planning and execution, particularly in the matter of swift transition from defence to attack and vice versa, which was where Mourinho's talent lay. It was not a guarantee of champagne football, although in that first season Chelsea's opponents were so unprepared that Mourinho's players were able to score four goals against Premiership clubs on no fewer than seven occasions, and twice more in the Champions League. That must have pleased Abramovich, albeit perhaps making him believe — along with many of the club's fans — that it was only a start, and that to apply even more money to the project would be like sprinkling water on a beautiful bud.

Mourinho, however, resented anything that did not fit into the pattern he had laid down, in which entertainment came a clear second to structure. He would rather spend less money on a player over whom he knew he would have influence than welcome the arrival of a fully formed superstar around whom the playbooks would have to be redesigned.

So when Abramovich presented him with Andriy Shevchenko and Michael Ballack in the summer of 2006, no doubt thinking that this was the equivalent of Santiago Bernabéu adding Ferenc Puskas to a Real Madrid side already containing Alfredo Di Stefano almost 50 years earlier, it was just about the last thing Mourinho wanted or needed, since it required him to disrupt the rigid planning on which all his success, in both Portugal and England, had been based.

Occasionally these "president's gifts" pay off. Bernabéu did not do badly, with five European Cup wins in a row. Nor did Silvio Berlusconi when he added Ruud Gullit, Marco van Basten and Frank Rijkaard to Arrigo Sacchi's squad at Milan. Berlusconi is still at it, recruiting Ronaldo from Real Madrid last Christmas in a deal over which Carlo Ancelotti had no jurisdiction but which the coach was happy to see result in the goals that helped the team overcome a points deduction in Serie A while giving his other strikers time to rest between the matches of their ultimately successful Champions League campaign.

Abramovich wants to be like Bernabéu and Berlusconi, distributing his largesse before enjoying the rewards and the acclaim from the presidential box. Many Chelsea fans will think that the departure of Mourinho is nothing short of bonkers but they will have to accept that their club has evolved into one whose sights are set firmly, as the chief executive, Peter Kenyon has said, on regularly capturing the European Cup, and that the model for such a project requires the regular turnover of head coaches whose functions are so restricted that they can no longer be called managers in the traditional English sense.

In England the sack has always been the reward for failure. In Abramovich's world it is the penalty for not enough success. We had better get used to it.

22|09|2007
What won't happen this week

Harry Pearson

....

Today: "We considered a minute's silence, or a minute's applause, but in the end we decided that this would definitely be the way he would have wanted to be remembered," a tearful Richard Scudamore tells reporters as the Premier League announces that, before kick-off at this weekend's matches, crowds will be invited to mark the departure of Jose Mourinho by joining in a minute's moody pouting.

Across the country the minute is generally impeccably observed, although there are unpleasant scenes at Anfield where sections of the home support choose to interrupt it by breaking out into enigmatic smirks and wistful grins.

"There are always a few idiots who are intent on spoiling the moody pouting," Radio Five's Alan Green tells listeners, though Liverpool fans later phone 6-0-6 to claim that their action was a protest against the Premier League, who "didn't see fit to mark the sacking of Gérard Houllier with a minute's lugubrious frowning because we're not a London club".

Tomorrow: Giving his first reaction to the departure of the Portuguese coach, Frank Lampard tells Frank TV: "Obviously this has been a big shock. It will take a while to sink in but I guess in a few days' time I am going to wake up and think, 'Oh wow, now I've got just the excuse I need to bugger off to Spain.'"

John Terry is equally upset by events. "As I say," he says, "this is a time when we as a squad have to really unite, pull together, grit our teeth, put our backs to the wall and say to ourselves: 'Please, please, please God, let Jose get the Real Madrid job.'"

Chapter 11
United's second coming: the Ferguson era

11/04/1997

Fergie's big break

It came at Firs Park for an Ayr reserve –
Lawrence Donegan meets the man who
first spotted a rare managerial talent

Willie Muirhead sparks a Bluebell match in the shelter of the fur collar of his sheepskin coat and lights another fat cigar. He is getting old now but it is not difficult to believe that back in June 1974 he was the proud chairman of East Stirlingshire FC.

He had not been near Firs Park, the Shire's home ground, for 18 years, though he made an exception for *The Guardian*. Manchester United are his team these days and, the 1-0 defeat in Dortmund notwithstanding, he fully expects them to win the European Cup. The trophy would give Alex Ferguson a justifiable claim to the title of "Britain's greatest manager". It would also confirm Willie Muirhead as football's equivalent of the man who discovered the Beatles.

If the dreams of the Old Trafford legions come true over the next month, they should each write a personal letter of thanks to this 77-year-old grandfather, because in June 1974 Muirhead took a chance on their future hero and gave him his first job as a football manager. The two men are still in touch. The United manager affectionately begins his letters to Muirhead, "Dear Faither …"

Ferguson was at Firs Park for the pre-season training, a failed League Cup campaign and 12 games in the old Scottish Second Division – not enough to merit a mention in the United manager's entry in the latest edition on *Who's Who*. It was less than four months but Muirhead can remember every day in forensic detail, from the morning he took a phone call from the former Scotland manager Ally MacLeod to the afternoon that Ferguson walked across the Firs Park pitch to tell him he had accepted an offer to manage St Mirren.

"I'll say now what I said then about him leaving: it was a bloody tragedy for East Stirling. He was the best thing that ever happened to the club." Muirhead shakes his head at the memory and glances around the modern-day Firs Park. One end

of the ground is hemmed in behind what looks like a prison wall. The terraces have crumbled away and the stand Muirhead bought 25 years ago looks fit to collapse. "If Alex had stayed we could really have been something," he said. "Not Manchester United perhaps but a really big club in Scotland."

East Stirlingshire's momentary flirtation with greatness began when the other directors went to Munich for the 1974 World Cup and left Muirhead to find a new manager. The previous incumbent left because the crowd was giving him stick for playing his son-in-law every week. The chairman interviewed a few people but none "had tickled my fancy".

"I was in the office one morning when the telephonist said there was a call for me from one of the other directors in Munich. He asked me if I'd got someone yet and, when I said no, he said there was someone who wanted to speak to me. Ally MacLeod, who was the manager at Ayr United at the time, came on the phone and said he had a reserve team player who was desperate to become a manager – an Alex Ferguson.

"I remembered him as a player with Falkirk," Muirhead recalls. He flaps his elbows like chicken wings and laughs. "He played with these. He was a good player but definitely no' great." The two men spoke on the phone and, after a brief hesitation when it looked as if Ferguson might take a coaching job with Queen's Park, they met with their wives at a hotel in Falkirk. "I was impressed straight away," Muirhead says. "He conducted himself very well. I was impressed by the fact he was a family man, a very trustworthy person. I knew straight away that I had got myself a manager far superior to the other people I'd interviewed."

After East Stirlingshire Alex Ferguson cut his teeth and cloth at St Mirren, getting them into the top division

Ferguson's hesitation in taking the job suggests he might have had doubts about the club. And who could blame him? He had only eight outfield players, including the son-in-law of the previous manager, a handful of untried kids and no goalkeeper. The team had finished near the bottom of the league the previous season and crowds had dropped below 500.

He did not have a contract. His appointment was announced in the *Falkirk Herald* on June 29. "I think I have enough experience as a player to have a go at being a manager," he told the local paper. "I have got a big job on my hands. Shire have been in the doldrums for a long time and it will be a long and gradual process to change the image of the team."

Muirhead and the board sanctioned a buying spree. "We gave him £2,000 – and he spent the lot on one player, Billy Hulston. I was on holiday at the time. I couldn't believe it," he says. "The rest of the players he signed were just cast-offs from other clubs – people no one else wanted – but he moulded them into a team straight away, a fighting team." For once Muirhead's memory lets him down. Ferguson's new team had a terrible pre-season and, when the *Herald* published the traditional team photograph, the Shire had gone six games without a win, conceding 17 goals and scoring five. The manager, in a fashion familiar to anyone who has followed the later years of his career, had already fallen into the habit of blaming injuries, the "silly" loss of points and acts of God for his team's failure to win every game.

Ferguson the strict disciplinarian did not take long to surface either. Two weeks into the new season the *Herald* reported that his star striker Jim Meakin had been suspended for "a breach of club discipline". "Meakin had booked himself to go to a wedding on a match day," Muirhead explains. "He was told he couldn't go but went anyway. And that was that. Alex suspended him and we backed his decision all the way."

The relationship between the fledgling manager and the directors was not always so harmonious. Muirhead remembers the night Ferguson was hauled in front of the board when without permission he spent £40 on hiring a minibus to bring some schoolboy players from Glasgow. "He stood up, took the money out of his back pocket, threw it on the table and walked out. I had to call him at home that night and persuade him to come back."

That argument was quickly forgotten as the Shire climbed the table. After 10 games Ferguson's side was in the top six and due to play their local rivals Falkirk. Muirhead remembers the derby match as the manager's finest hour. "You can see it in him these days: he had the Falkirk team so wound up they were beaten before they got on the park. He took our team down to the same hotel they were having their match-day lunch at and made sure they saw our lads laughing and joking around. Alex had convinced our lot they were supermen." The Shire won 2-0.

Ferguson's transformation of the ramshackle outfit had

not escaped wider notice. Crowds at Firs Park had more than doubled, to 1,200, and the *Herald* gave the first inkling that he could be on the move, linking him to the vacant job at St Mirren. Ferguson denied he had been approached, though he had in fact already spoken to the St Mirren chairman and turned the offer down.

"That was how we left it until we met up that day on the pitch," Muirhead recalls. "I knew straight away he had changed his mind. He said he had spoken to Jock Stein and he had told him to go to the highest point at their ground, Love Street, and survey all he could see and think about the potential the club had. Stein told him to then go to Firs Park and do the same." It was no contest. The view from Firs Park then, as now, was not an inspiring one.

12|05|1990
Cup fever may rage but it is ice cold for Alex

The Scot who has guided Manchester United to Wembley is a steely chip off three great heroes, says Frank Keating

When Frank O'Farrell was sacked as manager of Manchester United 20 years ago he described his treatment with bitterness. "It was," he said, "a death by a thousand cuts."

Alex Ferguson, the club's present manager, knows the feeling. Yet so far, for all the daggers, he has survived. This afternoon's FA Cup final is a watershed, both for Ferguson and for his team.

The sensitive Scot has needed to grow a thick skin since crossing the Border. A short-fused, passionate man, he is content enough to be perceived by outsiders as a sullen, cold fish.

You get straight to the nub when he tells you the three managers he has most admired: Bill Struth and Scot Symon, two legendary guiding lights of Rangers, and Jock Stein, to whom Ferguson was briefly right-hand man with Scotland.

Struth, who was in charge of Rangers from 1920 to 1954, was a fierce disciplinarian. One day he came out of his office at Ibrox and spotted a famous Rangers international chatting to a friend. The player had his hands in his pockets.

Struth walked quickly to the fellow and, without warning, punched him hard in the ribs and continued, without a word, on his way. Rangers men did not put their hands in their pockets.

Wee Alex Ferguson idolised Struth, along with every other "fitba daft" laddie from Govan. As a stripling centre-forward of 12 he played a trial match on the Ibrox school pitch but it was to be a few years before he was signed for Rangers by Symon, another taciturn toughie and one of only two men – Andy Goram, Hibernian's goalkeeper, is the other – to play soccer and cricket for Scotland (he took five for 38 against Bradman's 1938 Australians).

A sportswriter who once telephoned Ibrox on a Saturday morning to inquire about the weather conditions for the afternoon's match found Symon picking up the phone. "Is it foggy at Ibrox?" asked the journalist. After a long silence Symon finally came up with: "No comment."

"He was absolutely dominant with the team," recalls Ferguson. "All based on discipline. He didn't have to say much, nor did he need to. He just had this overwhelming aura of authority."

If Struth and Symon inspired in Ferguson the utter necessity of stern disciplines, it was Stein who taught him the value of another commodity which has been fairly useful to him in his stressful stewardship at Old Trafford since 1986.

Ferguson, of course, was alongside Stein on that touchline bench at Cardiff on the grief-stricken night when Stein died. It was a draining, passionate World Cup qualifier. The last words Stein spoke were to Ferguson, midway through the second half when the contest was reaching boiling point.

"Whatever the result," the wise old bear growled to his young assistant, "let us not forget our dignity. Win or lose, we must keep our dignity." Minutes later he was dead.

From a distance anyway no observer can fault Ferguson for dignity in the face of some fearful, at times nothing short of slanderous, assaults on his character and competence during this acrimonious season.

Ferguson is no stranger to the sack. Before his glorious term at Aberdeen he briefly cut his teeth in charge of East Stirlingshire and then, for four years, at backwater St Mirren. Remarkably he got the club up to the Premier Division but then ran into a series of rows with a couple of boardroom buffers who disliked his abrasive style and he was sacked.

Typically he fought back, taking the club to an industrial tribunal, where the club suddenly announced that he had been dismissed "for unpardonably swearing at a lady on the club premises".Ferguson cheerfully admitted that, yes, once when the office typist had cheekily sided with the chairman while he and Ferguson were arguing he had followed her out of the room and told her: "Never bloody do that to me again, lassie."

What other manager in any industry would not have done the same? Who wanted to work for such a club anyway? He dropped the case, and embarked on his stunning run with Aberdeen, winning the Scottish Cup four times. If United triumph today, he will become the first manager since the war to lift that trophy and the FA Cup.

His Pittodrie regime was strict. He once had four Aberdeen players publicly reciting a string of nursery rhymes Baa-baa Black Sheep, Little Miss Muffet, Humpty Dumpty, the lot after a landlady had reported them for damaging her airing cupboard during some high jinks. "If they act like children, I treat them like children," said Ferguson.

Another time his star striker, Steve Archibald, was presented with the match ball after scoring a hat-trick against Celtic at Parkhead. Ferguson insisted on him returning it, saying: "It's a team game: no big-headed superstars in my teams."

Archibald refused but the next day he threw open the manager's door, booted the thing into the office and shouted: "Here's your bloody stupid ball, man."

It was a discipline that Manchester United's board, weary of under-achievement by their team of swankers, liked the smell of. In dismantling the team he inherited Ferguson admits he was also looking to dismantle "Old Trafford's superstar syndrome of swaggering, socialite free spirits". He sold Norman Whiteside, affectionately nicknamed "the Shankhill skinhead", and Paul McGrath, the Irish international, after court appearances following motor incidents.

Soon Stapleton, Sivebaek, Moran, Olsen and Strachan were also pulling on other shirts.

Ferguson's first buy for United was the veteran defender Viv Anderson "less for his football, more for the fact that he's a teetotaller", said an anonymous insider at Old Trafford this week.

In all Ferguson made nearly £4m from his sales and spent an astonishing £13m in rebuilding the side in, supposedly, more of his own image and likeness. We shall see. The buck, you might say, stops at Wembley today.

The black comedies of the boardroom during the season cannot have helped his management of the team. The Cup run, all away ties, turned into Ferguson's lifeline, while the club, and the whole game, waited to see who would buy it. The chairman, Martin Edwards, says he will sell his majority holding this summer.

After United's shambolic 1-0 Cup win down among the dead men of the Fourth Division, at Hereford United, it was hard to recall a winning manager so tense, so taut, so strained.

By the time United had reached Wembley after those two epic semi-final ties against Oldham, one was fearing for Ferguson's health. "That second semi-final was the most draining thing I've ever been part of," he says. "The pressure got to me mercilessly.

"Never have I been so overcome, even at Aberdeen with the European cups. At Aberdeen I was in control, on top of everything. Manchester United is a different thing altogether, a totally different mythology if you like. But the great challenge of managing a football club, especially one as great as this one, is to have confidence in your ability to weather the storms, to know that you have faith in your own discipline and your own patience under pressure. If I wilt under the pressure, then what will the players do? I must be strong. I firmly believe that self-discipline is the key factor in the realisation of any great sportsman, or man who has been chosen to manage or lead them. And, yes, certainly shouting at players can get them motivated too.

"It's not 'ruling by fear' at all. People respond to anger, don't they? You don't put fear into people deliberately but how can any manager not help losing his temper when a player isn't giving 100 per cent?"

Ferguson admits that he once reduced a 16-year-old apprentice to tears when he caught him drinking half a pint of lager in a pub – "I've even cancelled contracts for less" – but nobody has ever accused him of being inconsistent about his sarn't-major approach.

"It got him where he is, and it will keep him where he is," says his old second-in-command at Aberdeen, Archie Knox. "When it comes to fighting back after any number of setbacks and adversity, Alex Ferguson is a very, very special man indeed. You'll see."

Eric Cantona's kung-fu attack led to an FA ban of eight months and 120 hours' community service

26|01|1995

Cantona lets fly

Crystal Palace 1 Manchester United 1

David Lacey, Selhurst Park

Manchester United failed to go top of the Premiership last night but that turned out to be the least of their problems. Yet again Old Trafford's season has been thrown into turmoil by the nitro-glycerine in human form that is Eric Cantona.

For the record, Crystal Palace deservedly took a point from a scrappy, scruffy match after Gareth Southgate had brought the scores level 11 minutes from the end, David May having given United the lead early in the second half. Thus Blackburn Rovers still lead the Premiership, albeit by one point, and they now have two matches in hand.

The rest paled into insignificance compared with the off-field activities of Cantona, who briefly went berserk four minutes after half-time. The Frenchman had a thoroughly unhappy evening: from the outset he was complaining about some of the tackling he received and when Shaw caught him from behind in the 48th minute the notoriously short Gallic fuse was reignited.

A linesman flagged as Shaw's tackle went in and, if the referee, Alan Wilkie, had stopped the play at that point, considerable trouble would have been avoided. As it was, Cantona kicked Shaw as the pair went for a high clearance from Schmeichel seconds later. Out came the red card and off went Cantona, for the fifth time in 16 months.

As he walked along the touchline towards the dressing room a young spectator raced to the front of the stand and as well as hurling abuse, verbal and digital, at the Frenchman he appeared to throw something as well. Cantona immediately leapt at the fan, both feet coming in chest-high. The Frenchman then threw several punches before police, stewards, team officials and other players pulled the pair apart. In the mêlée Ince appeared to swing a fist at another fan.

Two spectators were taken to South Norwood police station complaining of assault. Cantona now faces another ban for the dismissal and an even longer suspension by the Football Association which will, in turn, depend on what the police decide to do once they have studied the incident on video.

Chief Supt Terry Collins said that both Ince and Cantona, who were allowed to travel home, would be interviewed by police during the next 48 hours. "I've never seen anything like it in my life," he added. "There could have been a riot."

The Football Association was prompt in issuing a statement

last night which made the severity of the incidents clear and hinted at equally severe sanctions against Cantona.

The statement said: "The FA is appalled by the incident that took place by the side of the pitch at Selhurst Park tonight. Such an incident brings shame on those involved as well as, more importantly, on the game itself.

"The FA is aware that the police are urgently considering what action they should take. We will as always co-operate in every way with them. And as far as the FA itself is concerned, charges of improper conduct and of bringing the game into disrepute will inevitably and swiftly follow tonight's events.

"It is our responsibility to ensure that actions that damage the game are punished severely. The FA will live up to that responsibility."

The FA customarily takes a grim view of players and managers assaulting fans. Brian Clough was banned from the touchline for a spell after cuffing a pitch invader. Given Cantona's already poor disciplinary record, he may well be facing a lengthy suspension just when Manchester United need him most.

Gifted footballer though he is, the Frenchman has again demonstrated the fatal flaw in his temperament which eventually saw him quit league football in France after a series of run-ins with the authorities.

Since joining Manchester United from Leeds he has proved inspirational in the winning of two championships, as well as last season's League and FA Cup Double, but the devil in his make-up has never really gone away.

In last season's European Cup he was shown the red card at the end of the game against Galatasaray in Istanbul for calling the referee a cheat, having already punched the Turkish team's reserve goalkeeper as he sat on the bench.

Last March he was shown two red cards in four days, at Swindon and Arsenal, and he began this season under suspension having been dismissed at Ibrox.

Last night, on a heavy pitch which cut up badly and with Cole still ill-attuned to his new surroundings, Manchester United needed Cantona at his best, not his insufferable worst. After all, two seasons ago an outstanding goal from the Frenchman against Palace at Selhurst had set United up for the title.

Last night their passing did not improve until the few minutes allowed in the second half before all hell broke loose. Palace had created the clearer scoring chances up to that point but within six minutes of Cantona's explosion May headed Sharpe's cross past Martyn to score his first league goal for United since arriving from Blackburn.

"Strange: all the fuss seemed to affect us more than them," said Palace's manager, Alan Smith. Ten-man United did reorganise themselves well and, as Sharpe hit the bar, they seemed bound for the top of the Premiership once more.

Then May's slowness let in Salako, whose shot was blocked, and amid a tumble of bodies Southgate's cool shot brought the scores level.

29|04|2006
On this day … Kevin Keegan loses his cool

Sky's Geoff Shreeves relives the Newcastle manager's 'I'd love it' outburst after victory at Leeds in 1996

I was the floor manager that day, basically the eyes and ears of the director and producer. The job involves cueing kick-off, liaising with the referee and dealing with the managers and players when we need to interview them. In those days the managers would often speak to the studio direct rather than to a reporter but I had to take them up to the interview room.

The one thing I really remember is popping into our room at Elland Road after the game and one of the riggers had been farting like a trooper. He'd totally stunk the place out. The smell when I walked in made me want to retch. There was absolutely no way we could have interviewed anyone in there.

Obviously there aren'tmany floral air fresheners at football grounds, so to get this room hospitable I ran down to the dressing rooms and got the Leeds kit man, who was a friend, to lend me a deodorant. Then I ran back and sprayed the room. But for that deodorant the interview would never have happened.

I went to collect Kevin and he was calmness personified. Again after the interview he was his normal courteous self. He just said: "Thanks a lot, lads," and off he went. But you could see him getting animated as the interview went on. He starts the interview in a totally rational fashion but I think Richard Keys sensed there was a problem. I think you've got to give Keysie credit for asking the right questions.

Kevin always wore his heart on his sleeve and there's no chance he was putting it on. It was pure, live, raw emotion. But did he really crack or was it a rallying call? If Newcastle had won the league, people would have looked at that night in a very different light. You could see that what Sir Alex had been saying had really got to him. People tend to speak passionately in the moments after a match but this was something else. It was astonishing the emotion in that room.

Looking back, I think it has become one of the defining moments of the Premiership. When you think about the most remarkable quotes in football, I guess the 1966 World Cup final with some people on the pitch is out in front but this has got to be one of them.

Then what happened: Manchester United won their last game to clinch the title. Almost certainly, Keegan did not love it.

16|04|1999

Was this the greatest goal of all time?

Martin Thorpe retraces Ryan Giggs' glorious semi-final path to a strike worthy of winning the FA Cup

It started in his own half and finished up in folklore. Ryan Giggs dazzled a defence and then a nation with Manchester United's winning goal at Villa Park on Wednesday night, capping an evening of spinning emotions with a whirling-shirt celebration which not only revealed one of the hairiest chests in football but the footballing heart that beats beneath it.

There is already talk of this being one of the greatest goals of all time. The yardsticks have been measured: Ricky Villa at Wembley in '81, John Barnes in the Maracana '84, Maradona against England in '86, even David Ginola against Barnsley in the previous round of this season's FA Cup.

But subjectivity plays such a large part in these comparisons. One could say that the run of the ball helped Villa, that Barnes's goal came in a friendly, that the memory of his first strike soured the glory of Maradona's second and that Ginola waltzed through a First Division defence.

In that context Giggs, refreshed after coming off the bench, settled this semi-final replay by beating a tiring defence. But that would be nit-picking. In terms of skill and context his was a goal in a millennium.

Skill first. The key was speed. From the moment he picked up the ball 10 yards inside United's half to the moment he unleashed a shot high into the Arsenal net, Giggs ran 61.5 yards in 10 seconds. Not bad for someone with the ball at his feet and various Arsenal players at his elbows.

The move started innocuously enough. Three minutes into the second period of extra-time, with the score locked at 1-1, Giggs gathered the ball in the inside-left channel and began an unbroken sprint that would take him deep into the Arsenal area. Ahead of him he spotted four sentries in scarlet but his pace proved decisive, for it kept the quartet on the back foot, constantly trying to assess the right time to tackle this weaving, speeding foe and never certain enough of their judgment to act.

Giggs reached the halfway line and two things happened. Patrick Vieira came across to challenge but Giggs jinked left to avoid the half-hearted lunge of a player who has learned the penalty of impetuous tackles. And Dwight Yorke started a diversionary run from the middle to the left wing. This was to prove crucial.

Now the Welshman was in Arsenal territory and, next, Lee Dixon came across to confront the threat. Instinctively Giggs feinted right and went left, wrong-footing the full-back who seemed to console himself with the thought that, anyway, there were covering players behind. It proved a false reassurance.

Giggs approached Martin Keown and this was where Yorke's positioning came into play. It caught the England defender in two minds whether to cover a possible pass to the Tobagan striker out wide or to challenge Giggs's continuing run down that inside-left channel.

Taking full advantage, the United winger cut right to leave Keown off balance and capable only of hanging out a hopeful leg. As Giggs skipped by, Dixon reappeared to his right. Now, though, Giggs was inside the area and the full-back, wary of conceding a penalty, risked only a soft shoulder charge.

Unconcerned, Giggs employed his right foot for the first time in this merry dance to push the ball forward. It rolled to the left of the box six yards out and, without breaking stride, the 25-year-old fired for goal. With Tony Adams attempting a late, desperate covering tackle, the shot could, of course, have flown way over the bar and sullied perfection. But with an impeccable sense of occasion Giggs's left foot propelled United's winner into the top of the net.

David Seaman would have done better had he stood up longer. But Arsenal were too stunned to care, United too elated. Now Newcastle await in the final.

That was the skill. So what of the context? This was the second high-pressured semi-final these heavyweights had slugged out toe to toe in four days and, going into extra-time with the scores level, the tension was mounting. There were two goals already, another disallowed, a sending-off, a missed penalty. It needed a dauntless heart to break the deadlock. Enter Giggs.

It should not be forgotten either that this was not just any old defence but the lauded Dad's Army of Arsenal, the most parsimonious rearguard in the Premiership with only 13 goals conceded in 32 games and none in their previous seven in all competitions. But though age has not wearied them, Giggs's run certainly did.

And the upshot of his moment of magic? Universal applause and another ankle injury that leaves him slightly doubtful to play in next week's more important semi-final in Turin. Given United's yearning to lift the European Cup, it might have been sensible for Ferguson and his aides to leave Giggs on the bench on Wednesday. Thank goodness they did not.

Ryan Giggs wheels away after his goal that took Manchester United on to the FA Cup final (2-0 v Newcastle) and the treble

15|05|1999
Eleven days to shake the world

Alex Ferguson is urging his men to keep their nerve as they stand on the verge of an historic treble. By Michael Walker

Alex Ferguson knows Old Trafford inside out but this was something else: Thursday afternoon and Ferguson, one of British football's men of the century, never mind of the decade, the figurehead for 1,670 employees and the club with the largest turnover on the planet, the club on the verge of an achievement unparalleled in English football, was being asked his thoughts on the historic challenge ahead in a broom cupboard.

However, such is the media chaos at Old Trafford in the build-up to a possible treble that Ferguson's expression told of relief at locating a quiet corner, even if half a dozen tape recorders followed him in there.

The previous evening he had been in the Blackburn bunker witnessing Brian Kidd being relegated and now he was being asked about cups and conquests. It is zoom lens pressure from every direction but to Ferguson, in a managerial career that began at East Stirlingshire in 1974, it is an everyday tale of boot rooms, broom cupboards and trophy cabinets.

Beginning with Spurs at home tomorrow, the next 11 days could see Ferguson revisiting the cabinet with a polished double handful three times, but there is also the chance that he might not at all. With neither the FA Cup nor European Cup finals going to a replay, the three games against Tottenham Hotspur, Newcastle United and Bayern Munich are three one-offs which will test Manchester United's stamina, depth, ability and, crucially, their nerve. In their last two games, at Middlesbrough and Blackburn, Ferguson has seen signs of tension among his players.

"I think there are periods when maybe they're getting anxious," he said. "I made that point to them at half-time at Blackburn, not to force the game. I think they were trying to stampede their way through it instead of playing with their normal patience and control." Ferguson's concern is far from overwhelming, however. As he said: "I think it's a test of nerve when you go into a big game anyway but, if they had any lack of nerve, it would have shown itself in Juventus and they would have probably bottled it completely when they were 2-0 down. But they kept their nerve; it's a matter of keeping it rather than showing it.

"You have to break teams down. We had to break down Juventus and, look at their reputation at home, they'd never lost three goals and things like that. All these reputations are always going to stand until you do something about it. And I've got to look at what my players have achieved this season and how they've responded to the big-game situations. I mean the Juventus performance, and Milan, and Arsenal in the semi-final were all against teams of the highest quality.

"And they don't come any bigger than Sunday now, the players know they're going to have to produce their best-ever performance and I said that in Juventus and I said it in Milan. That is the nature of progress." Even in a cupboard Ferguson's unremitting presence is at work.

Given that victory tomorrow would mean a fifth championship in seven years, a lessening of the will would be only natural, yet this 57-year-old's is unyielding. Besides, tomorrow offers something new, clinching the title at home. Amazingly, in the four championships collected in England, to add to the three with Aberdeen, only once has the decisive fixture been at home. It was in 1985 at Pittodrie against Celtic and, when Ferguson was asked what it was like, he almost bit the air: "It's great." Against a Spurs side "which can be stubborn" United can finally seal it at Old Trafford — "something you'd like to do in your lifetime even if it's the last game, the last kick of the ball, a corner kick, free-kick, penalty kick, own-goal or a volley. Just somehow win it."

True depth
Jaap Stam's achilles is causing concern and Roy Keane is by no means a certain starter, although injuries have revealed the true depth of Ferguson's squad, without which, he said, "we'd never have got to this point". Ultimately, as David O'Leary suggested, it could prove the determining factor between United and Arsenal, though Ferguson said Arsenal's squad was "difficult to assess".

"He [Arsène Wenger] tends to play the same team all the time. I mean, what is Nelson Vivas? I have watched him play twice, whereas [Ole Gunnar] Solskjaer has 16 or 17 goals and is one of my fringe players." And with that Ferguson was off through a room where United's past triumphs were framed on the walls. Earlier in that same room Bobby Charlton had offered his perspective on what the next 11 days represent.

"These youngsters are very respectful when they look back, but they don't want to look back because this is their time. They could be the best, arguably the best there has ever been. There are three games to go, three games which could mark the greatest period in Manchester United's history — in fact, any English club's history."

Eleven days to shake the world.

27|05|1999

United snatch their treble chance: Sheringham and Solskjaer shatter Bayern at the death

Ferguson has his substitutes to thank for a stunning turn-about that regained the European Cup after 31 years

European Cup final
Manchester United 2 Bayern Munich 1
Martin Thorpe, Nou Camp

One-nil down with 90 minutes played: the prize was gone, the dream merely a mirage. Or so it appeared. In one of the most astounding climaxes to any game, let alone a European Cup final, Manchester United conjured up two goals in two injury-time minutes to snatch the European Cup from the seemingly secure grasp of Bayern Munich last night.

It was an unbelievable finish and never did Queen's triumphant anthem resound more meaningfully. "We are the champions, my friend, and we'll keep on fighting to the end."

In fact, in singing his team's praises before the game, Alex Ferguson had given the distinct impression that even he was surprised by the relish with which his players had risen to meet each new challenge this season. "They are special," he said. "I trust them and I'll be trusting them tomorrow."

His faith was not misplaced. Two goals from two substitutes, Teddy Sheringham and Ole Gunnar Solskjaer, brought the European Cup back to Old Trafford for the first time in 31 years, on what would have been Sir Matt Busby's 90th birthday, and back to England for the first time since 1984. It also, of course, clinched a unique treble which included the Premiership and FA Cup.

And so the task of lifting Europe's grandest trophy went fittingly to the hands which have saved United so often during his team's dominance of a decade. For Peter Schmeichel it represented a glittering conclusion to a brilliant career at United, for his team and manager an amazing end to the pursuit of the ultimate club accolade.

But United's start could hardly have been worse. The game was just over four minutes old when Bayern's giant striker Carsten Jancker was unceremoniously brought down by Ronny Johnsen some 19 yards out on the left.

As the Germans loitered over the free-kick, United arranged a long wall which Markus Babbel infiltrated. And when Mario Basler hammered his shot towards the crimson sentries, Babbel peeled off, taking the end of the wall with him and the ball fizzed through the hole, much to Schmeichel's anger.

In the absence of the suspended Roy Keane and Paul Scholes the United manager took a huge gamble in this, the most important game of his life, by risking David Beckham alongside Nicky Butt in the middle of midfield. The player constantly praised as the best crosser of the ball in Europe had filled this central role hardly at all in his career and once previously this season – in last Saturday's FA Cup final.

And the move did not entail just one risk. Ryan Giggs was relocated to an equally unfamiliar position on the right wing and Jesper Blomqvist brought in on the left.

Now, going a goal behind so early on, it presented an even stiffer test to Ferguson's brave redesign. But slowly, as they have done so many times before, United worked their way into the game. Bayern, though, were always dangerous and three times almost extended their lead. The substitute Mehmet Scholl hit the post with a 19-yard chip over Schmeichel before forcing the keeper to make a diving save from a fierce shot. Then, with only six minutes left, Jancker rattled the underside of the bar.

United were riding their luck and in need of a change of personnel if they were ever to find the winning post. And so off came Blomqvist to make way for last Saturday's man-of-the-match Sheringham while Solskjaer replaced Andy Cole.

And just when it seemed impossible, United finally found a winning hand. Forty seconds past the 90-minute mark Sheringham swept in a half-cleared corner to equalise and hardly had the refuge of extra-time been appreciated when on 92min 24sec Sheringham nodded on Beckham's corner for Solskjaer to shoot home from close range and leave Nou Camp in an unparalleled state of disbelief.

Alex Ferguson brings the European Cup back to Manchester after a gap of 31 years. Within three weeks he was knighted

12|08|1999

Fergie's unlikeliest fan ...

When City-loving Simon Hattenstone joined the United manager on his book tour, things took an improbable turn

Monday night, Manchester Waterstone's

I despise Alex Ferguson. He whinges when he loses – blames the referee or the other team or the fans or the underground heating or the stars. Anything. When he wins, he dourly chews gum and hints at a smile. He chooses weakened teams for the Worthington Cup because it's not worth winning, he withdraws from the FA Cup because there are bigger fish in the South American seas. As manager of Aberdeen he scrambled 11 trophies, at United he's fluked his way to five championship victories, three doubles and, last season, he stumbled his way to an outrageous treble. I despise Alex Ferguson.

And now there is this book. You may have heard about it – serialised in *The Times*, serialised in *The Sun*, on the front and back pages of every newspaper for the past couple of weeks. He is said to have been paid £1m and here he is in a back room at Waterstone's, signing copy after copy after copy, making himself even richer. The publishers, Hodder & Stoughton, look on in glee as the books are sculpted into the Wembley twin towers. In an hour's time the embargo will be lifted, the book goes on sale and already the queues are snaking back on themselves all round Deansgate.

Ferguson turns his head as I walk in. This is Simon, says Karen the publicist. He looks me up and down. "Aye! Got your medicine with you, Simon?" What medicine? "The medicine you take whenever you go to see City." How d'you know I'm a Manchester City fan? "Ach well, everyone knows round here." He seems to be smirking but it could be the famous Ferguson scowl. I show him my City scarf commemorating last season's

Wembley triumph – Manchester City, Division Two play-off final. City have not won a real cup for 23 years.

"My wife doesn't even like football," says Ferguson, "but she was jumping up and down when City scored at Wembley." Nice try. But I'm not so easily bought.

Downstairs the doors have opened and the fans have formed a neat procession. It's pouring but Waterstone's staff say it looks like a record attendance. Typical. They say there may be more than 1,000 people tonight.

The fans inch closer and closer, practising their lines, their hand shake, their thank-yous. The men are more rigid, more awed than the women. Some fluff their words. The women know exactly what they want to say: "Can I take a photograph?" "We think you're great" "We love you Alex, we do, we love you" "I had my hair done special for you," says one drenched woman. "How ya doin? Thanks," Ferguson returns.

I feel nauseous. Most of the fans have not even bothered to turn up in their kit. If it were the launch of City boss Joe Royle's autobiography, we'd all be there in blue wigs, frocks, inflatables. City fans know how to celebrate. They just don't get much opportunity.

The reporter from Sky is recording the tills burping away. Records have been broken. Roddy Bloomfield, Ferguson's publisher, walks in. "You know, it wasn't even finished till three weeks ago," he says. Hodder hope to sell a million copies.

Ferguson is still signing, with his how-are-yas and thank-yous. I notice something disturbing at the corner of both eyes – two triangles of lines, smile lines. You can see them on the cover of his book, and you can see them when he's talking to the fans. But everyone knows Ferguson doesn't smile.

Tuesday morning press conference, Old Trafford

As a child, I had a season ticket at City and vowed never to go to Old Trafford. And here I am in the Warwick Suite, where Manchester United plc plays host to the world's press, watching Alex Ferguson drink his Manchester United sparkling water. The sandwiches make me feel sick, thankfully.

I'm in an office looking over the perfect pitch. When the ground is empty, you get a spectacular view of this shrine to big business. Manchester United is planted in huge print over the main stand. Behind one goal the seats form into "Umbro", behind the other "Sharp", United's two main sponsors. Even the office's porthole windows are dedicated to capitalism – each one engraved with a sponsor's name. Who is football for these days?

Sports biographies tend to be bland or soppy. Hugh McIlvanney, the great sports journalist and Ferguson's ghostwriter, says this book was never going to be like that, because Ferguson "has a compulsion to tell the truth. It's not superficial, or light, it's a book about a life." Typically of Ferguson, he's written, or part-written, an extremely good and revealing book. Hence all the news stories – the £40,000 present from Andrei Kanchelskis's agent, reported as a bung; the fall-out with chairman Martin Edwards, who wouldn't up his pay and accused him of being unfocused; the vicious sectarianism early in Ferguson's playing career when he was scapegoated for being a Protestant; his criticism of Hoddle's treatment of Beckham when he played for England. All news stories, all selling papers.

And then there are the players who have come in for a hammering. Ferguson says the book is scrupulously fair and it probably is. The trouble is, we will remember only the criticism: Brian Kidd's moaning, the astonishing drinking feats of Norman Whiteside, Bryan Robson and Paul McGrath , Gordon Strachan's contract about-turn.

Back in the press conference the men from the dailies want hard news. Any regrets? Was he too hard on Kidd, his former No2? "No, there is no use fudging things." The bung? Ferguson says he is amazed it has been reported as a bung. After all, the money, which was promptly returned, was handed over three months after the transfer. Would he ever sign a Russian player again? Ferguson provides an off-the-record response and then a watered-down version for the record. "I wouldn't dismiss signing another Russian player …"

The press leave and Ferguson nudges me. "Ghastly isn't it?" In trot the Sunday papers for a more urbane chat. Yes, it was a shame that Shearer slipped away at his peak. But his great regret is not signing Paul Gascoigne before he went to Spurs. "What a great player he could have been at that age – courage, dribbling, change of pace, everything. He was made for here." Could he have tamed him, asks a member of the press corps. Ferguson smiles. Few players have stepped out of line in his reign.

'Aye! Got your medicine with you, Simon?' Red Ferguson and Blue Hattenstone in perfect step during the book tour

We're leaving Old Trafford by the secret exit via the players' tunnel. A group of children see us, and there is a shocked echo down the line. "My God! God!! GOD!!! It's Alex Ferguson!" I am within spitting distance of the pitch but control myself.

The journey to WH Smith

Alex Ferguson followed his dad into the Glasgow shipyards. And, like his dad, he became a shop steward, fighting a successful strike. It's a thousand dreams from the Sir Alex of today. In the book he says he became shop steward because no one else would do it. Is that all? "Well, there's always a cause worth fighting," he says. "You always try to get better conditions for yourself. But being a shop steward you also represent others. I think the injustice of the system in those days made you want to fight, made you want to represent people."

Was his family political? "My father was a strong Labour man, a strong socialist. And so was my mother."

I ask him whether he still wants to fight for others. "I don't think it leaves you. It doesn't surface as much because, as you can see, my lifestyle has changed dramatically."

Time for the Prescott question. Does he still consider himself working class? "Yeh, I do in the ethical part. Ooooh! Did you see the way that car came out of there?" One of his favourite words is loyalty. Back in Glasgow, he says, people were loyal to each other; they had to be. "People from my neck of the woods depended on each other because everyone went through a hard time at some time or other."

But hasn't loyalty disappeared from the game? Just look at the mercenaries such as Anelka, who demand a transfer every other season to cushion their lifestyle. "I've got plenty of examples of players' loyalty and people's loyalty to make you optimistic that life goes on," he counters.

The galling thing is that Ferguson is right. He nursed players such as Giggs and the Neville brothers and Scholes and Beckham from childhood, cautioned their behaviour, became their role model. And most players have repaid him with a loyalty unique in football. Few players leave Manchester United to further their bank balance.

Has money made or broken the game? He coughs by way of a rebuke. "Well, if you think money has brought Manchester United its success, I would disagree. Because, in proportion to other clubs' spending, we've been quite moderate and balanced. So I don't think it's down to money buying success, it's down to management and structure, and also a bit of luck. I don't think you can dismiss that." Ferguson knows he was probably within days of being sacked in 1990, when the club were drowning in the league. If only he had been. Of course, United went on to win the FA Cup.

The conversation turns to Murdoch's failed bid for the club. Was he glad when it was squashed by the DTI? "Funnily enough, I was indifferent, because I always felt if it did happen, as long as I had a football team I was happy. And that is really the nub of my life ... so long as I'm controlling the team." He says one of the problems with the sums of cash at stake in football now is that the directors want success yesterday – just look at the number of managers Manchester City have sacked over the past 20 years, he says, cruelly. "Managers don't have time to wait for youth development to happen. You sign a young boy at 13, you may have to wait for five years and by that time the manager may be gone. If you've got time and control you can have plans for five years ahead." That is why so many managers rush to buy experienced players from abroad – paranoia, plus the crazy inflation of Britain's transfer market.

But haven't the Premiership's imports improved the game? "Oh yeh," he says, licking his lips. "No doubt about that. You are not going to tell me the game is not better for players like Cantona and Schmeichel, Vialli and Vieira?" And Michael Vonk, the great Dutch centre-back who played for Manchester City? Ferguson giggles. Vonk was not the most skilful of players.

WH Smith

I wave at the crowds as I walk through the security cordon. "Fergie, Fergie," they roar at me. One man tells Ferguson he's skiving to be here. "Aye! I never did that!" Ferguson says. And you feel he probably never did. The skiver is sweating with anticipation. "My hands feel drunk," he says as he shakes with Ferguson. It's funny how none of the women asks Ferguson for a kiss. But I guess he's that kind of man – a leader rather than a lover. A woman asks him to sign his name as Sir Alex and he says he can't.

Doug, his driver for the day, says he doesn't know why he respects him so much. "It's strange. He doesn't ask for respect, and you don't notice you are giving him respect. You just do." Why's he not as surly as I'd hoped? "Well, I bet you expected him to be chewing all the time as well, didn't you?"

The journey to Asda

Why wouldn't he sign his name Sir Alex? "It's difficult that one, isn't it? You don't feel absolutely relaxed about it, you know." Did he have doubts about accepting the knighthood. "No, none at all. None at all." What does it mean to him? "I think for my family it was good. It's a tribute to all the work that's been done over a long period. When I got my OBE at Aberdeen, I wondered why I should get this type of thing. I tried to justify it, and say, what do other people think about this, you know. But when this knighthood came along ..."

Which manager influenced him most, I wonder? "Scot Symon and Jock Stein," he replies. What did the less famous Symon teach him? "When I came to Rangers I recognised the pressure he was under. About three months after I joined they sacked him. Rangers were top of the league, undefeated. What I recognised in him was that he'd never criticise his players publicly. He'd defend them to the hilt." Which is his policy? "Absolutely."

Ferguson busies himself with his phone. "Yes, chairman, he's about the same size as Andy Cole and Dwight Yorke. Very mobile. Good back-up." Ferguson fancies the South African, Quentin Fortune, currently playing for Atlético Madrid.

Next he is on to his wife, Cathy, telling her she wouldn't believe the number that have turned up for the signings. Is she really not interested in football? "Aye. She only goes to the Cup finals. She's interested in me, obviously. She worries about me all the time."

I wonder if her indifference to football has been helpful to their relationship. "Yes, I think it has, yeh. We seldom talk about football."

Ferguson has three sons – one, Darren, started out as a United footballer, another son works in the City. Is he a wheeler-dealer? "I think he's got a big job, yes. I'm very proud of him. But I don't want you mentioning who he works for, because he's a bit sensitive about that." For the benefit of my tape recorder he repeats: "Do not at any cost mention vere my son vorks. Your life iz in danger."

I laugh, then I remember myself. Why have so many great managers been from working-class industrial backgrounds, I wonder. "Matt Busby, Jock Stein, Bill Shankly, all were from mining backgrounds. There must be some influence to have made them what they were. All different types but all so determined." All Scottish, too. Ferguson may be the last of the line.

Asda

The biggest crowd yet. Rows and rows like a football match. We stay a couple of hours but run out of time. There are still kids left dangling their unsigned books. They start to cry, parents begin to shout, things get nasty. Especially when the Asda man announces: "Sorry, Sir Alex won't be able to do all the signings. He's got to be in Stockport by half seven. Hope you all had a great day." "No. We didn't. We didn't have a great day," says one woman. Soon the crowd is baying. A woman has an epileptic fit and her feet are kicking in the air uncontrollably.

On the road to Dillons, Stockport

Both Ferguson and the publicist are shaken by the Asda debacle. Ferguson turns the radio on to listen to the sport. Is it hard to motivate himself after the treble, I wonder? "No. No. Not a bit." What about the young kids who have already achieved the ultimate? "I don't worry too much about the players. I think the nucleus are solid citizens." A perfectly Fergie expression. "What are you going straight for?" he asks the driver. He is not the easiest of passengers.

I ask him about the compulsion to tell the truth that McIlvanney was talking about. He says they were all things he had to say, instances that affected the shape of things, that it would have been dishonest to exclude them. How does he think his former player, the Coventry manager Gordon Strachan, will react to Ferguson's conclusion, after a contract dispute, that "this man could not be trusted an inch". "Gordon has always written things about me that are not actually accurate. Gordon let me down. He was a mature man and I think your words are important at that stage of your life."

Reflecting on my Old Trafford visit, I wonder aloud who football is for these days? Is it not becoming unaffordable for normal people? "No. I don't think Man United are unaffordable," he says defensively. Chelsea? "I think it would be difficult to watch football at Chelsea, wouldn't it?" Yes, but Chelsea or United, isn't football in danger of being split from its roots? "That's possible," Ferguson says. "But it's like a cat with nine lives – when it gets to the eighth it's watching itself for the ninth." Ticket prices may reach a point where they threaten the game but, when it comes, the clubs will back off, he suggests.

Dillons, Stockport

Final call of the day. Ferguson is still uncreased in his black suit and shirt and tie but he's demob happy, sitting behind a desk singing Scottish folk songs. "D'you know City are playing Burnley tonight, what d'you think the score will be?" 4-0, I say. He just grins.

I ask him if he remembers the day City beat United 5-1. That was in '89, when he almost got sacked. Was it the worst day of his professional life, I wonder? He grunts. In the book he describes how he went home in morose silence, slapped the pillow over his head and tried to force himself to sleep. "You won't believe this but you had six chances that day. We had 14. Fourteen! We mur-dered ya! Mur-dered ya . . . so much that we got beat 5-1." So he enjoyed that day? "Aye! It gave me as much enjoyment as the British soldiers at Passchendaele."

The crowd move in. And it strikes me what ease he has with people. "Right, off to bed with you," he tells one little girl. A man tells him he's 65 and been following United all his life. "You know, it's you who should have got the knighthood," he replies. I think back to what he says about his players being solid citizens. A girl with Down's syndrome hugs her sister for asking Ferguson if he'll be at United's training ground on Thursday. She sticks two supportive thumbs at him. He sticks two big thumbs back in thanks. Thanks for everything, say so many fans. I have a lumpy throat.

There are no signs of the businessmen who fill the corporate seats, there is no sign of Manchester United plc. These are real fans. Even Man United has real fans. Of course, football is a cynical business, of course it rips off its followers. But their lives have been transformed by football, by Manchester United and Alex Ferguson, just as City gave me purpose and energy and belief when I was a kid. The only difference is that United win cups, while City just dream. At least City have the best fans in the country, don't they Alex? "They certainly have the most defiant," he says.

As the crowd finally drain away, I queue up with my book for Ferguson to sign it.

18/02/2003

Stitch in time is a small price to pay for putting the boot in

Kevin McCarra

David Beckham has shed blood in a good cause. He had no choice and, judging by his stern expression while driving away from his Cheshire home yesterday morning, team-mates should refrain from teasing him about that cut. The dressing on the stitches above his left eye, though, lent raw interest not only to his features but to his club's image.

He was an accident victim when Sir Alex Ferguson kicked a stray football boot into the air during a critique of Manchester United's performance in the 2-0 defeat by Arsenal. If that was primitive conduct by the Scot, it proves at least that the Premiership's richest club will not be asphyxiated by corporate culture while he is in charge.

His epic fury has been one of the glories of United and it would be hypocritical to tut over the petulance of it so soon after that rage was credited with reigniting the team. Following the defeat at Maine Road in the Manchester derby three months ago, he is reported to have had a sincere air while proposing that a potential lynch mob of fans be invited in. United won nine of their next 10 matches, including victories over Newcastle, Liverpool and Arsenal.

All of his peers communicate through tirade now and again but Ferguson is one of those whose career would be most at risk if he ever considered anger management classes. His tempestuousness is even a shock to himself. He once wrote of the bemusement he felt while looking back on his time at Aberdeen and realising the danger he had put himself in during confrontations with tough individuals such as the raw-boned Doug Rougvie.

Ferguson can be childish at times but there is something immature at the heart of sport itself. The crowds do not gather for shows of spectacle and moderation. It is the disproportionate character of the spectacle and the senseless importance of the result that lifts people beyond the chafing prudence of everyday life. As the United accounts show, human beings will pay handsomely for that.

There is no parallel between football and grown-up professions. A chief executive who occasionally smashed up the head office would find, for example, that he had stretched the trust of the company's shareholders and its bankers too far. Around Britain's football grounds, however, excess can enhance a reputation.

Trevor Francis's standing at Crystal Palace was certainly improved by an incident last August. It is claimed to have cost him the two weeks' wages subtracted by a club that was required to be censorious, as well as a £1,000 fine from the Football Association. During a match with Bradford City the reserve goalkeeper Alex Kolinko was alleged to have snickered when the visitors scored and Francis struck him on the nose.

Those well acquainted with the Selhurst Park scene declare that the crowd then started to develop a fondness for the manager while the squad formed a stronger bond with him. Francis, of course, was in the wrong but the transgressions are more reassuring to fans than they have ever been. They find relief in the proof that they are not alone in their visceral reaction to football.

With many players so perplexingly wealthy, the season ticket-holders are readily prey to the suspicion that they are alone in having an emotional stake in matches. How much, they wonder, do they still have in common with athletes who hurry away from grounds to get on with being millionaires? That characterisation is unfair to the competitive instinct of sportsmen

David Beckham, never shy of bodily markings, is none too happy about the unscheduled one above his left eye

but it is a relief to be furnished with the evidence that the final score still has a crazed relevance to men like Ferguson.

It is not strictly necessary to be Glaswegian in order to become constructively unhinged. Arsène Wenger commented yesterday that he has the same capacity for wildness, even if his demons are more heavily shackled than Ferguson's. Old Trafford has heard his tantrum and Robert Pires describes his manager as being "berserk" when Arsenal were 5-1 down at half-time there in 2001.

There can be no success without emotional engagement and fans are gladdened when they are witnesses to it. Glenn Roeder can make a good, logical case for his arms-folded demeanour but it is a further cause of fear to an Upton Park crowd that dreads relegation.

Beckham's anger will be honed by embarrassment at having to walk around with that now famous cut in open view. He must feel ridiculous and deserves an apology from his manager. But the player might also reflect that the uninhibited nature of the serial tea-service smasher has helped form his own character and career. Without the broken crockery, how could there ever have been so many cups for the Old Trafford trophy room?

29|09|2004
Rampant Rooney starts in unforgettable style

Old Trafford hails a stunning hat-trick debut by the £27m striker, who was a danger every time he touched the ball

Manchester United 6 Fenerbahce 2
Daniel Taylor, Old Trafford

....

Even by Wayne Rooney's standards of defying all reasonable expectations his first appearance for Manchester United will go down in the club's annals as the most impressive debut that Old Trafford has ever witnessed.

He did not quite manage to silence the boisterous Turkish supporters but his hat-trick here was notification that Sir Alex Ferguson is blessed with a player who can make up for whatever inadequacies exist elsewhere in the team.

Those deficiencies were evident in the second half when Ferguson's players allowed carelessness to infiltrate their performance but by then Rooney had ensured their first victory in Group D. The England striker left the pitch to a standing ovation with the match ball as his souvenir for a remarkable night's work, a performance which incorporated vision, finesse and the embryonic signs of a partnership with Ruud van Nistelrooy that could inspire trepidation in the world's most accomplished defender.

Rooney's mere inclusion was guaranteed to generate a crackle of excitement inside Old Trafford, but there was still something extraordinary about the way in which he consigned the likes of Van Nistelrooy and Ryan Giggs, well as they played, to a place in the supporting cast.

Every time Rooney took possession he was a danger. He showed anticipation, courage, immaculate control and his goals were exquisite, from the two thumping shots that helped United to a 3-0 half-time lead to the wonderfully taken free-kick with which he completed his hat-trick, eight minutes after the restart.

For aesthetic quality the best was probably the last but there was individual excellence attached to all three – first when Van Nistelrooy's through-ball split the visiting defence and Rooney's instinctive left-foot shot soared into the net. Then when the £27m signing from Everton picked up the ball and, unfazed by several defenders, drove a magnificent shot beyond Rustu Recber. Left foot, right foot – it does not seem to matter to Rooney.

It began to feel like a trick of the mind that Ferguson's experimentation elsewhere in his side had provoked so much disquiet before the kick-off.

The manager confounded everyone, not only by giving Roy Keane the night off but by demoting Cristiano Ronaldo and John O'Shea. The only logical conclusion to draw was that he regarded Fenerbahce as little more than a bunch of sightseers – an assertion which proved every bit as accurate as Rooney's finishing.

In came Eric Djemba-Djemba, Kleberson and, most bewildering of all, David Bellion. Equally surprising was Gary Neville's return to action only three weeks after suffering a hairline fracture of his kneecap in England's World Cup qualifier in Poland. His recovery, a full month ahead of initial expectations, will be encouraging for Sven-Goran Eriksson but not for Wes Brown, who faces a prolonged spell on the sidelines.

Still, Ferguson can hardly be accused of underestimating Fenerbahce. United were ahead after seven minutes, when Giggs glanced in a header from Kleberson's cross, and their opponents could not extend Roy Carroll throughout the opening 45 minutes.

Briefly the Turkish champions offered themselves a flicker of hope when Marcio Nobre made it 3-1 from a badly defended corner within a minute of the restart, but not even the most pessimistic United follower could have been fooled into thinking it would be the catalyst for the most unlikely of comebacks.

Seven minutes later Frank de Bleeckere awarded a questionable free-kick against Fabio Luciano 20 yards from goal. This was usually Giggs territory but the winger was happy to stand

aside for Rooney to curl his free-kick into the top right-hand corner. Even Eriksson, disregarding his usual decorum, jumped out of his seat at that.

To Ferguson's irritation, more dubious defending presented Tuncay Sanli with the chance to make it 4-2 soon afterwards. Indeed, United were beginning to look jittery until Van Nistelrooy scored the fifth, collecting Darren Fletcher's pass and expertly finishing from 12 yards.

Bellion added the sixth but there was no mistaking the fact this was Rooney's night and an unforgettable one at that.

19|11|2005

Roy Keane and Alex Ferguson: 1993-2005

Daniel Taylor tells the tempestuous tale as 12 years of mutual respect and club success collapse in vitriol

Perhaps the saddest part of Roy Keane's fall from grace at Manchester United is that he will be remembered in future years for the acrimonious nature of his departure rather than anything he did on the field. Ushered out of the door by the most ruthless manager in the business, Keane's exit could hardly have been less dignified but he can have nobody to blame but himself.

Even by Sir Alex Ferguson's standards, there was something remarkably brutal about Keane's final few hours as a United player. Two of the game's most combustible characters came together at United's training ground and by the time they had unloaded their vitriol it had become clear they would never deal with one another again. Twelve years of mutual respect and admiration had totally disintegrated.

This was at 9am, the beginning of a tumultuous day, but the turning point can be traced back to November 3, three days after MUTV had been forced to pull an interview with Keane because his criticisms of his team-mates were so vehement. This was the first time Keane had seen them since and it appears he refused to make any apologies. On the contrary he called them together and said: "If they aren't going to show you the tape, I'll tell you what's on it."

As he did so, Ferguson intervened and after an exchange led Keane and the rest of his squad to his office to watch the MUTV video. Ferguson's anger soon matched that of Keane's. He accused him of "ranting" and of bringing the club into disrepute. It is believed an apoplectic Keane made a reference to Ferguson's legal case over the Rock Of Gibraltar racehorse, a remark that the United manager would consider beyond the pale.

Now it was the turn of Ferguson's assistant, Carlos Queiroz, to intervene. Keane cut him dead, attacking him with the sort of tirade to which he famously subjected Mick McCarthy before walking out of the Republic of Ireland's World Cup squad. From that moment there was no turning back, though Ferguson stewed long on how he was to deal with what had occurred in his office, knowing his authority had been undermined in front of the squad. When Keane regained fitness, Ferguson would have to answer questions as to why he was not picking his captain. This explains the delay between November 3 and Thursday night's instruction to Keane that he would not be playing for United's reserves. Both men knew then that Keane's United career was over.

Yesterday Keane was in Ferguson's office again. Ferguson had summoned him, along with his solicitor Michael Kennedy and the club's chief executive, David Gill. Keane had known for two days that he would not be offered a new contract at the end of the season and now he was about to find out why.

The meeting degenerated into another furious row. Ferguson accused Keane of mutinous and unforgivable behaviour. Critically, he is then understood to have told Keane he would not continue as captain. Keane returned fire. He believed Ferguson was humiliating him and made it clear, in his inimitable style, he was not willing to stay. At 9.20am he stormed out.

At 11.30am Ferguson held his weekly press briefing and, asked for an update about Keane's contractual situation, replied: "Nothing to report. There hasn't been any decision about his contract."

Thirty-five minutes later the bombshell dropped in a statement from Old Trafford. "Manchester United have reached agreement with Roy Keane for him to leave the club with immediate effect. The club have offered Roy a testimonial in recognition of his 12 years at Old Trafford."

United's spin-doctors had supplied some quotes on behalf of Ferguson, describing Keane as "a fantastic servant, the best midfield player in the world of his generation, one of the great figures in our club's illustrious history".

Keane, in turn, had given his approval to a message that read: "While it is a sad day for me to leave such a great club and manager I believe the time has come to move on."

United claimed it was by "mutual consent" but it would be truer to say mutual contempt. There were no handshakes. As far as Ferguson was concerned, Keane had made one indiscretion too many. And nobody takes on Ferguson at Old Trafford and wins — not even Roy Maurice Keane.

19/03/2007

Ronaldo threatens to eclipse Best in arts of sorcery

Manchester Utd 4 Bolton 1
Daniel Taylor, Old Trafford

It is not a subject that Sir Alex Ferguson likes to discuss but there is a school of thought at Old Trafford — not least among some of the senior players — that, contrary to his public utterances, the oldest manager in the business may retire if Manchester United finish the season on a suitable high. "I am not going to leave this club as a loser," Ferguson once said, and what better way to bow out than with a Premiership and/or Champions League medal in his top pocket?

The alternative argument is that a crowbar would be needed to prise Ferguson away from his desk at a time when Wayne Rooney and Cristiano Ronaldo are engaged in this increasingly bewitching contest about who should be recognised as the most exciting exponent of their art in world football.

A whole host of superlatives would be needed to analyse their performances on Saturday, a match which could conceivably register as United's finest display this season given the list of absentees and the early loss of Gary Neville through injury. Rooney's goals were exemplary: a 60-yard dash and deft chip over Jussi Jaaskelainen for his first and a shot with a sharp arrowhead at its end for his second. Ronaldo had to go some to outstrip his colleague but he managed it so beautifully that Carlos Queiroz, Ferguson's assistant, described the winger as the best player he had worked with.

It was some compliment from a man who has coached, among others, Luis Figo and Zinedine Zidane, and the question was this: has any other player in United's history, even the great George Best, shimmered with such menace when in possession?

To see Ronaldo right now is to witness a man completely in love with his work, a footballer playing as though nothing comes more naturally. The Portuguese winger is still to cross

Cristiano Ronaldo 'is a man completely in love with his work, who makes his own rules when dealing with a football'

the line between great footballer and football great but he is firmly on course and the beauty of it is that he refuses to do it the conventional way.

He will flick the ball with the outside of his left boot while leaning back looking at the sky. He will conjure up shots that dip at the last moment like a beach ball on a windy day. He will look one way and caress a pass in the opposite direction. He is not easy to copy. Cristiano Ronaldo dos Santos Aveiro makes his own rules when dealing with a football.

Sam Allardyce, the Bolton manager, argued that his defenders had made Ronaldo look good. The truth was that Ronaldo had made them look bad. "He's a player that Manchester United cannot afford to lose," Allardyce acknowledged. "Whatever it takes to keep him they have got to do it and, after that, they just have to hope that he wants to stay. That's the key."

That last sentence suggests Allardyce is dubious about whether Ronaldo will sign a new contract and resist the lure of Real Madrid, having publicly declared a desire to move to the Bernabéu last summer.

"He can look at Spain later on, maybe, but he certainly shouldn't be moving there at this stage in his career," said Allardyce. "If it's Real Madrid, that would be a mistake because they're not the right club for him. There's no development at Madrid, there's only decline. Manchester United have a young team that is developing. They're top of the league and still involved in the three major competitions. This is the right club for Ronaldo."

Ferguson will drink to that after seeing Ronaldo inspire United to a 3-0 lead inside 25 minutes, setting up Park Ji-sung for both his goals, playing in Rooney for his first and generally exploding Allardyce's theory that Bolton could snuff out his danger by doubling up on him. Ronaldo wanted to take them all on. The upshot is that United need six wins from their remaining eight games to guarantee Ferguson's ninth title in 14 years. Chelsea's durability has to be admired in pressing them all the way but United look immune to stage fright.

Gary Speed's 87th-minute penalty was a mere footnote – the referee, Alan Wiley, taking a hardline stance about Nemanja Vidic's push on Abdoulaye Faye – and the home side's dominance was such that Ferguson could withdraw Ryan Giggs early in the second half with tonight's FA Cup quarter-final replay against Middlesbrough in mind.

Giggs was imperious again, having collected his player-of-the-month trophy before kick-off. Ferguson also had a prize to accept: his 19th manager-of-the-month award since the Premiership's formation. As for player of the year, only Didier Drogba can prevent Ronaldo making it a landslide vote.

09|05|2007

FC United rise and shine on a sense of community

The club born out of discontent at the Glazer takeover are winning titles and putting down roots, says David Conn

FC United of Manchester, formed by fans opposed to Malcolm Glazer's takeover at Old Trafford, have travelled a joyfully long way from mere rebellion. At Gigg Lane, a week before "Big" United were confirmed as Premiership champions, FC fans stood and sang throughout a 5-0 demolition of Formby, completing their own second season of record-breaking, championship-winning promotion.

In gorgeous weather surely never previously witnessed in April in Bury, in the raucous section of the Main Stand and the packed Manchester Road End, the fans belted out Sloop John B, customised as their season's anthem : "I wanna go home/I wanna go ho-o-ome/This is the worst trip/I've ever been on."

There is a depth to this commitment which quite unexpectedly caught me by the throat, got me in the eyes. FC United may have started in protest at the heart-sinking economics which devoured Manchester United but it is powered by the fans' heartfelt attachment to football and the collective belonging they feel it represents. The relationship with "Big" United is complex. Most FC fans still support the club – packing the pubs and Gigg Lane social club to roar United on to the 4-2 win at Everton before FC's game last week – but they grew alienated over time from the business which is Manchester United.

Mike Turton, 44, an electricians' supervisor, who was at the Formby match with his daughter Danielle and sons, Ryan and Thomas, is a typical FC founding father. An Old Trafford regular for 31 years, he packed in on May 12 2005 – they can all recite the date – when the Glazers, from their Florida base, finally acquired United with their £810m hedge fund-leveraged deal.

"I didn't leave because of the takeover," he said. "That was just the final push I needed to get out. It started in the 90s. Winning trophies was very nice but I didn't support United to win trophies. I'd stopped enjoying it. The prices were rising and I wondered why I was forking out to fund the players' ridiculous wages. I love what we've built here. It's in the best Manchester tradition of protest, along the lines of the suffragettes and the Trades Union movement, which have their roots here."

You hear this Manc pride a lot as well as bemusement that fans of other clubs have not protested against their takeovers – "Not even Liverpool," the FC fans all murmur. Here they have moved on, to building their own club according to the principles they argued for when campaigning: supporter-ownership, with members (2,500 of them) voting for the board and policies, ticket prices affordable at £7 for adults, £2 for under-16s, and an agreement with stewards that supporters can stand. The club has established a youth policy which seeks to work with junior clubs who often feel exploited by the way professional clubs' academies trawl for the best players. FCUM have also made partnerships with social welfare and community organisations, seeking to welcome marginalised groups and introduce football as a good presence in their lives.

Andy Walsh, the former Militant firebrand and leader of the United fans' anti-Murdoch and anti-Glazer campaigns, has been reinvented here into FC United's general manager, all trim in a blue check suit and club tie, directing details on his walkie-talkie – stewards, tickets, match day volunteers.

"Most people here still love United," Walsh said, "but they love their feeling for United, which grew from following the club for years, not the big business which came to exploit that loyalty. We're aiming to show a football club can be run by and for supporters, open to all sections of society."

The Formby match was designated a youth day, with under-16s allowed in free and young people before the game taking part in drama, banner-making and working with the Touch of Class rap collective, which promotes an anti-gun message. Thomas Cullen, a coach at Trafford Athletic Club, brought a group and

said he believed one lad had just been saved from exclusion by his school. "His teacher is here and she saw a different side of him," he said. "This is great for them. They're mostly black lads from Hulme and Moss Side but not one has ever been to a match at Old Trafford because they can't afford it."

Bill Evans, manager of Rochdale Children's Rights and Advocacy Services, brought 30 children, all in local authority care, saying it was a "positive way for them to feel included". Maxine Seager of the Tameside Youth Service, a disaffected "Big" United fan herself, came with 70 kids – "Two coach loads," she said, grinning and rolling her eyes.

"They're loving it, buzzing. They get so much out of this and we work our programmes, on anti-racism and social cohesion, around coming to the game."

The youth day events were organised by Vinny Thompson, who seemed staggered by his own football conversion: "To go from parading on terraces all over Europe to being a lentil-eating social worker in two years is pretty bloody amazing."

The thirty- and forty-something Stretford End veterans who formed FC United are painfully aware that Premiership ticket hikes have largely priced out the next generation of fans, so are replenishing their own ranks with the regular £2 entry price and this youth day. The place was teeming with kids, a sight long disappeared from top-flight football. One group of eight, aged 11 to 14, marching along with classic red, white and black scarves around their necks and not an adult in sight, seemed like a Life On Mars throwback to the 1970s. One eloquently explained why they come: "The atmosphere's mint."

The 3,847 who made it to the Formby game may not represent the dent in the Glazers' business plan some hoped for but it is many more than Bury had at their last home game, a phenomenon at the base of football's pyramid. The five goals strolled in took FC's total this season to 157 and a finish on 112 points; both are records. After the game the North West Counties League title was presented to Dave Chadwick, FC's mountainous captain, Walsh discreetly handing out the champagne. Beaming, bowing to shake hands with crowds of kids at the Manchester Road End, the players looked disbelieving, that tough semi-pro careers have turned out this glorious.

Karl Marginson, the former Rotherham United and non-league striker who has proved the perfect manager, said he has understood FC's philosophy more with time. "It's a very special thing to be part of. I try to instil its importance in the players, that this is the fans' club." In the celebrating stands they were mixing fond player ditties, anti-Glazer chants and pro-FC compositions. To the tune of Anarchy in the UK they roared: "I am an FC fan/I am Mancunian."

This is a football club they have fashioned for themselves out of belief and conviction. While Big United chase the Double at Wembley, they are off to the UniBond Northern Premier League next season. It seems like the best trip they have ever been on.

Followers of FC United of Manchester enjoy the passion of old-time fans, close to the action with a sense of identity

Ryan Giggs and Gary Neville lift the Premier League trophy in 2007, after three seasons without, and find it as good as ever

19|05|2007

How Ferguson took the fight to Chelsea

United's manager reinvented himself this season to break the Blues' dominance, writes Kevin McCarra

There may well be victory for Manchester United in the FA Cup final this afternoon but even the desolation of defeat by Chelsea would be short-lived. They know already that everything has been transformed. Sir Alex Ferguson can walk away from Wembley in the comforting knowledge that all the questions that had previously weighed on him now oppress Jose Mourinho.

The Portuguese, assuming he keeps his job at Stamford Bridge, is the one who has to review the signings made, identify the targets that ought to be pursued and decide whether his approach to the game has to be adjusted. Mourinho, after four astonishing seasons in Porto and London, has been introduced to self-doubt.

Ferguson, with the Premiership title once more stashed at Old Trafford, has triumphed over not only Chelsea but also the innumerable doubters among us who wondered whether the 65-year-old was a man stranded in a sport where he no longer belonged. After all, he had not won the league since 2003 and that made him a failure by the daunting standards he had set for himself.

Those who know Ferguson best held a deeper faith that he could react to even the emergence of a Chelsea plugged into a billionaire's wealth. Walter Smith, the Rangers manager, has been his friend and occasional colleague over the past 30 years. To him Ferguson is unique in adapting himself triumphantly to each new era. "When it comes to encompassing all the changes in football over the decades," said Smith, "he is better than any manager in history."

Normal life still bears Ferguson along through all the natural phases. A few years ago his wife, Cathy, rejected the suggestion that they buy a flat in Alderley Edge and now, instead, they are getting ready to leave the home they built in 1987 and move to a secluded and larger new house nearby that is more suited to

visits by 10 grandchildren. Nonetheless, Ferguson is not held prisoner by his age.

The Scotland manager, Alex McLeish, is struck by the fact that a footballer two generations younger than Ferguson is so swayed by him: "It was significant to me that someone like Wayne Rooney would say his man management is fantastic." McLeish himself was once the centre-half in Ferguson's great Aberdeen team and encountered a fierier, more regularly confrontational incarnation of the manager. Impressed by the sophistication of United's Carrington training ground, he once asked Ferguson whether he could deal with the contemporary footballer in the same fashion that he had those at Aberdeen. "Alex told me he had to be a psychologist nowadays," said McLeish.

He does not delude himself that men like Ferguson can be copied. "You always jump at the chance to watch someone like him or Marcello Lippi at work because you want to find out the secret," said McLeish, "but you don't really see anything different from what you do yourself. What they really have is a gift for getting the best out of a player and that is the biggest factor."

Smith agrees that "there is no Alex Ferguson template" for would-be imitators, pointing instead to the United manager's personality: "He loves what he does, so he wants to carry on doing it. He couldn't be successful otherwise."

It did look, all the same, as if Chelsea had changed the Premiership so radically that Ferguson would be unable to keep pace. There have been periods when he looked clumsy in the attempts to deal with the advent of foreign ownership. When arriving in Hungary for a 2005 Champions League game he was rebuked by fans enraged at acquiescence towards the Glazers' takeover. "I've got a job to do and 15 staff who come first," retorted Ferguson.

It was the unsatisfactory answer of a person taken by surprise and nearly implied that the backroom staff required his patronage to stay in work. Their interests were trivial by comparison with the impact of the Glazers on the club.

Ferguson had been more sympathetic to supporters fighting

189

Rupert Murdoch's earlier attempt to buy United. Later, though, he reflected on that and remarked: "As long as I had a football team I was happy." For all the complexities of United, he has never lost sight of the group of footballers at the core of the club, nor has his fascination with guiding them diminished.

The past four years without a Premiership title had raised debate about Ferguson's future, rather as the phase from his appointment at Old Trafford to the landing of the first trophy, the 1990 FA Cup, did. Danny Wallace, a member of the line-up that beat Crystal Palace in a Cup final replay 17 years ago, was not aware of whatever strain the manager might have been experiencing: "He didn't make us feel that there was any real pressure on him. We had some experienced players there and he made sure we knew what we had to do."

Ferguson's scheming and his confidence held up well under the Mourinho ascendancy of the last two seasons. "He has always insisted that he had talented people who were getting experience," said McLeish. "I didn't believe his time could be over. He's insatiable for football. When he changed his mind about retiring you sensed a new lease of life."

There is an inexhaustible curiosity about Ferguson, who has a passion for biographies of inspirational figures and keeps on recommending them to McLeish. His reading about such people reinforces the United manager's conviction that it is essential to square up to tough challenges.

Smith helped out Ferguson by spending a few months on the club's coaching staff early in 2004, when Cristiano Ronaldo was in his debut season. The Portuguese is a very different player from David Beckham but the contentious transfer of the latter to Real Madrid the previous summer had opened up a vacancy. "Alex has always been prepared to let players go when they were near the peak of their careers if he thought it was of benefit to the team as a whole," Smith said, "and people should see that he has been capable of changing United again and again." Wallace was bemused by the sale of Ruud van Nistelrooy but agrees that "he always knows when to buy and when to sell".

The manager, too, has been judicious during Chelsea's domination. "He has been bringing players in for a while," said Smith, "and he has been prepared for them to mature and reach a high level of consistency." The Rangers manager felt, too, that it was unrealistic to suppose that Stamford Bridge could have perpetual ascendancy in England with its history of competitiveness: "It has been a great achievement for Chelsea to win as many games as they did in the last two seasons and it's hard for anyone to stay at that level."

While admiring Ferguson's capacity for reinventing himself, Smith appreciates, too, the respects in which the fundamentals do not alter at all. "Formations can change," he said, "but not the philosophy of out-and-out attack with passing football that has brought United success."

Ferguson has evolved and evolved again while remaining unmistakably the extraordinary manager he has always been.

Chapter 12
The Premiership years: for richer, for poorer

Alan Shearer is back where he and Newcastle fans believe he belongs. In the next 10 years he did not disappoint them

07|08|1996

'The money won't change me — I'm only a sheet-metal worker's son from Newcastle'

The entire city appeared to be wrapped in black-and-white to hail their hero Alan Shearer's return. By Jim White

She is 63, gets £67 a week state pension; he is 25 and scrapes by on £30,000 a week, or maybe £35,000 or possibly even £42,000, depending on which tabloid you read. Her last pair of shoes cost her £9.99 from a discount warehouse; he gets paid £500,000 a year to wear his. She lives in a £40,000 house in Denton Burn, a Newcastle suburb with a fashion bypass; he is said to be looking for a place in snazzy Ponteland, something for around £750,000. But the moment Barbara Donaldson heard Alan Shearer was coming to her town, she thought she was the lucky one.

"The morning he signed for us I went to get my pension at the post office," said Mrs Donaldson. "Normally, they're a right grumpy lot but that day everybody in the queue had a smile like a Cheshire cat. If you'd put us in for the Olympic high jump that morning, we'd have set a world record."

Mrs Donaldson was by no means alone in her reaction to the purchase of Shearer for £15m. On the day he was presented to his army of new lovers (fans is too slight a word) the entire population of Newcastle appeared to be wrapped in black-and-white striped nylon.

Everywhere you looked people in replica Newcastle shirts were heading for St James' Park, Newcastle's ground which stands on top of a hill dominating the town. And Newcastle were not even playing. Fifteen thousand people just wanted to be there, to roar and chant as the new man was paraded.

Mrs Donaldson was luckier than most. While the 15,000 were left in a car park along with the press and 1,400 invitees sent tickets by Newcastle's sponsors, she found herself inside the stadium itself.

"I've been offered £100 for my tickets," said Brian Bloomfield from Gateshead, sitting next to Mrs Donaldson. "But I wouldn't take it. It wouldn't be fair on him," he added, pointing to his son, Dean, aged nine, who was beaming beside him. "He has to be here on this of all days."

Now this is an unexpected thing. Shearer cost enough to equip a hospital. He earns more in four days than a teacher will earn in a year. In a town where unemployment is endemic, you might think spending so much on a mere footballer would be regarded as wanton extravagance. But you could find few in Newcastle yesterday who did not think he represented the biggest bargain this side of a Marks & Spencer prawn sandwich.

"I'd have paid the money myself if I had it," said Brian Bloomfield. "This is the best thing to happen to this town since I can remember."

Which is the point about Shearer. On the BBC's Match of the Seventies broadcast on Monday night, we saw footage of Malcolm Macdonald, a previous incumbent of the No9 shirt Shearer is about to make his own, signing for Arsenal. That was the way things used to be around these parts: every time someone made good he went down south: Gascoigne, Waddle, Cole, they all migrated. Now the real thing was coming Newcastle's way. Not only that, he is a Geordie coming home. Better still, he was snatched out of the grasp of traditionally bigger, richer rivals.

"There's real pride in that," said Mrs Donaldson. "That we are in a position to compete with Man U, who just seem to be able to get whatever they want."

Thus the very size of Shearer's fee, the weight of his wage, are seen locally as symbolic of a new muscular ambition abroad in the town, the Nineties equivalent of the grandiose town halls the Victorians used to build.

"This sends out a signal to the rest of the world," Kevin Keegan, Shearer's new manager, said.

And the man who provided the funds to bring Shearer back to Newcastle was everywhere yesterday, making sure this point was made. "Football has always been part of our tradition," said Sir John Hall, Newcastle United's owner, bouncing around St James' Park in a pair of unexpectedly pointy blue shoes. "Football has never left the area. It's the talent that's gone away. What we're saying here is you don't have to leave Newcastle."

And, indeed, there will be economic benefits to the place from buying Shearer. Dozens more staff have been taken on in the club shop to process orders for Shearer shirts.

Thousands of extra pounds have flowed through pub tills toasting the new arrival. Hundreds more Scandinavians will flock in for football and shopping weekends.

The cynic might suggest the chief beneficiary of the Shearer boom will be Sir John Hall, owner of Britain's biggest shopping centre, the Metro Centre in Gateshead: in an economy built on retail, to be in possession of a brand as potent as Shearer is to be king.

But then there was no place for cynics around St James' Park yesterday. "Of course, Sir John's making money out of this," said Dave Trainer, from Darlington, at 25 the same age as Shearer but earning slightly less as one of the area's unemployed. "But without him, we'd have none of this," he added. "Sure, I can't afford to come and watch them but I'd rather not be able to afford to watch my team with Shearer in it than get in to see rubbish."

As for the man himself, well, Shearer clearly prefers his venomous right foot to do his talking: his press conference pronouncements were not in the sardines and trawlers class. Blinking modestly in the flashbulb blaze, he limited himself to talking of "giving 110 per cent" and saying "for me the season can't come quick enough".

He also declared: "If money comes my way, that's fine. I'll deal with that when it comes along. It certainly won't change me. After all, I'm only a sheet metal-worker's son from Newcastle."

Mrs Donaldson was thrilled by the man. "He's lovely, everything a mother dreams her son to be," she said. "Not one you'd lust over, mind. Not like Sir John. Power, now that's the real aphrodisiac."

Meanwhile, outside the stadium, the 15,000 fans waited for their new man to appear on the stage. A sense of parochial triumphalism was on their minds as they ignored the rain and sang as one: "Are you watching, Sunderland?"

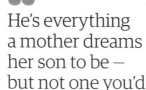

He's everything a mother dreams her son to be — but not one you'd lust over, mind

---

15/08/1996

Has-been who never was talks up Posh

Paul Kelso finds Barry Fry, owner and manager of Peterborough, mending gutters and champing at the bit

....

While most Premiership managers were plotting transfer coups and finalising team selection for the season's opening day, Barry Fry, the new owner-manager of Second Division Peterborough United, had more pressing problems. It had been raining for four hours and the gutters on the new Family Stand could not cope. "It bucketed down all afternoon and the gutters couldn't take it. You could effin' swim in a couple of the executive boxes after an hour," he said.

Such are the trials of life in the lower divisions, where club finances can be parlous. Keeping the Posh in the black while making sure they retain their present status is the immediate task for Fry, who fulfilled his long-held ambition to own a club by paying an estimated £500,000 for a 75% stake in Peterborough 2½ months ago.

Sacked by Birmingham City in May, he was hunting for a job when Peterborough's chief executive, Chris Turner, his former assistant at Barnet, invited him to be manager. He agreed on condition that he be allowed to buy into the club.

"I couldn't have come here only as manager," he says. "If I'd been successful I'd have moved on in two years, leaving Peterborough in the lurch. And it was no good me just bringing a bit of cash and enthusiasm. The club's got bags of potential but I've got to get the fans interested."

The Fry effect seems to be working. Season-ticket sales are up and all home games have been sponsored in advance for the first time. On the field things are looking up too.

'We beat Sheffield Wednesday 2-0 three weeks ago and got a standing ovation. When you speak to the supporters, they just want to finish in the top half of the table, having come 19th last year. I want promotion in the first year. Being realistic, I've got a three-year plan to get us out.'

Watching Fry on the training ground it is clear his dual

Barry Fry has done 'just' management. As Peterborough chairman (until 2006), at least he was safe from the sack

06/11/2002
I'm posher than you lot, Mrs B tells Peterborough

Paul Kelso

One is a struggling second division football club, the other a struggling pop star, and all they have in common is a nickname. But by the time Peterborough United and Victoria Beckham have finished with each other there will be only one Posh.

Beckham, aka Posh Spice, this week began proceedings aimed at preventing the club from using its 68-year-old nickname "the Posh", threatening it with ruin and prompting outrage from supporters.

Four years ago the club chairman, Peter Boizot, received trademark rights to use the terms "Posh" and "the Posh" on merchandise, leisurewear and other items sold at the club's London Road ground. But on Monday the club was informed that lawyers acting for Beckham had objected to Peterborough using the names on the grounds that, since her former band, the Spice Girls, shot to fame in 1996 she had been known around the world as Posh Spice.

"I was staggered to think that anyone would think we are not entitled to be known as the Posh," said the club's chief executive, Geoff Davey, yesterday. "We've been known as the Posh since the 1920s and certainly since we became a professional club in 1934." Michell Chapman, who chairs the Peterborough United Supporters' Club, said: "It's a joke that she thinks she can come along and claim the name."

The club, currently languishing one place off the bottom of the Second Division, cannot afford a lengthy legal battle.

A spokesman for the patent office confirmed Mrs Beckham had registered an objection and said she would now be asked to make her case.

The football club will have to do likewise in a process expected to take several months.

It's a joke that she thinks she can claim the name. We've been the Posh since the 20s

responsibilities have not diminished his enthusiasm. Wearing only shorts and boots he cajoles players on two pitches at once, looking every inch the "51, fat and happy fella" he claims to be.

Yet his transformation from training-ground drill sergeant to boardroom boss is effortless. Having promised the players a weekend away so they can all "get a bird, get pissed and play 18 holes of golf", a now double-breasted Fry gives a grand tour of the club's London Road ground. As we pass the club secretary's office he looks in and signs a couple of players' contracts. He has always liked collecting players. For Peterborough he has already signed nine.

His relish for the game is born of a desire to atone for past failures. When he was an apprentice at Manchester United in the 60s Matt Busby told him he would be the next Jimmy Greaves. To a degree Busby was right, only Fry skipped the scoring feats and went straight for the drinking. "I'm the has-been who never was," he says.

But Fry does not dwell on the past. Even his sacking from Birmingham – "the biggest surprise I've had in football" – has not left him bitter. "I've never looked forward to a season as much as this one. I've got to do the business on the field but I also want to see if this silly football manager can run a club."

As for his fluctuating fortunes, he says: "Football's football. There are no ethics or fairness. It's a cut-throat business but at least these days I don't have to plead for money to buy a player. I haven't got to answer to anyone. The only certainty in management is that you'll get the sack and, of course, the beauty of this job is I can't."

20|12|1996

Keep on keeping on and on

Paul Weaver explores the forces that have driven Peter Shilton through glory and bankruptcy to his 1,000th game

The story of Peter Shilton is that of no ordinary footballer or man. It is about an obsessive, from the time he marched into Leicester City's Filbert Street as a 10-year-old and demanded a trial, who then stretched his frame by hanging weights from his feet as he suspended himself from the banisters of his parents' Leicester home.

It is the story of an outstanding sportsman but also of a single-minded perfectionist who can make Geoff Boycott and Nick Faldo look like dilettantes and who today, like them, finds himself strangely exiled from the nation's deepest affection.

This is the man who became England's greatest goalkeeper, winning a record 125 caps and playing in the finals of three World Cups. He was Britain's highest-paid player, earning £250,000 a year at Derby nine years ago, owned three homes and bred racehorses. Today, after more than 30 years in the professional game, he is penniless and living in a rented home near Coventry. He has been destroyed, financially, by a hopeless addiction to gambling that has forced him to put retirement on hold.

On Sunday, at Leyton Orient's unfashionable little ground in London E10, and at the age of 47, he will make his 1,000th league appearance against Brighton in the Nationwide Football League Third Division. The match will be live on Sky Sports but it might be more at home on UK Gold.

Shilton's is a colossal achievement. Behind him comes Terry Paine, with 824 appearances, while his two great contemporaries between the posts, Ray Clemence and Pat Jennings, made 758 and 757 respectively. To call Shilton a veteran is a little like suggesting Methuselah was knocking on a bit.

He played his first League match for Leicester in May 1966, the days of The Beatles, false eyelashes and the E-type Jag. England had not yet won the World Cup. Arkle was the toast of Cheltenham and John Pulman was world snooker champion after beating Fred Davis. Gary Sobers led West Indies against England, Jack Brabham was the Formula One world champion and Spain's Manuel Santana won Wimbledon. It was not just another football season; it was another age.

That Shilton is still playing at all is remarkable. Yet such is his self-belief that he has negotiated a clause in his Orient contract that would release him if he is approached by a Premiership club. It is the same massive confidence he had as a 17-year-old at Leicester when he told the club they had to choose between himself and the great Gordon Banks. Leicester thought about it and sold Banks.

"I was hoping to play my 1,000th game in the Premiership," he said this week. "I feel I could still do a job there and, who knows, I still might get the chance. I've not had a bad year. I played 12 games for West Ham reserves and let in seven goals, and I've conceded three in four games for Orient. The Premiership is where my heart lies and I believe I'm still good enough. I'm training as hard as ever and I don't know when I will call it a day." All this sounds a little sad. He paints a picture of self-deception, of someone stumbling through a wonderland that might have been landscaped by Peter Pan and Walter Mitty. Yet it is Shilton's considerable achievement to turn outrageous ambition into reality.

"He is the most headstrong, determined man I've ever met," says his friend and biographer Jason Tomas. "You can never write him off because, like his old manager, Brian Clough, he has this genius for pulling off the impossible.

"Sometimes I think he's a little demented, a very difficult but fascinating man. And he never does anything by halves, whether it's goalkeeping, gambling – where he has taken ridiculous risks – or drinking, where he has thought nothing of going on a two-day bender." Barry Hearn, his Orient chairman who is planning a Chris Eubank-style entrance for him at Brisbane Road on Sunday, says: "No one will ever break this record. I can see him playing at 50. I've always thought that, if the world was to end in an hour, Boycott would go and have a net and Shilts would go through his exercises.

"But he can be a stickler with a contract. Our negotiations were hilarious. In the end I threw the piece of paper at him and told him to write in what he wanted." There are also stories about Clough, who wanted to sign him when he was manager of Derby and Leeds, smashing his squash racket against his office wall at Nottingham Forest as he became frustrated by Shilton's excessive demands. "He is the most single-minded man I've ever come across," says his former agent, Jon Holmes. "In many ways he doesn't have a life beyond goalkeeping." His long-suffering wife of 26 years, Sue, would testify to that. Shilton was fortunate to have devoted parents, who met over a milk stout after a spell as war-time pen pals. They encouraged their son's precocious ambition and even moved house because they feared that living next to a working men's club would disturb his preparation. Les and May Shilton ran a cafe and remember their 15-year-old son returning from training during a busy lunchtime to complain that his bed had not been made.

Sue Shilton needed to be even more supportive when the property slump left the couple with negative equity on three properties, and when his horses failed to win. Shilton turned to gambling with disastrous results. At one point she was forced to sell her Mini, a Christmas present from her husband, and buy a bicycle.

There were repossessions, a bankruptcy notice from the leading trainer Martin Pipe and court hearings – one for the non-payment of a TV licence. There was also a drink-driving conviction after he had been discovered with a married woman in his car, an evening Sue still refers to as "Peter's accident".

She added: "Peter always demanded this perfect home, with everything spotless. I knew nothing about many of the financial problems. When I found out I felt this anger towards him." There were professional problems too. He was sacked as manager of Plymouth. John McGovern, his former Forest teammate, had already quit as No2 claiming Shilton had failed to repay a £9,000 loan.

None of this is likely to be paraded at Brisbane Road on Sunday. Instead the footballing world will pay homage.

"Peter is truly, truly amazing," says the former Arsenal keeper Bob Wilson. "He has this magnificent obsession and, if Clemence hadn't been around, he would have won nearly 200 caps. He was not as naturally elastic as Ray and was not wonderful on crosses. But in the end he was the better keeper. His preparation and fitness were wonderful and he was one of the first goalkeepers to psychologically and physically intimidate other players, much as Peter Schmeichel does today.

"He made younger keepers model their game on his. He even got me looking at my game and I was eight years older." John Burridge says Shilton could still play in the Premiership. "I was the oldest goalkeeper to do so at 43. Peter is my all-time hero. The only thing you lose when you're older is the respect of other people who see you concede a goal and blame your age." No Orient player would dare do such a thing this weekend.

"

If Ray Clemence had not been around, Peter would have won nearly 200 caps

"

04/04/1997
Constant failure keeps us happy

Harry Pearson charts Middlesbrough's tortuous route to Wembley after 121 years of character-building failures

On Match of the Day recently Alan Hansen offered the opinion that Middlesbrough would willingly swap Sunday's Coca-Cola Cup final and next week's FA Cup semi-final against Chesterfield for a place in next season's Premiership.

As a Boro supporter I have to say this is abject rubbish. I can see why he might think it, though. Despite his outward appearance of lean fitness, the years at Liverpool have taken their toll on Hansen. He is a man grown soft on a rich diet of victory.

In Hansen's mind relegation means crossing the threshold of some arid and brutal place. We, however, are used to the First Division. Trying to scare us with the drop is likely to meet with as much success as an attempt to deter Roberto Duran by slapping him across the cheek with a damp J-cloth.

Middlesbrough, it is true, are staring relegation in the face but this is nothing new. In fact, it is an occurrence so common I imagine relegation is staring right back at us, a look of irritation playing about its countenance, muttering: "Oh no, not you again." It's for the best, anyway. As in the bedroom scenes from a Fifties movie, sometimes in football you have to keep one foot on the floor to preserve some semblance of decency.

The Coca-Cola Cup final and the FA Cup semi-final are new experiences for Middlesbrough. You wait 121 years and suddenly they both come along in the same week. Of all the accusations levelled at foreign players such as Juninho, Ravanelli and Emerson, the one about them having no understanding of English footballing tradition is, in this case, surely the most accurate.

Their arrival on Teesside and the subsequent victories over Stockport and Derby have brought the end of an era. Boro fans may be tempted to gloat at this change in fortune but they have not got the hang of it yet. It is not as if we have had much practice. My grandfather started taking me to Ayresome Park when I was six. He had been following Middlesbrough since 1912. Over the years the disappointment had curdled into a bleak pessimism and then solidified into something far darker.

He was not alone. The town was full of people like him. At the old Opera House an actor once gave a dramatic recital of Dante's Inferno. When the account of gnashing teeth and burning flesh was finished, a member of the audience jumped to his feet and shouted enthusiastically: "That sounds champion. Are there any vacancies in June?" To my grandfather the trip to Ayresome Park took on the mood of a bi-weekly penitence. If Boro embarked on a Cup run or edged too close to the top of whatever division they were in, he stopped going. He had come to see the endurance of failure as a badge of masculinity. Success was an affront to his manhood.

Such attitudes pass down through the generations. During Emerson's voluntary exile a Teessider who had previously shown limited enthusiasm for football remarked to me that it was "the usual fiasco at the Boro, then". I might have been tempted to disagree. I didn't bother for two reasons: first, there was a kernel of truth in the remark and second, experience has shown there is no sense arguing with my mother.

It is not that Boro are a vastly unsuccessful club. They have spent only a couple of seasons outside the top two divisions, unearthed great players and regularly fielded teams packed with internationals. No, what has marked them out has been their unmatched ability to lurk near the top while avoiding major honours with all the studied nimbleness of a Highland sword dancer skipping around a set of glittering, crossed claymores.

My grandfather's hero back in the days when he was merely disgruntled was George Camsell. Camsell is, in some ways, the key to understanding the near-missability of Middlesbrough Football Club. Born in the Durham coalfield before the Great War, Camsell was an archetypal old-time centre-forward.

His socks bulged with shinpads the size and thickness of futons, his hair glistened, teeth were a distant memory. During the 1926-27 season Camsell scored 59 goals in 37 league games. It was an English record. He was feted as a hero and seemed destined to go down in the history books. The following season Dixie Dean of Everton scored 60. There are many words you might use to describe this episode, but "bloody typical" will probably suffice for now.

The first true Boro-style failure I witnessed (or rather, didn't, my grandfather having withdrawn in protest after a third-round victory over West Ham) came during the 1969-70 season when Boro advanced to the sixth round of the FA Cup.

This was the team of John Hickton, idol of all Teesside, whose penalty run-up was so long Wainwright could have written a book about it, jug-eared Bill Gates, side-burned Derek Downing and goalkeeper Willie Whigham, whose startling facial resemblance to the Sea Devils from Dr Who still gives me unsettling dreams.

Before the draw for the quarter-finals the manager, Stan Anderson, boldly announced that he wanted to play Manchester United next. As an eight-year-old fan this struck me as complete folly. Why would he want to play Manchester United? Manches-

ter United had won the European Cup. They had George Best and Bobby Charlton. They were, let's face it, better than us. Much, much better.

Surely Stan Anderson should want to play a team who were worse than us, someone we could beat. Sensing that in my childish naivety I was probably missing some subtle nuance of Boro's master strategy, I addressed these concerns to my grandfather. "Why do we want to play Manchester United?" I asked. "Because the chairman needs a new Rolls Royce," he replied, it seemed to me at the time cryptically.

Ah, yes, Middlesbrough's chairman, under whose direct orders, rumours on Teesside had it, the club had displayed a capacity for self-destruction that would have drawn gasps of admiration from a room full of kamikaze pilots.

Whatever, Stan's wishes were met. Boro played Manchester United, drew at Ayresome then lost at Old Trafford. ("A replay," my grandfather cackled cynically.) And so it went on. In 1974-75 we reached the quarter-finals again. By now we were in the top flight. We drew Birmingham City at St Andrew's. We had beaten the Blues 3-0 home and away in the league. In the Cup we lost to a Bob Hatton goal.

The following season we reached the semi-finals of the League Cup. In the first leg at Ayresome Boro beat Man City only 1-0 but nobody was particularly concerned. This, after all, was Jack Charlton's team. The defenders (Boam, Craggs, Maddren) had the names of rocks that oil tankers founder on. You would, people said, back those lads to defend a one-goal lead anywhere in the world. Except Maine Road, obviously. We lost 4-0.

I could go on and on. And I will. 1978. FA Cup quarter-finals again. This time Leyton Orient at Ayresome Park. Orient were mid-table Second Division. Boro were top-half First Division. Never mind the manager, never mind the chairman, this was the draw I wanted. This was a team we were better than. No doubt about it. Definitely. We drew 0-0 and lost the replay 2-1.

Think you've got the picture now? You haven't, believe me. 1981. FA Cup quarter-finals. Wolverhampton Wanderers. At Ayresome. We had beaten them earlier in the season. Beaten them comfortably.

The result (a 3-1 replay defeat) was predictable, the aftermath less so. Within a year the manager John Neal had gone, good young players such as Craig Johnston, David Armstrong and Mark Proctor were sold, home attendances almost halved and the club was relegated. Five years after John Richards's winning goal at Molineux Middlesbrough went bankrupt.

Eleven years later here we are. Pundits keep pointing out that Middlesbrough could still lose both big games and get relegated. But so what? Whatever happens, we have taken a step forward into unknown territory and the Boro fans have survived worse.

In the desert of footballing despair Alan Hansen may well be a croaking, sweating greenhorn. We are the Apache.

14|04|1997

So near, so far: suffering Spireites dream on

FA Cup semi-final
Chesterfield 3 Middlesbrough 3 (*aet; 2-2 at 90min*)
Martin Thorpe, Old Trafford

This was very nearly the greatest FA Cup tie in the competition's 125 years. In the end it had to make do with being one of the greatest.

Put together for £320,000, the fourth-oldest club in the world were 20 minutes away from beating a Middlesbrough side that cost £21m to become the first team from outside the top two divisions to play in an FA Cup final. And had the referee, David Elleray, not controversially ruled out what appeared a good Chesterfield goal when the Spireites were 2-1 up, they would probably have achieved that.

In the 68th minute, Jon Howard found himself free in the area with the ball at his feet. He turned smartly and hammered a shot which hit the bar and came down over the line. To everyone's surprise Elleray blew for an infringement, but no one was clear what the offence was, least of all the referee.

After the game he at first said that the whistle was for an offence by Andy Morris after the ball had hit the bar and rebounded off the pitch, implying that he did not feel the ball had crossed the line. Later he had a different story: "I've seen the replay and I accept the ball crossed the line," he said, adding that he had blown up for an infringement before the ball hit the bar. It was the sort of refereeing controversy which has plagued this season, and which gallant and spirited Chesterfield did not deserve.

But Middlesbrough's escape was not all about good fortune. Fabrizio Ravanelli and Juninho have shown the doubters since they arrived here that they really are prepared to sweat as well as swagger. Having been 2-0 down after 60 minutes, they

Chesterfield went wild. It is difficult to blame them but they probably went too wild

helped to pull their shell-shocked side to 2-2 after 90 minutes and a goal ahead with one minute of extra-time remaining.

Chesterfield had given everything and looked dead on their feet. Then Chris Beaumont, a late substitute with more strength than his team-mates, hoisted a last hopeful long ball into the Boro area. Kevin Davies, Chesterfield's biggest threat all afternoon, jumped with a defender and the ball fell to Jamie Hewitt on the penalty spot.

With one last summoning of will the defender leapt higher than the red shirts gathered around and steered a looping header past the flat-footed Ben Roberts into the top corner.

It is Hewitt's 30th birthday on May 17, the day of the Cup final, and he made sure that Chesterfield at least have a chance of being there to play Chelsea. They must replay this fixture at Hillsborough a week tomorrow.

Chesterfield had calmly asserted themselves from the whistle but the first real turning point came after 37 minutes. Vladimir Kinder had already been booked for kicking the ball away needlessly at a free-kick when the skilful Davies beat him down the right. Kinder twice pulled back the striker and was sent off for a second bookable offence.

Nine minutes after half-time Chesterfield took advantage of the extra man when Howard got past the substitute Clayton Blackmore down the right and fired in a cross to the ubiquitous Davies. His shot was deflected past the keeper, and the 6ft 4in striker Morris had only to tap the ball in at the far post.

Six minutes later Chesterfield went 2-0 ahead. Morris again steamed into the area and was upended by, or fell over, Roberts's diving body. Elleray judged it to be the former and Sean Dyche hammered in the penalty. Chesterfield went wild. It is difficult to blame them but they probably went too wild and found it impossible to clear from their minds the dream of achieving the impossible. They paid the price.

Within four minutes Boro had pulled a goal back: Emerson sent Blackmore clear down the left and Ravanelli bundled in the cross for goal No28 of the season.

When, two minutes later, Elleray gave a penalty to Middlesbrough after Juninho seemed to run into Dyche, it only compounded the injustice in Chesterfield's minds. Craig Hignett equalised from the spot, squeezing the ball under Billy Mercer's body.

Thirty minutes of extra-time was a daunting prospect to tired Chesterfield and Boro duly applied a firmer grip to the game. The impressive Mercer produced a flying save from Juninho and blocked well from Ravanelli. It seemed inevitable that Boro would score and, when Robbie Mustoe's shot cannoned off the bar and bounced over the advancing Juninho, the ball fell to the defender Gianluca Festa, who drilled it past Mercer.

But Chesterfield come from defiant stock and were not about to give up then. "I'm so proud of my players and everybody associated with the club," said their manager, John Duncan. "It was an extraordinary, emotional day, the best of my career."

09|05|1997

Why I love Steve Bull

Charles Ross

Wolves are at Crystal Palace in the play-offs tomorrow. Steve Bull stands on the verge of achieving his ultimate goal: getting his beloved Wolves back into the top flight. No one could deserve it more.

It is impossible to convey just how much Bully means to Wolves fans. When he was offloaded to us by near but not very dear West Brom back in 1986, Wolves were in the lower half of the old Fourth Division and on the road to extinction. Over 300 goals later and still he is at Molineux, living proof that loyalty does exist in football. Now 32, Steve Bull has sacrificed his career to drag Wolves back where they belong.

There have been any number of enticing offers to leave: more money, more international caps, the chance to win things. Two years ago, after the heartache of a play-off defeat at Bolton, Graham Taylor accepted a bid from Big Fat Ron to send Steve to Coventry. Wolverhampton went berserk. Two days later Steve announced he was staying put "because of the fans". Come the

new season and Molineux reverberated to "We don't care what Taylor thinks, Stevie is our king". It was Taylor who left.

That Steve might ever leave us has been a recurring nightmare, not least because any subsequent promotion achieved without him would have felt empty. He is the one destined to kick off in our first match in the Premiership, the Wolves renaissance complete. That is how the plot is written.

Bully epitomises Black Country values: honest, direct, fiercely loyal and no false airs and graces. Like his football, in fact. He scores proper goals: running on to through-balls, brushing off defenders and smashing shots into the net. No easy tap-ins or penalties. The only penalty in his tally was, bizarrely, scored for England B; "no one else fancied it".

This is his testimonial year. It seems to be less a money-making exercise than a means of saying thank you – for fans and player alike. Keen to do something special for the hard-core supporters he volunteered for a question-and-answer session with fanzine readers – free of charge.

He spent a riotous two hours on stage one wet winter's night in the upstairs room of a Wolverhampton pub. At the end of it he declined the offer of a swift and private exit down the back staircase. "I'll come downstairs and have a pint with you lot," he said, "if that's OK." But neither his avalanche of goals nor his unswerving loyalty suffice to explain fully the place this bloke holds in our affections. The Hayward family millions may have rescued us financially but Bully has put the heart and soul back into Molineux. How else do you explain average gates of 25,000 for the last three years in the Division From Hell? He plays the way a fan would. He does now know what a lost cause is.

True, we have not seen Wolves play in the top flight since the early Eighties but we have been privileged to follow the greatest story this proud club has ever seen.

A generation from now, our children and grandchildren will turn round and ask us "what was Bull like?" The videos will be there to capture the goals but not the emotion. Our eyes will mist over because we will remember that, whenever Bully left that tunnel wearing the Old Gold No9 shirt, a little bit of each of us took the field with him.

Promotion beckons. Wolves fans will end up in tears, of joy or despair. We will be crying not so much for ourselves but more for Steve Bull.

Charles Ross is editor of A Load of Bull, the Wolves fanzine

Steve Bull stuck it out at Wolves for 13 years and stuck it in, too, with more than 300 goals. No wonder they loved him

17|04|1999
Carlisle – from Derby day to doomwatch

Charles Burgess reveals the agonies of watching a small-town club rise right to the top, then fall right back down again

It was 24 years ago this month that I stood on the emptying terraces of the Baseball Ground, around five o'clock. Many of the delighted crowd of 38,000 had already headed home having seen Derby County crowned as League champions after a goalless draw.

But it had been their opponents I had gone to see. My town, my team, Carlisle United, were finishing their one and only season in the then First Division.

As the detritus of the crowd, the discarded papers and sweet wrappers, swirled around the stadium, I lingered, looking at the silent stands and knowing I would never, as a supporter, see the top division again.

It was sad but not surprising. After all we were a small-town club who had amazed the football world and ourselves by getting there in the first place.

And then we had astounded everyone by winning our first three matches in the top flight and being top. Top of the whole 92-club league, above Liverpool, Arsenal and certainly above the fancy dans of Manchester United, who had been relegated to the Second Division. I still have the *Sunday Express*: played three, won three, points six. Chelsea at Stamford Bridge, Middlesbrough and Spurs at Brunton Park.

Now, 24 years later, having leapt up and down the lower divisions and latterly having enjoyed or, some would say, endured one of the most charismatic chairmen in football, the situation is so different and so desperate. Carlisle, bottom but two in the Third Division, are odds-on to drop out of the League, having played more games than their two rivals in distress. And with it will go a part of my life.

There was never a question of whom to support. It came with the territory and, as fans of lowly clubs will know, much of it is a matter of duty rather than pleasure. But though the sad times, or just plain boring times, outnumbered the good, they were all worth waiting for, shared with a few fellow sufferers.

Remember that 3-0 victory over Mansfield to get promotion from the Third when we ran on the pitch and kissed the turf, the away trip to Bolton when a bus driver saved us 12-year-olds from some nasty-looking yobs, the hours we spent thinking of phrases involving a midfielder called Train, contriving all our Subbuteo tournaments so that Carlisle would win the FA Cup, changing the words of hymns so that Chris Balderstone was the King?

And then, when we were older and had moved south, we would search out the games in or near London and stand with the other exiles and watch a lot of poor football, interspersed with a minute or two of clever stuff. And often when the players applauded us at the end I wanted to get on the team bus with them for the long journey home. Balderstone, a midfield player with a cracking left foot and an eye for the long pass, was one of the last men to play League football and county cricket, and we were glad that he did it while playing for Carlisle.

There are other factoids we would recite. Did you know that Ivor Broadis became the youngest manager in the Football League when he was appointed in 1946, aged 23? And that he became the first manager to transfer himself when he moved to Sunderland for £18,000 in 1949? And that his replacement was Bill Shankly? Yes, that one.

Carlisle have always had to sell to survive. The last big one to go was Matt Jansen, now at Blackburn Rovers but sold last year to Crystal Palace. Jansen is the son of a local policeman and we first saw his abilities in a match at Wycombe Wanderers. He was a yard faster than any of his team-mates and it was obvious he was not long for our world.

The man doing the selling recently has been Michael Knighton, who you may remember very nearly pulled off the astonishing coup 10 years ago of buying Manchester United for about £10m. He had the vision to see that big football clubs were vastly undervalued and that television revenues would transform their wealth. He must have wondered what might have been when BSKyB offered Martin Edwards and friends £623m. Ouch.

Knighton came within a whisker of acquiring United and no one really knows what went wrong. He blames the press for undermining his position, others say he was unable to raise the last few pounds to fulfil his ambition. But ambition he had and, after a few years as an Old Trafford director, his ambition fell on my team. They were in a mess in 1992 and finished bottom but Aldershot had already gone out of the league that season, having gone bust and failed to complete their fixtures.

No one else wanted Carlisle and Knighton, full of plans and chutzpah, bought the club for a song. We might have gone bust without him and it was fun for a while. He talked of a football museum and hotels and centres of excellence and built a stand. We even got promotion to the Second Division twice and went to Wembley twice for the final of the Auto Windscreens Shield, winning it once.

But for many Knighton's bluster was looking preposterous. He said soon after taking over: "I predict that within 10 years we will be among the 10 wealthiest clubs in this country. We will be competing in Europe and will have one of the finest stadiums."

He was reported as saying he had seen UFOs over a northern motorway and he took to writing long, rambling justifications of his thoughts and actions.

Then at the start of last season he decided he could manage the team, sacking the manager Mervyn Day. Knighton, no mean footballer in his youth and unquestionably knowledgeable about the game, called himself the director of coaching. The team chopped and changed, players came and went so quickly that we joked that the crowd knew one another better than the players. But it was no joke and Nigel Pearson, the former Middlesbrough player, was brought in this season to manage.

Before last month's transfer deadline other players were sold, a few more came in and Knighton, much of whose property portfolio in Carlisle is up for sale, announced that he would rather go down than go bust.

No one knows, apart from Knighton and his fellow directors, the real state of the finances at Brunton Park or how much money has been taken out or put into the club, and right now, quite frankly, that is not important.

Today Carlisle go to promotion-seeking Rotherham. There is a month to go in which League status can be retained. Broadly we need to win and Hartlepool, whom we still have to play, and Scarborough need to lose.

It is as simple as that. The club needs it, the town needs it, I need it.

Please.

24/04/1999
This cottage industry of dreams

Once a music-hall joke, Fulham are getting serious down by the river. Well, almost. Donald McRae reports

....

These are dizzying times for Fulham. This week's confirmation of their Second Division championship, with speculation that the little old club by the river may yet smash an English league record by reeling in 108 points for the season, seems almost surreal to their wry band of long-suffering supporters.

Even a recent sighting of Michael Jackson at Craven Cottage, or news from the Vatican that the irresistible rise of Kevin Keegan's Black-And-White Army is being monitored closely by the Pope, appears less bizarre than the belated but still mildly shocking arrival of footballing glory in SW6.

For Simon Wallace and Tom Greatrex, who have amassed 35 years of Cottage chaos and heartache between them, Fulham's customary gloss of eccentricity has always coated failure rather than success at the club. While still in their mid-20s, the two suddenly bewildered fans are steeped in Fulham's history of comic drama. The support of a hardcore Cottage man, like His Holiness, is as familiar to them as the fact that their real saviour, Mohamed Al Fayed, followed comedians like Tommy Trinder and Jimmy Hill when unexpectedly he became Fulham's chairman in May 1997.

Vatican in the know

"The Pope is a bit different from Michael Jackson," Greatrex suggests blithely, "because he really did support Fulham. When he was based at a seminary in Roehampton just after the war he used to watch Fulham regularly. This latest story came about because some idiot rang up the Vatican and asked if the Pope would say a prayer for Fulham. The Vatican spokesman already knew that Fulham were playing Wigan next and so he apparently said that the Pope was hoping for a good result."

On April 10 Fulham beat Wigan 2-0 and before the match Fayed went on his 'Victory Walk' around the Cottage. "Al Fayed does that before every game," Greatrex says, "because he loves the applause. But on that particular afternoon we couldn't hear the announcer. We just thought it was the usual thing of Al Fayed and his bodyguards having a stroll. It was only when they came round the corner where we stood that we said, 'Who's that with him?'

"He was dressed all in black and he wore shades," Wallace remembers, "and we wondered if he was one of those look-alikes. We only realised it was the real Michael Jackson when the sun suddenly came out and he wouldn't carry on until somebody put up an umbrella to stop him melting."

Stand-up jokers around the country are already lifting lines of new material from Craven Cottage's dream life. "Have you heard about the night Michael Jackson, the Pope, Mohamed Al Fayed and Kevin Keegan went down the Rat & Parrot to celebrate Fulham winning the title?" will echo repeatedly before this season ends.

Yet Fulham's rich burst of achievement under Al Fayed and Keegan has been trailed by decades of despair. As recently as January 1996, Fulham were only one place from the bottom of the entire Football League. The Third Division club below them, Torquay United, then trotted out and won 2-0 at Craven Cottage.

Mere footballing misery, however, was far less significant than the threat posed by various schemes to redevelop the ground between 1986 and 1996. Apart from razing the Cottage, such greed looked set to devour the club itself.

"The lowest moment for me," Greatrex says, "was when I heard they were planning this merger with QPR into something called Fulham Park Rangers. Football almost became a secondary concern. That's always been a problem for Fulham, because all our previous owners eventually realised that in an area like this, where property prices are so high, the ground was worth more than the players and the club put together."

After a Hill-led consortium had briefly salvaged Fulham in the mid-90s the way was open for Fayed to make his conclusive bid. "We were all worried," Wallace says, "because Al Fayed was not noted for his love of football. There was a lot of scepticism. And things didn't improve when Micky Adams was sacked in only the second month of the new season. We all loved Micky because he'd done a brilliant job in getting us up from the Third. So those early doubts about Al Fayed intensified."

Twenty months on, and despite the "typically Fulham" calamity of losing to Grimsby in last season's play-offs, the up-front combination of Fayed and Keegan has finally moved the focus away from a droll but dismal past. Fulham has usually been a gentle reminder to someone that their grandad or their uncle's best friend used to watch them in the 60s when they had Johnny Haynes. Frustrated by such nostalgia, a younger fan like Greatrex points more dryly to another ancient Cottage hero George Cohen. "See," Greatrex confirms, "England have never won the World Cup without a Fulham player in the team."

The new Mohamed 'n' Kev Show hit the promotion road at speed and now rolls with the swagger of a club generous enough to loan out their manager to a needy England. After facing Wrexham at home this afternoon, Keegan leads England into Hungary, secure in the knowledge that he and Fayed have fulfilled the first stage of their glorious, if still vaguely crazy, plan to bring Premiership football to Fulham by August 2000.

On Wednesday Fulham outclassed Millwall 4-1, displaying the verve which encourages Al Fayed's pre-game ritual. As he saunters around the pitch, doffing his Fulham cap and giving a royal wave of the black-and-white scarf, his milking of the gratitude is as relentless as it is interesting. For one of Britain's richest men, he seems exceptionally pleased to greet his small choir. But then "Fayed For England" is not a chant he would have heard outside Craven Cottage.

United's toughest game

Keegan obviously grew accustomed to such echoing hymns more than 25 years ago. After the worship of the Kop and St James' Park, he is more practical when assessing both Fulham's current delight and expectation. So Keegan has tempered his chairman's earlier claim that Fulham could become "the Manchester United of the south". Instead Saint Kev says: "I think you're talking round about West Ham-size."

But Keegan emphasises Fayed's financial investment and increasingly emotional attachment to the club remain the defining features of Fulham's resurgence. "Without wanting to sound blasé, I expected it," he said as Fulham exulted in their first title for 50 years. "When you have Mr Al Fayed's backing you expect it." He points to Fulham's next target, a Football League record. "We've now got 96 points. We've won 30 games out of 46, with 15 on the trot at home. If we win our last four games, which we're capable of doing, then we'll reach that record 108 points. That drives us on. But we've a way to go yet."

When the conversation turned to Manchester United's victory in Turin, Keegan became more mischievously chirpy. Fulham's 1-0 reverse at Old Trafford in the FA Cup shone even more magically as a noble defeat by the European Cup finalists. "That was probably their toughest game this year," Keegan cracked.

For the aptly named Wallace and Greatrex, such quips suddenly sound cheerfully optimistic rather than ridiculous. They even grin helplessly when Wallace says: "We've put aside our doubts about Al Fayed. You can't question either his motives or his commitment to the club any longer. The same goes for Keegan. We've had so many false dawns at Fulham but this feels fantastic. We're just going to enjoy it, however long it lasts."

19|08|2000
Blackburn mourn the death of Uncle Jack

Daniel Taylor

....

The first bouquets started arriving just before 11am. It started as a slow trickle, followed by a steady flow. Very soon, as the news reverberated across the old cotton town, Ewood Park had become the focal point for the mourning of a club and its community.

Not only Blackburn but football had lost one of its greatest fans when Jack Walker lost his lengthy battle with cancer.

"We never met ... but I always felt I knew you," read one floral tribute. "Thanks, Jack, for everything," said another.

Robert Coar, the Blackburn chairman, summed up the mood. "No tribute from us, no matter how long or how detailed, could ever do justice to Jack Walker's achievements here.

"Jack was our No1 supporter in every possible sense. His love for Rovers knew no boundaries his loyalty and commitment were never in question. It goes without saying how much we will miss him but he has left us with some fantastic memories."

The tributes were led by Alan Shearer, the former Rovers

striker who, perhaps above all, had the closest relationship of anyone to the man known throughout Blackburn simply as Uncle Jack.

Before every game of their 1994-95 title-winning season Walker summoned a bookmaker to his office to find out the odds on his most prized asset scoring the first goal. "Alan never lets me down," he would chuckle. And his affection for Shearer never diminished even after he had departed for Newcastle.

"Football has lost a true friend," the retired England captain said yesterday. "Jack was a kind, generous and emotional man. He gave pride to the town of Blackburn. Those memories of winning the Premiership will stay with me forever."

An adversary then but sharing in the tributes now was the Manchester United manager Alex Ferguson, who said: "If ever there was someone who lifted a club by its bootlaces it was Jack Walker with Blackburn Rovers. Nobody there will ever forget him."

Of Blackburn's current players, David Dunn, having been affiliated to his hometown club since the age of 11, probably knew Walker better than anyone.

"He was a big one for coming in the dressing room before games and putting his arm around us all. He would speak to every player and wish us all the best," said Dunn. "We hadn't seen him since last season. We kept hearing he was ill but, even so, it has not lessened the blow."

Typically Walker had made contingency plans to safeguard Blackburn's financial future. When the gravity of his illness became clear he instigated a board meeting in which he announced he would be leaving a significant part of his fortune to a special trust fund.

"We know he is looking after us," said Pauline Perkins of the club's supporters' association. "He was Blackburn through and through. His influence on this club cannot be overstated."

The association plans to fund its own memorial. "We have already discussed the idea and hopefully we can raise the money by arranging a match against a top team," she added. "They have a statue for Bill Shankly at Liverpool and it would be lovely to have something similar at Ewood Park for the man who made it all possible for Blackburn."

For Graeme Souness, the best tribute possible would be promotion. "When death comes along it doesn't matter when it comes or how it comes, it's always a very hard time, always a very hard thing to accept," he said.

"Jack will be remembered as Mr Blackburn Rovers, which is only right after all he has done. He has transformed them from a little club to one of the most high-profile clubs and built a stadium that is absolutely fantastic, plus a training ground and a youth academy that are second to none.

"Jack has put down the foundations down for the club to sustain Premiership status and, make no mistake, we will be trying our damnedest to get there for him."

07|05|2001

Interview: Peter Ridsdale

Jim White meets the Leeds chairman who has driven his club to heady European heights in extreme adversity

It is the morning after the biggest night of his career in football, and the chairman of Leeds United is full of apologies because he is five minutes late for this interview. After watching his team play in the semi-final of Europe's top club competition for the first time since 1975, five days late would have been understandable. But still Peter Ridsdale apologises, explaining that he lives over in the foothills of the Pennines, 90 minutes' drive from Leeds, and had not got home from all his glad-handing duties until one o'clock that morning.

"Usually I'm in here by eight," he says, gesturing round his modest office over the road from United's Elland Road stadium. "Yesterday it was six. But I thought I was entitled to lie in a bit, then I misjudged the traffic. I'm so sorry."

Apart from apologetic, though, how does he feel as Leeds's European expeditionary force rolls on? "Exhausted. I am exhausted," he says. "It has been an emotionally draining season. I can't remember being this tired in my life."

Tired he may be but Ridsdale does not look like a man on the brink of collapse. There are no dark glasses, no stifled yawns, no demands of his secretary for the intravenous application of double espresso. There is an air about him. It is partly of prosperity, particularly in the waist department, which even the most expensively cut suit struggles to disguise.

But after a moment or two's conversation, about the game the night before, about how his boys will score in Valencia, about how he has never seen a Leeds side with so much potential, you realise it is not just success he exudes. It is happiness. The look Peter Ridsdale wears is of a cat which has just glanced down and discovered it has grown an extra tail overnight.

"Yes. Yes I am, I'm very happy," he says. "It was great last night. A fantastic night. I'm even happy to be this tired. It's a tiredness I wouldn't swap for the world."

Ridsdale's is the happiness of the fan who got his hands on the train set. He has supported Leeds all his life, doing his time on the terraces, living the Revie years. It's a family thing. His son was one of the first infants to be popped in the newly installed match day crèche at Elland Road back in the 80s. In 1986 he became a club director.

A high-up in Sir Ralph Halpern's Burton group, he brought to the table the "Top Man" shirt sponsorship deal that accompanied the Howard Wilkinson years when Leeds won promotion in 1990 and the championship in 1992. He took on the chairmanship four years ago. "I don't think most directors have a clue the huge leap it is becoming chairman," he says. "I didn't."

What he took over back then was a club suffering not so much from crisis as mediocrity. That 1992 championship win was followed by the worst defence of the title since Ipswich in 1963, Wilkinson was let go in 1996 and George Graham, newly emerged from bung disgrace, was invited north as his replacement. Graham was in charge when Ridsdale took over and there was little sign he would repeat his Arsenal trick. But Ridsdale, casting inquisitive eyes over the Pennines to see how a club should be run, was an advocate of continuity. What a stroke of luck, then, that Graham decided to pack his bags for Spurs

"I think I made the right choice in his successor," says Ridsdale. Notwithstanding all that disingenuous, wearisome blarney about how green he and his boys are, David O'Leary has been some selection. The proof of it is in the condition of the Leeds squad he has built. Leeds supporters watch Robbie Keane, Olivier Dacourt and Rio Ferdinand and think it was only a couple of years back that their places were filled by Darren Huckerby, David Hopkin and Alfie Haaland. But to rebuild the squad O'Leary needed access to a chequebook. As a fan, does Ridsdale find that his natural inclination to behave like a kid in a sweet shop conflicts with his fiscal obligation as a chairman?

"My first duty is to the shareholders of this company; we are a plc," he says. "But the way to maximise their investment is to win things, so that pleases the fans. People said at the time of the Ferdinand transfer that we were mad because there was a chance that the transfer system might have been scrapped and thus Rio's value would have been wiped out overnight. But it really wouldn't have worried me if the transfer system had gone the day after I signed the cheque. We were investing in making the football team a more competitive proposition. We wouldn't have had this European run without this squad. And already it

has almost paid for Rio." That is why, he adds, all his investment so far has been in the team. "Win things first," he says. "That brings an audience and that fills a bigger ground."

Not that it is necessary to win things these days to find yourself in the money. As a fan, does he not find it sad that lifting the FA Cup is now regarded as less of an achievement than finishing third (next season fourth) in the Premiership, thus ensuring entry to the till-filler that is the Champions League? "I want us to win every match we play but the priorities are obvious. We have to make this club a top-four side every season."

And to do that, what is his role? "I think what I bring to the party is in the relationship I have with the manager. Gone are the days of Cloughie and his anecdotes about throwing the chairman off the team bus. Good lord, who did he think the bus belonged to? There is no question that the manager is the most important employee at the club, but the way you handle that manager also counts. I think David and I have a relationship which allows everyone to get on with their job."

The other thing Ridsdale has become renowned for is his media savvy. Every time there is a Leeds crisis – the plane crash at Stansted, the court case we must not write about (though in private his views are trenchant) – he is there, in front of the cameras, being statesmanlike. His exemplary way in a disaster first came to attention after two Leeds fans were murdered in Istanbul before a Uefa Cup match with Galatasaray.

"I made a decision to take leadership," he says. "It's what I felt the chairman of a plc should do." And was he advised by PR men? Is there an Alastair Campbell at Elland Road?

"Nobody advised me to do it," he says. "In fact, if anything, they told me not to but to sit tight and see what happened. All I knew was we had a lad dead and another in hospital dying. I simply behaved as I felt appropriate. If with hindsight that turned out to be the best thing in terms of the public image of the club then so be it. But that was never the intention."

Arrived at by good fortune or not, he has a public image most club chairmen would sell their shareholders for. Alan Sugar, Martin Edwards, Michael Knighton: how they must look on Leeds and wonder. The fans love Ridsdale in a way only the real sugar daddies of football have previously managed. Last summer he spent every weekend out in the neighbourhood, opening fetes, pressing the flesh. "I've got to learn to say no," he says. "I owe it to the family to put some time in."

But if Leeds pull off the incredible on Tuesday and beat Valencia, the invites are unlikely to stop. "Oh, we will do it," he says. "It'll be a 1-1 draw. You'd be very unwise to bet against me. A fan came up to me yesterday and gave me £100. Apparently I'd bet him after we'd lost at home to Manchester City that we'd qualify for Europe again. I hadn't remembered the bet, but he had. I told him to send the money to the local hospice."

The PR man to the last. And if they do get through tomorrow night, you suspect even this most exhausted of chairmen will have energy enough to open a bottle or two.

We are investing in making the team win things. And that pleases the fans

30|04|2007

Bad news for Leeds — Bates and Wise vow to stay on as fans bring extra sour note to a dark Yorkshire day

Leeds United 1 Ipswich Town 1

Jeremy Alexander, Elland Road

Ken Bates, in his chairman's notes, made "an impassioned appeal for all fans to stay off the pitch at the end of the game". He said nothing about during the game. Mayhem ensued. In the last minute of six added on, with Leeds staring at the uncharted waters of the third tier, hundreds of fans charged on to the pitch. The next charge will surely come from the Football Association. If Bates conforms to type, electric fencing may be raised too.

The FA, promising a full-scale investigation, says it will be "very unusual for a points deduction for next season". Leeds may start on level terms with Hartlepool.

They had led from the 12th minute to the 88th, a win becoming more urgent once Hull went ahead at Cardiff (executive chairman, Peter Ridsdale) after half-time. Strictly they are not condemned yet but the arithmetic demands a nine-goal swing next Sunday, when they must win at Derby and Hull lose at home to Plymouth. Pigs invade pitches before they fly.

Leeds fans have tried more than once to influence a result. In April 1971, chasing the League title, they objected to Ray Tinkler's decision to overrule his linesman's offside flag and West Brom made it 2-1. Arsenal did the Double and Leeds had to play their first four home games of the next season on neutral grounds. They were also fined £750. With inflation, West Ham's £5.5 million penalty and the FA's holier-than-Europe line on crowd trouble, Leeds could be hit by as much as Ridsdale left them in debt in 2002. Their invasion was more violent in 1982, when defeat at The Hawthorns dropped them to the second tier.

The referee here, Michael Jones, made no attempt to stay on the pitch when the crowd chose to share it. The delay was 32 minutes, during which the PA hardly drew appealing breath — for "support, kindness, common sense and co-operation". Ipswich fans made good their escape, rightly proud of their team's effort with nothing at stake. If Francis Jeffers had not been a mole in a hole for an hour they might have threatened sooner. If Leeds, after a goal made by Alan Thompson's twist from his marker and 50-yard diagonal pass, had pressed on instead of retreating to a cagey 4-3-1-2, Alan Lee might not have brought on the trouble with his glancing header.

The majority of fans chanted "You're the scum of Elland Road" and the scum slowly seeped out, many physically abused by fellow fans. There was no sign of stocks outside but, if the club's CCTV was operating at the other end of the scale of efficiency from the stewarding, none of the culprits will see the inside of Elland Road again. "It's a criminal offence to encroach on the pitch," the FA said yesterday.

"You may not be aware of the state of the game," said the PA. "Leeds have been awarded a corner and the referee has indicated there are 45 seconds to play." The goalkeeper went up and the referee played twice that — until he was in pole position for the tunnel. Jim Magilton, the Ipswich manager, said: "It was shambolic and a poor decision. The players were worried about going back out. If any had got hurt I would have been knocking at his door."

Six years ago Leeds were looking forward to a Champions League semi-final and Bates, having failed to get his way with Wembley, was two years from his profitable exit from Chelsea. Eleven months ago Leeds were one play-off game from the Premiership. Six months ago Dennis Wise was riding high as new manager of Swindon in League Two. Having lifted Leeds from 23rd to 22nd, he may now meet them coming the other way.

"I haven't done what I came to do," he said. "It's a sad day for everyone and I take full responsibility. We are big people." No one likes to see a big club in distress but some find it easier to bear if it is Leeds. After the madness a presentation was made to Gary Kelly, retiring after 16 roller-coaster years. Good Leeds fans honour their heroes. The players followed for a lap of laughable honour.

Bates, trying to engage with fans, ended his notes: "The future is bright, the future is White." The present is clearly black but Wise, given a vote of confidence from his son's godfather, said: "I'm here for the long haul." Just now it is a haul of shame.

A presentation was made to Gary Kelly after 16 years. Good Leeds fans honour their heroes

26|01|2004
Cobblers admire the view, then trudge back to a grim reality

Northampton fans turned out in force for United's visit, but Matthew Engel finds the great divide greater than ever

Sub-editors all over the country must have been itching yesterday to write a headline along the lines of "Fergie Held By The Cobblers". It looks increasingly as though his enemies might have engineered precisely that — but that has nothing at all to do with Northampton Town Football Club.

Northampton's great day came and went. Everyone got money's worth. At 3-0 the score fell somewhere in the no man's land between heroism and humiliation. The players shook hands at the end as fellow pros intimating mutual respect. Then Manchester United went back to their world, and a place in the fifth-round draw of the FA Cup, while Northampton contemplate reality: Doncaster and Rochdale.

This game will not be replayed and recalled endlessly 34 years hence, should the two teams happen to meet again — partly because in 1970 George Best scored six goals on his own against Northampton, and this time United got only three between them, all of them frankly a bit scraggy.

It is also rather dubious whether an occasion like this will even exist in 2038. The Cup's value is now a matter of open debate. Even a tuppenny-ha'penny club like Bolton Wanderers are openly dissing the whole thing, though an outsider might think that a team like that, without a hope of winning the Premiership, might cherish a second-chance competition.

Manchester United, who began the Cup's downward spiral by skipping a year and playing in Brazil, abided by the traditions and courtesies yesterday. But the modern equivalents of George Best did not appear. It was not quite a youth team such as they might put out for the Carling Cup when they are actively trying to find a way out. But it was sufficiently second-rate to include England internationals and similar kinds of spear-carriers.

It was a bit like one of those pre-season benefit games for a Third Division stalwart, when the manager prevails on old acquaintance, and Fergie promises to send his first-team squad, which is of course rather large. He does not promise that Ruud van Nistelrooy will ever get off the bus or, in the case of this fixture, even get on it.

The Northampton fans greeted the arrival of the three United substitutes, who were not household names, with loud cries of "Who?" — though in the case of Kieran Richardson they nearly found out because he was just about the liveliest man on the park.

Minute by minute Northampton were often a match for this version of United. Determination and their sense of occasion kept them in the game, if not the contest, all the way through. They are in any case the sort of team traditionally ripe to do some giant-killing: gifted performers at their level who happen to be underperforming in the league. And had the luck gone a bit differently either way, it might just — improbably — have been 1-1, or then again, 5-0 to United.

But there were moments when the difference seemed unbridgeable, when United swung the ball wide and then in again, managing somehow to be playing with a sphere that was at once heavier and faster than when Northampton kicked it.

What has happened is that the gulf has turned into an ocean. The old Fourth Division was full of top-flight players: many of them were real stars, either on the way down or the way up. Most of them were nearly-men, the sort who could have been contenders but lacked a little something — a brain, quite often, or simply the ambition.

But modern Premiership players, even in the unlikely event of them being English, do not need to stop off at Northampton on the way down; they have enough money, thank you. And the clubs' scouting networks pick up youngsters faster than ever. The top and bottom of football used to be different worlds. Now they are different galaxies.

But in other ways the difference yesterday was not great enough. Had this been at the grotty old County Ground, United's players would have been horrified. But the dressing room was adequate, the pitch was in beautiful condition and the crowd was too damn respectful.

Northampton turned out in force. The main stand was a claret lake of a depth not seen since the EU also had a butter mountain. But the supporters just sat there awe-struck. The United fans corralled in a Conference-sized stand at the end, stood throughout and, although outnumbered six to one, never shut up. A little club has to intimidate opponents like this or they have no chance.

Sadly Sixfields is no place for a miracle. This little ground, apparently built from Meccano, is one of the mini-stadiums of the future, set among a dreary late-Elizabethan edge of town, a wasteland of theme pubs and chain restaurants. Its one eccentricity, the hill from which it is possible to see a third of the pitch and one of the goals for nothing, was primly cordoned off yesterday: health and safety.

So we could have been anywhere. Only the traditional defeatism of Northampton supporters made it seem real. There were some real old-style Cobblers fans in front and after 24 minutes, the scores still level, one yelled out: "Take your time, Cobblers," hoping against hope for a replay.

It was never a real hope. For the second half Diego Forlan came out wearing gloves, as though hinting that he really did not have to be doing this. The United contingent chanted that they would sit down only if he scored. In the event he did, they didn't.

Last night, with greater events than this swirling round Old Trafford, Sir Alex Ferguson was the more worried manager. The great managerial careers, like political ones, nearly always end in failure: think of Ramsey, think of Clough. Ferguson may be brought down by events that have little to do with football.

But the real worry is for those who care about days like this and the right of all the Northamptons to take on the great teams, just sometimes, as equals. Don't hold your breath for the 2038 FA Cup.

08|08|2005

Harry and Clive just Carry On Regardless

Barney Ronay

Great TV sitcoms tend to stick to certain well-worn rules. Take a couple of slightly flaky characters from different walks of life. Stick them in an office, a scrap-yard, prison or an ambitious South Coast football club. Then repeat until funny. The laughs tend to come from a feeling that neither of these characters, like it or not, is getting away from the other.

On the face of it the sandwiching-together of Harry Redknapp and Clive Woodward at Southampton has the makings of a classic "you say vine-ripened organic tomato, I say ketchup" double act. Unfortunately it will probably not last that long.

This weekend Redknapp somehow became the most important person on the planet. Or at least on a planet where nobody does anything except watch sport on TV. Or possibly just round at my place. The start of the Championship football season was all about Harry. Everywhere you looked his Droopy the Dog face was already there – trailed as always these days by the invisible ghost of Sir Clive, with his earpiece radio mic and his motivational PowerPoint presentation. Harry

kicked off the day as star guest on the first-ever *Guardian* Sport Show. Woah, you might be thinking, the *Guardian* what show? The *Guardian* Sport what?

In case you missed it – and as you might expect of a Saturday morning telecast by Britain's finest left-leaning metropolitan broadsheet newspaper – the first show featured a report on the all-Islington non-competitive tofu straining championships, an interview with a Ukrainian Marxist weightlifter and Noam Chomsky, Sienna Miller and Ashley Giles in a round-table debate on post-Premiership anxiety in a hierarchical football league pyramid.

Actually the show was not bad. The host, Clive Anderson, batted a light sporting debate around among his guests, Steve Claridge and some journalist types, and before long Harry was on the sofa fielding his first question about the other Clive. "I am one million per cent in charge of the team," he declared, while Woodward's role was described as "sports science, the academy, that kind of stuff". "I won't give anyone the chance to sack me, Clive, I promise you that," Harry said, the words tripping so lightly off his tongue that you wondered whether he'd already said exactly this to someone else. Anderson was not to be deflected. "We share an office," Harry admitted, conjuring up in an instant the template for the first episode of The Dugout, a new 22-part BBC3 comedy series.

In fact the best way to understand the Woodward-Redknapp relationship is to reimagine it as an early black-and-white Carry On film. Cravat-sporting Clive, played by Jim Dale, is the boss's nephew sent in to modernise the local bidet factory, which is managed by Harry (Sid James, with Bernard Bresslaw as side-kick Jim Smith). Before long Harry is tearing his hair out ("Where's the bladdy bidets gorn?") as the young squire puts into place his hair-brained whims. After a brief diversion that sees Rupert Lowe (late-career Kenneth Williams) being chased around his office by an amorous Claus Lundekvam/Hattie Jacques, Woodward comes round to the old way of doing things and teams up with Harry, Charles Hawtrey and Barbara Windsor (Dennis Wise) to save the factory from a team of censorious visiting bidet inspectors ("Ooh I say, put that thing away!").

Before our next episode of Harry and Clive, however, we had a Sky Sports B-feature, an underwhelming season opener starring Sheffield United and Leicester City. It is hard to take the start of the football season seriously. The midday sun creeps in under the curtains in your living room. You have dozed off under a family packet of Morrison's herb and onion quavers. And suddenly Chris Kamara is shouting "you have to say that is poor, poor goalkeeping" in your ear with the kind of throaty conviction usually heard onlyon the top deck of the bus from men in brown raincoats who seem convinced the CIA are communicating with them by thought experiments.

The biggest problem with the lunchtime curtain-raiser was that it did not have Harry in it. This was put right by the teatime trip to Southampton at home to Wolves. There was Harry again, on the touchline in short-sleeved blue shirt and the same biscuit-coloured slacks as the morning. In the studio Gavin seemed to have eaten something stimulating for lunch. "It's time to forge new futures," he rasped. It is true: with Harry in town the pitch looked greener and even the officials were wearing Premiership-lite kiwi coloured shirts. And there was Clive at last − sitting high in the stands with the words "Technical Director" inscribed beneath his head which, with its light beige tan, is now roughly the shape and colour of a large celeriac.

At his post-match interview Harry looked just as fresh as at nine o'clock that morning. He did scoot off rather quickly at the end, though. Back to the office probably. ("Put the kettle on, Clive mate." "Espresso or raspberry bracer?" "Gor blimey, how did I end up stuck in here with you?" "Sssh, Rupert's coming, for God's sake try to be nice.") Let us just hope they get a second series.

14|01|2006

Reading fans should rejoice in their most reluctant of heroes

Steve Coppell's team are running away with the Championship — yet he isn't having fun, he tells Jon Brodkin

....

Steve Coppell's tone and expression often make it hard to know whether he may just have won the lottery or lost his life savings. One idea that might be expected to rouse this even-keeled manager, though, is the prospect of mixing again with Arsenal, Liverpool and other giants. Having played for Manchester United and taken charge of Crystal Palace in the top flight, Coppell has spent much of his working life among the elite.

The 50-year-old's excellent stewardship of Reading has him heading back in that direction, his team perched top of the Championship with an 18-point advantage over third-placed Leeds, who have a game in hand. Even if Coppell insists he does not look at the table, and sometimes gives the impression he views it upside down, he must know he is more than well placed to work in the Premiership for the first time since 1998 with Palace.

Subsequent spells at Brentford and Brighton suggested Coppell might never get another crack at that but it appears he was not bothered. Ahead of a "big week" which sees Reading play

Coventry today, West Bromwich Albion in the FA Cup on Tuesday and Palace next weekend, Coppell insisted the thought of the Premiership does not excite him. "No," he said. "Management is management. I got the same excitement when I was working at Brentford as I do at Reading. It's not heightened the higher up you go."

Not even with the crowds and international stars? "You give everything as a manager and when your players kick off it doesn't matter at what level," he said. "I'm sure every Sunday league manager can sympathise with me. Once the whistle's blown the Sunday league manager gets the adrenalin rush, the drive, the motivation, sometimes losing your head. All those feelings are to the fore and they don't get even more heightened the higher you go."

Mick McCarthy's experience at Sunderland has shown Premiership management can be dispiriting and, while Coppell calls promotion to the top division "the biggest prize in football" and by no means suggests he would prefer not to work there, he hardly craves the attendant spotlight and media inquisitions into his character. "Do I like reading about myself? No. Am I introspective normally? No. You ask me questions I never ask myself. I've got to give you answers and I don't really like doing it."

Coppell did not duck a single issue, though, and his honesty is to be admired. There was no pretence that his work provides constant pleasure. "No, I don't enjoy it," he said. "Nobody can enjoy it. People say to me 'Do you enjoy management?' and I say 'No, you can't enjoy it.' When you look back at the end of the season you think 'We've done all right' and then you can put it more in perspective. It's a demanding job."

So why continue? "I suppose I enjoy being on a beach and playing golf," he said, "but I would soon get bored with that." Football is in his blood. "When I finished as a player I did have things I wanted to do but I soon found when I was trawling through any list I had made that they weren't as [much] fun as winning football."

Coppell knows how to build a winning side. Witness his promotion, third place in the top flight and FA Cup final with Palace, his transformation of Brentford in 2001-02 before losing in the play-offs and a 27-game unbeaten league run with Reading now. He will not go into detail about his abrupt departure from Manchester City but says he derives an intense thrill from victory, even if that is not etched on his features.

"Is it jump-up-and-down-and-run-round-the-streets? No. It's just a nice feeling," he said. "I can liken it, I suppose, to when I got my O-level results. I just felt 'I've worked hard and I've done well.' It's that feeling, like when you pass your driving test."

The caution Coppell adopts on Reading's position — he calls it realism — is understandable when 11 games without a win last season destroyed his play-off hopes and his career as a winger was ended prematurely by an injury. "If I'd had a full playing career I doubt if I would have gone into management," he said. "When I finished I lived in Amsterdam for three months and every Sunday morning I would go to Dam Square, get the English papers, have a cup of coffee and pore over the English football news for three hours. When I came back I thought there was obviously something in my system regarding football which needs to be removed. I made the decision then that I would give it a bash."

Football does not seem close to being out of his system now. "Probably not. I signed for a year [until May] and I've got a year's work to do. Once the year's finished I will see what I want to do then. But I don't want to make that an issue . . . That's just the way I am, comfortable working for a year at a time."

As Coppell struggled through his first year at Palace in the mid-1980s, he did not imagine seeing many more seasons. "Did I think I would last after that first year? No. Toothache would have been more pleasurable than that first year. Now it's a routine."

He believes management has become tougher with a decrease in boardroom patience and the Bosman ruling. His astute signings, such as Kevin Doyle and Bobby Convey, have strengthened Reading but more investment would be needed in the Premiership. The chairman, John Madejski, has said he would think about his position with promotion but Coppell does not expect the millionaire to stand down.

"I think you've got to say realistically it won't happen," he said. "I'm sure one of his many goals when he took over the club was to get in the top division." Coppell shares that ambition but being there would not enhance his excitement.

Cup fever: Steve Coppell is one of football's most understated managers, claiming that no one can actually enjoy the job

17|03|2007
In New York's ad-land, Bolton have designs to stay ahead of the game

Mike Forde wanders the globe making sure his club punch above their weight. Dominic Fifield hears how

The continuing quest for improvement took Bolton Wanderers' performance director to New York recently but not to scrutinise the sporting techniques of the Giants, Knicks or Yankees. Instead Mike Forde sat in a 16th-floor office at Saatchi and Saatchi's headquarters high above Greenwich Village as the advertising company's world CEO, Kevin Roberts, talked ideas. "People wonder what a Premiership football club can learn from a business like Saatchi, but the similarities in what we're aiming at were actually stunning," said Forde. "Both of us are always asking, 'How do we stay ahead of the game?'"

Bolton travel to Manchester United this lunchtime attempting to maintain another campaign spent apparently punching above their weight near the top of the Premier League. They will end the weekend in fifth place, yet they are blazing their own trail off the pitch in order to remain hugely competitive on it.

It is eight years since Sam Allardyce recognised the need to find an edge that would hoist his side clear of the also-rans. Forde, the man behind Big Sam whether in the stands or at the training ground, is one of a few key staff at the Reebok Stadium seeking to guide this club's long-term vision. The 31-year-old, whose background is in sports science and psychology, oversees a strategy that should keep Bolton competitive in the years to come.

Forde's job effectively entails scouring the globe for innovations that may be relevant to the club, whether they be in IT, scouting, psychology or people-management. This week he met Roger Draper, CEO at the Lawn Tennis Association, to examine its infrastructure, following up visits to 25 teams in the United States, from NFL to NBA, and a spell with Honda observing formula one testing in Barcelona.

Later this year he will meet the All Blacks before the rugby World Cup. "They've just appointed a guy whose job is to blue-sky, ignoring this year's tournament but exploring sports science and coaching techniques to see how they are going to win the next World Cup in 2011. In any leading business there's always someone whose job is to pinpoint what's around the corner because what was extraordinary yesterday is very ordinary tomorrow.

"Every six weeks I take the staff away for a strategic-planning day: we'll examine the next phase of the season, then spend half a day brainstorming. I presented what I'd learnt from Saatchi's, showing how we can link it with what we do. They have a handful of designers as talented as the players we have and, like us, probably spend a high percentage of their costs on a small percentage of staff. But they have created a framework which allows them to be successful today while planning for tomorrow. It ties into the quantum changes we've had at this club."

When Forde was recruited by Allardyce and his then assistant, Phil Brown, in 1999, Bolton had an ambitious Championship side, a fine new stadium but a decrepit training ground. Steered by the manager, with Forde overseeing development in the background, they have finished eighth, sixth and eighth in the top flight over the past three years and their ability to attract such players as Nicolas Anelka, Jay-Jay Okocha and Youri Djorkaeff to a small town near Manchester is remarkable. The full-time backroom staff has swollen from five to 21, covering coaching, medicine, sports science, performance analysis and administrative support.

"And the scouting operation has gone through the roof," said Forde. "We've created a no-excuse environment which will allow our players to flourish. The squad has gone from 80% British to 80% foreign and we ensure whoever we bring here can settle. It's about the small things: opening bank accounts, finding schools or houses, showing them where they can eat out or where their local mosque or church is.

"But we also offer a unique experience. At one stage our squad boasted 25 championships, two World Cups and seven Champions Leagues. Fernando Hierro had played for Real Madrid for 14 years but his desire to plan for a career beyond playing – like Gary Speed – meant that he recognised us as a fantastic opportunity to learn from our coaching, sports-science and game-analysis techniques.

"Last year every member of our squad had played on average for six different teams, eight managers and in 250 games. We looked at where they had each been most successful and picked out anything we could from that environment we could replicate here. It's a very deductive process but it might be the smallest thing. A player might have come from a bigger club where he was a fringe player and he might relish having a bigger role here.

"Our screening process is so extensive. We recruit possibly eight players every year on, say, an average wage of £1m. If you went into the private sector, the due diligence around recruiting someone on that amount would be incredible. We're making the same investment here, so we have to be as thorough. It's actually quite difficult to sign for this club because of the due diligence we undertake."

Those recruited benefit from a revamped training ground, complete with tranquil suites with Chinese medicine techniques to hand. The international players are accompanied by club masseurs, fitness staff or nutritionists when abroad with their countries. "We can't control the environment they're in when they're away but we can influence it. We want to keep them thinking: 'I am a Bolton player.' It's about making the players feel wanted and creating the conditions for success. You can never guarantee you'll win, but how can you take away the excuses for failure?"

On-pitch analysis is adding to Bolton's options. They were one of the first Premiership clubs to adopt ProZone, the player-tracking service which produces detailed data of every move, kick or spit that occurs in a game. Dave Fallows has been recruited from ProZone as the club's head of technical scouting, with his seven-man team scrutinising matches on-site. "Any club can have ProZone but some use it better than others," said Forde. "We have a fantastically talented analysis team who, on matchday, are wired up and give constant feedback. The future of sport is real-time science.

"Our IT suite can, on request, call up certain passages of play. When Sam walks in at half-time he can play those incidents on screen. It's a 15-minute window of opportunity and another competitive edge we exploit."

Such innovative thinking has attracted interest from around the globe, with Aussie Rules clubs and the LA Lakers visiting the Reebok to view Bolton's techniques. At Old Trafford this lunchtime the Wanderers will have a high-profile stage on which to put them into practice.

23|04|2007

Screen Break: Jacqui cracks the glass ceiling

Martin Kelner

....

It has been a long hard struggle, what with those plucky Pankhurst girls defying the establishment, risking arrest and imprisonment, Emily Wilding Davison throwing herself in front of the king's horse in the 1913 Derby, then all the bra-burning in the 70s and feeling obliged to read those Germaine Greer and Marilyn French books. But it has all been worth it.

Finally a woman gets to commentate on a Premiership football match on Match of the Day. All right, it was only Fulham v Blackburn Rovers but what a triumph for female emancipation as Jacqui Oatley got to say things like "Jason Roberts found himself in acres of space there", "Fulham caught totally square at the back" and "What a crucial goal that could be", all statements previously thought – and still thought by Dave Bassett and the *Daily Mail*'s Steve Curry – impossible to utter without being in possession of a penis.

I worked with Jacqui in Leeds, where she produced my local radio programme a few times. What with that and following Wolverhampton Wanderers, she clearly has not had an easy ride. She certainly has not been plucked from the chorus line by the BBC as some sort of gimmick and probably does not need me or anyone else to patronise her by saying she is sharp, intelligent and witty and loves the game of football – and, as it happens, has quite a capacity for dealing with arsy presenters.

Whether she wants faint praise or not, though, she was destined to get a little of it on MOTD – you would expect nothing else – when Gary Lineker pointed out that "even the presence of our first female commentator could not inspire Fulham to victory" and the pundit Lee Dixon said, "She did well, though, didn't she?" to murmured assent.

The view from the rehearsal room, where my local women's theatre collective is preparing for a new sparse production of The Vagina Monologues, is that only when Jonathan Pearce is patted on the head in this fashion by the panel will any kind of equality have been achieved, and for the time being Dixon and all other men remain potential rapists. They added: "Mike Newell, Dave Bassett, Jim Davidson, the late Benny Hill, your boys took one hell of a beating."

The Vagina Monologues, you may recall, was considered too rude a title to appear on a theatre marquee in Florida, so the play was renamed The Hoohaa Monologues, which struck me as an apt way to describe some of the coverage last week previewing Jacqui's TV debut. She was, after all, merely following in the tradition whereby the six or seven minutes of highlights of one of the Premiership's less interesting matches are allocated to one of Radio Five Live's people.

Like most of her predecessors in this slot, Jacqui talked too much. Radio commentators always do when they start in TV, what with dead air being anathema more or less on the radio. The added pressure brought on by the shards of glass as she smashed through the ceiling probably did not help either. But once Jacqui has the confidence to let the pictures do more of the work, we may wonder what all the fuss was about.

> **Whether Jacqui wants faint praise or not, she was destined to get a little on MOTD**

21|01|2008

Screen Break: Bong! Door in Newcastle might open soon. Bong!

Martin Kelner

Never go back, they say. Returning to the scene of former glories, hoping to recapture the magic, is almost always a mistake. And that is certainly what it looks like this time; a lacklustre start against less than impressive opposition. Frankly, I think you were foolish to take the job, Sir Trevor McDonald.

Three point eight million against the BBC's four point eight; it is not what the fans were expecting. Sure, you cut an impressive figure on the training ground and the younger members of the News At Ten team will be in awe of your dazzling achievements first time round – "Good evening", that was one of yours, "And finally ..." another – but times have changed, and the days when stand-in firemen could be relied upon to rescue a cat from a tree and then run over the cat on their way back to the station, giving you a zinger for the end of the bulletin, are long gone.

You have been out of the game too long, Trevor. I believe you haven't even watched any television for the past three years, preferring instead to concentrate on your academy for young newsreaders, where you get them to say – with portentous pauses between each word – things like: "More problems for John Major's government and why Percy the Parrot won't be going home for Christmas. Join us after the break."

Well, those days have gone. The game is pacier these days. What is more, what you considered light-hearted items to prop up a bulletin now ARE the bulletin. Only the other day, Trev, nearly half the news was devoted to the appointment of football manager Kevin Keegan.

Like yourself, Kevin is charged with reviving an ailing enterprise, in his case Newcastle United, and you would not be human if you were not just slightly envious of the enormous fund of goodwill that has come his way.

As a member of the Amalgamated Guild of Writers of Semi-Humorous Sport on TV Columns, I welcome Sir Kevin with open notebook. The BBC, I suspect, will be similarly exultant. From a Newcastle manager who would not talk to them they have gone to one who will not shut up.

I have been pining for King Kev ever since he went awol from Manchester City, as anyone who has heard my mobile 'phone ring tone – "Al tell you, 'e's gone down in my estimation" – will testify. Away with dull aitches at the start

Kevin Keegan enjoys — or perhaps not — his second, or strictly third, coming at St James' Park. It was Newcastle 0, Bolton 0

of words, I say. Let us enjoy what most commentators are dubbing "the third coming".

Predictably Sky Sports News was more excited than even I was, dispatching its top man, Ian Payne, to the North-East and broadcasting pictures from the press room at St James' Park a full 20 minutes before the Messiah manifested himself. As a result the cameras were mostly fixed on the door through which the sainted one was scheduled to enter.

"This is the door that Kevin Keegan will be walking through," confirmed Payne, ratcheting up excitement levels round my gaff, which were in no way lessened by the fact that the picture remained the same, as the director seemed to have taken the opportunity for a last toilet break before the great man addressed the masses. "We're just looking at pictures of the door as we wait for Kevin Keegan to come in," said Payne. "We're told he will come in in about 30 seconds, so we will keep watching the door."

This was a press conference as directed by Andy Warhol and a challenge to which Payne rose manfully. As 30 seconds turned into five minutes, he continued: "You're watching Sky Sports News. These are live pictures of a door, as we wait for Kevin Keegan and Chris Mort to come through it and sit on those seats."

And lest we were in any doubt that Sky was bringing us history in the making, Payne reminded us that first news of Keegan's appointment came in a text message to Sky's man in the North-East, David Craig. "We probably all remember where we were when we first heard it," said Payne. Yes, with chronically bad timing I was standing outside the Texas Book Depository.

Helping Payne cover the pictures, and fill the unforgiving minutes, was something called "The Voice of Warren Barton, Newcastle United 1995-2002". The Voice's view was that, unlike the hero of Ray Davies's song Lola, Sir Kevin was the world's most passionate man.

"You can see the buzz on his face," it announced, although it could not decide about Kevin's eyes. "The spark's back in his eyes and he's got a skip in his step," the Voice said at one point, later amended to "there's a glint in Kevin's eye" before finally: "He looked really focused, with determination in his eyes."

And then He was back and, boy, was it good to enjoy once more that exhilarating mix of good humour, common sense, and — you should pardon the expression — complete bollocks. What, for instance, was all that stuff about Geordies working hard all week and needing entertainment at the weekend? As I understand it, nobody is knocking dirty great rivets into ocean-going liners up there these days or mining coal. They are eking out a living much like the rest of us; cutting each other's hair, driving taxis, delivering pizzas to one another. One is inclined to tell Kevin to get real, as modern parlance has it. But the day that happens is when the fun stops.

Chapter 13
England: the hurting years

05|07|1990

Gazza's tears, England's penalty heartache

World Cup semi-final
England 1 West Germany 1
(aet: West Germany won 4-3 on pens)
David Lacey, Turin

England went out of the World Cup last night just when they were ready to take on the world. After proving themselves the equals of West Germany, and sometimes their betters, over two hours of absorbing football in Turin, they lost their semi-final on penalties, which is a sadistically cruel way for any team to be beaten at this stage. Russian roulette should be left to the Russians.

Bobby Robson's ambition of ending his eight years as manager by taking England to the final of the World Cup for only the second time ended when Chris Waddle lifted the fifth penalty of the shoot-out high over the crossbar.

There was no need for the West Germans to complete their quota, for Stuart Pearce had driven England's previous kick into Illgner's diving body. The Germans took their penalties with rather more assurance than they had played the match.

Paul Gascoigne, Peter Shilton and the whole of the defence were England's outstanding players. Gascoigne was cautioned after his foul on Berthold, his second yellow card of the tournament, and would have missed the final. As it is he will miss the third-place match against Italy in Bari on Saturday.

Thus the 1990 World Cup final will be a repeat of 1986, with West Germany meeting Argentina, the holders, in Rome on Sunday. This time the Germans will be fancied to win although it would be unwise to write off Argentina, even though they do have four players suspended. One of the biggest ironies of last night's match is that England have shown Diego Maradona and his colleagues just how vulnerable the Germans can become under pressure.

How England would have loved another chance to grip the Hand of God and how close they came to achieving what a month ago would have seemed an idle fancy, the stuff that dreams are made on. Poor Waddle: he had hit a post at the end of the first half of extra-time and one felt that, had England scored, even the opposition's noted powers of recovery would have been stretched beyond reasonable limits.

England's run of luck ran out when they deserved it most. The goal from Andreas Brehme with which West Germany went ahead a minute before the hour was the result of a chance deflection off Parker, and penalty shoot-outs are always a lottery.

This is the first time that both World Cup semi-finals have been decided this way and the England manager's suggestion that playing on for the first goal would be a more genuine way to settle games seems a reasonable one.

Watching Robson's side it was hard to believe that a similar team had performed so wretchedly against the Republic of Ireland and Cameroon. Last night they reproduced the character and determination which had marked their more recent matches but they also played good football, taking the game to the Germans in the opening stages, defending solidly and efficiently for long periods, then returning to the attack in extra-time.

In the middle period of the game England's dominant players were usually defenders. Because Wright's gashed eyebrow made regular headers a risk, Robson took the chance of playing Butcher as sweeper while Wright and Walker marked Völler and Klinsmann. This might have exposed Butcher's lack of pace.

In fact, the defence operated so well as a unit that the effectiveness of the German strikers was severely reduced and lost more impact when Völler was forced off seven minutes before half-time with a leg injury after a tackle by Walker.

With Parker and Pearce curbing the threat of Brehme and Berthold on the wings, England always had a broad, confident base for their own attacks. In fact they started the match by setting up a base just outside the West German penalty area, forcing three corners in the opening 90 seconds.

It was during this period that Gascoigne established a chirpy command between the penalty areas that the West Germans never really overcame. Germans rarely come across players like

Paul Gascoigne is overcome as England go out of the World Cup. Twice booked, he would have missed the final anyway

Gascoigne and did not know what to make of him. Even when they tackled him successfully, he would get up with the ball still at his feet.

The early England pressure petered out for want of a consistent partner for Lineker. Once again Beardsley was his faithful servant but he did not look like scoring himself. A lob from Waddle struck from just inside the German half was England's most spectacular scoring attempt of the first 45 minutes.

West Germany continued to mount piecemeal raids in the second half but England met nothing with which they could not cope until the 59th minute. Then Pearce fouled the busy little Hassler as he tried to take the ball wide and Thon tapped the free-kick to Brehme, whose shot ricocheted off Parker as the full-back tried to intercept it. The ball flew over the defence in a high arc and Shilton, caught a couple of yards off his line, could not get to the ball as it floated in under the bar.

Franz Beckenbauer replaced a troubled Hassler with Reuter, which gave the Germans more pace on the right. Robson, as he had done against Cameroon, replaced Butcher with Steven and played with a flat back four in order to give himself a better chance of saving the match.

Gascoigne, sending Waddle clear only for Berthold to make a covering tackle, still looked the man most likely to inspire an English goal. In fact the honour went to Parker. With 10 minutes of normal time remaining the right-back's cross found Kohler and Augenthaler, the sweeper, in a dither. As the ball dropped, Lineker dragged it wide of Augenthaler and placed it firmly past Illgner's flailing right hand for his fourth goal of the tournament.

Shades of the 1966 final and now, surely, it was England's turn again. As Shilton saved superbly from Klinsmann, who then shot wide after Augenthaler's delicate lob had sent him through, England looked well favoured. Waddle's low, tightly angled shot beat Illgner but rebounded from the inside of the far post.

Buchwald's shot, the only one to beat Shilton directly, hit the right-hand post and would have been a worthy winner but by that time England had done more than enough to earn the right to take their chance with penalties. A pity Lineker could not have taken all of them.

Chris Waddle lifted the fifth penalty high over the bar. In extra-time he had hit a post

03|06|1996
Flashpoint for 'El Tel'

Brian Alexander, *The Sun*'s sports editor at Turnip time, assesses Terry Venables' likely treatment during Euro 96

You can bet your last pound taxed at 40% that every newspaper has a colour supplement prepared to mark Tony Blair's election triumph, future royal separations and Gary Lineker's knighthood. And any sports editor worth his weight in one-liners will have the headlines and the archive images prepared for the moment Terry Venables fails to beat Germany in the European Championship final by anything short of three clear goals. A one-all bore, with an 89th minute winner, will not do at all.

The start of Euro 96 on Saturday is our biggest sporting event since the World Cup in 66. After all those embarrassing Olympic bids by Manchester and Birmingham we actually have a decent event on our own doorstep and, even better, we did not have to go through that rather degrading qualification process.

1966 was the year we won the biggest prize of all under Alf Ramsey, a man famed for his love-hate relationship with the press. He told a press conference: "I have to make a living just like you. I happen to make mine in a nice way. You happen to make yours in a nasty way."

I dread to think how Sir Alf would react now. In his day newspapers published mono pictures. Today the photographs are in colour but the opinions of those newspapers are chillingly black and white. England are either inspired or inept; Venables is either brilliant or baffling; Gazza is either our most gifted performer or an overweight, lager-sodden lout. Take your pick. But in this tabloid game nobody is the winner.

On June 18 1992, I was sports editor of *The Sun*, having been hired to make the sports pages "intelligent", to quote the editor who appointed me. It did not quite work out as planned but on that evening, when England made their exit from the European Championship, a sub-editor called Dave Clement produced one of the best headlines since 1966: Swedes 2 Turnips 1.

A day later, with that headline firmly in our minds, Taylor the Turnip came to life. Like a bad meal the Turnip has kept coming up. And like all repeats the original was probably the best. As I tried explaining, with a degree of success, to the England manager when we met a month or so later, it was meant to be a bit of fun. No real malice was intended, unlike some of the attempts at humour recently, such as the noose round Venables's head on one back page.

Taylor, to his eternal credit, did not pin me against a wall at his Lancaster Gate office, preferring to ask me how the image had been created. He was genuinely interested, although the hurt I had clearly caused his family was sobering. The longer you are removed from the tabloid environment, the shorter is your patience with what they do.

The treatment England managers receive represents the pent-up frustration of tabloid journalists who are mostly regular blokes with a regular interest in football and who are simply trying to reflect the views of their readers. But that frustration is based on a tricky premise: that England have a divine right to win every international and with plenty of Latin flair.

No doubt the tabloid teams have contingency plans to put Venables firmly in his place if he fails in the next few weeks. The opening game against Switzerland should be points in the bag for England. The tabloids, judges and jurors of English football, will take a harsh line if the game is goalless. "Swiss Roll England Over" or "You Taking The Swiss Terry?" are possibles.

Then the showdown of all showdowns, England v Scotland, will be upon us. The Euro 96 draw from hell. England 0, Scotland 2 and all hell breaks loose. The back page shows Venables wearing a kilt. To the right is a wee caricature of Scotland's manager, Craig Brown, lifting Venables' kilt to reveal … two deflated footballs. "What A Load of B****cks", screams the headline.

Defeat by Holland will be just too much to bear. "Dutch 2, Clogs 1" may be a contender or perhaps Venables's face will be squeezed inside a tulip.

When Venables became England coach, his repartee with the football correspondents augured well — he even referred to the Turnip during his first press conference: "If you're going to turn me into a root vegetable, that's no problem with me," he said. "I'm used to it. I was called Terry Vegetables at school."

Venables knows how to deal with the media, although he has found the *Mirror*'s one-man campaign to oust him hard to fathom. Of course, he has no need to worry. His swan song will be to win it and win it well, beating the Germans 3-1 in the Wembley final.

Then the back-page cartoon will show a crown on his head and the headline, "Hail King Terry!" But he will see through the mist of tabloid schizophrenia, sip a gin and tonic with the journalists he has trusted and catch the first flight to Spain to begin his lucrative new career.

If you want to turn me into a root vegetable, fine. At school I was Terry Vegetables

---

A game that no one man deserved to lose

Euro 96 semi-final: Richard Williams reports on a classic match between two historic sparring partners

There will be a game of football at Wembley on Sunday night and they will call it the final of the European Championship but goodness knows how it can hope to equal, never mind surpass, the drama that played itself out at the old stadium last night, when the footballers of England and Germany gave everything they had, every ounce of skill and thought and effort, to justify a pre-match build-up of almost intolerable intensity.

If ever a game justified the controversial Golden Goal idea, this was it. When the two sides entered the unknown territory of sudden-death extra-time, with its short history of suffocating timidity, they immediately behaved as though Uefa had paid them a special bonus to demonstrate the potency of the concept. Ignoring the physical effects of the first 90 minutes they tore at each other with renewed vigour and redoubled courage, chances coming by the minute at both ends.

There was no fear, no hesitation, no sense of anything other than a prize there to be won. Mere patriotism dissolved in the spirit of a game played for its own sake.

It seemed as though almost everyone on the field had a chance to go down in history as the first man to decide one of the tournament's matches with a sudden-death goal: first Anderton, then Kuntz, then Moller, Kuntz again, then dear old Gazza, twice in three minutes, then Ziege, then Platt, then McManaman, then Adams. All of them will be seeing those chances again in their dreams, only the Englishmen will wake up sweating.

There was barely a cigarette paper between the two sides all through a night when both these old enemies appeared to have signed a pact to do away with caution. Who would wish to choose between the elegance of Sammer and the wholehearted-ness of Adams, between the mad invention of Gascoigne and the chilling deftness of Möller, between the ferocity of Pearce and the athleticism of Ziege? It was a contrast of style but rarely of quality and there must have been many in the stadium who, moved by the sheer generosity of the players, regretted the necessity for either side to lose.

And certainly not to lose through one man's mistake. Well, of course, we can say that penalties are an authentic part of the game, and that it is best to decide such a match by using a legitimate technique. But at the end you just wanted them to draw lots for a place in the final so that luck could be blamed, not a man. No one deserved to be remembered for losing this one by his error, as poor Gareth Southgate will be at the end of a tournament which he entered as an international novice before establishing himself as one of England's most skilful and perceptive players.

It was Stuart Pearce, inevitably, who was first to reach Southgate as the distraught defender made his way back to the centre circle knowing that his failure had ended the nation's hope of an even bigger party than the one we have been enjoying for the past 2½ weeks. Pearce was the only one who knew exactly how Southgate felt and in the months ahead his example should be of some comfort to a man who will wake up today feeling the entire burden of elimination weighing on his shoulders.

"I am proud of the whole lot of them," Terry Venables said afterwards, emphatically including Southgate. "It can be a cruel game but it can be wonderful." When he saw how much his players were prepared to give him he could have been forgiven for believing that last night was not going to be one of the cruel ones.

Before the start the big question concerned the true condition of Jürgen Klinsmann's damaged calf muscles. Were they torn, strained or merely bruised? Someone who had seen him the night before said that he could hardly walk but there was suspicion that Berti Vogts might use him in emergency, if only as a talismanic figure warming up on the touchline, to put fear into English hearts. The Germans had spent the night before the match in a hotel a couple of hundred yards away from Madame Tussaud's, which prompted the thought that perhaps Vogts was planning to borrow the wax effigy of the 1995 Footballer of the Year to send out at the head of the team like Charlton Heston in the final scene of El Cid.

In Klinsmann's absence England took the lead after two minutes. Did they think, in that moment, that they had it won? There have been times during this tournament when what they needed to animate their game was a goal; without one they looked anxious and incoherent. Well, they got one last night, with Shearer's devastating swoop, but it had the opposite effect. It put them to sleep.

For the next 13 minutes and for the only time in the match they sat back on their lead and watched while the Germans pulled themselves together and began to move the ball around. At first tentatively but soon with gathering confidence, Sammer and Möller started to mark out a steady tempo on which a variety of rhythms could be imposed.

England could not have chosen a more dangerous strategy. This German side is not equipped for breakaways. It moved forward as a unit, favouring short passes at damaging angles to men already on the move to accept the ball on the understanding that there would be someone else arriving to receive it in turn. England's unwillingness to force the pace after taking the lead presented the Germans with exactly the opportunity they required to recover from the jolt caused by Shearer's strike, and the move leading to Kuntz's goal, after Platt's poor control had given the ball away in the centre cirle, unfolded with implacable logic.

Eventually England pulled themselves together and, if there was a player who consistently rose above the throng, it was Darren Anderton. Overshadowed by McManaman in the early matches of the tournament, he fulfilled the wing-back's role on the right in the first half last night before relinquishing the task to his Liverpool counterpart and using the consequent freedom to invent most of England's best moves. Had his shot gone in rather than hit the post in the second minute of extra-time some sort of justice would have been served. But on we went instead to the unbearable unfairness of the penalties.

No one can deny that the footballers of the Czech Republic have earned the right to their appearance in Sunday's final of Euro 96. And, if they win it, to call themselves champions. But they can count themselves honoured to be facing the winners of a match in which both sides played as if they had nothing to lose, the way it is in dreams.

03|06|1998
It won't be a proper war without Gazza. What else is football for?

Jonathan Freedland

....

It's lucky I'm not the England coach as I would have picked Paul Gascoigne. OK, I know next to nothing about football but I do know that, if you're the England manager, picking Gazza is part of the job description. Glenn Hoddle's decision suggests he doesn't understand what football is all about.

England's coach seems to think it's a bloodless exercise in technical efficiency and robotic prowess. His talk of physical condition, fitness levels and soccer "athletes" suggests he is less concerned to build a football team than a well-tuned machine.

But what we soccer outsiders know is that football is not precision science. It's about passion, fervour and deep emotion — areas in which Gascoigne remains a world-class performer.

That's why Gazza had earned his place in France but it's also why football has become the most important game on earth. The politicians understand it, so do the money men and so do Mr Hoddle's fellow international managers. Unlike him they realise that soccer is much more than a mere sporting contest, contingent on such minor matters as a player's form. Stronger forces of national pride, tribal identity and human drama are at work — a lesson we are set to learn all over again in a tournament which will dominate British life for the next five weeks.

Sky TV showed it understood soccer's devotion when it promoted its Premiership coverage under the slogan, "It's Our Religion". Coca-Cola tagged along with "Eat Football, Sleep Football". The latest edition of Sponsorship News predicts that "early in the millennium the World Cup will overtake the Olympic Games to become sport's greatest money-spinner".

Politicians drew that same conclusion decades ago, ruling that football was far too important to play games with. It's striking that the World Cup is the only major global sporting event never to have fallen victim to an international boycott. While the Moscow Olympics of 1980 and the Los Angeles Games of 1984 both became battlefields of the cold war, the World Cup went ahead in 1982 without a hitch.

It helped that those arch-boycotters, the Americans, did not find their footballing feet until after the fall of communism: by the time they competed in Italia '90, there was no Soviet bloc worth boycotting. But the chief cause of the World Cup's immunity from geo-politicking is governments' fear of the power of the game. Most leaders of footballing nations know that soccer is bigger than they are — and that to suggest pulling out of the quadrennial soccer-fest is to risk popular insurrection.

How else to explain the absence of a campaign to keep Nigeria out of the coming finals? The Abacha regime's appalling human rights record has made Nigeria an emerging pariah nation and the object of heavy EU sanctions. Since those apply to France, Nigeria should have been blocked from taking part. Yet almost no one — except the lone voice of Glenys Kinnock, raised in the European parliament — has suggested the ban be implemented. It's as if boycotts are all very well for the boring old Olympic Games — but football simply matters too much.

As Bill Shankly famously remarked, "Football's not a matter of life and death — it's much more important than that." The Colombian defender Andres Escobar proved the point in 1994 when, days after he had scored an own goal against the United States which led to his team's ejection from the tournament, he was shot 12 times outside a bar in Medellin. "A costly error," as John Motson might say. And there was 1969's Football War between Honduras and El Salvador — an armed conflict which began with a dispute over a soccer game and left 6,000 dead.

What explains this degree of fervour, apparently peculiar to soccer? It helps that football is the people's game: the rules are simple and, with no need for special equipment, it costs nothing to play. But the appeal is deeper. My guess is that it beats the likes of tennis, boxing and Olympic athletics because it is about teams. Whole peoples can get behind a football team because they are bigger than any one individual: they become instead representatives of the tribe. "They are wearing the flag and going to war," says Channel 5's sports anchor Jonny Gould. Football is battle by other means, with the 11 men our chosen force. No wonder Saddam Hussein is said to have beaten the soles of the Iraqi national team after its failure to qualify for this month's finals: they had inflicted a collective humiliation on Iraq no less than those soldiers cut down on the road to Basra.

So much more is at stake on the football field than mere gymnastics with a plastic sphere. The heroes of the game understood that: that's what makes them magical. Their home nations understand it, too. That's why Italy has sent Roberto Baggio to France even though he is, like Gazza, 31 years old. Germany would not be without Lothar Matthäus even though he is a creaky 37. And the Saudis have found a place for their own Gazza, Saeed Owairan — even though he was jailed for six months for immoral behaviour.

Paul Gascoigne is like them — not fast or clinical, but capable of inspiring his team-mates and pulling off an 89th-minute dash of brilliance. If football was played on a computer spreadsheet, then maybe Gazza should have been dumped. But since it involves human flesh and blood, with an uncanny way of entering hearts across the globe, Paul Gascoigne — unlike football itself — should not be coming home.

Paul Gascoigne brings something different to the game — in this case cut-out cards of Diego Maradona and Ruud Gullit

David Beckham collects footballers' autographs but not referees'. Kim Milton Nielsen brandishes the red

02/07/1998

What now for outcast David Beckham?

The £8m-a-year glory boy put one foot wrong against Argentina and may pay a heavy price. By Richard Williams

As it happens, David Beckham collects footballers' autographs, like any young fan. When he joined the England squad, less than two years ago, Glenn Hoddle's signature was immediately added to his collection. A few weeks before the World Cup he successfully cornered Pele.

He also collects shirts. At the end of England's victory over Colombia last week, he dashed over to Carlos Valderrama, the opposition's captain, and exchanged tops with a man playing his last match at the end of a legendary international career.

Beckham is a hero-worshipper. And the man he worships most fervently, the man whose shirt and autograph take pride of place in his collection, is Eric Cantona, his former Manchester United team-mate.

"Eric was my role model," he said recently. "He's the best I've ever played with. A great guy. One day I'd like to be as charismatic as him."

In one respect, at least, Beckham has now matched Cantona's standing. His flick of a foot at Diego Simeone in St Etienne on Tuesday night may have lacked the theatrical element of Cantona's kung-fu kick on Matthew Simmons at Selhurst Park in 1994 but it has earned him similar notoriety.

Although Cantona's doom was widely forecast, he survived the ordeal once the facts of the case had been examined. Solid in his private life, strong in his idiosyncratic philosophy, silently contemptuous of his critics, the Frenchman returned from a long suspension to win more trophies with the club before slipping quietly into retirement last year, at the age of 30. Whether Beckham has the mental resources to cope with a similar public crucifixion is another matter.

It will probably be some time before one of his England colleagues breaks rank to tell us what, if anything, was said to Beckham in the dressing room after the rest of the team had returned in defeat on Tuesday. Not much, probably. His fellow professionals would recognise the misfortune inherent in a dismissal for a gesture far less offensive, however stupid, than many which went unpunished in the same game. They would know, though, that in such cases the referee can never be blamed for playing it by the book, and the book said Beckham had to go.

The England coach, however, has already infringed one of the unwritten rules of the game by suggesting that Beckham's exit probably cost his side the game. Alex Ferguson, Beckham's manager at Manchester United, would never have allowed himself to level such an accusation at one of his own players, however provoked.

Ferguson, who has guided Beckham through all the stages of his professional life, from apprentice to superstar, believes that internal criticism should be made behind closed doors. To do otherwise can only give comfort to the enemy, whether that be the opposing team or the media. The wisdom of his policy can be judged by the intensity of the storm that broke over Beckham's head yesterday.

At 23 Beckham is the boy with everything. No current male pop singer enjoys the degree of popularity experienced by Beckham and Michael Owen, his 18-year-old England team-mate. They are heroes and stars at once, blessed with natural talent, good looks and pleasant manners, benefiting from the extraordinary increase in the popularity of their sport over the past decade.

"There are some mornings when I wake up and have to pinch myself to know that it's real," Beckham recently told Erik Bielderman of *L'Equipe*, the French sports paper, before the tournament began. He has a Porsche, a Jaguar coupé and luxurious homes in Manchester, where he plays, and London, where he grew up.

He is engaged to be married next year to Victoria Adams, aka Posh Spice, with whom he exchanged rings costing as much as suburban family houses.

They appear to enjoy a mutually supportive romance: he

says loyal things about the Spice Girls being the best group in the world; she was in the grandstand to watch him take the field against Argentina. He likes nice cars, they both like clothes.

He is one of the few men in England who can be pictured with his girlfriend going for a holiday stroll while wearing a sarong and not look stupid. As a couple they filled the hole left by Charles and Diana and then by Liz and Hugh as the nation's temporary sweethearts – their idylls celebrated only in order, it seems, to be destroyed.

But this is all a byproduct of his talent. In his own words, Beckham was born to be a footballer. Although he is a Londoner, he was constantly taken to watch Manchester United by his father, who travelled to every game. His mother often went with them. Once he demonstrated a gift for the game his future was not in doubt.

At Old Trafford he came under the eye of Ferguson, whose extraordinary success at the club has been largely based on a policy of finding and grooming young players. Understanding what damage can be done to young men in their situation by constant media exposure, Ferguson has carefully restricted and monitored the public utterances of Beckham, Ryan Giggs, Paul Scholes and the Neville brothers. All are in their early 20s, all have medals and international caps in their trophy cabinets and yet they remain essentially private figures.

Their taste in girlfriends ensured that Beckham and Giggs moved eventually from the back pages to the front, emerging from Ferguson's shield to become public property. In the Britain of the late 90s a young millionaire footballer going out with a blonde TV presenter or a pop singer is likely to be scrutinised as closely as the Prime Minister. They enter a different world, a Hello-land, given no training to help them cope with a new set of rules and tests.

Beckham shares an agent with Alan Shearer, the England captain, whose ability to deal with superstardom by playing a dead bat even to the most anodyne question has long been the despair of journalists, broadsheet as well as tabloid. Beckham admires the skill with which the 27-year-old Shearer covers his back as much as the skill with which he scores goals, but it is the younger man's instincts on the pitch that have led him into the kind of trouble Shearer has so assiduously avoided.

Although Beckham's soft voice and diffident delivery make him seem young for his age, as a footballer he is known to display a combative, even rancorous temperament, seemingly at odds with his status as one of the few English players capable of real artistry. He disputes decisions with referees and occasionally he lashes out. As Bielderman pointed out to him, this can give the impression that he is a bit of a brat and too big for his boots.

"I've never been sorry for anything I've done on the pitch," he responded, with an echo of Cantona. "Sometimes I've committed a foul and afterwards I've told myself I shouldn't have done it but football is a contact sport and there's a lot of pres-

sure. On the pitch and off it I'm two different people. On the pitch I know there are people who hate me."

It was Beckham's fate that his reaction to Simeone's original foul occurred only a few feet away from Tuesday night's referee, Kim Milton Nielsen of Denmark. In less pressurised circumstances Nielsen might have quietly reprimanded both men and waved play on, knowing that a dismissal would disrupt and perhaps even ruin the pure narrative of what had, for 45 minutes, been a magnificently spectacular match, easily the most compelling of the 55 so far played in the 1998 World Cup.

Beckham might have noted the reaction of the French public when Zinedine Zidane, their most gifted and important player, got himself sent off in France's second match for walking over the back of a Saudi player. Zidane was suspended for the next two matches, a punishment which almost cost the hosts their place in the quarter-finals. But although journalists and the public expressed regret at his action, there was neither outrage nor recrimination.

In Thatcherised and Murdochised Britain, where sport and celebrity and money and the media are locked together in a dervish dance, that sense of proportion appears to have been suspended.

"I always dreamed," David Beckham has said, "that one day people would look at me the way I looked at the big stars of the game when I was a boy." But no one looks at stars that way any more.

02|02|1999

Hoddle may once have had the world at his feet, but the bitter end is not such a surprise

England's sacked coach was determined to fulfil his destiny but the self-destruct button was always there. By Jim White

Glenn Hoddle must have known that he was in trouble the moment the Prime Minister abandoned him. Tony Blair, the man with his antennae most attuned to the public mood, chose that vital platform for disseminating government information, ITV's This Morning With Richard And Judy, to express his distaste for Hoddle's idiosyncratic views on disabled people.

Glenn Hoddle, in charge of England at the 1998 World Cup, was determined to realise the greatness within him

"If he said what he is reported to have said in the way he is reported to have said it," the Prime Minister told a waiting nation, or at least those watching morning telly, "then I think that was very wrong."

But how has it come to this? How could a man who apparently had the world at his feet barely 18 months ago have fallen so far, so quickly? And more than that: where will a man who has become the biggest social pariah this side of Bernard Manning go now?

Oddly enough, it is possible to see evidence of his potential for self-destruction even on that triumphant autumn evening in Rome. On October 11 1997, a fortnight before Hoddle's 40th birthday, England drew with Italy to secure their place in the World Cup finals. Everything he had planned for his team had worked that night, everything he wanted them to do had fallen into place. He wore a smile so wide it must have hurt. In that moment Glenn Hoddle looked fulfilled.

The next day he returned to England to the kind of press football managers dream about. Reading the papers this week, it may be hard to believe but on that morning tabloid and broadsheet alike trumpeted praise. Column inches were filled with eulogies to his team. Most papers carried profiles of Hoddle. The articles talked about his calmness, his drive, how his spirituality was such an asset in a job as tricky as his.

And they talked about his family, about how having a secure background gave him the stability to strive in his workplace.

That evening Hoddle returned to his wife, Anne, at their home in Ascot. Typical Glenn, that: the family man whose adherence to things domestic was obvious in the Shredded Wheat commercial screened at the time which showed a happy breakfast in the Hoddle household. But this occasion was different.

This was the night of all nights that Hoddle chose to tell Anne he was leaving. "The marriage had run out of steam" was his brusque epitaph for an 18-year relationship. Though subsequently it appeared a more significant factor was a relationship involving the wife of a former acquaintance coming to the boil.

In football as in any other profession marriages break up under the strain of frequent absence. There was nothing unusual in the end of this one, except its manner and timing: curt, matter of fact and ruthlessly executed.

It also revealed all sorts of clues about the way Hoddle sets about his life. The timing was appalling. Not just for his wife – how must she have felt looking back at those pictures of him cavorting around the Roman turf knowing that in the forefront of his mind the decision to leave her was floating around? But also for his public image: why risk souring the moment when there was plenty of time to do this sort of thing later?

The answer to both questions was the same: Eileen Drewery. Hoddle had discussed his marriage with the woman who has been his spiritual adviser since he was a teenage starlet at Tottenham and she told him to follow his heart and make the break as quickly as possible. And there is no one he pays more heed to than Drewery.

But something else was revealed in Hoddle's callous treatment of his wife that night: he thought he was unassailable. It was not just the win in Rome that convinced him of his own invincibility. He had been like that all his life.

Man in a hurry

From the earliest days this is what everyone says about Hoddle: how utterly determined he was to realise the greatness within him. What you do not hear are yarns, gags and anecdotes. A book of uproarious incidents from Hoddle's life would be about as extensive as the William Hague guide to hair care.

He has never had time for the lightweight, the inconsequential, the silly. Which may be why he could not get on with Paul Gascoigne. He was a man in too much of a hurry to be distracted. He was a man trying to fulfil his destiny.

It was clear to him early in life what it was, his destiny. All footballers have immense reservoirs of self-confidence; it is a prerequisite for the job to believe you are up to it. But Hoddle was different. He told his dad at the age of 11 he would play for England. At 12 he told him he would manage his country too. Born with the supra-natural grace and balance of the real athlete, he was also blessed with single-mindedness.

As a child he would practise on his own, for at least two hours a night, every night, perfecting his technique in his back garden in Harlow, Essex. That natural skill of his took an awful lot of work.

When he met Drewery, and she healed a nagging injury, that sense of destiny gained a focus. There seemed to be, in her hotch-potch philosophy and grab-bag spirituality, an explanation which legitimised his enormous sense of self. She told him he was chosen. From that moment he behaved as if he was.

So it must have come as something of a surprise that so many of the managers presiding over England teams when he was a player failed to share his own assumptions.

As the country's most talented player it seemed astonishing to him he was chosen for the national team on only 55 occasions, particularly as he was so dedicated to the cause. He did not drink, had a steady home life, trained like a Trojan.

His only sign of deviant behaviour was once releasing an execrable record called Diamond Lights with Chris Waddle and singing it on Top of the Pops while wearing cast-offs from the wardrobe for Miami Vice.

Thus, since as a player he had been prevented from realising his destiny, he could not wait to be a manager — particularly after his appetite had been whetted by a spell as a player in Monaco, where he was coached by Arsène Wenger, who helped him appreciate that it is possible to be a football manager without behaving as if on the army parade ground.

Destiny calling

It was obvious, from the briefness of his tenure at both Swindon Town and Chelsea, that from the moment he became a manager in his early thirties Hoddle was ambitious. In 1996 he angered Ken Bates, chairman of Chelsea, with the speed of his departure. But Hoddle did not mind whom he upset: destiny was calling in the shape of the England manager's job.

In truth the blazers at the FA were delighted a man of Hoddle's calibre was happy to take on the position. It had been dubbed by a previous incumbent "the impossible job", such was the pressure from a public hungry for success and a popular press hungry for another scalp. But Hoddle paid no heed to such talk: after all, he was destined for the job — Eileen told him so — and God, or whatever name he gives to the strange eternal being he reckons is directing the film of his life, would look out for him.

So in 1996 he became England coach. He decided to do things his way and some of his theories were good ones. He inherited a reasonable side and the respect he generated from those who remembered him in his prime as a player meant he had a willing audience for his tactical ideas.

At first he did well on the pitch, topping his World Cup group in some style. And, while he was winning, the fact he made no allowances for the press did not matter. Ironically, given what happened subsequently, he came into the job determined to give nothing to a press which he believed had contributed to the downfall of several predecessors.

"He's never been comfortable with the press," said Paul Miller, his friend and former playing colleague. "He's never liked them. He could never forgive them from early on for the criticism they levelled at him. And one thing about Glenn, he never forgets." He even once refused to do an interview with the FA's own in-house magazine. "I have been stitched up by FA magazines before" was his explanation. Stitched up? By your own house organ? Surely not even Alastair Campbell is that paranoid.

But the World Cup, the tournament he thought was finally going to provide him with his fulfilment, was the beginning of the end for Hoddle. He made mistake after mistake, tactically and in his man management.

It culminated in his diary, in which he made huge financial capital disclosing information which should have remained confidential. He was losing the respect of his players, who began to question the central importance that he placed on Drewery ("it's like joining the Moonies," said one senior player) and publicly wondered why training sessions consisted largely of their manager showing off his ball skills to the watching cameras for 45 minutes. When the qualifying campaign for Euro 2000 began, Hoddle was overseeing an increasingly discontented squad.

Typically, Hoddle blamed everyone else for the problems. His only mistake was not taking Drewery to France, he said, a remark which made several senior players wince. And, as he started losing, he found he had no allies in the media.

Thus, when his spin doctor, David Davies, suggested a charm offensive of the papers to restore some confidence prior to this spring's qualifying campaign, Hoddle reluctantly agreed. Unfortunately such was his assumption of invincibility he did not appear to listen to Davies's advice that the interviews be about "football, football and football".

So came the fateful interview with *The Times*, when he seized the opportunity to proselytise his views on the disabled. Since then he has dug the hole he finds himself in ever deeper, laughably trying to blame the reporter. Given that the views expressed in the piece were entirely consistent with what he has said before, that he has a history of denying on-the-record comments and that nobody could have made up such nonsense anyway, perhaps only Drewery has accepted his assertion that he was misquoted. He may not have meant the meaning to come out like that, but he said the words.

Whatever happens, Hoddle is finished, the author of his own demise. No one can work with him again, not because he has offensive views — football is riddled with those whose opinions would appal London cabbies — but because he is too arrogant, inept and misguided to keep them to himself.

That and the fact that his England team are faltering. Such is the place football holds in the national consciousness that, had he been winning on the pitch, we would have forgiven him anything.

09|10|2000

King Kevin abdicates again: where now for England?

David Lacey

Of the 10 men who have been in charge of the England football team over the past 54 years Kevin Keegan will be remembered as a cheerleader who denied Wembley one last hurrah and then quit while he was behind.

Keegan's sudden resignation five minutes after his team had lost Saturday's World Cup qualifier 1-0 to Germany concludes the most bizarre period yet in the quirky history of national managers.

The England coach had taken over 20 months ago after the Football Association's decision to sack Glenn Hoddle once the Prime Minister, put on the spot in a day-time television chat show, had muttered that, if Hoddle really had implied the disabled were paying for the sins of past lives, he ought to go.

In view of what has happened now Hoddle might have been referring to the FA international committee, for if ever a body is reaping the whirlwind of past misdeeds it is surely this one.

Bobby Robson took England to the semi-finals of the 1990 World Cup but his contract was not renewed, Terry Venables had already decided not to sign a fresh contract by the time England reached the last four of Euro 96, the committee having expressed doubts about his legal wrangles with Alan Sugar and the Department of Trade and Industry, and Hoddle's sin was to express his beliefs clumsily to a national newspaper.

The timing of Keegan's departure was totally predictable. His temperament and lack of tactical nous made him a bad choice from the start.

When he originally agreed to take the job for four matches, while remaining manager of Fulham, he promised that the players would sing the national anthem with passion and bring a similar mood to their performances. Well, not all of the team were singing before Saturday's match and not enough of them were in harmony during the game to form a barbershop quartet.

Keegan also stressed that he would not leave Fulham once his four-match stint had ended. After two games in charge, however, he decided that "it's time to stop playing games: I want the job". On Saturday he again decided it was time to stop playing games, only now he believed he was not up to the job

Kevin Keegan ponders England's 1-0 defeat by Germany before admitting he did not know what to do and resigning

after all. In other words, after taking the England post saying I'm sorry I'll read that again, he has abandoned it admitting I'm sorry I haven't a clue.

Keegan's plea of *mea culpa* ("I'm blaming nobody but myself. I wasn't good enough"), the revelation that during England's awful first half he did not know what to do, his apparent self-sacrifice in order to hand the squad over to someone with more knowledge and the hardly original thought that he wants to spend more time with his family will cut little ice with experienced Kev-watchers.

He has walked out after a defeat that made it imperative that he stayed for at least four more days in order to give England the best chance of repairing the damage, serious though hardly mortal, to their chances of qualifying for the World Cup caused by an initial home defeat. Instead of which Howard Wilkinson, the FA's technical director, will again pop up like George, the inflatable automatic pilot in Airplane, to take over the team for Wednesday's qualifier in Finland.

When Don Revie quit on England during a World Cup qualifying campaign the FA tried, unsuccessfully, to ban him from football for 10 years. True, Keegan did not conduct covert negotiations with the United Arab Emirates before giving his resignation exclusively to a newspaper, but his defection is scarcely more admirable.

If, as he insists, he enjoyed the full support of everybody at the FA from the chairman to the Lancaster Gate cat, then surely he could have given the job one more chance.

Keegan's excuse that the fans who clamoured successfully for his appointment had helped him make up his mind on Saturday by booing him as he left the arena is barely worth consideration. If every England manager had walked out after being jeered at Wembley Alf Ramsey, Ron Greenwood, Bobby Robson, Graham Taylor and Glenn Hoddle would not have lasted anywhere near as long as they did.

According to Adam Crozier, the FA's chief executive who has limited experience of these things: "It is never easy to say I'm not going to be England coach any more. To walk away from that is a very courageous thing to do." Yet surely it would have been even more courageous to stay put, tough it out and risk the probability of being ditched by the FA if the team also lost in Helsinki.

It is not as if Keegan had a rough ride from the media, who let him down relatively lightly after the debacle of Euro 2000. He was never vilified in the press as Robson was more than once. He was never lampooned as cruelly as Taylor nor hung out to dry like Hoddle. The heat in Keegan's kitchen barely rose above gas mark one.

Crozier was nearer the mark, albeit unwittingly, when he observed that "I think Kevin Keegan knew he was making the right decision for Kevin Keegan". That is surely the point.

On Saturday Keegan made all the right self-deprecatory noises in the interviews. He is a master of the soundbite and it is a pity that his tactical know-how in handling reporters' questions was not matched by an ability to organise the England team.

"I just feel that for Kevin Keegan there is nothing more in football I want to do," he said, a trifle wistfully. Presumably this precludes returning to TV as a soccer pundit. Surely he can never sit in judgment on England again having admitted that he did not know enough when he was in charge.

England's sweetest revenge

World Cup qualifier
Germany 1 England 5
David Lacey, Munich

Now all of England is on fire. The pessimism of 11 months ago had already given way to guarded optimism but after the extraordinary events here on Saturday night English joy has, for the moment at least, good reason to be unconfined.

Beating the Germans at football always did lift the nation's hearts. Beating them 5-1 in Germany will have come close to blowing the nation's minds. This was ecstasy in spades.

For 35 years England have lived on the tale of the day a World Cup was won against West Germany at Wembley. Shortly before the countries met in the Olympiastadion here to contest automatic qualification for the 2002 tournament Geoff Hurst was on German television recalling his hat-trick.

From now on talk of hat-tricks against Germany will revolve more around Michael Owen, each of whose goals on Saturday certainly crossed the line. Having wrought havoc in the Bayern Munich defence for Liverpool in the Super Cup in Monaco, Owen returned to Bayern's home ground to give Muncheners the full Monte. As gaps in Rudi Völler's awful defence yawned he simply tore along the dotted lines.

"For me Michael Owen has something very special," enthused Sven-Goran Eriksson, whose stock as England's coach is now in the upper stratosphere. "He's a good footballer and his technique is excellent but he also has two things which are difficult to find in a player: he's very cold when he gets a chance and he's very quick. When you have that combination it's a killer."

David Beckham, groin strain forgotten, commanded an England performance as he had never done before. Equally crucial were the tactically adroit performances of Steven Gerrard and Paul Scholes, who denied Germany the midfield mastery they

The Germans may have wished Munich's Olympiastadion was less well appointed in its scoreboard

had been so meekly allowed at Wembley last October, when Dietmar Hamann ran the match and scored its only goal.

That Germany victory, a swift revenge for England's 1-0 win in Charleroi that had bundled them out of the European Championship, begat Kevin Keegan's resignation and the glum scoreless draw in Finland under Howard Wilkinson which finally persuaded the Football Association to look abroad for the next man to run the national squad.

Eriksson always did seem a sound choice by the FA. Now the appointment has taken on the touch of genius. England, three points behind with a game in hand, can finish only level with Germany in Group Nine if Germany win their last game against Finland, but crucially Eriksson's side are four in front on goal difference and will still go through automatically if first place has to be decided on the head-to-heads. Of course they still have to beat Albania in Newcastle on Wednesday and Greece at Old Trafford on October 6. Even in the heady aftermath of Saturday's match Eriksson tried to keep a sense of proportion.

"After a victory like this there is always a danger of thinking that you can put out a shoe or a foot or a leg just to win a game," he said. "The game on Wednesday is not so glamorous, so tomorrow we must try to forget this victory and be focused on Albania. It would be a small disaster if we beat Germany away and then lose to Albania at home. Then this victory tonight would be worthless, more or less."

Those are wise words, though it is hard to imagine his cool England team being carried away even by Saturday's historic win: the first time Germany have ever lost in Munich, only their second home defeat in World Cup qualifiers, their heaviest to

Michael Owen's hat-trick had Sven-Goran Eriksson saying: 'He's very cold when he gets a chance and he's very quick'

England at full international level and the most dramatic turnaround in a return bout involving German opposition since Joe Louis battered Max Schmeling to a jelly.

On Saturday Germany's defence suffered a similarly nightmarish, if less physically painful, experience. When in the sixth minute Carsten Jancker punished some ball-watching by the England defence, prodding the ball past David Seaman after Oliver Neuville's header had surprised Sol Campbell and Rio Ferdinand, some bad memories came floating back.

In the event the sloppiness of falling behind merely made the manner of England's recovery even more impressive. Eriksson's plan was to exploit the narrowness of Völler's back three by getting Gary Neville and Ashley Cole behind the German wing-backs Marko Rehmer and Jörg Böhme while Owen and Emile Heskey advanced through the inside-forward channels.

Chronically inept German defending played its part but so did England's character. "I think the reason why we came back into the game was that our players believe we have a really good team and that we can do good things," Eriksson said. "If you don't believe that, it doesn't matter how good you are. These things must always start in the head.

"I told the players before they went out that, if you play football as you can, we can beat anyone. If we want to play as we did against Holland [to whom England lost 2-0 in a friendly at White Hart Lane], we can lose against anyone. Either way it's very easy. But if we can go on like this in important games, we can lose a friendly now and then and it doesn't matter."

Eriksson pointed to the shot rifled into the left-hand corner of the German net by Gerrard in first-half stoppage-time as the crucial moment. "To go in leading 2-1 instead of drawing 1-1 was a great difference both for us and for them."

Owen's equaliser in the 12th minute, a sharp volley after Gary Neville's forward header had caught the defence moving out too late and left Nick Barmby onside when he nodded the ball square to the Liverpool striker, might still have been dashed by offside against other players but the flag stayed down. On another night Sebastian Deisler might have scored a crucial goal at a crucial time for Germany instead of dragging the ball wide and just before Gerrard's goal Seaman made his most important save, keeping out a low snap-shot from Böhme.

Although England needed only two minutes of the second half to increase their lead, Beckham's sharp centre enabling Heskey to nod Owen through for his second goal, how different might things have been had Jancker not directed a free header the wrong way just before the hour.

Once Gerrard had neatly dispossessed Michael Ballack before setting up Owen's hat-trick, to be followed by Beckham and Scholes combining to send Heskey through a thoroughly dilapidated and depressed defence for England's fifth goal, the Olympiastadion was emptying in droves.

Long before the end the German supporters did not think it was all over. They knew.

24|06|2002

Why a weary England will never win

A League season of too many games plus no winter break equals shattered dreams, writes David Lacey

Nothing quite becomes England in major tournaments as their leaving of them. Before Sven-Goran Eriksson's players flew home from Japan on Saturday the proprieties were observed with a smoothness born of frequent practice.

England were disappointed not to have gone further in the World Cup but had learned a lot and hoped to do better next time. The lads had done their best but it was not to be.

The scene has now been played out in a dozen World Cups or European Championships since England's success in 1966.

England fans in Shizuoka absorb the same old story after Brazil end their hopes in the quarter-finals

Unless the domestic fixture list relents sufficiently to allow the national coach more time with his squad and the players more rest between engagements, the script will not change.

When the Football Association sanctioned the breakaway which led to the formation of the Premier League 10 years ago, it did so in the belief that the move would help the national team. England, the FA stated in its 1991 Blueprint for Football, would be at the apex of a new pyramid of which the Premier League would be an integral part.

The reality is that the Premier League, or Premiership, has become its own pyramid with Mammon at its apex and the England team as helpless an onlooker as the Sphinx. Far from benefiting the development of the national side, moreover, the Premier League has hampered its progress with foreign imports.

True, Manchester United, Liverpool, Arsenal and Leeds United have between them provided a solid England side who have done better than expected, given the severity of the draw, the loss of Steven Gerrard and Gary Neville, David Beckham being no more than 60% fit and, to rub it in, facing Brazil with Michael Owen able to last only half the match.

Yet there is no escaping the fact that among the leading English clubs most goals are scored or made by foreigners, the best passers are foreigners and, with the exception of Rio Ferdinand, the best defenders are foreigners. It would help England if their footballers could play less often. Since taking over the squad 18 months ago Eriksson has been pressing the point that no other European country places so many demands on its players.

He is echoing his predecessors but few clubs could stand the loss of income this would involve and even fewer players would accept the reductions in salary that might be necessary.

Not surprisingly, therefore, Eriksson has more or less given up hope of seeing the burden on his squad eased. He will have to qualify for the 2004 European Championship, and from a group containing newly potent Turkey, under the usual conditions.

"We need less teams in the Premier League but that's impossible," he said, just before England flew home. "We also need them to have a winter break but I don't know if we will get that." A glance at the Boxing Day attendance figures should put him right there.

It is surely no accident that going into the World Cup the fittest player in the England squad was Owen Hargreaves, who plays for Bayern Munich in the 18-team German league where a footballer's career is less of a treadmill. Before Eriksson took his squad to Dubai to begin training in earnest, fitness and blood tests revealed that his Premiership players were showing worrying signs of fatigue.

This may explain why, in each of their five World Cup matches and particularly against Sweden and Brazil, England fell away after half-time. Eriksson put this down to tiredness – a bit of a handicap in a team relying so much on pace.

"Eriksson talks about pace," said the Brazilian coach Luiz Felipe Scolari after his 10 men had passed England to oblivion

231

in Shizuoka. "But nothing can run faster than the ball." Perhaps that was the trouble. England spent too much energy running after the ball because they could not run well enough with it.

There is a counter-argument, though. England have had a better World Cup than France, Italy and Argentina, who had more gifted squads and whose players have a lighter domestic workload. Even Arsenal's French contingent gets a rest when Arsène Wenger rotates the team.

It also needs to be remembered that the successful club sides of the past, notably Liverpool, regularly used fewer players in seasons involving 60 matches or more, although they did not have to divide their attention between the League Championship and the Champions League.

Yet the intensity of the game is even greater now than it was then. The relaxation of the offside law, for example, means players have to cover more ground at a greater pace.

In general, levels of fitness in English football have never been so high. It is just unfortunate that, when the England team needs the players to be at their peak, so many of them are battered, physically and mentally, by the labours of the previous nine months. Lions in winter, lambs in spring – that is England and nothing is going to change.

After a short break the members of Eriksson's squad will be reporting for pre-season training and in next to no time memories of Japan will be overtaken by a resumption of Sir Alex Ferguson's moods and Wenger's myopia.

Not to worry. A date for the next England inquest has provisionally been arranged for some time in June 2004. And the verdict will be the same: natural causes.

I founded Matrix in 1999 with three other photographers: Trevor Adams, Jonathan Bushell and my long-time Sardinian sidekick Marco Deidda. In this business you go through lean times and busy times, often irrespective of how hard you work. I think it's about karma every now and again, something will land on your lap.

Stenning is one of about 10 London-based freelance photographers on our books. His patch is Knightsbridge and Chelsea. I wouldn't say he's the highest earner but occasionally he comes up with a corker. Two years ago he brought in a picture of Tara Palmer-Tomkinson in her car, smoking an interesting-looking home-made cigarette.

Two weeks ago he photographed Nick Faldo and his girlfriend. No one knew it then but the photo showed she was pregnant, so that made a newspaper and a few magazines.

This time it had really happened for Stenning. The funny thing was, it had happened nearly a week before. When we sent out the Sven picture, people asked why we had sat on it for four days. The truth is it was complete accident that we saw it at all.

On Thursday July 3 I left work at 5.30pm and was walking to the car when I got a call from the office to say Stenning was on the phone. One of his regular informants had told him that Sven was going to drop in on the new owner of Chelsea FC.

It was raining and dark and Martin works on foot, so we needed to send back-up. In those conditions you increase your chances by 100% if you have more than one angle. We wanted someone there, in a car, and fast, but as we were taking down the address Stenning's phone died. I uttered a

Another day, another picture: Sven-Goran Eriksson arrives at FA headquarters in Soho Square

14|07|2003

A shot we nearly shelved

Max Cisotti tells Will Pavia how a discarded picture made the front pages a week later

Last Wednesday Martin Stenning came into the Matrix office with a big smile. His photograph of Sven-Goran Eriksson entering the home of Roman Abramovich, the new proprietor of Chelsea football club, was front-page news for most papers and the story was getting all-day coverage on the radio.

few four-letter expletives. We'd just have to hope Martin got some good shots. We weren't that surprised when he called that night to say he had a few images but they were too poor to be of use. I don't think he realised how important the story was.

Forward to the next week. Stenning comes into the office on Tuesday morning to deliver some photos of Mrs Abramovich shopping in Harrods. The Matrix office is rectangular: we sit on two large benches, set in a few feet from the walls. I don't have my own presidential suite; I'm on the benches with everyone else. We are 12 right now: four directors, seven regular employees, plus a chap called Andrew MacDonald, who is doing work experience before he goes to university.

MacDonald was sitting next to me, downloading Stenning's picture card, when I spotted it. There was Sven and – hang on, where was he going? It was all there (thank God it hadn't been deleted) and it had a good frame. Give me a good frame between my teeth and I'll do the rest. I brightened it, added some contrast and got straight on the phone.

As it was a photograph of "national importance", I decided it couldn't be sold as an exclusive. We'd offer it to every newspaper that wanted it. Everyone did. The only nationals not to use it were *The Independent* and the *Daily Record*. Even *The Guardian* bought it.

In terms of remuneration it probably worked out about the same and everyone got a piece of the action. As for Stenning, he should be able to take a nice summer holiday now, thanks to a photo at the back of his card that he never got round to deleting.

22|06|2004

Queue to sign Rooney snakes around Europe

Euro 2004's leading scorer has turned himself into the continent's hottest property, reports Daniel Taylor

The first biography about Wayne Rooney, published with a mixture of financial acumen and obscene hastiness before he had turned 18, stretched to 217 pages. The updated version might have to be twice the volume. Watching Rooney bewitch Euro 2004 once again last night, it was difficult to leave without the sensation that the world's second most important football tournament is witnessing one of the great stories in the making.

This is a competition that cherishes new heroes. Rooney left the pitch to a standing ovation against Croatia, and it was possible even to feel a twinge of disappointment that Sven-Goran Eriksson had decided to substitute him. A hat-trick was beckoning and Rooney did not seem in any mood to spare his opponents.

So the leading scorer as we near the midway point of Euro 2004 is an 18-year-old who can still be found occasionally kicking a tennis ball around the streets of Croxteth, where some of his mates are so young they risked being shooed away from the pub, Rooney's, that has been named in his honour.

At the end of all the back-slapping from his team-mates, the rich tributes from Eriksson and the modest little wave with which he acknowledged his name being bellowed out by England's followers, one wonders how Everton must feel. Mixed emotions? Only the accountants at Goodison Park can truly be happy because it is starting to feel faintly ridiculous that Rooney could be back in a fair-to-middling club side again next season.

One of the guests at Estadio da Luz was Joan Laporta, the president of Barcelona. A delegation from Real Madrid was here in sharp suits and dark shades and both of Roman Abramovich's yachts have been docked in Lisbon's Doca da Marinha for a fortnight. Last night Abramovich, Chelsea's manager, Jose Mourinho, and Peter Kenyon, the chief executive, were here to see the player Eriksson compared to Pele. The capture of Rooney would offer Chelsea's Russian oligarch another rare butterfly to show off to his friends.

"Everton are a very good and very important team but I know for a fact that a lot of clubs want Rooney," Laporta, that notorious mischief-maker, volunteered. "He has been the star of Euro 2004 so far.

"He is at Everton now but maybe he already has an agreement with another club? Talking with other managers and coaches, everybody is impressed with him. In football nowadays there are not enough players with that quality, the kind of player who you can tell is different. Everywhere in Europe it is: 'Rooney, Rooney, Rooney.' All the time."

This used to be the territory of Michael Owen. Not long ago he, not Rooney, was the darling of English football, the cute teenager who smiled sweetly, then played with such ruthlessness you wanted to check his birth certificate.

Another disappointing night for Owen should not be overlooked in the next wave of Rooney-mania. Identifying a struggling player is easy; establishing the cause is difficult. In

Owen's case maybe only he truly knows and we will have to wait to see whether he decides to share that information.

There is certainly no logical reason, however, why at times in this tournament, not least on this cool Lisbon evening, it has been difficult to equate this hesitant, even clumsy player with the coltish young daredevil who enthralled the world when he hared away from the entire Argentina defence in St-Etienne six years ago. By his own admission Owen's recurrent misfortune with injury has deprived him of an element of the blistering pace for which he was famed but 24 still seems depressingly young for a player of his repute to be on the wane.

In Owen's defence he might never have expected he would have to wait until five minutes before half-time before receiving a pass from which he could extend his legs and establish whether he had the beating of Croatia's centre-halves.

When Frank Lampard finally obliged with the sort of measured ball that Owen relishes, his scuffed shot failed to beat Tomislav Butina but caused enough mayhem for Rooney to head the rebound goalwards for Paul Scholes to apply the finishing touch. Owen could at least say he had made a worthy contribution but by squandering his solitary chance in the second half he will have left with differing emotions.

He made his name as a predator but has not scored any of England's eight goals. Rooney has half of them and gives the impression there are more to come. Owen, once the baby-faced assassin, has had to make way for Rooney, the assassin-faced baby.

Wayne Rooney enjoys scoring against Switzerland. He was injured in the quarter-final; England went out on penalties

03|07|2006
Complacent to the last

In Germany Sven-Goran Eriksson and his players got what they deserved – absolutely nichts. By Richard Williams

In the aftermath of a punishing defeat no man should be called to account for his impromptu remarks. But when Frank Lampard said on Saturday night that England had "deserved" to win the match in which defeat had just eliminated them from the World Cup, he was inadvertently exposing the problem at the heart of the team's consistent inability to scale the highest peaks.

David Beckham had used the same word earlier in the campaign. England would get to the World Cup final, the captain said, because they "deserved" to be there. Since no deeper analysis was forthcoming, his listeners were left to infer that the evidence in support of his contention might have included any or all of the following: England's historic role as the game's mother country; the vast popularity of the Premiership at home and abroad; the inflated pay and celebrity status of its players; and the attention lavished on the public appearances of their wives and girlfriends.

When Sven-Goran Eriksson also spoke about the team "deserving" to reach the final, he tried to suggest that it was because of the quality of their football. Strictly on the basis of their successive performances against Hungary, Jamaica, Paraguay, Trinidad & Tobago, Sweden and Ecuador, however, it would have taken a battalion of the world's finest legal advocates to make a case for the justice of their arrival in the final rounds of the biggest international football tournament of all.

The attitude represented by the words of Lampard and Beckham represents a culture of complacency at work and it could be seen in the climactic shoot-out against Portugal, when three of England's penalty takers failed with attempts in which the slackness of their body language and their shooting spoke of men who were ready to put their trust in the belief, as England players have believed for several generations, that their reputations alone would be enough to ensure their success.

A successful apprenticeship in the upper reaches of English football wraps such an effective comfort blanket around a young player that he is seldom exposed to the harsh realities of the outside world and never confronts those moments in which failure really does mean disaster. When they are called to summon reserves of resilience at moments of extreme pressure, they discover those reserves either do not exist or have been depleted by the demands of domestic football.

Where, on Saturday, was the Englishman prepared to take control of the game as Zinedine Zidane would do in France's defeat of Brazil later that night? The only candidate was Owen Hargreaves, who both converted his penalty — the one Englishman to do so — and secured the man-of-the-match award with 120 minutes of non-stop tackling, intercepting, running and passing. Alone among his colleagues he displayed a dynamism that seemed to come from within. What also makes him unique among the squad, of course, is that he has never lived in England. The two things may not be unconnected.

Before Hargreaves was born, his parents left Britain to make a new life for their family in Canada. They succeeded and, in so doing, may have laid the mental foundation for their son's career. Owen Hargreaves arrived in Munich at 16 and began a long struggle to establish himself among the superstars in the first team at Bayern, in a country where he knew no one and had to learn the language from scratch. When times were difficult, when he was dropped or suffered injuries, his parents' example of ambition and self-sufficiency can have done him no harm.

Hargreaves may also have benefited from the Bundesliga's 34-match season and its mid-winter break. Whereas he faced up to Portugal's challenge with what the English like to see as their characteristic qualities of energy and doggedness, his native-born team-mates struggled to turn their talent and desire for success into the currency of coherent football.

Individually there was much to admire in their display — in Ashley Cole's gradual return to form, in John Terry's obduracy, in Aaron Lennon's zigzag runs and in Peter Crouch's sheer willingness — but collectively they could only demonstrate the difficulty they experience in achieving, even sporadically, the kind

of momentum that the better sides in this tournament have maintained virtually from first whistle to last.

Eriksson, permuting his resources for the fifth time in five matches as he responded to the opposition's strengths and his own squad's injuries, asked Hargreaves to provide a screen for the defence while a midfield quartet attempted to support Wayne Rooney, the lone front runner. That it took the coach so long to reach this conclusion, after having Hargreaves in his squad for almost five years, is among the most serious indictments of his regime.

The fatal flaw in the way the formation was applied was the use of Rio Ferdinand as the launchpad for attacks. On countless occasions the ball was given to the centre-back in the expectation that he would make the first significant pass. He would take a touch to control the ball, look up, take another touch, look up again, have another think and then, after a delay often of six or seven seconds, play it - not always accurately — to a team-mate.

By the time he was ready to part with the ball, two things would have happened: first, his team-mates had effectively come to a standstill; second, the Portuguese defenders had been given the time to move in to cover them. So almost every England move would start from a static position, with the opposition well prepared for counter-measures.

Although Ferdinand is a decent passer of the ball, he is not Andrea Pirlo. Neither is Hargreaves but he should have been encouraged to become the kind of pivot that Claude Makelele represents for Chelsea and France, taking the ball from the defence and recycling it to the midfield with the minimum of fuss or wasted time, acting as the team's metronome. Then England might have had a chance to develop the kind of rhythm and movement that we sometimes see from Arsenal, Chelsea and, less frequently nowadays, Manchester United, but at which English-born players in general have never been adept.

When the Football Association hired Eriksson as England's first foreign coach, it was reasonable to expect that an improvement in fluidity was among the benefits the players could expect from his long experience in Italy and Portugal. All they got, really, was a swift application of common sense to a formerly chaotic selection policy and a discovery that Eriksson's notion of an acceptable standard of living matched their own five-star expectations.

His inability to get Englishmen to play football together with a combination of spontaneity and consistency means that, after a promising start, the Eriksson era must on balance be counted a failure. Sadly, given the unfailing courtesy with which he confronted an often hostile environment, he was not the man to dismantle the mental barrier that prevented his players from turning their talents into real achievement at international level. In the end they, and he, deserved no more than they got.

> **The Eriksson era, after a promising start, must on balance be counted a failure**

17|09|2007

Screen Break: A triumph of Hope over Dick van Dyke any day

Martin Kelner

I hate to take issue with a colleague, but I think Barney Ronay, who wrote in this paper on Saturday that women's football is great to participate in but not to watch, is wrong. I am having great fun watching the women's World Cup. Barney's problem is that he has a day job, which prevents him from watching too much daytime TV, so maybe he does not realise that an entirely different set of criteria come into play when you are judging TV broadcast between the hours of 10am and 4pm. You do not have so much to lower the bar as to bury it.

Wait till you have watched a few programmes about people buying properties in Spain, or Dick van Dyke being a detective, and you will look on women's football more favourably. Daytime telly is what I like to call sub-prime TV (have you seen Loose Women?) and into these dismal schedules the women's World Cup matches, mostly shown on BBC2 at around 12.45pm, have come breezing like a welcome, er, breeze. I find they fill the afternoon nicely.

Only the other day someone asked me what I do all day and I explained wearily that once I have done the *Guardian* crossword and updated my Facebook profile there is not much of the day left. Well, now I have live sport to shoehorn into this busy schedule and, if my feminist friends, bless them, will forgive my being mildly patronising, it is not half bad. Again, I have to disagree with Barney, who reckoned it was like "watching men who aren't very good at football playing football". I think that he may be confusing it with England in the rugby union World Cup, which is like "watching men who aren't very good at rugby playing rugby".

Most teams in the women's World Cup seem to me to have two or three very good players, half a dozen passable performers and one or two who are so bad you wonder how they ever got picked for any team, let alone a World Cup squad and here I think I may have stumbled upon a major difference between the sexes. We boys will make it brutally clear — even as infants picking teams in the playground — whom we reckon are the no-hopers, and they are summarily dispatched to the chess club or to cry alone in the corner. Should one of them, like Bernard Jackson for instance, make it on to the team-sheet, he will be insulted in the most pointed and personal

fashion should he make a mistake, like selling goalkeeper Frankie Hampson short with a suicidal back pass. (I am sorry, Bernard, but it was a long time ago and it had to be said.)

Girls, on the other hand, are mostly much gentler than us and more likely to put an arm around an underperformer, dry her tears, and give her a place in the team anyway, possibly in goal. I may be generalising wildly but this is the only explanation I can think of for the Swedish and the Argentinian keepers. This niceness spills over into the BBC studio, where Karen Walker, the former Doncaster and Leeds player — who has a South Yorkshire accent so broad she makes Sean Bean sound like Brian Sewell — the Charlton player Jo Potter and token male Gavin Peacock are reluctant to criticise even the most flagrant howler. They are in that difficult position — part pundit, part unpaid PR for a sport that is growing in popularity but remains desperate for recruits — and their tendency is to do as Bing Crosby once recommended, in an entirely different context, and accentuate the positive.

Gabby Logan, who seems to have used the close season to spend more time with her hair straighteners (sorry, but I would say the same if it were Gary Lineker) may, however, be overdoing it. Before both the Japan and the Germany games she said: "Let us meet the 11 players with the nation's hopes on their shoulders," which seemed to be slightly overselling the importance of the tournament in the national psyche.

I polled a random selection of people in Leeds and very few said that their hopes and dreams rested particularly on the shoulders of the England women's football team. Some said the progress of the team was not in their thoughts at all — an unrepresentative sample maybe, but that was certainly the feeling on Friday afternoon outside the Northern Rock Building Society.

There are frustrations in watching women's football, especially when one of the less accomplished players insinuates herself into a flowing move and invariably misplaces the pass, but incidental pleasures too like finding a favourite gender stereotype confirmed, when the England striker Kelly Smith took her boots off and kissed them after each of her two goals against Japan. How appropriate, I thought, for the women's game to come up with a shoe-related celebration.

Finally, an apology. Last week's column may have given the impression that we felt something pretty deep was going on beneath the still waters of the England rugby coach, Brian Ashton, and expected impressive crisis management for the South Africa match.

Unfortunately, we confused him with the women's football coach Hope Powell, who despite looking as if she would be more at home managing a feminist bookshop in New York, skilfully masterminded England's goalless draw against Germany. In comparison, Argentina this afternoon should be plain sailing and, if the crossword is not too difficult, I will be there.

08|11|2007

The day McClaren went missing in inaction

Marina Hyde

To the match the world was watching, then, as we turn our thoughts to the continued fallout from LA Galaxy's clash with Hollywood United on Sunday evening and rue the irony that Without A Trace's Jack Malone was in goal for the visitors.

Special Agent Malone is head of the FBI's Missing Persons Unit and, had he not been shipping 12 goals at the Home Depot Center – not all that bad for a 48-year-old with a plastic hip – he might have been prevailed upon to use his legendary sleuthing skills to pinpoint the whereabouts of the England manager.

Steve McClaren, you see, was not even at the game. He had flown to Los Angeles, watched a training session and visited David Beckham's well-appointed Beverly Hills home. But contrary to initial reports, it has now emerged that he chose to forgo the opportunity of watching Beckham wrongfoot Def Leppard's Viv Campbell. (It is not known whether representatives from the Croatian set-up made the spectacle part of their preparations for the Euro 2008 qualifier later this month.)

Sounding faintly uncomfortable, a Football Association spokesman confirms suggestions that McClaren did not actually attend the match with the words: "It looks that way . . ." As for where he was, it has not requested a breakdown of his move-

66

Steve McClaren, surviving on a salary of £2.5m, is clinging on for his severance

99

ments, despite having funded the trip. He may have been flying home. He may have been glued to one of the 37 Without A Trace re-runs that grace US basic cable each day. We may never know. And in fairness the lacuna in McClaren's schedule is unlikely to become a mystery to rival Agatha Christie's 11 missing days.

But it would seem to mark the moment his tenure as head coach tipped beneath low farce. At some level one has to marvel at McClaren's knack of finding a concealed basement in any barrel the bottom of which he happens to be scraping. Remember his response when questioned in March as to how he planned to reverse his run of five games without a win. "Keep going, keep going" was the answer. "Keep doing the same things."

And so with last weekend's hokey-cokey. If there is one thing that looks worse than his skipping Arsenal-Manchester United to watch David Beckham turn out against a side featuring a 52-year-old former Sex Pistol, it is his skipping Arsenal-Manchester United not to watch David Beckham turn out against a side featuring a 52-year-old former Sex Pistol.

If only that were it. Alas, perhaps dimly aware of the even dimmer view being taken back home, a "source close to the England boss" let it be known on Tuesday that McClaren had determined not to resign should England not qualify and that, if the Football Association wished to remove him, it would have to sack him. He had "found it difficult when he took over because the players were still on a downer after the World Cup," ran this view, "but they have a strong spirit again now".

Having had to survive on a salary of £2.5m, it is hardly a surprise to find McClaren clinging on for his severance. Yet, in any sane universe, the very fact of the Californian jolly might have given the FA a chance to fight having to make the full pay-out.

Its chief executive, Brian Barwick, might well have had a case for alleging the trip was so idiotic as to constitute misconduct. Unfortunately the universe is far from sane and the FA has been forced to concede that Barwick actually went so far as to endorse the luminously pointless odyssey.

In which case the chief executive's latest blinding piece of judgment must serve as yet another reminder that Barwick's and McClaren's jobs are bound to be seen as symbiotically linked, as they have been since the moment Barwick began whitewashing over his fiascoid attempt to hire Luiz Felipe Scolari by claiming that McClaren had always been his choice. It would be yet another disastrously retrograde step for England if he was somehow ring-fenced when the P45s are handed out.

To return to the realm of mysteries, the chief executive has been a version of Sherlock Holmes's dog that didn't bark, a creature whose failure to act at any point should be seen as highly significant. As for McClaren, to the list of his oversights can be added the failure to ensure a photographer presence as he stepped Chamberlain-like off the flight from LA. There would have been something suitably bathetic to his triumphantly waving a piece of paper, identified as a declaration of David Beckham's fitness.

15/12/2007

Capello could yet turn out to be Ramsey revisited

David Lacey

Stanley Rous's autobiography was predictably pompous and dropped names like confetti. Yet the man who was secretary of the Football Association for 27 years and later Fifa president surely got it right when he defined the nature of the England job. "It can be a very frustrating experience to change from the bustle of club management to the isolation of national team manager," he wrote, "where a couple of bad results may be followed by months without a match or a squad to train. The long periods of waiting can ferment too many new ideas and encourage excessive change." It needed someone of strong determination to stick to a consistent basic plan which might not always be appreciated by the public "or those who are more concerned with entertaining quotes or fanciful ideas than solid results".

Rous was referring to Alf Ramsey but the same has applied to all those who have led England since. Certainly Fabio Capello does not come across as someone who will be sidetracked by a need for entertaining quotes let alone fanciful ideas. Ramsey gave little away and neither did his better teams. Capello could turn out to be Alf revisited.

The Italian was the last opponent to score against Ramsey's England, finding the net three minutes from the end of a

> **Another leading foreign coach will not in itself solve the problems of the English game**

friendly in November 1973 that gave Italy a first ever win in England. The following morning's headlines were scathing and conditioned by the fact that a month earlier England had failed to qualify for the 1974 World Cup after being held to 1-1 by Poland. "L-plate England" and "Alf's final humiliation" summed up the general mood. Ramsey was sacked the following spring.

The Italy match also saw Bobby Moore win his 108th and, as it turned out, his last England cap. Neither Moore, Ramsey nor anyone else trudging home from Wembley that night could have imagined that the Juventus midfielder who had been England's nemesis would eventually be picking the England team.

Selective quotes can make or malign a man. To some it may appear that having failed to land an egocentric, Jose Mourinho, the FA has opted for an egomaniac. Clearly Capello does not suffer fools but neither did Ramsey. The Italian's manner will not matter provided he restores England to roughly where they were when Steve McClaren succeeded Sven-Goran Eriksson and makes them serious challengers in international competitions instead of born quarter-finalists.

As football coaches bred in the pressurised world of Serie A Capello and Eriksson are two of a kind. Their approach is cautious. Their teams attack from a solid defensive base and, once in the lead, protect the advantage in numbers – Mourinho's philosophy, though it can be assumed Capello will not be forced out if his England side keep winning without entertaining.

Language will not be a problem. Capello, like Eriksson, will quickly grasp sufficient English to get his ideas across. Vocabulary is seldom a strong point with England managers anyway. Ramsey struggled with his aspirates, Ron Greenwood said "irrevelant" when he meant "irrelevant", Bobby Robson warned his squad against sunbathing because of "those ultra-ray violets" and Glenn Hoddle never said them things.

The appointment of another leading foreign coach to manage England will not solve the problems besetting the English game. The Professional Footballers' Association wants a quota of three or four home-grown players to be included in clubs' first teams – a nice idea but try telling that to managers of struggling sides who see the transfer window as a chance to buy cut-price salvation from mainland Europe.

The absurdity of asking seven-year-olds to play on full-sized pitches while dwarfed by full-sized goals and harangued from the touchline by parental wanabees was a point made by Greenwood when he succeeded Don Revie as England manager 30 years ago. Greenwood took over too late to qualify for the 1978 World Cup, the damage having already been done in Rome, but his team did beat Italy 2-0 at Wembley playing positive, flowing football. Capello represents almost everything Greenwood hated about the modern game but, if the Italian gets England to major tournaments and breaks the habit of going out to the first decent team they meet, he will have earned his enormous salary. And if things do get a bit boring ... well, there is always the Mexican wave.

Results

World Cup finals

1930
Uruguay 4 - 2 Argentina
Hosts: Uruguay

1934
Italy 2 - 1 Czechoslovakia
(aet: 1 - 1 after 90mins)
Italy

1938
Italy 4 - 2 Hungary
France

1950
Uruguay
(decided by league format vs. Spain, Sweden and Brazil)
Brazil

1954
West Germany 3 - 2 Hungary
Switzerland

1958
Brazil 5 - 2 Sweden
Sweden

1962
Brazil 3 - 1 Czechoslovakia
Chile

1966
England 4 - 2 West Germany
(aet: 2 - 2 after 90mins)
England

1970
Brazil 4 - 1 Italy
Mexico

1974
West Germany 2 - 1 Holland
West Germany

1978
Argentina 3 - 1 Holland
(aet: 1 - 1 after 90mins)
Argentina

1982
Italy 3 - 1 West Germany
Spain

1986
Argentina 3 - 2 West Germany
Mexico

1990
West Germany 1 - 0 Argentina
Italy

1994
Brazil 0 - 0 Italy
(aet: Brazil won 3 - 2 on pens)
United States

1998
France 3 - 0 Brazil
France

2002
Brazil 2 - 0 Germany
South Korea & Japan

2006
Italy 1 - 1 France
(aet: Italy won 5 - 3 on pens)
Germany

Women's World Cup finals

1991
USA 2 - 1 Norway
Hosts: China

1995
Norway 2 - 0 Germany
Sweden

1999
USA 0 - 0 China
(aet: USA won 5-4 on pens)
United States

2003
Germany 2 - 1 Sweden
(aet: won by golden goal)
United States

2007
Germany 2 - 0 Brazil
China

European Championship finals

1960
USSR 2 - 1 Yugoslavia
(aet: 1 - 1 after 90mins)
Hosts: France

1964
Spain 2 - 1 USSR
Spain

1968
Italy 1 - 1 Yugoslavia
(aet: Italy won replay 2 - 0)
Italy

1972
West Germany 3 - 0 USSR
Belgium

1976
Czechoslovakia 2 - 2 West Germany
(aet: Czechoslavakia won 5-3 on pens)
Yugoslavia

1980
West Germany 2 - 1 Belgium
Italy

1984
France 2 - 0 Spain
France

1988
Holland 2 - 0 USSR
West Germany

1992
Denmark 2 - 0 Germany
Sweden

1996
Germany 2 - 1 Czech Republic
(aet: 1 - 1 at 90mins)
England

2000
France 2 - 1 Italy
(aet: 1 -1 at 90mins)
Belgium and Holland

2004
Greece 1 - 0 Portugal
Portugal

European Cup finals

1955/56
Real Madrid 4 - 3 Reims
Venue: Parc des Princes,
Paris

1956/57
Real Madrid 2 - 0 Fiorentina
Santiago Bernabéu,
Madrid

1957/58
Real Madrid 3 - 2 AC Milan
(aet: 2 - 2 at 90mins)
Heysel Stadium,
Brussels

1958/59
Real Madrid 2 - 0 Reims
Neckarstadion,
Stuttgart

1959/60
Real Madrid 7 - 3 Eintracht
Frankfurt
Hampden Park, Glasgow

1960/61
Benfica 3 - 2 Barcelona
Wankdorf Stadium,
Berne

1961/62
Benfica 5 - 3 Real Madrid
Olympisch Stadion,
Amsterdam

1962/63
AC Milan 2 - 1 Benfica
Wembley Stadium, London

1963/64
Inter Milan 3 - 1 Real Madrid
Prater Stadium, Vienna

1964/65
Inter Milan 1 - 0 Benfica
San Siro, Milan

1965/66
Real Madrid 2 - 1 Partizan
Belgrade
Heysel Stadium,
Brussels

1966/67
Celtic 2 - 1 Inter Milan
Estádio Nacional,
Oeiras

1967/68
Manchester United 4 - 1
Benfica
(aet: 1 - 1 at 90mins)
Wembley Stadium, London

1968/69
AC Milan 4 - 1 Ajax
Santiago Bernabéu,
Madrid

1969/70
Feyenoord 2 - 1 Celtic
(aet: 1 - 1 at 90mins)
San Siro, Milan

1970/71
Ajax 2 - 0 Panathinaikos
Wembley Stadium, London

1971/72
Ajax 2 - 0 Inter Milan
De Kuip, Rotterdam

1972/73
Ajax 1 - 0 Juventus
Crvena Zvezda Stadium,
Belgrade

1973/74
Bayern Munich 1 - 1 Atlético
Madrid
(aet: Bayern won replay 4 - 0)
Heysel Stadium,
Brussels

1974/75
Bayern Munich 2 - 0 Leeds
United
Parc des Princes, Paris

1975/76
Bayern Munich 1 - 0
St Etienne
Hampden Park, Glasgow

1976/77
Liverpool 3 - 1 Borussia
Mönchengladbach
Stadio Olimpico, Rome

1977/78
Liverpool 1 - 0 Bruges
Wembley Stadium,
London

1978/79
Nottingham Forest 1 - 0
Malmö
Olympiastadion, Munich

1979/80
Nottingham Forest 1 - 0
Hamburg
Santiago Bernabéu,
Madrid

1980/81
Liverpool 1 - 0 Real Madrid
Parc des Princes,
Paris

1981/82
Aston Villa 1 - 0 Bayern
Munich
De Kuip, Rotterdam

1982/83
Hamburg 1 - 0 Juventus
Olympic Stadium Spiros Louis,
Athens

1983/84
Liverpool 1 - 1 Roma
(aet: Liverpool won 4-2 on
pens)
Stadio Olimpico, Rome

1984/85
Juventus 1 - 0 Liverpool
Heysel Stadium,
Brussels

1985/86
Steaua Bucharest 0 - 0
Barcelona
(aet: Steaua won 2-0 on pens)
Sánchez Pizjuán,
Seville

1986/87
Porto 2 - 1 Bayern Munich
Prater Stadium, Vienna

1987/88
PSV Eindhoven 0 - 0 Benfica
(aet: PSV won 6-5 on pens)
Neckarstadion,
Stuttgart

1988/89
AC Milan 4 - 0 Steaua
Bucharest
Camp Nou, Barcelona

1989/90
AC Milan 1 - 0 Benfica
Prater Stadium, Vienna

1990/91
Red Star Belgrade 0 - 0
Marseille
*(aet: Red Star won 5-3
on pens)*
Stadio San Nicola, Bari

1991/92
Barcelona 1 - 0 Sampdoria
(aet: 0 - 0 at 90mins)
*Wembley Stadium,
London*

1992/93
Marseille* 1 - 0 AC Milan
(later stripped of title)*
Olympiastadion, Munich

1993/94
AC Milan 4 - 0 Barcelona
*Olympic Stadium Spiros Louis,
Athens*

1994/95
Ajax 1 - 0 AC Milan
*Ernst Happel Stadium,
Vienna*

1995/96
Juventus 1 - 1 Ajax
*(aet: Juventus won 4-2
on pens)*
Stadio Olimpico, Rome

1996/97
Borussia Dortmund 3 - 1
Juventus
*Olympiastadion,
Munich*

1997/98
Real Madrid 1 - 0 Juventus
*Amsterdam Arena,
Amsterdam*

1998/99
Manchester United 2 - 1
Bayern Munich
Camp Nou, Barcelona

1999/2000
Real Madrid 3 - 0 Valencia
*Stade de France,
Paris*

2000/01
Bayern Munich 1 - 1 Valencia
(aet: Bayern won 5-4 on pens)
San Siro, Milan

2001/02
Real Madrid 2 - 1 Bayer
Leverkusen
*Hampden Park,
Glasgow*

2002/03
AC Milan 0 - 0 Juventus
(aet: Milan won 3-2 on pens)
*Old Trafford,
Manchester*

2003/04
Porto 3 - 0 Monaco
*Arena AufSchalke,
Gelsenkirchen*

2004/05
Liverpool 3 - 3 AC Milan
*(aet: Liverpool won 3-2
on pens)*
*Atatürk Olympic Stadium,
Istanbul*

2005/06
Barcelona 2 - 1 Arsenal
Stade de France, Paris

2006/07
AC Milan 2 - 1 Liverpool
Olympic Stadium, Athens

Uefa Cup finals
Two-legged finals (aggregate
results are shown)

1971/72
Tottenham Hotspur 3 - 2
Wolverhampton Wanderers

1972/73
Liverpool 3 - 2 Borussia
Mönchengladbach

1973/74
Feyenoord 4 - 2 Tottenham
Hotspur

1974/75
Borussia Mönchengladbach
5 - 1 Twente

1975/76
Liverpool 4 - 3 Bruges

1976/77
Juventus 2 - 2 Athletic Bilbao
(Juventus won on away goals)

1977/78
PSV Eindhoven 3 - 0 Bastia

1978/79
Borussia Mönchengladbach
2 - 1 Red Star Belgrade

1979/80
Eintracht Frankfurt 3 - 3
Borussia Mönchengladbach
(Frankfurt won on away goals)

1980/81
Ipswich Town 5 - 4
AZ Alkmaar

1981/82
Gothenburg 4 - 0 Hamburg

1982/83
Anderlecht 2 - 1 Benfica

1983/84
Tottenham Hotspur 2 - 2
Anderlecht
(Tottenham won 4-3 on pens)

1984/85
Real Madrid 3 - 1 Videoton

1985/86
Real Madrid 5 - 3 Cologne

1986/87
Gothenburg 2 - 1 Dundee
United

1987/88
Bayer Leverkusen 3-3
Espanyol
*(Leverkusen won 3-2
on pens)*

1988/89
Napoli 5 - 4 Stuttgart

1989/90
Juventus 3 - 1
Fiorentina

1990/91
Inter Milan 2 - 1 Roma

1991/92
Ajax 2 - 2 Torino
(Ajax won on away goals)

1992/93
Juventus 6 - 1 Borussia
Dortmund

1993/94
Inter Milan 2 - 0 Salzburg

1994/95
Parma 2-1 Juventus

1995/96
Bayern Munich 5 - 1 Bordeaux

1996/97
Schalke 1 - 1 Inter Milan
(Schalke won 4 - 1 on pens)

One-legged finals

1997/98
Inter Milan 3 - 0 Lazio
Parc des Princes,
Paris

1998/99
Parma 3 - 0 Marseille
Luzhniki Stadium,
Moscow

1999/2000
Galatasaray 0 - 0 Arsenal
(aet: Galatasaray won 4 - 1
on pens)
Parken Stadium, Copenhagen

2000/01
Liverpool 5 - 4 Deportivo
Alavés
(aet: match decided by
golden goal)
Westfalenstadion, Dortmund

2001/02
Feyenoord 3 - 2 Borussia
Dortmund
De Kuip, Rotterdam

2002/03
Porto 3 - 2 Celtic
(aet: match decided by
silver goal)
Estadio Olímpico de Sevilla,
Seville

2003/04
Valencia 2 - 0 Marseille
Nya Ullevi, Gothenburg

2004/05
CSKA Moscow 3 - 1 Sporting
Lisbon
José Alvalade Stadium, Lisbon

2005/06
Sevilla 4 - 0 Middlesbrough
Philips Stadion, Eindhoven

2006/07
Sevilla 2 - 2 Espanyol
(aet: Sevilla won 3 - 1 on pens)
Hampden Park, Glasgow

Cup-Winners' Cup finals

1960/61
Fiorentina 4-1 Rangers
(two-legged final, aggregate
result shown)

1961/62
Atlético Madrid 1 - 1
Fiorentina
(aet: Atlético won replay 3 - 0)
Hampden Park, Glasgow

1962/63
Tottenham Hotspur 5 - 1
Atlético Madrid
De Kuip, Rotterdam

1963/64
Sporting Lisbon 3 - 3
MTK Budapest
(aet: Sporting won replay 1 - 0)
Heysel Stadium,
Brussels

1964/65
West Ham United 2 - 0
1860 Munich
Wembley Stadium,
London

1965/66
Borussia Dortmund 2 - 1
Liverpool *(aet)*
Hampden Park, Glasgow

1966/67
Bayern Munich 1 - 0
Rangers *(aet)*
Frankenstadion,
Nuremberg

1967/68
AC Milan 2 - 0 Hamburg
De Kuip, Rotterdam

1968/69
Slovan Bratislava 3 - 2
Barcelona
St Jakob Stadium,
Basel

1969/70
Manchester City 2 - 1
Gornik Zabrze
Prater Stadium,
Vienna

1970/71
Chelsea 1 - 1 Real Madrid
(aet: Chelsea won replay 2 - 1)
Karaiskakis Stadium,
Piraeus

1971/72
Rangers 3 - 2 Dynamo
Moscow
Camp Nou, Barcelona

1972/73
AC Milan 1 - 0 Leeds United
Kaftanzoglio Stadium,
Salonika

1973/74
Magdeburg 2 - 0
AC Milan
De Kuip, Rotterdam

1974/75
Dinamo Kiev 3 - 0
Ferencváros
St Jakob Stadium,
Basel

1975/76
Anderlecht 4 - 2 West Ham
United
Heysel Stadium,
Brussels

1976/77
Hamburg 2 - 0 Anderlecht
Olympic Stadium,
Amsterdam

1977/78
Anderlecht 4 - 0 Austria
Vienna
Parc des Princes,
Paris

1978/79
Barcelona 4 - 3 Fortuna
Düsseldorf *(aet)*
St Jakob Stadium,
Basel

1979/80
Valencia 0 - 0 Arsenal
(aet: Valencia won 5 - 4
on pens)
Heysel Stadium, Brussels

1980/81
Dinamo Tbilisi 2 - 1 Carl
Zeiss Jena
Rheinstadion, Düsseldorf

1981/82
Barcelona 2 - 1 Standard Liège
Camp Nou, Barcelona

1982/83
Aberdeen 2 - 1 Real
Madrid *(aet)*
Nya Ullevi, Gothenburg

1983/84
Juventus 2 - 1 Porto
St Jakob Stadium,
Basel

1984/85
Everton 3 - 1 Rapid Vienna
De Kuip,
Rotterdam

1985/86
Dinamo Kiev 3 - 0 Atlético
Madrid
Stade de Gerland,
Lyon

1986/87
Ajax 1 - 0 Lokomotiv Leipzig
Spiros Louis Stadium,
Athens

1987/88
Mechelen 1 - 0 Ajax
Stade de la Meinau,
Strasbourg

1988/89
Barcelona 2 - 0 Sampdoria
Wankdorf Stadium,
Berne

1989/90
Sampdoria 2 - 0
Anderlecht *(aet)*
Nya Ullevi,
Gothenburg

1990/91
Manchester United 2 - 1
Barcelona
De Kuip,
Rotterdam

1991/92
Werder Bremen 2 - 0 Monaco
Estádio da Luz,
Lisbon

1992/93
Parma 3 - 1 Antwerp
Wembley Stadium,
London

1993/94
Arsenal 1 - 0 Parma
Parken Stadium,
Copenhagen

1994/95
Real Zaragoza 2 - 1
Arsenal *(aet)*
Parc des Princes,
Paris

1995/96
Paris St-Germain 1 - 0
Rapid Vienna
King Baudouin Stadium,
Brussels

1996/97
Barcelona 1 - 0 Paris
St-Germain
De Kuip,
Rotterdam

1997/98
Chelsea 1 - 0 Stuttgart
Råsunda Stadium,
Stockholm

1998/99
Lazio 2 - 1 Mallorca
Villa Park,
Birmingham

Photography

Writers

Index